Calgary's
GRAND
story

The Making of a Prairie
Metropolis from the Viewpoint of
Two Heritage Buildings

Donald B. Smith

UNIVERSITY OF
CALGARY
PRESS

© 2005 Donald B. Smith
Published by the University of Calgary Press
2500 University Drive NW, Calgary, Alberta, Canada T2N 1N4
www.uofcpress.com

Library and Archives Canada Cataloguing in Publication

Smith, Donald B., 1946-
    Calgary's grand story : the making of a prairie metropolis from the
viewpoint of two heritage buildings / Donald B. Smith.

Includes bibliographical references and index.
ISBN 1-55238-174-9

    I. Lougheed Building (Calgary, Alta.) 2. Grand Theatre (Calgary,
Alta.) 3. Calgary (Alta.)—History. I. Title.

FC3697.7.S54 2005   971.23'3802
C2005-903462-9

We acknowledge the financial support of the Government of Canada
through the Book Publishing Industry Development Program (BPIDP),
the Alberta Foundation for the Arts for our publishing activities. We
acknowledge the support of the Canada Council for the Arts for our
publishing program. We acknowledge the support of the Alberta Lottery
Fund – Community Initiatives Program.

Printed and bound in Canada by Houghton Boston
∞ This book is printed on 80 lb. Chorus Art silk paper
Cover design, page design and typesetting by Mieka West.
Production by Danny Miller

Cover exterior photo of Lougheed building from
Glenbow Archives NA-5434-7

To Nancy, who inspired and made this book possible

TABLE OF CONTENTS

ACKNOWLEDGEMENTS

As the dedication indicates, I give great thanks to my wife, Nancy Townshend, who shared me with this book for five years. Our sons David and Peter also deserve my profound thanks for their support.

When did this all begin, this desire to tell the twentieth century history of Calgary from the vantage point of two heritage buildings? Unconsciously it began in 1974 when I first arrived in Calgary from Toronto to teach Canadian history at the University of Calgary. My first evening in the city in mid-August 1974 I stayed at the now demolished Carlton Hotel (originally the King George, built in 1911) opposite the Palliser Hotel. That evening I saw a movie in a theatre by the old Greyhound Building (originally the Herald Building, built in 1913), the Grand Theatre. Through my research the following winter (1974-1975) on Chief Buffalo Child Long Lance, a colourful Calgary character in the early 1920s, I met a number of people born at the turn of the century, people then in their 70s and 80s, who took me back to the Calgary of the early twentieth century. One gentleman, Hugh Dann, a good friend of Long Lance's, mentioned that he had an apartment in the Lougheed Building, next to the Grand Theatre, in the early 1920s.

Conversations over the years with, among others, my colleague in the history department, the late Henry Klassen; and Calgary historians—Hugh Dempsey, Max Foran, Harry Sanders and Jennifer Cook Bobrovitz—greatly deepened my appreciation of Calgary's history. My colleague Lou Knafla, now professor emeritus, University of Calgary Department of History, assisted greatly with questions about Alberta's legal history. I profited greatly from talks about the Calgary Stampede and theatres in Western Canada with Robert and Tamara Seiler in the Faculty of Communication and Culture at the University of Calgary. My colleague Doug Francis in the history department endured more conversations about the Lougheed Building and Grand Theatre than I think he would like to remember. My late father's work in the early 1970s to save the endangered Union Station in Toronto (he died in 1973, the year before I came to Calgary) led me to join the campaign which began in the summer of 1998 to save the Lougheed Building and the adjacent Grand Theatre.

Immediately before the provincial government announced its decision not to designate the Lougheed Building and Grand Theatre provincial historical resources in November 1999 I conceived the idea of a book on these two historic landmarks. The Minister of Community Development's negative decision convinced me of the necessity to proceed, if simply to record the incredible shortsightedness in allowing the obliteration of two vital city landmarks. The owners of the Lougheed Building had commissioned an historical resource impact assessment of the buildings in August 1998, the

Forseth Report. In 1999 it became a public document. Prepared by Gerald Forseth, architect and project leader, David Mittelstadt, historian, Colin Campbell, structural engineer, the report provided me with a quick X-ray image of the two buildings. Together with the notes I had already collected, the Forseth Report gave me a great start. Early in 2000 the granting of a Killam Resident Fellowship for the following year made the project possible.

I am extremely grateful to the Trustees of the Killam Resident Fellowship for their award of a Killam Resident Fellowship for the Winter Term 2001 (January 1-April 30). I thank as well my employer, the University of Calgary, for a Sabbatical Leave in the Fall Term 2002 (July 1- December 31), which advanced my project immensely. At first the task appeared much less imposing that it actually was. I am very grateful to Brian Brennan, who has contributed so much to a greater popular knowledge of Alberta history through his "Tribute" column in the *Calgary Herald* during the 1990s, and most recently in his recent books on the province's past, for looking at the first draft of my initial six chapters in the summer of 2003. He provided very helpful advice. In the fall of 2004 I completed a project first anticipated to end with the Killam Resident Fellowship in April 2001.

Many individuals assisted with my research, generously giving of their time. In the section on "Sources" I acknowledge the invaluable assistance of a number of individuals who helped in various archives and institutions with information for my research. To that list I first add all those individuals who shared direct memories of the building and/or theatre with me; and secondly, all those who assisted by providing research materials, or memories of those connected with the buildings. If I have omitted anyone in these acknowledgements, I offer my profound apologies; all blame lies on the shoulders of this scribe, who tried his best to record all contributions given. Marmie Hess and Helen Thomson assisted greatly with the names of contacts for my study. As her parents had been good friends of the Albrights, Kathleen (Kay) Coutts replied to numerous enquiries. Marmie, Helen and Kay, as well as Hilda Doherty, Jeff Lydiatt, Margaret Lydiatt, the late Peggy Tregillus Raymond, Grace Lydiatt Shaw and Harcourt (Tobe) Smith assisted with the re-creation of the atmosphere of Calgary in distant days.

For those who had personal memories of these two structures I thank in alphabetical order: Rod and Mary Anderson, Tom Anderson, Jack Anschetz, Bonar Bain, Pat Tolerico Baldwin, Bob and Cleo Barron, Dick and Jean Barron, Scott Bennie, Jim Black, Clara Blackstone, George Braithwaite, Ed Bredin, Archie Brown, Dennis Burton, Hy Calman, Jim Cameron, Ron Campbell, Terry Carter, Christina Chan, Kelley Charlebois, Bill Chomik, Gordon Clarke, Martha Cohen, Fred Colborne, Rowena Cooper, Steve Cosburn, Cindy Davidson, Art Davis, Constance Deslandes, Tom Dixon, Marianne Doherty, Jacqueline Nowlin Donoghue, Judy Dundas, C. H. (Dave) Dyke, Bill Epstein, Gordon and Joan Evans, Rhonda Fenton, Dean Firmaniuk, Phyllis Chapman Ford, Ethel Garnett, Thelma Gerlitz Garrett, Will Ghazar, Harold Gibson, Patrick Gobin, Harold Hanen, Clayton Hare, Dorothy Hare, Lois Wood Hollingsworth, Verna Hopkins, John Howse, Ernie Hutchinson, Robert Ingles, Bonnie Jacobs, Jill Jamieson, Bill Joiner, Amund Jonassen, Coleen Kauth, Mabelle Lee, Shelagh Nolan Lester, Ada Kelter, Jean

"Calgary's Grand Story" owes a great deal to Izaak Walton Killam, whose estate allows for the Killam Resident Fellowships at the University of Calgary. Appropriately he owned Calgary Power, which had an office in the Lougheed Building in the mid-1920s. The financier also was a major shareholder in Famous Players, who leased the Grand Theatre from 1926 to 1932. Izaak Walton Killam appears on the far right of this photo; next to him is Max Aitken, the future Lord Beaverbrook. R.B. Bennett stands next to Aitken. Taken around 1913. Beaverbrook Papers, House of Lords Record Office, London, England.

Donald Smith and Bill Joiner, son of Maynard Joiner, manager of the Grand Theatre for most of the 1920s, Surrey, B.C., 24 November 2001. Photograph by Fran Joiner, Bill's wife.

Kendrick, Aubrey Kerr, Abbas Keshmiri, Ken Knudsen, Tom Kurzaj, Bonnie Jacobs, Jill Jamieson, Amund Jonassen, Don LePan, Christine Logan, Don Lougheed, Peter Lougheed, Margaret Lydiatt, Wally McDill, Morley McDougall, Richard MacInnes, Allan McLennan, Alan Macpherson, David Marshall, Dick Matthews, Jim Millard, Ted Mills, Doran Moore, John Moreau, Jim Morris, Gordon Moss, Alexandra Munn, Barry Nelson, Jim Nesbitt, Jim Ogle, Ruby Beck Olmstead, Don Palmer, Gordon Palmer, George Parker, Doug Parnham, Ed Patching, Edythe Rosen Pearlman, Joan Powell, Ivan Radke, Grant Reddick, Will Robson, Lorne and Margaret Roberts, Keith Rolfe, Pauline Sande, David Semmens, Grace Lydiatt Shaw, Art Sick, Don Sinclair, Aileen Smith, May Smitten, Stanley Smith, Jenny Chow Soo, Don Spicer, George F. G. Stanley, Bob and Marlene Tavender, John Third, Len Treleaven, Ted Trafford, David Trimble, Harlow Tripp, Dick Tullson, Blanche Upton, Art White, Neil and Hazel Whittal, Marion and Robert Williams, Millicent Stanford Willis, Fred Wolf, John O. Wood, Steve Wood, Bill Yee, Jeffrey Zhang.

For those who assisted with information about the two buildings, twentieth century Calgary or put me in touch with individuals directly linked to the two buildings (or supplied information about them), I thank in alphabetical order: Flora Allison, Denise Anderson, Alan Andrews, Cheryl Avery, Frank Bailey, Beth Lee Baker, Paul Banfield, Josh Barron, Judith Beattie, Muriel Bell, Marlene Bird, Robert Blackburn, Brian Brennan, Lorna Brooke, Mary Burns, Geoff Burtonshaw, Colin Campbell, Darryl Cariou, Doreen Catley, Gian-Carlo Carra, Mary Lou Charles, Bill Chestnut, Pamela Clark, Pat Cleary, Jamie Coatsworth, Winn Coatsworth, Kay Coutts, Eve Crawford, Karen Crosby, Lois Daly, Suzanne den Ouden, Art Dixon, Cynthia Downe, Audrey Dubé, Lawrie Duff, Jackie Durrie, David Elliott, Sandra Elliott, Barry Elmer, Maria Eriksen, Peter Fitzgerald-Moore, Catherine Ford, Gerald Forseth, Peter Fortna, Franklin Foster, Ben Fullalove, Curley Galbraith, Jeffery Goffin, Bruce Gowans, Rob Graham, Mel Gray, Rick Green, Matias Grum, Mary Guichon, Sandy Haesaker, David Hall, Jonathan Hanna, Charlie Hansen, Larry Harnisch, Catherine Harradence, Carmen Harry, John Hawitt, Blane Hogue, Norm Holden, Andrew Homzy, Frederick Hunter, Les Hurt, Alan Hustak, Jay Joffe, Jane Brown John, Glen Johnston, Wayne Juke, Peter Jull, Harry Kiyooka, Nancy Kuenz, LeRoi LaFlèche Sr., Sandra LaFlèche, Bob Lampard, Brett Lougheed, Jopie Lougheed, Grant Luck, Albert Ludwig, Fay Lukenoff, Gordon Lydiatt, David Matthews, Viviane McClelland, Robert Macdonald, Al McDowell, Marion McKenna, Jim Mackie, Marcia McClung, Ernie McCullough, Russell McKinnon, Steve Mackinnon, Bill McLennan, Mike McMordie, Al McNeil, Bill McWilliams, Sidney Madden, Muriel Manning, Orlando Martini, Daniel May, Mel Merrells, Mark Miller, Dave Mittelstadt, Sean Moir, Margaret Moore, George Morrison, Cindy Murrell, Terry Nail, David Neill, Brian Norford, David Ogden, Andy Ogle, Daniel Oliver, Patrick O'Neill, André Ouellette, Ken Patton, Maxime Pearson, Ken Penley, Peter Penner, Damian Petti, Nancy Pierce, Jim Pietryk, Del Pine, Sandra Pope, Georgina Protheroe-Beynon, Bill Quackenbush, Kate Reeves, Craig Reid, Marjorie Reid, Janine Richardson, Myra Riches, Peter Ridout, Mary Roaf, Curtis Royer, Bev Sandalack, Bill Sayers, Angela Schiwy, Harold Segall, Roger Shaw, Ethel

King-Shaw, Allan Sherwin, Brock Silversides, Lorne Simpson, Art Smith, Cal Spankie, Norman Sproule, Ron Staines, Jim Stott, Marie Strang, Don Sucha, Vic Sweetnam, Jack Switzer, Peter Tassie, Jim Taylor, Wendy Theberge, Christine Thompson, Gord Tolton, Joan Van Housen, Dan Van Keeken, Jane Vincent, Peter Waite, Nancy Walton, Anne White, Frank Ellis Wickson, Larry Winter, Patricia Wood, Myken Woods, Maurice Yacowar, Bill Yeo, Barry Yzereef.

I thank those that assisted with the search for the identity of Len Wardrop, the architect of the Grand Theatre and the Lougheed Building: Burtch Beall, Jacky Durrie, Barry Elmer, Peter Goss, Nancy Hadley, Don Hartley, Robert G. Hill, Gwen Kingsley, Matt McLain, Lynne Merrill-Francis, Doug Misner, Elizabeth Mitchell, Cathy Phillips, A. LaVonne Brown Ruoff, Grant Smith, Les Wardrop and Sylvia Wardrop.

My neighbour Dave Crowe helped with invaluable computer assistance in the final stages of the writing. My sons and Dave's son, Aran Crowe, tutored me on earlier occasions. I enjoyed several talks about the buildings with my neighbour Manfred Grote, a Calgary architect.

In particular I thank Shawn England for all his help with the proper formatting of the footnotes as well as for the excellent copy-editing of the text of *Calgary's Grand Story*. Marilyn Croot drew the map showing the location of the Lougheed Building and Grand Theatre, which appears in the Introduction. Many thanks as well to Walter Hildebrandt, Director, and John King, Senior Editor, of the University of Calgary Press. I also enjoyed working with others at the Press: Peter Enman, Greg Madsen, Kellie Moynihan, Wendy Stephens, and Mieka West. My sister, Barbara Nair, generously prepared the index.

A supplementary note to the reader of "Calgary's Grand Story" — The documentation provided in end notes reveals the author's research on individuals and events, from archival sources, interviews and newspapers. The availability of many Calgary newspapers on the World Wide Web in *Our Future, Our Past: The Alberta Heritage Digitization Project* allows the reader access to the early twentieth century theatrical and musical reviews themselves. The Web address is : <http://www.ourfutureourpast.ca> The reader can make his or her own assessment of Grand performances from the 1910s to 1930s, by looking up the events as reported in *The Calgary Herald* or *The Albertan* on the Web, from the dates supplied in *Calgary's Grand Story*.

Please note that all attempts to locate the rightsholder of the photo of the opening scene from "The Passing of the Third Floor Back," which appears on page 7, and the scene from the filming of "Arms and the Man," on page 198, have been unsuccessful. If you have any information on these two images please contact the University of Calgary Press.

Many thanks to Philip McCoy and Jack Pecover for their careful reading of the published text before the second printing.

INTRODUCTION

Calgary firefighters reached the six-story Lougheed Building at the southeast corner of 6th Avenue and 1st Street S.W. just after four o'clock on the morning of 10 March 2004. From the roof smoke poured out from the two-story elevator mechanical structure beside the penthouse. Flames jumped up in the darkness. Just after the advance team entered the building, one of the elevator's two motors crashed through the roof narrowly missing several firefighters before it wedged itself on the fifth floor. Using their Bronto Skylife, two aerial ladder trucks and two cranes, the firefighters fought back, bringing the hot spots under control and removing debris. Speedy action limited the damage to the mechanical building and penthouse on the roof, and to the Lougheed's fifth and sixth floors. Fortunately no one was hurt. An investigation of the site by fire officials ruled out arson, leaving the cause undetermined.

The fire's threat to personal safety led to the re-routing of traffic in the downtown core. For much of the day police closed several city blocks: 6th Avenue, between Centre Street and 2nd Street S.W.; and 1st Street between 5th Avenue and 7th Avenue S.W. The closures caused huge traffic backups during rush hour. Calgary's radio and television stations broadcast updates all day; the media also covered the previously scheduled aldermanic committee meeting on the fate of the Lougheed Building.[1]

Until 10 March 2004, few Calgarians walking or driving past the Lougheed Building and the adjacent Grand Theatre gave them any thought. In this city-in-a-hurry the office building's and the theatre's great days had long since faded out of public memory. In the 1940s the Lougheed appeared in the centre of panorama photos of the city of 100,000 people. Over half-a-century later the six-story red-brick-and-sandstone building and theatre stand hidden by surrounding skyscrapers, in particular by the shadows of its giant neighbour to the north, the Petro-Canada Centre, almost ten times as high.

March 10th began as a day of despair for the Lougheed, with its threatened immolation. It ended with the venerable building still standing, and with hope of restoration. By a strange coincidence the city's Standing Policy Committee on Finance and Corporate Services had weeks earlier scheduled to review the owner's restoration plan that same day. Visibly shaken by the early morning events, owner Neil Richardson participated in the discussions. Once word came from fire officials in the early afternoon that the building was salvageable, the committee made an extraordinary decision. In a 6 to 1 vote it recommended to City Council that the Lougheed Building receive $3.4 million in tax relief and annual grants for the next fifteen years to allow the owner to restore and rehabilitate it. In addition, the motion recommended that "best efforts" also be made to save the Grand, to which the office building is joined by a party, or shared, wall.

Calgary's "Grand Story" began on the evening of Monday, 5 February 1912, with the spectacular opening of what the *Morning Albertan* termed, "Canada's Finest Theatre." It might well have ended on Wednesday March 10th, if the firefighters had failed to contain the blaze. But instead of death, the events of the afternoon of March 10th offered hope. The committee's recommendation that the City contribute financially to the restoration was accepted at a full Council meeting on March 22nd. This decision marked the essential first step for the owner to approach other levels of government, and the private sector, for help.

Today these two historical icons, both completed in 1912 when Calgary had just 50,000 people, stand in the downtown core of a metropolis of almost one million. In terms of both their cultural value and their physical framework they provide a strong symbolic link with the city's economic, political and cultural pioneers. They add variety to the commercial corporate atmosphere of the city's centre. Vitality comes from diversity. The Lougheed's use of local brick and sandstone reflect the geology of southern Alberta. The colour of the brick and sandstone are irreplaceable. If the downtown core consists entirely of shiny high-rises like the Petro-Canada Centre, the glass will have nothing to reflect.

Calgary's Grand Story recounts, from the vantage point of two heritage landmarks, the history of the city to Alberta's 100th birthday in 2005. The Lougheed and the Grand are used as vehicles to tell the entire story of the Foothills City during the two buildings' lifetime. This urban biography uses the lens of individual personalities and important events to review Calgary's story, particularly in the early twentieth century, the office building's and the Grand's "salad days."

The book begins with the Grand's opening night, a marvellous evening of suspended disbelief, with the presentation of a play in which virtue soundly triumphs over evil. With the arrival of a first-class performing arts centre in the city the "C" in Calgary increasingly stood for "Culture." The genius of the Lougheeds in placing a state of the art office building adjacent to an outstanding theatre merits our esteem nearly a century later. The two following chapters review the lives of the builder, Senator James Lougheed, and his wife, Belle Hardisty Lougheed. In many respects the office building reflects his personality: straightforward, practical, business-like. In contrast the ambiance of the theatre best represents hers: complex, imaginative, artistic.

Having introduced the Lougheeds the book's scope widens. Chapters four and five look at the site's immediate neighbourhood and the construction process itself. Three biographical chapters, six to eight, follow on tenant Will Tregillus, lawyer Fred Albright and theatre manager Jeff Lydiatt. They recall the buildings' first decade when the structures truly served as centres of gravity for both Calgary's business and cultural communities. Chapters nine and ten review their continuing grandeur in the 1920s, a prosperity which continued for four more years after Senator Lougheed's death in 1925. Chapter eleven looks at the impact of the Great Depression of the 1930s, which very

nearly added the Grand Theatre to its list of victims. Belle Lougheed died in 1936 at the very depths of the Grand's misfortunes.

The second last chapter introduces the two buildings in the mid-twentieth century, from the late 1930s to 1960s. Thanks to major tenants: United Grain Growers, the Alberta Wheat Pool, Home Oil and the leading accounting and law firms located there, the Lougheed Building retained its status as an important downtown address into the 1950s. The purchase of the Grand by the Barron Family in the late 1930s led to more active use of the Grand for live performances into the mid-1950s. But with the completion of the Jubilee Auditorium in 1957 it became exclusively a movie-house. Then the departure of Home Oil from the Lougheed in the mid-1950s, followed by the Alberta Wheat Pool in 1959, removed two of the office building's largest tenants. Subsequently Harvey and Morrison, the Alberta Wheat Pool's accountants, and Allen, MacKimmie, Matthews, Wood, Phillips and Smith, the Pool's legal advisors, withdrew as well. The United Grain Growers remained until the late 1970s, then it left after over six decades in the Lougheed Building.

The final chapter reviews the phenomenal urban growth, fed by the oil and gas boom in the 1950s and 1960s, that transformed the Foothills City. By the late 1960s towering skyscrapers stood throughout the old downtown core. Subdivisions expanded in all directions served by regional shopping centres. The city with the headquarters of Canada's oil and gas industry now stood separate from its agricultural hinterland, formerly its life force. It now depended on "black gold." The new metropolis bore little resemblance physically to the Calgary of the 1940s.

By the early 1980s it appeared only a matter of time before the wrecking ball struck down both the Lougheed and the Grand. In 1998 the then-owners of the buildings filed an application with the City of Calgary to make way for an office tower twenty-two stories high. In November 1999, and again in May 2000, the provincial government of Alberta declined (on account of the owners' objections to the designation) to protect the Lougheed/Grand by declaring them provincial historic sites. But then, in a dramatic reversal, in February 2003 the owners sold the buildings to a new buyer, Neil Richardson, who came forward and announced his intention to try and save them. On 22 March 2004, Calgary's City Council took the vital first step by granting badly needed financial assistance, to help save and restore the Lougheed Building. Richardson intends to preserve the exterior of the historic structure, bringing it to match the original appearance of 1912 as closely as possible. He will restore the main entrance to the Lougheed Building, the Lougheed's lobby and the entrance to the Grand Theatre, to match their original appearance in 1912. The second floor will also be restored to match its 1912 original appearance as closely as possible. He will modernize the other five floors to meet the most-up-to-date office standards.

More good news followed in early September 2004 when the local theatre company, Theatre Junction, purchased the Grand Theatre. It plans to undertake a massive renovation of the already drastically altered interior. By early November 2004 capital fundraising had raised over half the $10.3 million needed (including $2.7 million from the province of Alberta). Then the theatre company learned on November 22nd that

the Calgary City Council committee approved a $1.5 million municipal grant. Theatre Junction hopes to open its newly-designed contemporary theatre space in late 2005. To quote Mark Lawes, Theatre Junction founder and artistic director, "We have a vision of bringing it [the Grand] back to its original purpose, for live entertainment that is not just for theatre but for dance, music and film."[2]

This year Alberta celebrates its 100th birthday. Gone at last is the haunting fear of the demolition of both structures. The exterior forms of these nearly-century-old buildings whose story encapsulates the business and cultural history of twentieth century Calgary will live on. Changes will occur inside the two structures, as they must. New lives will be lived here, new events will occur. But the unseen presence of those who came before, a feeling of those who lived at a time distant from our own, with their own cycle of sadness and joy, of hope and despair, will remain.

Writer Constance Martin, whose grandparents came to Calgary in the 1890s,[3] made an eloquent plea for the retention of heritage buildings in a 1981 article in *Western Living*: "There is no way of rebuilding the past if its reminders are destroyed, and without such reminders any city becomes a bleak place indeed."[4] Why do we need a sense of the past? Nellie McClung, whose husband worked in the Lougheed Building for six years in the 1920s, best explains the conviction: "People must know the past to understand the present and to face the future."[5]

28 June 2005

The Calgary of
CALGARY'S GRAND STORY

Calgary City Limits

DOWNTOWN
CALGARY
MAIN MAP AREA

Bow River

N

5 Avenue SW

6 Avenue SW

LOUGHEED BUILDING
& GRAND THEATRE

7 Avenue SW

HUDSON'S BAY
COMPANY

CENTRAL UNITED CHURCH

CLARENCE BLOCK

CITY
HALL

Stephen Avenue Mall

GRAIN
EXCHANGE
BLDG

ALBERTA
HOTEL

BURNS
BLDG

9 Avenue SW

PALLISER
HOTEL

10 Avenue SW

11 Avenue SW

12 Avenue SW

MEMORIAL PARK
LIBRARY

THE
RANCHMEN'S
CLUB

LOUGHEED
HOUSE

13 Avenue SW

14 Avenue SW

15 Avenue SW

McCLUNG
HOUSE

0   100   200   300   400
METRES

PETRO CANADA
BUILDING

CHAMBER
OF
COMMERCE

6 Avenue SW

HERALD
ANNEX

LOUGHEED BLDG

GRAND
THEATRE

TELUS
TELEPHONE
BUILDING

HANOVER
PLACE

1 Street SW

FITZPATRICK BLDG

HERALD
BUILDING

LEN WERRY
BUILDING

TELUS
BUILDING

RENFREW
BUILDING

Centre Street

7 Avenue SW

CENTRAL
UNITED
CHURCH

DELAWARE
BLDG

Chapter One

OPENING NIGHT!

5 FEBRUARY 1912

THE NEWS SPREAD ACROSS THE BOW RIVER VALLEY LIKE A GREAT STAGE whisper. Johnston Forbes-Robertson, one of the greatest stars of the English stage, and his touring London company would open Alberta's most luxurious theatre—the Sherman Grand—with "The Passing of the Third Floor Back." The play had run an incredible three hundred continuous performances in London, and over two hundred in New York.[1]

Monday, 5 February 1912. Just before noon the celebrated actor-manager and his troupe arrived at the Canadian Pacific Railway (CPR) station. It was a fine February morning, "fair and cool," to quote *The Albertan* newspaper. Upon arrival Forbes-Robertson commented: "I am surprised at your climate. I have always imagined it was cold here. It was our Mr. Kipling, I think, who put this beautiful country in bad by writing of Canada as Our Lady of the Snows."[2]

Leaving their private railway car Forbes-Robertson and his leading players travelled to the Braemar Lodge, located on 4th Avenue, the city's fashionable residential street. They had arrived in a bustling city. Horse-drawn buggies, electric streetcars and automobiles made the narrow streets at times impassable in economically booming Calgary.[3] The sounds of the daytime city traffic reverberated. With the horse as the prime mover, and polluter, one crossed carefully over city streets. The crew dispatched the stage sets and costume trunks from the railway baggage car to the Sherman Grand. All afternoon the stagehands assembled the set.

The playhouse greatly impressed Forbes-Robertson. In an interview with the *Calgary News-Telegram*, one of the city's three dailies, the world-famous actor praised the Sherman Grand as "one of the finest and most commodious theatres in all of Western Canada."[4] No expense had been spared in its construction. Fellow English actor John Martin-Harvey, in fact, later commented that if one piled all the lighting features and stage accessories of the London theatres together, they would still be short of one or two items belonging to the Grand Theatre.[5] Just after dinner the actors dressed in the theatre's modern changing rooms below the stage, all fifteen equipped with hot and cold water as well as electric lighting.[6] The theatre was completely fireproof in every sense of the word, with a stage fitted with a modern automatic sprinkler system. The solid red brick structure, constructed with reinforced concrete and steel, had walls twenty-one inches thick.[7]

Hundreds of out-of-town visitors arrived in Calgary for the theatre's opening. Some came by train while others arrived by horse and buggy. They came from Banff and Canmore to the west; from Strathmore and Gleichen to the east; from Balzac and Airdrie to the north; from Okotoks and High River to the south. A number of out-of-towners stayed at the Alberta Hotel on 1st Street, just two blocks south of the theatre.[8] The sun set just after 5:30 that evening. Fortunately the good weather continued with no blinding snowstorm or plunging Arctic temperatures. The thermometer read a comfortable twelve degrees Celsius below zero.[9] Horse-drawn cabs, carriages and an assortment of automobiles pulled up continuously before the Lougheed Building. All bundled up, the elegant first-nighters descended from their unheated vehicles. Those who lived in the immediate neighbourhood walked briskly toward the glowing temple of light at the southeast corner of 6th Avenue and 1st Street.

Several electric streetlights, and the glare of automobile headlights, illuminated the theatre's entrance. The automobiles made more noise than the streetcars. The still uncompleted L-shaped office building enclosing the theatre remained obscured in inky black darkness. Banished were the sounds of workers and constant hammering. From inside the theatre, all aglow, music filtered out onto the street.[10] In long lines extending out along the sidewalk, men and women stood bundled up in their warm winter gear. The doors opened at 7:30 sharp. Immediately the crowd began to enter the long, elegant theatre lobby with its special tile floor and wainscoting of marble. Copper-leaded stained glass enclosed the box office on the left. Theatre staff took tickets at the entrance to the foyer. Uniformed female attendants accepted theatre patrons' coats at the checkroom to the left of the lobby. Seeing others and being seen in the foyer and seating area added to the audience's excitement.

A profusion of cut flowers decorated the entire theatre. Just beyond the foyer stood the Italian Renaissance-style playhouse itself, the interior painted in warm brown and beige colours, with ornate carvings on the walls and ceilings, and a magnificent proscenium arch. Large oil paintings from Italy hung on both sides of the theatre adjacent to the boxes. One work represented the balcony scene from "Romeo and Juliet."[11] An English pastoral scene decorated the asbestos fire curtain.[12] The theatre overflowed with people, the main floor and the balcony ablaze with jewels and new gowns.[13]

Female ushers in smart black and white uniforms, an innovation for Calgary, welcomed the 1,500 guests: many men attired in tuxedos, the women in lavish dresses.[14] The 1,350 regular seats, upholstered in green leather,[15] were roomy and comfortable with 810 on the main floor and 540 in the gallery.[16] Along the front of the gallery were twelve loges with six chairs each. The theatre also contained twelve boxes each with six seats.[17]

A special ramp on the right, for the purposes of decorum, rose from the lobby to the balcony. This allowed ladies in long dresses to ascend to the balcony, in the words of Calgary theatre historian Alan Hustak, "without worry of gentlemen catching a glimpse of their ankles."[18] On the left hand side others chose the staircase. From the sunken orchestra pit the theatre orchestra played "English and American Airs," the overture by Laurandeau.[19] The musical program was directed by Professor A. C. L. Augade, the Grand's newly appointed musical director. "Johnny" Augade, a violinist, had trained at the Paris Conservatory of Music before moving to Calgary in 1895.[20]

Just before the houselights dimmed and fire curtain rose, Belle Hardisty Lougheed, the wife of the building's owner, took her seat in the Lougheed family box, banked with masses of golden daffodils and roses. A woman in her early fifties, she wore a striking orange charmeuse satin gown with diamond ornaments.[21] She was joined by her sons, Clarence, Edgar and Norman, along with Norman's wife, Mary; and their friend, Newton Stirrett. Norman, the Lougheed's second son, the first to marry, had married Mary Stringer the previous May on Victoria Day.[22]

Years later, over seven decades later to be exact, Calgary historian Jack Peach wrote that when Belle entered the family box, "she was given a standing ovation as the first of the Lougheed family to use the box."[23] As no other source confirms this; perhaps myth has overtaken reality. But even if imaginary, the story confirms the family's importance in the creation of the theatre.

Belle's husband, Senator James Lougheed, in his late fifties, a federal cabinet minister and government leader in the senate, the individual who had paid for this ornate palace, unfortunately could not attend the opening night. Urgent unexpected government business called Calgary's most important federal politician away to Ottawa. The senator owned both the six-story office building and the theatre, but leased the theatre to impresario Bill Sherman to manage. In the midst of Calgary's phenomenal boom Sherman originally hoped that the senator would build twin theatres on the site, one seating 1,800 and the other 1,200.[24] But instead the city's most successful developer decided instead to construct just one, a truly palatial performing arts centre. The senator named his theatre the "Sherman Grand" after the man he chose as its first manager.[25]

That afternoon Forbes-Robertson met the flamboyant Bill Sherman, an eccentric dresser who wore a diamond on his ring finger "that looked like the headlight of a CPR locomotive."[26] What splendid opposites they were. The American-born theatre operator, then in his early forties, stocky and overweight with a voice rough and coarse, and the English actor-manager, one year short of sixty, lean and tall, with a dignified bearing and a cultured accent. So articulate in fact was Forbes-Robertson that George Bernard Shaw once seriously proposed recording his speech phonetically as a standard for spoken English. So highly did Shaw regard the actor's entire presentation of himself that he wrote his play, "Caesar and Cleopatra," for him to perform.[27]

Johnston Forbes-Robertson came from a privileged intellectual background. His mother was in her own right an accomplished painter, his father the distinguished art critic for the *London Times*. His parents belonged to an intellectual community which included some of the most talented artists and writers in England: Ford Madox Brown, Dante Gabriel Rossetti and Holman Hunt, who, with Rossetti, was one of the prophets of the pre-Raphaelite movement, a brotherhood of English painters and poets formed in the mid-nineteenth century to protest against the current low standards of British art. In his parents' friends' homes he gained access to the world of painting and literature. Johnston's education was that of a gentleman. He attended the famous English public school, Charterhouse. Equally genteel was his hobby, golf, which he played most frequently at St. Andrews in his native Scotland.[28]

Lobby of the Sherman Grand, September 1912. Photo from Albert Marche, Flesher Marble and Tile Ltd., Calgary. Glenbow Archives/ NA-1469-30.

Interior of the Sherman Grand Theatre. The architect's drawing first appeared in The Calgary Herald, 21 September 1912. This illustration is from The Western Standard, 12 June 1913. Glenbow Library.

In contrast, Bill Sherman, crude and unrefined, had a rough-and-tumble background. A self-made man, he attended school for a few years in his hometown of Coshocton, Ohio, but left early. He obtained his real education in the circus. From age seventeen to thirty-three he travelled on circus trains throughout North America with different shows, including Ringling Brothers. Before entering the management side Bill had a short, undistinguished vaudeville career involving the exhibition of a trained goat. But he excelled as a theatre impresario. After arriving in Calgary in 1905 Sherman built Calgary's Sherman Rink, a combination roller rink, dance hall and multi-purpose auditorium. By 1912 he also leased and efficiently operated several theatres in Western Canada, including Senator Lougheed's Lyric Theatre. Over the years Calgary's theatrical magnate had booked many well-known performers for his Western Canadian theatres.

Bill Sherman thought big. Only six weeks before the Sherman Grand opened he announced that he planned to have the celebrated dancer Anna Pavlova inaugurate it.[29] Whether or not he actually invited the famed Russian ballerina made little difference, for the "announcement" fed the buzz about his theatre's opening. Pavlova did not cross the North Atlantic to perform in the Sherman Grand; but, for a hefty $5,000 guaranteed fee,[30] Bill booked Forbes-Robertson, then in the midst of an extensive North American tour.[31]

The curtain rises. The overture ends. Calgary's "Grand Century" begins.

"The Passing of the Third Floor Back," a contemporary morality play, had a simple theme—that considerate, well-meaning behaviour could redeem even the most depraved individuals. Playwright Jerome K. Jerome set his play in a rather run-down boarding house, which provided shelter for a group of eleven outrageous vulgarians. All three acts occur in the parlour of an ancient London mansion turned second-rate rooming house. As *Leslie's Weekly* summarized the opening: "The curtain rises on the interior of a Bloomsbury boarding house, with a catty, tricky, gossipy landlady, an immoral, thieving and saucy serving maid and a gathering of boarders, each one emphasizing some special vice—vanity, selfishness, snobbishness, etc. The saucy maid gulps down half a pitcher of milk and pours in water to refill the pitcher. One boarder is detected by the audience stealing candles, and another sneaks a silk hat half full of toast."[32]

Three loud, long raps sound at the street door. The maid, just released from an industrial school, opens the door to find a slight stooping figure, in clothes somewhat old-fashioned, yet with an atmosphere of dignity around him. He has a remarkably sensitive-looking face. The mysterious stranger explains he has come in response to the "Room for Rent" sign in the window. At first the landlady tries to cheat the newcomer, but his sincerity and kindness cause her to change her mind. Much to her own amazement she reverses herself, and asks the fair price.

After taking the small back room on the third floor, the new lodger, Christ-like in his behaviour, morally rehabilitates his fellow lodgers. In turn all feel his influence. To every insult "The Third Floor Back" returns a pleasant word; for every malicious remark, a compliment. He recalls their dead and forgotten youthful ideals. The first act shows the characters in their unreformed state, the second after the stranger has begun

The opening scene from The Passing of the Third Floor Back. The Passer-By, played by Johnston Forbes-Robertson appears in the centre.

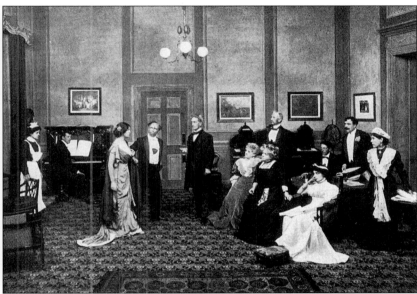

to transform them. In the third and final act we see them regenerated. Through his faith in the best of each of them, their "Better Self" comes out.

In the audience sat two of the province's leading cultural personalities. The first was Mrs. Annie Glen Broder, an attractive-looking white-haired woman in her mid-fifties who loved to wear crimson velvet gowns with touches of lace.[33] The city's foremost music critic was born in India at the fortress of Agra, within sight of the Taj Mahal. Her father, Reverend William Glen, taught at the Oriental School run by the Indian government. Her grandfather, the first Rev. William Glen, translated the Old Testament into Persian and actually presented the first copy to the Shah himself.[34] Although born in India Mrs. Broder had close cultural links to the mother country. Raised in England, she studied piano at the National Training School for Music in London when Sir Arthur Sullivan served as Principal. At the invitation of Sir Arthur himself Annie attended early performances of Gilbert and Sullivan at the Savoy Theatre in London. Very impressed by her musical and writing talent, he described her as "a woman of exceptional gifts."[35] She had been present at Albert Hall for the first performances in England of Wagner's music, with the composer himself conducting. A brilliant student, she wrote an authoritative textbook, *How to Accompany*, which went into its second edition in just six weeks. Queen Victoria commanded a copy. A popular lecturer, she spoke on piano accompaniment throughout Britain, including Oxford University. After her Oxford lecture with musical illustrations, Professor Friedrich Max Mueller, the German philologist and renowned Orientalist, invited her to join him for lunch. In London she was an acquaintance of a number of celebrities, including playwright Oscar Wilde and his brother Willie Wilde.

Immediately after her 1903 arrival in Calgary with her husband, Richard,[36] Mrs. Broder assumed the central role in the city's musical world. Instantly she became the Grande Dame of Calgary's small musical universe: the organist at the Anglican Pro-Cathedral Church of the Redeemer, a highly regarded music teacher, recitalist, composer and the music critic of choice for local newspapers. Shortly after her arrival Annie Glen Broder wrote one of her most popular pieces, a march, "The Ride of the Royal North West Mounted Police." The song she wrote to accompany the composition enthusiastically celebrates the men in scarlet.[37]

In 1911 the *Free Press* in Winnipeg engaged Mrs. Broder as their special correspondent at the coronation of King George V in Westminster Abbey. Earlier, in 1902, she covered the coronation of Edward VII for both the *Free Press* and the *Toronto Globe*. When she passed away in 1937 *The Calgary Herald* wrote of her as "a figure of Victorian elegance, retaining a Dresden-like distinction until the end. When she swept down the aisle at concerts to her critic's chair, her befeathered hat swathed in pink tulle was known to half the audience."[38]

Mrs. Broder's formidable counterpart, Mrs. Lydia Case Winter, southern Alberta's leading drama critic, also was in attendance. She ruled Calgary's dramatic world just as Annie Broder dominated the musical. The daughter of a British diplomat and his Spanish-Portuguese wife, Lydia Case was born on-board ship in San Francisco harbour in 1859. As a child she lived with her parents in Japan, China, Ceylon, Spain

and Portugal before beginning a stage career as a professional actress and singer in England.[39] She came to Calgary in 1893, with her lawyer husband, Roland Winter. Mrs. Winter's Calgary biographer describes her as "a buxom five feet four inches tall with an erect carriage and a resonant contralto voice that swelled from deep within her."[40] This mother of seven children, a woman of boundless energy, gave a great deal of her time to develop amateur theatre in her adopted province—acting, directing and teaching. Only a year earlier she played Katisha at Senator Lougheed's Lyric Theatre in the Calgary Amateur Operatic Society's production of "The Mikado." *The Calgary Herald* found her "thoroughly at home in the part, which is hardly to be wondered at when one remembers that Mrs. Winter played it at the Savoy theatre, London, Eng., in the heydey days of the famous Gilbert and Sullivan collaboration."[41]

The reigning monarch of Calgary theatre world had her own eccentricities. Although a robust woman Lydia Winter always carried a gold-headed cane, which she used to accentuate the dramatic gestures she loved to make.[42] Even in the hottest summer weather her distinctive wardrobe included knit skirts almost to her ankles. She loved large hats tied with a veil over her face to protect her from the ravages of the southern Alberta sun. This outlandish British woman, who taught fencing, and was an accomplished horsewoman, had a wonderful sense of humour. When people mistakenly called her "Winters" instead of "Winter," she always corrected them: "The name is Winter—because I am a very singular person."[43] Years later Elaine Catley, a contemporary of both women, provided short sketches of the two leading ladies of Calgary's cultural world. "Mrs. 'Judge' Winter," she wrote, "sailing along in her Gainsborough hat, and saying just exactly what she thought in her clear, English voice—Mrs. Annie Glen Broder, with her limitless knowledge of music, and her beautifully written reviews of all the concerts."[44]

Two well-dressed men with newspaper connections also awaited the play's beginning. The first, Bob Edwards, fifty-one years old, edited the "semi-occasional" *Calgary Eye Opener*. The portly editor with a bushy moustache wore clothes well-tailored to fit his 5' 7" frame.[45] Appearances can deceive. Although conventional in dress and "quiet and retiring" in terms of speech,[46] he was highly original and forceful in his writing. "Eye-Opener Bob," the paper's editor, publisher, manager, reporter and errand boy all rolled into one, feared no one. In his columns he harpooned many institutions and public figures to the joy of his readership. He targeted graft, hypocrisy and pomposity. On his maternal side his grandfather was Robert Chambers, the famous Scottish publisher. At home Bob received a good education in the best Scottish tradition, including attendance at Glasgow University. Fifteen years earlier he arrived in Alberta from Scotland via a Wyoming ranch and an Iowa farm.

The *Eye Opener* came out irregularly due to its editor's love of the bottle. He was a binge drinker whose benders occasionally left him hospitalized for treatment.[47] Regardless of its irregular appearance his readers loved the *Calgary Eye Opener* and made it the most widely read newspaper in Alberta. By 1912 it enjoyed a circulation of over 30,000, a figure greater than that of any other Canadian newspaper west of Winnipeg.[48] Bob's caustic wit and total unpredictability were essential parts of the *Eye*

Opener's success. But on the evening of 5 February 1912, Bob stepped through the lobby, the foyer, then into the Grand's spacious auditorium, already favourably disposed to the elegant theatre. In the *Eye Opener* one week earlier the important Calgary opinion maker praised the new structure, done in "such excellent taste": "This will be the finest playhouse in the Dominion, outclassing anything they have in Winnipeg, Toronto or Montreal."[49]

The second gentleman, Jim Davidson, known to his friends as "Big Jim,"[50] was a large man (almost six feet tall) with broad shoulders.[51] A fellow Rotarian later wrote of this dynamic individual: "Everything about him was big: body, head, brain, voice, laugh, straight look of the eyes, heart, purpose, ideal, and love of Rotary."[52] He looked older than his thirty-nine years. Highly successful in several different fields of endeavour including diplomacy, business and journalism, Jim Davidson was one of the leaders of the American community in Calgary.

Davidson had probably the most exotic background of anyone in the theatre that evening. When barely twenty-one, the young Minnesotan participated in Commander Peary's second Greenland expedition. A persistently bothersome foot, which Jim had frozen on an ice cap, often reminded him of his year-and-a-half Arctic adventure.[53] From Arctic Greenland he went to tropical Formosa as a war correspondent in the Sino-Japanese War of 1895. Jim spent over a decade in Asia. In 1905 he served as the American consul-general in Shanghai. He owned one of the first two automobiles in the Chinese city.[54] The world citizen arrived in Calgary in 1907 to join his brother, banker Charles Davidson. Together with John Beiseker, allegedly the richest man in North Dakota,[55] Charles had bought 250,000 acres of Canadian Pacific Railway lands northeast of the city, at what became known as the Beiseker district. Charles later developed sections of Hillhurst and Sunnyside.[56] Jim himself built up a successful lumber business, Crown Lumber, which by 1912 had fifty-two yards in the province.[57]

The morning after opening night, Jim Davidson praised the Sherman Grand in *The Albertan* as "The Greatest Theatre in Western Canada." "Calgary," he wrote, "now has perhaps the finest and most modern theatre in the Dominion, with a stage that in size and equipment is not excelled." In Western Canada, he added, only Winnipeg's celebrated Walker Theatre, owned by theatre magnate C. P. Walker, came even close to rivalling it. But the Sherman Grand exceeded the Walker in size, as it did Toronto's Royal Alexandra, to that point reputed to be Canada's finest theatre. Then Davidson, with the precision of one of his American consular reports, supplied the exact details. While both the Royal Alex and the Sherman Grand had the same stage width and identical seating capacity of just over 1,500, the Grand extended four feet higher than the Royal Alex from stage to roof. In depth of their stage, from footlights to rear wall, the Grand surpassed the Royal Alex once again by an additional four feet.[58]

Forbes-Robertson, the distinguished actor-manager, whose acting career extended back nearly four decades, instinctively knew the Sherman Grand's importance to this bustling Western city. All afternoon he heard all about Calgary's amazing growth, about the "city that has risen in a night."[59] The federal census found it had grown tenfold from 1901 to 1911, from 4,400 to nearly 44,000 people. Calgary boosters went

further and alleged that its true population in 1911 was closer to 60,000.[60] Without any overriding plan new residential areas expanded in all directions. Boosters insisted enough prairie land existed within the city's limits to provide half a million building lots and factory sites.[61] But this cultured British visitor knew the importance of the arts in newly settled communities. Humanity cannot live by bread alone. In fact, just before the second and last intermission after the second act, he made a short impromptu speech to congratulate Calgary on its splendid new theatre.[62]

At the end of the third and final act the Calgary audience boisterously made known its appreciation. The cast received half a dozen curtain calls. The man billed in the *Provincial Standard*, a Calgary weekly paper, as "the Greatest English-Speaking Actor,"[63] stepped forward with his company to acknowledge the tumultuous applause. After their last bows the final curtain descended. The audience rose to sing "God Save the King"[64] before leaving the auditorium still spellbound by the powerful performance. Outside, the sub-Arctic night air brought to lower altitudes those still suspended in another world. Well beyond midnight hotel restaurants hosted lavish theatre suppers for Calgary's gilded upper crust. For one incredible evening, downtown Calgary had the atmosphere of London's West End, or the theatre district in New York.

The critics praised "The Passing of the Third Floor Back" as strongly as the public. Mrs. Broder called Forbes-Robertson's performance as the Third Floor Back "a triumph," then added: "Apart from the physical endowments of Forbes-Robertson, which have always marked him out for great parts, he possessed in a marked degree the power of concentration without visible effort, and staying power that is no less intense. To keep a character at a sustained elevation throughout a long performance is—simple as it may seem—an extraordinary tour de force." As for Mrs. Winter, her words soared even higher. She wrote, "It is not presumption on the part of a long time worshipper at the shrine of dramatic art, to say that his work in the 'Passing of the Third Floor Back' was the most absolutely perfect and spiritually beautiful portrayal that has ever been seen on any stage." Even the hard-nosed Eye Opener Bob reacted warmly. He judged the play, "a brilliant affair. Everything passed off beautifully... The role of the Passer-by was magnificently played by Forbes-Robertson."[65]

The next day the *News-Telegram* announced the audience's verdict: "The hundreds of Calgarians who attended the first night performance were unanimous in endorsing the play and endorsing Forbes-Robertson and his company as the greatest play and the greatest company of players that have yet appeared in the city."[66] When the High Riverites who attended opening night arrived home the *High River Times* wrote, "they all report a delightfully interesting evening with the great English actor."[67] Jim Davidson, president of Calgary's Town Planning Commission, sent a telegram of congratulation to Senator James Lougheed in Ottawa: "The Calgary Town Planning Commission wish to express their appreciation of the beautiful theatre you have erected in our city and to congratulate you on the successful, opening tonight which can truly be regarded as one of the great events in the onward movement of our City."[68]

In his phrase, "the onward movement of our city," Jim Davidson repeated the City of Calgary's one-word motto: "Onward." Henry Orr Beattie, twenty-one years old,

was in the audience on opening night. He wrote his name on his program and kept it all his life.[69] Henry Beattie had local roots. His grandfather, Wesley Orr, mayor of Calgary in 1893, selected the city's motto.[70] Now, at last, the motto rang true. The splendid new theatre proclaimed the city's arrival as a metropolitan centre. Orr's grandfather urged the development of electric light, water and sewage systems for Calgary. To advance agriculture in the dry land east of the settlement he promoted irrigation.[71] Yet, in spite of his commitment and unswerving faith in Calgary's future, the depressed economy defeated him. Wesley Orr died in February 1898, a few years before the world economic situation lifted leading to a settlement boom in Western Canada. By 1905, the year Alberta became a province, the settlement of the "Last Best West" truly began.

On account of its tenfold growth from 1901 to 1911 Calgary was a city of newcomers. As one once wrote, "A residence of over ten years accords you the title of 'old-timer,' of over twenty, that of 'pioneer'."[72] Most Calgarians, apart from individuals like Henry Orr Beattie with strong links to the city's past, had no sense of place or appreciation of the area's past. Throughout late January and February 1912, for example, the Rev. John McDougall presented a series of weekly lectures on Western Canada as he first saw it nearly half-a-century earlier.[73] But interest in the past, in a city with such obvious potential for the future, remained low. Many newcomers still mentally lived in worlds they had left behind—in Britain, Eastern Canada and the United States. The veteran Methodist missionary's evening lecture on 26 January attracted only fifty people,[74] in a city with a population of approximately 50,000.

"The onward movement of our City"— stirring words by Jim Davidson, but the phrase masked an inner tension within Calgary's upper elite in early 1912. The issue of free trade had just deepened the divide between the Conservative and Liberal Party factions in the city. Conservatives feared for Canada's future. Just four months earlier the protectionist Conservatives defeated the governing Liberals, advocates of free trade with the United States. Locally, Senator Lougheed and R. B. Bennett, his partner in the law firm of Lougheed and Bennett, led the Conservative Party. They presented free trade as treason, as a prelude to political annexation to the United States. After the Conservative victory the senator, a veteran of twenty-two years standing in the Senate, joined the federal cabinet, and R. B. Bennett entered the House of Commons as Calgary's Member of Parliament, the only Conservative elected in Alberta.[75]

In 1912 Canadians of British ancestry dominated in Calgary. Calgary was a British-Canadian town with strong British values and attitudes. Other groups formed identifiable communities, which gave the city a modest multi-cultural flavour, but in number the continental European and French-speaking communities remained small. The largest groups consisted of German-speakers from Central Europe and Russia (6%), Eastern Europeans, mainly Russians and Poles (3.3%), Scandinavians (2.2%), and French-speakers from Eastern Canada and Europe (1.6%).[76] Protestant Christianity dominated the religious landscape in 1912. Protestants outnumbered Roman Catholics by roughly eight to one. A tiny non-Christian world existed. The city contained a small Jewish community of about six hundred. Several hundred Chinese residents appear listed in the census of 1911 as "Buddhist and Confucian."[77]

Calgarians of British ancestry embraced Forbes-Robertson and his touring company. The English spoken on the stage on opening night, and during the following two evenings and afternoon matinee, warmly brought instant memories of the "old country." In the case of native-born Anglo-Canadians from eastern Canada or the United States, the accents of British-born parents or grandparents returned. Ethel Heydon, *The Albertan's* city hall reporter originally from St. Thomas, Ontario, described the personal impact of the play in this manner: "Their speech is something to marvel; with all the variations of dialect from Cockney to Devon, the dialogue of the play becomes a concert worthy of hearing."[78]

Most women attending the Sherman Grand's opening night came as escorted guests of husbands or gentleman friends. Few women had independent sources of income. In 1912, most married women worked inside the home as housekeepers and mothers. Ethel Heydon, who the following year married her employer, W. M. Davidson, editor of *The Albertan*, was one of the first female journalists in Calgary during the 1910s.[79] Males of Western European—particularly British Canadian—background enjoyed special privilege in Calgary in 1912. Women still laboured without many civic rights, including the right to vote both provincially and federally. In terms of numbers in this male-dominated town, men outnumbered women three to two.[80]

Individuals of African or Asian ancestry, and the Native Peoples, faced considerable challenges. One Calgary newspaper's comment on the "Passing of the Third Floor Back" speaks volumes about contemporary racial attitudes. The day after the Grand's opening the *News-Telegram* wrote of the Passer-By, the play's key character: "He comes in, attracted by an advertisement, to inquire about a room on the third floor back. He is a very chivalrous and courteous gentleman, and treats the boarding-house keeper and even the 'slavey' like the first ladies in the land. He is a white man through and thorough."[81]

Robert J. C. Stead, an Ontario-born columnist for the *High River Times*, covered the event for his paper. He termed the play "extraordinary," in his review.[82] Previous to his appointment in 1911, Bob Stead published a book, *The Empire Builders and Other Poems*. After reading it, Earl Grey, then Governor General of Canada, sent a congratulatory note: "You have a great power, and I rejoice to think you are exercising it for noble ends."[83] The editor of the *High River Times* liked it so much he gave a free copy to anyone taking out a new subscription to his paper.[84] One of Stead's poems, "The Mixer," speaks volumes about the racial attitudes in Canada at the time. Within the author described how the country turned immigrants into Canadians, "all but the yellow and brown."

> In the city, on the prairie, in the forest, in the camp,
> In the mountain-clouds of color, in the fog-white river-damp,
> From Atlantic to Pacific, from the Great Lakes to the Pole,
> I am mixing strange ingredients into a common whole;
> Every hope shall build upon me, every heart shall be my own,
> The ambitions of my people shall be mine, and mine alone;

Not a sacrifice so great but they will gladly lay it down
When I turn them out Canadians—all but the yellow and brown.[85]

Most of the dominant Anglo-Canadian community in Calgary arrived directly from Eastern Canada, others came indirectly via the United States. The British-born came from the United Kingdom, or also via the United States, with a small number coming from the outreaches of the empire. According to the census of 1911 over seventy per cent of the population was of British descent.[86] As the census failed to distinguish between those of British descent who were of Canadian or American origin it is impossible to say how many Americans actually lived in the city. Western Canadian historian James Gray has written that the 1911 census only listed four thousand Americans in Calgary, or one-tenth of the population, "but several pioneers of the era put the number as high as a third of the population."[87]

Ethel Heydon Davidson later recalled the early Americans' participation in the community: "U.S. immigrants led in financial speculations, but were not otherwise outstanding."[88] Her statement hints at her British Canadian viewpoint. Other British Canadians made their imperial allegiance well-known. R. B. Bennett told a Calgary Canadian Club audience some years earlier, "We would not and will not be assimilated to the United States."[89] Just a few months before the opening of the Sherman Grand, Bennett personally intervened in a local controversy over a residential real estate subdivision known locally as "American Hill."

The exclusive district of Calgary (in which Jim Davidson and a number of other Americans lived) was originally owned by the CPR, the city's largest landowner. In 1906 it began to open up the 320-acre hill on the southwestern boundary of the city as a luxury suburb. The CPR chose a number of historic street names for Mount Royal, named after the mountain in Montreal. To give northern Mount Royal a distinctive Canadian flavour, it selected the names of several Northwest Territories' governors, including Cameron, Forget and Royal. The last two were French Canadians from Quebec, while Cameron came from British Ontario. In southern Mount Royal, it added British administrators and governors of early Canada: Amherst, Hope, Carleton/Dorchester, Sydenham, Colborne, Bagot and Durham. On the western boundary it chose the names of British Governor-Generals of Canada: Monck, Dufferin, Lorne, Lansdowne, Stanley, Aberdeen, Minto and Grey.[90]

But unanticipated events upset the CPR's plans to have a Canadian face to its luxury suburb. Immediately after the CPR opened its sale, well-to-do Americans settled on Mount Royal's northern slopes, including James Davidson, who himself purchased three lots on Royal Avenue in 1909.[91] So many Americans, in fact, bought land that the daily newspapers, the city directory and many Calgarians themselves began to call the area "American Hill." In October 1911, just after the federal election, the CPR acted again. R. B. Bennett himself passed complains about the Americanization of Mount Royal to the CPR land commissioner in Winnipeg. Subsequently the commissioner selected a second batch of names, most from the history of the French regime, and the final struggle for control of northeastern North America, fought between Britain and France.

He chose names such as Cartier, Champlain, Talon, Laval, Frontenac, Joliet, Marquette, Vercheres and Levis. Western Canadian historian James Gray learned that when the CPR's land commissioner in Winnipeg chose the French names he chortled: "There, let them damn Yankees try to pronounce these names when they tell their friends where they live!"[92]

R. B. Bennett, British-to-the-core, had fanned the flames of Yankee-phobia in the election campaign of September 1911. But Senator Lougheed, while also publicly voicing pro-British sentiments and opposing free trade with the United States, acted more discretely, not wishing to burn any bridges with Calgary's American community. Already he maintained close economic relationships with two Americans in Calgary— his theatre partner Bill Sherman and, apparently, Jim Davidson. Years later Marjorie Davidson Abramson, Jim's daughter and only child (born in 1915), recalled being told that her father oversaw the construction of the Sherman Grand and the Lougheed Building during the senator's many absences on parliamentary business in Ottawa.[93]

On the evening of 5 February 1912, Calgary's British-Canadian and American elite forgot their free trade skirmish. At the Sherman Grand's gala opening even the lowest priced ticket cost one dollar at a time when twenty cents an hour constituted a fair wage. In 1911 the average worker in the Canadian West received $15 to $18 a week.[94] The top-end box and loge tickets for the Sherman Grand's opening sold for $5.[95] In terms of current dollar values this is almost $100 today.[96] A working class person could not afford to pay over a third of one day's wages for even the lowest price ticket. But the city's Anglo-Canadian and American economic elite came out in force, except for the man most responsible for the event, James Lougheed. Prime Minister Borden needed his senate leader, a man described by the Montreal Gazette as "in the prime of middle age; capable, energetic and respected,"[97] in Parliament. Borden wanted his seasoned Conservative Party gladiator to defend in the senate the government's proposed multi-million dollar gift to the Royal Navy, to strengthen Britain's mastery of the seas, now threatened by the resurgent German Empire.

Chapter Two

JAMES LOUGHEED

HIS STORY

Who WAS THE MAN WHO BUILT THE BUILDING THAT NOW BEARS his name? Shortly before James Lougheed's death in 1925 the national Canadian magazine *Saturday Night* identified him as "A man of charming personality, courteous and well-versed in the arts and graces of leadership, he is not only an outstanding figure in the Senate, but a public man of wide experience, with a broad grasp of national questions."[1] Other favourable opinions include his obituary in the *Ottawa Citizen* on 2 November 1925, which states that he was "one of the ablest and also one of the most popular men of his party."

General William Griesbach, a fellow Alberta senator, had a less positive view. The former Edmonton mayor and World War One veteran[2] served under Conservative Senate Leader Lougheed as his party whip for four years in the early 1920s. The decorated war hero, over twenty years Sir James's junior, recalled him as, "a very clever man with a wide knowledge of many subjects." The general admired his punctuality, always in time for all functions, but noted as well a distinct authoritarian side to his character: "He could meet a delegation and be as sweet as pie, but finally having made up his mind he became a boss and was vigorous and sometimes ruthless in carrying out his ideas." His paternalism could grate. Often they went golfing, and the younger man remembered: "Normally, I used to beat him at every hole but that did not prevent him from telling me what was wrong with my stance, what was wrong with my driving and the like." Lougheed, he continued, was "the exact opposite" of Dr. Brett, Alberta's Lieutenant Governor in the late 1910s and early 1920s, whom Griesbach recalled "as a kindly man, very considerate of the opinions and feelings of others."[3]

Sir James said little about himself, as the *Toronto Star Weekly* commented in a feature article in July 1921: "He is a man of few words."[4] The fact that he left behind no personal collection of papers also makes any assessment of his character challenging. Without any doubt he owed his cherished role in the governing class to competence. Even if one accepts Griesbach's reservations about his lack of concern for others and capacity for occasional ruthlessness, the general also recognized his administrative ability. Lougheed's selection as Conservative senate leader, and later as a cabinet minister by both Prime Minister Robert Borden and his successor, Arthur Meighen, confirms the respect he enjoyed among his peers. But his meteorite-like emergence in Alberta from a modest background in Ontario requires additional explanation. Time and circumstance also played a key role. This man of relatively humble origins from East Toronto had the good fortune to arrive early in the settlement of Alberta. Even more importantly, James Lougheed's rise to power and wealth in Calgary owed much to his wife, Belle Hardisty. Through his marriage into the Hardisty family, he instantly became well connected. His wife, so skilled socially and such a natural person, also helped to give the recent arrival from Eastern Canada a boost upward to higher altitudes.

In the early 1880s Belle's uncle Richard Hardisty, Chief Factor at Fort Edmonton, oversaw the Hudson Bay Company's (HBC's) entire operations throughout the North Saskatchewan River Valley—an area larger in size than the British Isles. Both his father, Richard Hardisty, Sr., and his maternal grandfather, James Sutherland, rose to become chief traders in the Honourable Company. After his father's death in 1865 Richard's mother, Marguerite Sutherland Hardisty—described in her youth as "a dark, petite women of remarkable beauty, undoubtedly derived from her mixed-blood or Indian mother"[5]—employed fourteen servants at the family's home at Lachine, just west of Montreal.[6] An astute business person himself, with excellent administrative ability, Richard Hardisty amassed a fortune estimated in 1883 at $40,000 in cash, mortgages, stocks and bonds.[7] This was a huge sum indeed when compared with the $2 to $2.50 day wage that a labourer earned on the prairie section of the CPR.[8] Several of Richard's five brothers also obtained responsible positions in the HBC.[9] His oldest brother William served as Chief Factor in the Mackenzie River Valley. Upon his death at Lachine in 1881 he left a substantial estate to his widow, Mary, and their children.[10]

Few knew the prairies and its investment possibilities as intimately as Chief Factor Richard Hardisty, a veteran with over thirty years experience in the company's service. He spent his working life at posts strung out along the North Saskatchewan River from Cumberland House northwest of Lake Winnipeg to Rocky Mountain House in the Alberta foothills.[11] While still Aboriginal country in the early 1880s, it was changing fast. In a letter written in June 1882, the Chief Factor at Fort Edmonton commented on the momentous changes to the south: "People are flocking in, in connection with the Canadian Pacific Railway and cattle ranches, besides others going in for the purpose of settling down on farms."[12]

The following summer, Chief Factor Richard Hardisty transferred the headquarters of the company's Alberta operations from Fort Edmonton to the railhead at Calgary. In mid-August the HBC began shipping its goods to Calgary from Winnipeg on the CPR.[13] Richard and his wife, Eliza McDougall Hardisty, moved to Calgary themselves that summer. Shortly after their arrival at the junction of the Bow and the Elbow rivers Richard invited Belle Hardisty, his late brother William's lively and spirited twenty-two-year-old daughter,[14] to visit them in Alberta. By early fall 1883 the once arduous journey suddenly became much easier. The CPR reached Fort Calgary that August.

Just a few weeks before the CPR reached Calgary, Jim Lougheed arrived from Medicine Hat. In one of his few personal references he once told fellow Conservative senator Gideon Robertson, his deskmate in the senate from 1917 to his death, that he entered first Calgary on foot, having walked from the railhead.[15] The ambitious young lawyer came without benefit of influential family or friends.

Belle Hardisty Lougheed's paternal grandparents, Richard Hardisty and his wife Margaret Sutherland Hardisty, taken around 1860. Archives of Manitoba.

In the tent village on the east bank of the Elbow, Jim became an active member of the local Methodist Church as soon as he arrived. In December 1883 at a Methodist congregational meeting held at the home of Richard Hardisty, he became one of the first church stewards.[16] He later served as the Sunday School Superintendent from 1884 to 1888. He also joined the choir.[17] During those early months in Calgary his social life revolved completely around the Methodist Church. Although shortly before his death he appears to have affiliated with the Anglican Church, in his early years in Calgary he identified himself as a Methodist.[18]

An emerging romantic interest helped to keep Jim in the Methodist ranks. At church he met Belle Hardisty, the newly-arrived church organist, with whom he found he had a great deal in common.[19] She had a delightful personality and a zest for life.[20] His personal drive and ambition did not upset her. In 1884 the *Calgary Herald* reported both Jim and Belle among the performers at a church concert that packed the small frame and canvas church on Good Friday.[21] At age twenty-nine Jim proposed and Belle accepted. Exactly two weeks after Jim's thirtieth birthday, they married in Calgary's Methodist Church on 16 September 1884. Eliza Hardisty's brother, the Rev. John McDougall, married them. A delighted Richard and Eliza Hardisty held a reception for the newly married couple immediately after the ceremony.[22]

In contrast to Jim, Belle had always stood at the top rung of the social hierarchy. The daughter of the Chief Factor of Mackenzie River Valley had attended two well-respected private schools—Miss Davis' School in the Red River and the Wesleyan Ladies' College in Hamilton, Ontario. In Montreal she frequently visited her Uncle Donald's and Aunt Isabella Hardisty Smith's huge stone mansion on Dorchester Avenue. Donald A. Smith had become one of Canada's first multi-millionaires through his holdings in the Hudson's Bay Company, the Bank of Montreal and the CPR. Belle had the poise and self-confidence that came from a privileged background. From both her schools in Manitoba and Ontario she had a deep grounding in the arts—particularly in art and music.

Jim had more modest origins. Perhaps to give himself sufficient gravitas for his legal practice in Calgary, he took to calling himself James.[23] Born in Brampton in 1854, just east of Toronto, James Alexander Lougheed, to use his full name, was raised from the age of three or so in Cabbagetown, the poor east end of the city. East Toronto emerged in the mid-nineteenth century as an important destination point for British immigrants to Ontario, particularly for Irish Protestants. The growth of railways and industries in Toronto created large numbers of jobs for urban workers north of the new rail and factory complex at the Don River end of the harbour. After immigrants spread in the 1840s along both sides of King Street East, they settled on the vacant land to the northward. There the newcomers built squatter shacks and planted essential gardens. Hence the district's name—"Cabbagetown."

John Lougheed, his carpenter father, set up his workshop at the junction of King and Queen, just west of the Don River Bridge. Here, in a succession of modest rented houses,[24] young Jim grew up with his parents and younger brother Sam. Cabbagetown, a district of drab frame houses, stood close to the dirt, debris, and fumes

The British Isles's relative size
as superimposed upon Western
Canada. Courtesy of Dr. William
C. Wonders, University Professor
Emeritus, Department of Geography,
University of Alberta.

Tent city on the east bank of
the Elbow River, 1883. Glenbow
Archives/NA-1315-9.

of the factories. In his boyhood the Lougheeds lived in thinly built homes with back-yard privies but without central heating.[25] For elementary school Jim attended Park School, one noted throughout the city for its high absenteeism, a widespread problem in the poorer city schools.[26] Although both of Jim's parents were of Protestant Irish background, John Lougheed had been born in Upper Canada, as Ontario was then known. Jim's mother, Mary Ann Alexander Lougheed, arrived directly from Ireland.

Twenty years younger than her husband, Mary devoted herself to her older son's advancement. James always credited his mother for his success. She taught him the value of hard work, and the importance of honesty. As the Canadian Press reported in its notice of his death in 1925: "Though Sir James has often been called a self-made man, he has often attributed his success in life to his mother, Mary Ann Alexander, a beautiful Christian woman, an active worker in Berkley [Berkeley] Street (Toronto) Methodist church."[27] Nothing is said about his father's influence.

Mary Lougheed insisted that Jim attend two Sunday Schools on Sunday. He went to her church in the afternoon and to Little Trinity Anglican Church on King Street in the morning. Even at the age of fifteen he was very conscientious. On 15 October 1869, his teacher at Little Trinity gave him a prize book, "for punctuality and attention." The volume, entitled *A Life's Motto*, contained this advice from Ecclesiastes 9:10 on its title page: "WHATSOEVER THY HAND FINDETH TO DO, DO IT WITH THY MIGHT; for there is no work, nor device, nor knowledge, nor wisdom in the grave, whither THOU goest."[28] He kept the book all his life and brought it with him to Calgary.

Jim attended both Sunday Schools with his lifelong friend, Emerson Coatsworth, Jr., who later became an important Orange Lodge leader in Toronto, a mayor of the city (1906–1907), and a York County judge. The boys were taught to renounce worldly habits. Berkeley Street Methodists, Emerson Coatsworth recalled three-quarters of a century later, "did not play cards or dance. We did not attend the theatre or the races."[29] (Once one knows of Jim's plain, culturally deprived childhood, one can better appreciate the impact that Belle had on him from the moment of their first meeting in Calgary.)

John Lougheed intended that his sons follow him into the trades, which James and Sam both did after leaving school. Years later James recalled walking miles to building sites.[30] In 1869, William Pearce, who like James also later became one of Calgary's leading citizens, briefly worked with him. His testimony provides a glimpse of young Jim the same year he won his Sunday School prize. With the characteristic precision of a surveyor, Pearce recalled years later that he first met Jim "on Sept. 30, 1869, on which date I entered an office in Toronto in which he was engaged."[31]

Pearce, then twenty-one years old, five years older than Jim Lougheed, had just left the School of Engineering at the University of Toronto. "Finding that the course of studies there was not teaching me what I anticipated," he departed after completing only one term.[32] He then articled with the Toronto surveying firm of Wadsworth and Unwin on Adelaide Street.[33] For three years William went out on survey parties throughout northern Ontario learning his profession. Like young Jim Lougheed, William was ambitious and recognized the same trait in his young friend. Both William Pearce and James

A LIFE'S MOTTO.

ILLUSTRATED BY

Biographical Examples.

" WHATSOEVER THY HAND FINDETH TO DO, DO IT WITH THY MIGHT;
for there is no work, nor device, nor knowledge, nor wisdom, in the grave,
whither THOU goest."

BY THE

REV. THOMAS PELHAM DALE, M.A.

RECTOR OF ST. VEDAST WITH ST. MICHAEL,
AND LATE FELLOW OF SIDNEY COLLEGE, CAMBRIDGE.

WITH A FRONTISPIECE BY J. D. WATSON.

LONDON:
JAMES HOGG & SON, YORK ST., COVENT GARDEN.

Lougheed met again in Calgary in the mid-1880s, and became life-long acquaintances. The veteran surveyor never forgot his first impression of the young Jim Lougheed in 1869: "He was then a very young man, in fact he was regarded as a boy, but he was very industrious and aggressive."[34]

While John Lougheed might have been pleased to have Jim assist him as a carpenter's helper, his wife was not. Carpentry, or even basic office work, might be a good choice for Sam, but not for Jim, who had natural leadership abilities and a real aptitude for school. Although Jim was still only in his early teens the church officials at the Berkeley Street Methodist Church noted his maturity. They made him a local, or unordained, preacher, "before he was old enough to grow a moustache."[35] Mary Ann Alexander Lougheed had great ambitions for her elder son. She wanted him to consider options other than the building trades. Further encouragement for a career change came one day, totally unexpectedly.

Through his involvement in the Sunday School at Little Trinity Anglican Church, Jim met Sam Blake, committed evangelical Anglican and eminent city lawyer. Sam was the brother of Edward Blake, the premier of Ontario from 1871 to 1872.[36] The young volunteer served as Little Trinity's assistant librarian. The library distributed Bibles to the Sunday School classes. In his new post Jim frequently met the "Hon. Psalm Blake," as one journalist later dubbed him. Blake took a liking to the polite, well-spoken young man. One day he said to him: "Boy you have too good a head to be a carpenter, why don't you take up law?"[37] The influential lawyer's remarks nourished the seeds of ambition his mother had carefully sown.

Years later James Lougheed confided to fellow senator, Raoul Dandurand, that after Sam Blake spoke to him about a legal career, "he devoted all his spare time to self-improvement."[38] As soon as he saved enough money he entered Weston High School, in the neighbouring village of Weston (population 1,000) immediately west of Toronto. He might have attended Jarvis Collegiate, closer to home, but he did not. Perhaps he selected Weston to be near his relatives in Peel County. Maybe his father had opposed his decision making it uncomfortable to remain at home. In any event, the school had an excellent reputation, which no doubt attracted him.[39] After his studies at Weston he returned to Cabbagetown. He and his boyhood friend Emerson Coatsworth then prepared together for their matriculation exams, which they both passed in 1875.[40]

Upon his return, Jim, his brother Sam, Emerson, and a half-a-dozen other young men formed the Awscal Literary Society at Berkeley Methodist Church. The word "Awscal" was derived from the initials of the members of the group.[41] A hand-written financial account by treasurer Coatsworth survives of their oyster supper on 30 December 1876.[42] Nearly half-a-century later, only months before his death in November 1925, James Lougheed told a reporter that he received his "early training as a speaker" at the Awscal Literary Society. His life-long debating style also reflected his early training as a carpenter. As one parliamentary reporter later described him in action: "Nothing subtle, or nimble, not a trace of rhetoric or sentiment about him. But his words came direct and crashing, his facts were driven home with pile-driving force."[43]

Jim joined the Toronto law firm of Beaty, Hamilton and Cassels as an articling student in 1877.[44] Right from his articling days he wanted to explore all aspects of the

John Lougheed, James's Lougheed's
father, late nineteenth century.
Photograph by Thomson and Son,
Toronto. Glenbow Archives/R.510.53.

law and its enforcement. One day in the early summer 1880, Nicholas Flood Davin, one of the firm's criminal lawyers, received a finely engraved card inviting him to the execution of one of his clients, whom he had failed to save from the gallows. Davin, who considered the decision a horrendous miscarriage of justice, tossed the card into the waste paper basket and put his head into his hands. Jim saw his despair. When the distraught man finally looked up Jim seized the moment. He boldly asked if he might take the card. The senior lawyer replied, "Do what you damned well please about it." Accordingly, on the execution day Lougheed went to the prison yard, presented Davin's card and obtained a ring-side seat.[45]

As an active member of the Toronto Young Men's Conservative Club and an Orangeman, young Jim campaigned for Sir John A. Macdonald in the federal election of 1878.[46] The Conservatives favoured the establishment of a strong central government and a policy of tariff protection. Macdonald argued for a National Policy, a high protective tariff for Canada, which the free-trade Liberals, then in office, fiercely opposed. Young Jim worked hard at Macdonald's Toronto rallies. Canadian historian Peter Waite recreates the atmosphere of the mid-nineteenth century political meetings: "One thinks of those audiences, dead and gone now, the noise, the whiskey, the laughter, the tobacco, the smell of unwashed humanity...."[47] Now a valued party worker, Jim loved the excitement of politics.

Jim's membership in the Orange Order brought with it a political identification with the Tories, the dominant faction in Cabbagetown. The Orange Lodge celebrated the British Crown and Protestantism. "No Surrender" was the Order's rallying cry. To be an Orangeman in nineteenth century Toronto was, almost without exception, to be a Conservative.[48] In retrospect it is truly amazing that James Lougheed, years later, in the early twentieth century, enjoyed such a warm relationship with Quebec Senator Raoul Dandurand, a Liberal and a Roman Catholic. That acquaintanceship shows the enormous distance James Lougheed travelled in his lifetime from his narrow Orange beginnings in Cabbagetown.

Formed by Irish Protestants in Ireland in 1795, the Orange Order spread rapidly throughout Ireland and England. It came to British North America in the 1820s. By 1870 Canada had more than a thousand Orange Lodges, with the largest number in Toronto. The Orange Order opposed Catholic schools and the use of the French language outside Quebec. Anti-Catholicism was the glue that tied the Order together. As John McAree, a prominent Toronto journalist, wrote in *Cabbagetown Store*, his memoir of his late nineteenth century East Toronto: "Catholics were generally spoken of as Dogans, a term of contempt, I suppose. They were considered as foreign as if they had been Italians, and were viewed with suspicion."[49]

Catholicism was the issue, not "race." In fact, the Orange Order in Canada allowed Protestant First Nations and African Canadian males to join.[50] This reflects an interesting detail about James Lougheed; perhaps on account of his Orange beginnings he remained remarkably free of the common racial prejudices of his day. But in his boyhood he embraced the Order's anti-Catholic code. Catholic and Protestant communities must never be integrated. Orangemen solemnly swore never to embrace

Catholicism or to marry a Catholic. All members promised to observe July 12, the date of William of Orange's victory at the Battle of the Boyne in 1690, which led to the Protestant minority's maintenance of its domination of Ireland.[51]

Orange lodges had elaborate rituals and regalia: secret passwords and hand-shakes, initiation oaths and hierarchical structures. Apparently young Jim loved all of this, for he became a member of the Orange Young Britons, organized in the 1860s to strengthen the Orange community. Some members of the Orange Order's youth wing were overly zealous in the late nineteenth century, as John McAree recalled: "A really militant organization was the Orange Young Britons, made up of husky, strutting young men, mechanics and labourers who were extremely provocative. They would parade frequently and always made it a point of invading a neighbourhood east of Parliament Street and south of Queen Street where there was quite a Roman Catholic settlement. These parades always wound up in fist fights and the throwing of stones."[52]

But there was another side to the organization. The Orange community in Cabbagetown did a great deal to benefit its members and their families. It served as a social club and a mutual aid society to which even the lower classes could afford to join. Lodge members assisted each other in times of sickness. A primitive insurance system existed to cover burial costs and provide lump-sum payments to widows. Under the obligation to assist, Orangemen helped fellow members find work. Due to its political power in Toronto the order was a powerful force in the city's administration, which controlled city patronage.[53] Jobs under the order's control in Toronto included those at Toronto's post office and the federal customs house, as well as the City of Toronto's gas-works, waterworks, police and fire departments.[54] As a young man without influential or affluent relatives, Jim participated fully in the Orange community's activities. Many years later his first cousins Jane and Elizabeth Lougheed recalled that while "still a stripling" he served as a chaplain in the Orange Young Britons. He "wore a white gown and carried a Bible at Parades."[55]

Politics interested Jim from his teenaged years. His growing political involve-ment with the Conservatives enlarged his viewpoint. According to the Misses Lougheed his political interests always ran deep: "He was never known to be idle—his spare time was spent at Church meetings or at the Houses of Parliament where he liked to listen to the speeches."[56] In politics he learned the necessity of working with everyone, including Catholics.

In January 1882, Jim, now a practicing Toronto lawyer, decided to move west to Winnipeg. His younger brother Sam also left home for good at about the same time. New opportunities beckoned in the Canadian West soon to be crossed by a transcon-tinental railway. Their mother had died in June 1880, leaving their father a widower. After his sons left, their seventy-year old father eventually moved back to board in the Cabbagetown neighbourhood where they lived when Jim was a teenager. Old John Lougheed, content with his modest life and social position, died there in 1904, at the age of ninety-three.[57]

Jim Lougheed entered a good Winnipeg law firm—Aikins, Culver and Hamilton—headed by J. A. M. Aikins, the son of Manitoba's Lieutenant Governor,

James Cox Aikins.[58] The younger Aikins was western solicitor for the CPR.[59] Sadly, Jim's timing was poor. The Winnipeg boom which saw the city's population jump in one year from slightly over six thousand in 1881 to almost fourteen thousand in 1882, suddenly collapsed.[60] Greater opportunities beckoned farther west.

Early in 1883 Jim left Manitoba and followed the CPR construction teams then at work a thousand kilometres to the west. He saw a sea of buffalo grass across the treeless prairies, but no live buffalo. By the tiny CPR stations stood gigantic mounds of buffalo bones awaiting shipment east to be ground and used for fertilizer.[61] The great herds had disappeared on the Canadian side of the border in 1879. According to a story he later told fellow senator Raoul Dandurand, he left Winnipeg with a letter of introduction to the CPR's chief engineer and superintendent of construction, which sufficed to secure some legal work at the construction camp at Medicine Hat.[62]

At Medicine Hat Coulee where the CPR crossed the South Saskatchewan River, Jim set up his shingle again, this time on his tent by the riverbank. The Native name "Medicine Hat," or "The Hat" as locals called their town, had a smack of romance to it.[63] The young lawyer was intellectually curious. Years later he wrote, "Most of life's charms are those of the unanswerable kind—solve the puzzle and you at once drop the solution."[64] While living at Medicine Hat he learned several explanations of how it obtained its name. James Sanderson, renowned Metis scout, railway contractor and livery stable owner, recorded a First Nations' tale. Below the cliffs where the ice never froze dwelt a huge water serpent capable of communicating with humans. The giant snake approached a warrior and promised to make him a great warrior and medicine man if he sacrificed his wife and placed her body in the opening in the water. If he did as he was told, the serpent would direct him to the hiding place of a charmed hat—one with great powers. To protect their community the man's wife expressed her willingness to die. The warrior sacrificed her and presented her body to the serpent, which in turn directed him to a hat trimmed in ermine. If worn in battle, the hat would ensure victory. "The tradition has it," Sanderson concluded, "that the Indian became famous as a medicine man and warrior."[65] Stories like this welcomed the twenty-eight year old Torontonian to the western plains.

In Medicine Hat Jim adapted quickly to his new environment, and became known as a "capable young barrister."[66] The future railway divisional point stood in the midst of what explorer Captain John Palliser reported as an arid desert covering a large expanse of southeastern Alberta and southwestern Saskatchewan. Smack in the centre of what has ever since been called Palliser's Triangle stood the well-watered oasis of Medicine Hat. Taking advantage of an offered business opportunity, the young lawyer also became part owner of a store in the bustling hamlet.[67]

Around Winnipeg, the massive eastern migration of the late 1870s and early 1880s made the First Nations and Metis a minority in their homeland. But the First Nation and Metis still constituted the majority of the population in southern Alberta into the late 1880s.[68] Treaty Seven had only been signed in 1877. Fundamentally the two sides had different understandings of what the agreement meant. The newcomers believed Treaty Seven was a land surrender, which gave them title to over ninety-eight

percent of the First Nations' land, now free for the taking.[69] In contrast, the Blackfoot believed Treaty Seven a peace treaty, which only allowed the newcomers to use their land with permission. As a lawyer trained in British and Canadian law, Jim Lougheed naturally assumed that southern Alberta belonged outright to Canada. In return for approximately fifty thousand square miles the Canadian government now simply owed the First Nations of the Treaty Seven area a Christian education and training in agriculture.

Despite a good beginning in the new community Jim stayed only a few months before moving further westward to the end of steel, then just east of Fort Calgary. Evidence exists that he found the price for lots on the Medicine Hat town site too high.[70] Maybe, as well, he simply sensed better opportunities awaited him in Calgary. Open range ranching had established itself in the district. Once the railway reached the tiny community of several hundred people a lawyer could make a good living there. Clearly Calgary would become an important supply centre for neighbouring ranchers.

Years later the lawyer recalled how the village looked on his arrival: "The only landmarks of civilization to be then found that antedated the arrival of the railway were the old Hudson's Bay Company Post on the east bank of the Elbow, the Northwest Mounted Police stockade, and the trading post of I. G. Baker & Co., on the west bank."[71] In anticipation that the CPR would place their station at or near Fort Calgary on Section 14 by the Elbow River, people settled there at the confluence of the Bow and the Elbow rivers.

Jim established his law office by the Elbow River, but he did not live in the surrounding settlement.[72] Speculators already occupied the east bank of the Elbow, opposite the North West Mounted Police fort, in expectation that the station must go where the population lived. Lougheed did not try to obtain property on the east bank at all. He elected to stay at the CPR construction camp situated nearly two kilometres from the Elbow River between the site of today's Calgary Tower and, to the west, Gulf Canada Square.[73] During his first few weeks in Calgary, Jim again lived in a tent, his tent mate being CPR civil engineer Peter Turner Bone.[74]

Ambitious, self-confident and blest this time with perfect timing, Jim's star rose quickly in Calgary. The CPR, with which he had already been associated in Medicine Hat, named him their solicitor in the tiny community of several hundred. His position gave him an insider's knowledge of the railway's plans for Calgary. It had no intention of building its facilities on or even near property already in private hands. Ten days before the end of track reached Calgary in August 1883, John Egan, the railway's western superintendent, had advised William Van Horne, the railway's general manager: "At Calgary on section 15, there is a very good location for a town site. No squatters are on this section, as the mounted police have kept them off there. Mr. Hamilton has arranged to lay out a town, and I have no doubt that when you see the place it will please you."[75]

In December the CPR instructed its surveyor to "lay out 15" for townsite purposes, revealing that the permanent station would be located on Section 15, which they controlled, not Section 14.[76] Jim moved quickly. At the first CPR land sale on 15

January 1884, the newcomer from Toronto acquired five lots close to the new station.[77] He knew the western townsite nearly two kilometres west of the original Calgary would prevail, and it did. The CPR offered to donate land on its own section for a town hall and a fire station.[78] Anxious to be near the station, the postmaster relocated in February. Attracted by the offer of a fifty percent rebate from the CPR to those who built a frame structure on Section 15 before 1 April 1884, others followed suit.[79] In the words of one local resident, the east side "got up suddenly one morning and moved itself westward across the Elbow—two hundred tar-papered shacks, half a hundred unpretentious wooden buildings, and a few log structures."[80] James invested wisely. His five lots close to the station quickly increased in value.[81]

Jim's marriage in September 1884 to a self-confident and talented woman whose family had immense power and wealth linked him with the Hudson's Bay Company. His new family connection with Richard Hardisty, his wife's uncle, helped him enormously. By 1885 he served as solicitor for both the CPR and the HBC in Calgary.[82] Such close ties with both commercial giants meant he no longer needed the Orange Lodge. He dropped all his connections with it and never renewed them. Initially his alliance with both the HBC and the CPR alienated him from some townspeople. Nominated to stand for the new seven-member Calgary Civic Committee, James lost by four votes.[83] Ironically, this future federal cabinet minister was never elected to office at any level of government.

In the Calgary district Sam Lougheed tried to become a rancher. Without any agricultural background, except perhaps short visits to relatives' farms in Peel County west of Toronto, the two brothers bought a herd of cattle. In James's name they selected a brand, the nicely styled "A" of his signature, "James A. Lougheed."[84] Sam ran cattle for a couple of years, until 1888 at least. At that point, defeated by ranching, he gave up and returned to carpentry. In the mid-1890s he found work as a carpentry instructor at Indian Industrial schools. He taught first at Red Deer to the north, and then at Battleford in Saskatchewan. Eventually he and English-born wife, Sarah, whom he had married in Calgary in 1889, moved to Winnipeg, where Sam worked as a carpenter for the CPR.[85]

James had alternatives. He and Sam both had the carpenter's broad powerful hands. They both knew how to do hard physical work and how to relate with those who did. But what separated James from Sam was an excellent education giving him additional marketable skills. His knowledge of the law, his ability to draft contracts, including Richard Hardisty's contacts, helped him advance in the hamlet, which two years after his arrival boasted a population of roughly one thousand. In 1885 the small commercial centre on the CPR mainline served the needs of the Bow Valley's two thousand or so residents, many of whom lived and worked on surrounding farms and ranches.[86] Seven years later it became the rail gateway to Edmonton with the opening of a branch line to Edmonton. Later in the 1890s, rail links to Fort Macleod to the south and to the Kootenay mining fields in southeastern British Columbia expanded Calgary's role as a supply centre. Now regarded as suitable for farming the Calgary district stood at the turn of the century on the cusp of phenomenal agricultural development. Extensive irrigation in the early twentieth century would greatly bolster the southern Alberta economy.

James first became a wheeler-dealer in real estate speculation in Calgary. He introduced other wheeler-dealers to each other. He soon became the local solicitor for the Bank of Montreal. As part of the advance guard he knew that a human tide would soon arrive from crowded eastern Canada. When the CPR's subsidiary, the North West Land Company, opened up lots for sale on the new Calgary townsite west of the Elbow River, he bought as many as he could. As Alberta business historian Henry Klassen has written, "Beginning on a relatively small capital base in the mid-1880s, he gradually expanded his land business and spread his risks widely."[87] Money came from many sources, including large-scale borrowing. As soon as he could afford to do so, James became a builder. He constructed rental properties on his land. By the end of the century he owned a number of Calgary buildings including the two named after his oldest sons, Clarence and Norman.

Fortunately James's all-consuming ambition was, in his early years at least, tempered with a sense of fun. Hardly any of his personal letters survive, but one, written in Calgary on 25 November 1885, does. Writing to his wife's uncle Richard Hardisty, then visiting Fort Edmonton, he light-heartedly wrote, "It appears to me that the Edmonton air does not fit you so well as the Salubrious atmosphere of Calgary, eh? I have no doubt by this time you are in the throes of winter's chilly blast in Edmonton ... while here we revel in sunshine, orange groves, banana fields...."[88]

With the defeat of Louis Riel and his Metis followers at Batoche in central Saskatchewan, the future looked very rosy. Yet, underneath the happy tone of the letter runs a underlying note of sadness; Belle's brother Richard, just twenty-one years old, had been shot dead in the final attack against the French Metis stronghold of Batoche on May 12.[89] He had been named after his uncle Richard. The danger of the Riel resistance had been real in Calgary. Belle's brother Frank joined the Rocky Mountain Rangers in southern Alberta. Years later he recalled that if the Blackfoot Chief Crowfoot had brought his warriors into the struggle behind Riel, "Calgary would have been wiped out in half an hour."[90]

James's letter to Belle's uncle indicates how well connected the neophyte lawyer, only three years removed from Toronto, had become. He had a surprising new acquaintance, his wife's uncle, Donald A. Smith. In his note to Richard Hardisty in November 1885, he added; "Hon. Donald A. was up here a few weeks ago. He telegraphed me to meet him at the station. I did so & we had quite a chat with the worthy driver of the last C.P.R. Spike."

James was a good conversationalist. He had acquired a wide range of experiences, and was, as result of all his efforts at self-improvement, well read. Years later the *Ottawa Citizen* wrote in their obituary of the senator: "He was a man of cultural charm, an engaging conversationalist, thoroughly informed, not only in parliamentary procedure and history, but familiar as well with the best in literature."[91] Very busy with his law practice, reading was one of the few hobbies James allowed himself. He knew the classics. When Charles Parlow, one of the witnesses at his and Belle's wedding in 1884, married, James and Belle Lougheed gave the former HBC employee and his wife the complete works of Shakespeare in twelve volumes as a wedding present.[92] Thanks

to his constant reading James could make interesting historical and literary references. Years later, for instance, he referred to Belle's uncle, Donald Smith, as having come to Canada in the late 1830s, "a period when men were living who lived when Montcalm and Wolfe had fought on the Plains of Abraham."[93]

Despite his defeat in his one and only Calgary electoral contest in 1884, James advanced quickly in public esteem throughout southern Alberta, strong Conservative country. He distanced himself completely from his Orange roots. In 1889, he and Peter McCarthy, his law partner of two years standing, welcomed into their partnership Nicholas Beck, an important local Conservative. Surprisingly Beck was a Roman Catholic who just six years earlier converted to the faith. This strong advocate for the Roman Catholic community in Alberta remained with the Lougheed and McCarthy firm until he moved to Edmonton in 1891.[94]

James Lougheed served on both the Reception and Address Committees organized to greet Sir John A. and Lady Macdonald on their visit to Calgary on 20 July 1886.[95] The fact that Prime Minister Macdonald in 1888 named Richard Hardisty as the first senator from the District of Alberta, also helped James's standing in the Conservative Party in Western Canada. In 1887 he formed a partnership with Peter McCarthy, a prominent local Conservative from St. Catharines, Ontario.[96] He had been at Aikins, Culver and Hamilton in Winnipeg at the same time James worked there.[97] Although McCarthy fifteen years older than James, had greater legal experience, they agreed the law firm's title should be Lougheed and McCarthy, as Lougheed first established the firm.[98] Their legal practice thrived. By 1889 James Lougheed's net worth, the *Calgary Tribune* estimated, stood at nearly $70,000, a phenomenal sum, almost double the assets of Richard Hardisty at the time when James came to Alberta six years earlier.[99]

Shortly after his arrival in Calgary the recent Torontonian became a strong public advocate of western interests. Charles Dudley Wood, the editor of the *Fort Macleod Gazette*, wrote of him in late 1890: "He is an Alberta man first, last and everytime."[100] The ambitious lawyer knew how successful political parties worked. Adherents generally paid slavish loyalty to the current party leader and expected to benefit from patronage once in power. During the volatile politics of the late 1880s Lougheed remained a staunch Macdonald loyalist. He endorsed the National Policy, or high protective tariff, even though many in the North West Territories loathed it. As for patronage, James Lougheed openly defended it into the early 1920s: "What reason is there why a good party man should not get a good public office provided he is equal to the duties of the post?"[101]

Richard Hardisty died after a freak accident in October 1889. He was thrown from his wagon and broke his back. Although a resident in the District of Alberta for only six years, James Lougheed emerged as a leading candidate to replace him in the

Senate. In contrast to someone like D. W. Davis, the first Member of Parliament for the District of Alberta elected in 1887, Lougheed was presentable. Davis, American Civil War veteran and former whiskey trader, had a lawless background.[102] Rev. John McDougall remembered him after his death as being of "the wildest type."[103] As a young employee with I. G. Baker, the American fur trading company, Davis once killed two Indians for trying to "steal horses." This occurred in the period immediately before the Mounties came west in 1874. In Parliament he said little, but he once broke loose physically. In one all-night session of the House of Commons in April 1888 the *Calgary Herald* reported: "He danced the Blackfoot Indian war dance. The dancer held his body in an erect position, but dropped his head on his breast, separated his feet several inches and without a motion of his body jumped along the table on which he was performing, uttering blood curdling yells."[104] Davis was an embarrassment.

Peter McCarthy advanced his partner's candidacy for the senate. He wrote Prime Minister Macdonald on October 21: "Mr Lougheed is a resident of Calgary and has been since 1883 and has taken an extensive part in supporting the Conservative cause in the Territories and I believe fully qualified for the position."[105] Four days later Rev. Leonard Gaetz, a Methodist minister and leading Tory in the Red Deer district, added: "Mr. Lougheed is incomparably the best name we can offer. He is a gentleman of culture, ability & position with thorough knowledge of and faith in Alberta, a Conservative of the Conservatives, a good address, and will make I believe a first class representative."[106]

Lougheed's unquestioned support of the Conservative Party now received its reward. On 10 December 1889, Sir John A. Macdonald appointed the Calgary lawyer, at age thirty-five, to the senate. For years to follow the Alberta senator remained one of the youngest members of this geriatric institution (no mandatory retirement existed in the Red Chamber until 1965). While James Lougheed served in the Canadian Senate, it held the distinction of including in its ranks some of the oldest parliamentarians in the world. James knew both of the office record-holders, two centenarians. The first was his fellow Conservative, David Wark from New Brunswick. Appointed in 1867, he served until his death in 1905 at the age of 102. He also knew the second senator who lived to see a hundred and more. Appointed in 1907 at the age of 80, the Quebec Liberal Georges C. Dessaulles sat until his death in 1930, also at 102.[107] Eventually oil portraits of Wark, Dessaulles and the long-serving Lougheed would hang together in the Senate Smoking Room.[108]

For the next thirty-six years James Lougheed moved back and forth between Ottawa and Calgary. His friend Raoul Dandurand, a Liberal senator from Quebec, best described his early years in the upper chamber. At first he "rather modestly sat at the feet of the elders and imbibed their wisdom."[109] In one reporter's words, in the senate he, "may not have proved himself to be amongst its most brilliant members, but he has certainly been one of its ablest."[110] Gradually, however, Dandurand and his fellow members of the Red Chamber became aware of the Alberta senator's strengths: "He was courteous, he was genial, he was resourceful—perfectly equipped legally and mentally. He had considerable commercial and financial experience; he knew the West as few men knew it."

Since Confederation the Upper Chamber has experienced considerable criticism. As an appointed and unelected body renowned for partisan appointment—until recent times for life—the senate has commanded little respect. Critics have called it "simply a fifth wheel on the governmental coach."[111] Political scientist MacGregor Dawson in his *The Government of Canada* described it as "a shelter for those whose active life is almost over and who are primarily concerned with a pleasant, secure, and not very strenuous old age." Dawson also noted "the sense of futility" in the chamber itself: "Few people listen to the speeches; the usual drama and excitement of politics are lacking; no vital issues hang on the Senate's votes; there are no reputations to be made; there are no fresh, aggressive, stimulating young minds to satisfy."[112]

With all those limitations why did an ambitious young man like James Lougheed stay for over a third of century (until his death in 1925) in what he himself called "the Old Men's House"?[113] Several possible reasons come to mind. His senate seat provided invaluable political and economic contacts. As long as his party ruled the country, which they did to 1896, and then again from 1911 to 1921, he had access to patronage. Without any doubt he enjoyed his high standard of living in Ottawa, where he often stayed in his early days at the Russell House Hotel, the late nineteenth century equivalent of the Chateau Laurier. Later in the late 1910s to his death, he had a suite in the exclusive Roxborough Apartments on Laurier Avenue.[114] He also regularly dined at the top of Ottawa's social pyramid, the Rideau Club, just opposite the main gate to Parliament Hill.[115] More good news: the unelected senator did not have to run in elections. Then too, initially at least, his senate post required a minimal amount of time and energy, a vitally important detail as James Lougheed was already in the early 1890s heavily involved in real estate and other investments.[116] Another reason certainly existed. He came to believe in the institution, and saw it performing a useful function. As a Conservative he came to believe in social hierarchy. The upper house existed to keep check on popular enthusiasms. In his own words, the senate was "a bulwark against the clamor and caprice of the mob."[117] James Lougheed stayed in "the Old Men's House" because he enjoyed belonging to the ruling class.

Yet, the Calgary lawyer's summons to the senate had at least one very negative consequence. It caused jealousy. His appointment, in fact contributed to the break-up in 1893 of the seven-year old legal partnership of Lougheed and McCarthy. Originally the two men had been the best of friends. When James and Peter formed their partnership, they agreed, in McCarthy's words, "that if either party to the said partnership should become aware of any speculation which might seem advantageous it should be communicated to the other and the same should be entered into for the benefit of both parties." The two men even located their large sandstone homes in the same area, on 13th Avenue, immediately south of the centre of town. But now, "the Senator's" new prominence apparently led to his law partner's resentment. Ill feeling existed over Lougheed's phenomenal success in real estate, the profits of which remained entirely with him, separate from those of their law firm. Peter McCarthy became so embittered with his younger partner that he launched a lawsuit against him. McCarthy, who had so enthusiastically recommended Lougheed for Alberta's senate seat in 1887, six years later accused him in a court statement of using others to get ahead.[118]

McCarthy lost, but memory of their quarrel remained vivid to both men for years. The former partners continued to be immediate neighbours. The McCarthys lived on the north side of 13th Avenue, by 7th Street opposite the Lougheeds.[119] Although their law partnership ended acrimoniously, James Lougheed did serve as pall bearer at McCarthy's funeral in 1901,[120] suggesting that they reached a reconciliation before his former partner's death.

The senator's political and social role in Calgary, with its population in the 1890s of about four thousand,[121] had necessitated a larger home. Belle knew how to entertain on a grand scale. In 1891 the Lougheeds built "Beaulieu," a French word meaning "beautiful place," their elegant sandstone mansion, on grounds comprising sixteen town lots. Calgary used its local sandstone for construction after the major fire of November 1886. Up to this point William Pearce's "Bow Bend Shack," in East Calgary, where the Bow River bends to the south, was the finest home in Calgary. Richard Hardisty himself had playfully suggested the name "shack" for the Pearce's big fifteen-room sandstone house, and it stuck.[122] Piped for gas, it was also one of the first Calgary homes equipped with indoor plumbing and hot and cold running water.[123]

Beaulieu, or Lougheed House, surpassed Bow Bend Shack in splendour. The interior of the two-and-a-half-story sandstone villa included Spanish mahogany, Italian marble, elaborate stained glass windows and electric lighting in all rooms. In the 1890s townspeople could see to the south the imposing sandstone mansion on the open prairies with its roof covered with metal singles painted a rich red. Lougheed House had seven fireplaces, and hot and cold running water.[124] The staff in 1900 included a male Chinese cook, an English labourer, and a female housemaid from Ontario.[125] Again in 1906 the census reveals that they had three servants, including a male Chinese cook.[126] The staff helped run the mansion and assisted with the continual welcoming of guests. Belle welcomed 150 guests at their initial housewarming in 1892. An orchestra played dance music to 2:30 in the morning.[127]

Within fifteen years other Calgary magnates built their residences along 13th and 12th Avenues West, on what Calgary historian David Mittelstadt has called "Millionaires Row."[128] Around Beaulieu and the McCarthy's home sprang up Calgary's first neighbourhood of fashionable houses. In 1901 Pat Burns built his mansion on 4th Street between 12th and 13th Avenues (the site of today's Colonel Belcher Hospital), following a design created by the well-known architect Francis Rattenbury of Victoria. Rancher and entrepreneur William Roper Hull built his magnificent Langmore in 1905 on 12th Avenue, just north of Lougheed House and immediately west of Pat Burns's baronial home.[129]

From the late 1890s into the new century the senator's star, politically, economically and socially (despite any lingering damage from Peter McCarthy's charges) continued to rise. Politics received more and more of his attention. Lougheed's flexibility, his skill at political legerdemain, made him a great success. He consolidated his position as one of the top Alberta Conservatives.[130] In the first years of the twentieth

century James moved into the privileged inner circle in Ottawa. In 1906 his colleagues elected him leader of the Conservatives in the senate. After the Conservative victory of 1911, he joined the federal cabinet as a junior member, as minister without portfolio.

Despite his new political responsibilities James Lougheed kept up his personal business interests. Harold Daly, a Manitoba lawyer who worked with him as a staff officer in Ottawa in the mid-1910s, had known him from childhood in the 1890s. He liked him: "I had known the Senator since I was 12, and he treated me as if I were still in short pants, but was very nice to me, and took me when he went on any inspection trip." His father, Thomas Mayne Daly, a prominent Manitoba Conservative politician, had served as the federal Minister of the Interior from 1893 to 1896, the time at which Harold's memory of Senator Lougheed began. Years later Harold recalled him as "a dapper little man, inclined to be close in money matters and a very large holder of real estate in Calgary and Edmonton."[131]

To replace himself in the courtroom, the Senator in 1897 hired Richard Bedford Bennett, R. B. Bennett, a young New Brunswick lawyer, as a partner. Bennett, a tall man for the day, nearly six feet tall,[132] soon became a familiar sight on Calgary streets. James Gray, his biographer, has provided this vivid word-picture of the young R. B. in his new city: "His black bowler hat, white scarf, stylishly cut overcoat, sharply pressed pants, and polished shoes identified him from 100 feet as a stranger in a town where short 'reefer' coats and never-pressed frontier pants were the accepted norm in men's clothing."[133] In the early years of Lougheed and Bennett the partnership worked well. Totally committed to the twelve-hour workday,[134] R. B. allowed James Lougheed to focus on his business and political interests. Soon the New Brunswicker himself became involved in business as well. More than a law office, Lougheed and Bennett took on mortgage, insurance and financial business, as well as real estate.[135] Harold Daly later recalled: "Lougheed and Bennett had a lot of dealings with the Department of the Interior, and made money out of government lands, which I suppose, they had a right to do, but they were not very popular with Government officials."[136]

By 1910 Lougheed and Bennett represented in Calgary, among other corporations and banks: the CPR, Bank of Montreal, Bank of Nova Scotia, The Hudson's Bay Company, Massey-Harris Co. and Manufacturers Life Insurance.[137] The senator also continued to make enormous sums in real estate speculation. In 1911 alone he sold ten lots on 7th Avenue to the Hudson's Bay Company for $250,000; and one of his buildings on 8th Avenue to the English politician and investor, William Dudley Ward for $150,000.[138] He also sold an expensive corner of land at 1st Street and 7th Avenue West to the Southams for their new Southam, or Herald Building.[139] In 1911, flush with cash, at the height of Calgary's great economic boom, the senator made his major investment move. He decided to erect the Lougheed Building, his real estate empire's new showcase, on the site of Alfred Terrill's greenhouses at the corner of 6th Avenue and 1st Street West. But he acknowledged from the outset that life should mean more than commerce alone, and added a theatre to accompany the office building. This was really quite an innovative idea for Canada, as only one other theatre in the country at this time was located in an office building, the Monument National in Montreal.[140]

"Canucks" by Cartoonists

Some of Calgary's Citizens.

SENATOR JAS. A. LOUGHEED,
Politician, Lawyer and Capitalist.

Chapter Three

BELLE LOUGHEED

HER STORY

E ARLY IN THE NEW CENTURY JAMES LOUGHEED BUILT TWO SMALL vaudeville houses in Calgary—the Lyric in 1905, and the Empire in 1908.[1] In the summer of 1911 the senator announced his new plan to open a modern office building adjacent to a truly first class facility for plays, concerts and operas. As Jim Davidson mentioned in *The Albertan*, "a very passable theatre could have been constructed with the same seating capacity for little more than half the cost," but this time he wanted the best.[2] His wife heartily approved. She regularly attended performances at the Grand Theatre from its opening night in 1912 until several months before her death in 1936.[3]

Belle Lougheed loved culture and the arts. At the age of seven she studied at Miss Davis's School in the Red River; and then boarded from age eight to fifteen at the Wesleyan Ladies' College, a private girls' academy in Hamilton, Ontario.[4] Music and the fine arts received special attention in the curriculum of the well-respected Hamilton school.[5] At the Wesleyan Ladies College she learned to paint, an interest Belle continued all her life.[6] She also studied piano, and later the organ.[7] The college was more than just a finishing school for the daughters of the wealthy, as the following introduction to the English program indicates: "We deprecate the feeling, all too prevalent in some quarters, that in a lady's education music, painting and kindred accomplishments should constitute the essence and chief attraction, often to the depreciation of a good English education and the mental culture that results therefrom."[8] Belle received an enviable academic training at a time few women in Canada had more than a limited number of years in elementary school.

Although constantly preoccupied with his political duties and business interests, James listened to his wife's advice and acted upon it. The very name of their sandstone mansion reveals her influence. The name "Beaulieu" undoubtedly was her suggestion, inspired by her memory of an important Mackenzie River Valley Metis family that her family knew well there.[9]

Belle's knowledge of the north came from her early childhood at Fort Simpson and later from the several years she spent with her family after her return from the Wesleyan Ladies' College.[10] Her father wanted to send her away to school, because, as he later wrote to her first teacher, Miss Davis in the Red River: "It is very difficult in this District to keep the children away from the Indians who are always about the house & my children labour under this further disadvantage that their mother has no education...."[11]

Fort Simpson, the headquarters for the Hudson's Bay Company's Mackenzie River Valley operation, had an attractive location. Charles Camsell, who served as Canada's deputy minister of mines in the 1920 and early 1930s, and later as deputy minister of mines and resources in the late 1930s and early 1940s, came from this area. His father, Julian Stewart Camsell, replaced Belle's father as Chief Factor in 1876. In his memoirs, *Son of the North*, Charles recalled Fort Simpson: "The Post was beautifully situated on an island at the junction of the Mackenzie and the Liard Rivers and was first known as the Forks of the Mackenzie. It faced on Mackenzie River which here flowed by in a smooth stream almost exactly a mile wide. The view up the stream was a magnificent one, perhaps the best on the whole river."[12] All her life Belle remembered the Mackenzie, as she told a Calgary reporter in 1922: "That is a wonderful river."[13]

Belle's self-reliance owed a great deal to her northern upbringing. At Fort Simpson her mother Mary Hardisty drove a train of dogs and also kept rabbit snares.[14] True, Mary had the assistance of First Nation and Metis servants,[15] including one English-speaking Native woman, Charles Camsell's mother, Sarah Foulds, the daughter of a Yorkshire man and his Native wife.[16] But still hardships existed. Challenges to survival arose. After Belle returned from Hamilton, for example, the food shortage at Fort Simpson reached such proportions her father sent his family to Fort Rae at the junction of the Mackenzie River and Great Slave Lake, where white fish abounded. "We were given fifty pounds of flour as our share of available provisions. For seven months we lived on that and white fish from Great Slave Lake."[17]

From Belle's northern experiences came independence and an openness to change. After years in southern Ontario she found life full of surprises in the north, even as to what constituted day and night. As Charles Camsell's sister, Louise, later recalled: "At Fort Simpson the sun sets about half past two in the afternoon in midwinter and rises about half past ten in the forenoon. It does not go high in the sky. We used to say it came up over the end of one of the buildings and went down over the other end of it. In the summer we used no lamps for about six weeks, and we had to have thick window blinds so that we could sleep during the bright night time."[18]

Belle loved adventure. The story of a proposed motor trip to Banff from Calgary reveals her high spirits. In the summer of 1909 the Lougheeds' second and third-oldest sons, twenty-year old Norman and fifteen-year old Edgar, suggested motoring to Banff, a journey that James promptly overruled: cars were prohibited in the national parks. But, shortly after issuing his decree, duty called the Conservative senate leader back to Ottawa. Once he left Belle reversed his decision. She fully supported her sons, and Norman's fiancée, Mary Stringer.[19] They should do it. Belle declared the Calgary to Banff road trip on.

One bright morning Belle joined her two sons and Mary, and they all piled into the family car, a big red Pope-Toledo, and set off with an extra tank of fuel and a huge hamper of food. Norman took the wheel wearing his driving cap with goggles. Friends in two other cars joined them, but when conditions on the old wagon trail proved too arduous for them, the faint-hearted turned back. Finally the Pope-Toledo, despite all the challenges of driving on a narrow dirt road, reached the village of Banff. No grand

Mary Allen Hardisty, Belle's mother. She was the daughter of Robert Allen, an English sailor in the service of the Hudson's Bay Company; and Charlotte Scarborough, the daughter of a sea captain, also in the company's service, and a Native woman. She was probably born at Fort Vancouver, around 1840. The photo is by Notman and Sandham, Montreal. Glenbow Archives/NA-2758-1.

Belle Lougheed with son Clarence, late 1880s. The photo is by William Notman and Son, Montreal. Glenbow Archives/NA-3232-4.

welcome awaited them; instead the park authorities impounded the Pope-Toledo. Only after the Lougheed party made a firm promise to depart the park immediately did the authorities release it.

Unfortunately the drive back proved more difficult than the ride in. About a third of the way to Calgary a tire suddenly blew. The car bounced off the road, down a slope, and smashed into a tree. After a long walk the quartet reached the small railway stop at Kananaskis. Although she had swollen feet at the end of the hike, Belle had surprised the others with her tremendous show of energy. The foursome flagged down an eastward bound train and made it back to Calgary. A wrecking crew and some local Stoney First Nation people dragged the stranded Pope-Toledo onto a flat car a few days later.

The boys' and Mary's appointment with destiny came with the senator's return. As luck had it, the first glimpse he had from his railway car window in Calgary was a glimpse of his prized automobile, battered and bent. Fortunately for her two sons, and the future Mrs. Norman Lougheed, Belle successfully smoothed things over. She explained to her husband that the park's regulation was ridiculous. With some improvements in the trail, cars could easily and safely reach Banff. Several years later, when the Conservatives came to power, Senator Lougheed convinced the federal minister responsible for national parks to rescind the prohibition of cars in Banff.[20]

On account of the senator's frequent trips away from home, Belle made many of the parenting decisions alone. Unfortunately few of her letters survive, one of the few being a note she wrote on 24 November 1903, six months before the Calgary to Banff road trip. The children were younger then, and at the time of writing she was six months pregnant—her last child, Marjorie, arrived in February. In late 1903 the Lougheeds had five children: Clarence, eighteen, then staying for a few months in Edmonton with his great-aunt Eliza McDougall Hardisty; Norman, fourteen; Edgar, ten; Dorothy, four; Douglas, two. As she was temporarily without a housekeeper Belle's life had its challenges. As she wrote to her aunt, Eliza Hardisty: "I have had to do all the housework for nearly two months, so that my health nearly gave way. The doctor ordered me off to bed one day, and there I had to stay for a week or so, which accounts for the report that I was very ill. However, I am glad to say that there was nothing to it, and I am getting quite strong again. You know there is a great deal to do in a house of this size."[21]

In addition to raising their children, the "Senator's Wife" was expected to entertain on a lavish scale. Fortunately this vivacious woman had complete social confidence and knew how to organize large functions. On account of James's political role in Calgary she entertained a great deal. In November 1898, for example, she opened her house to nearly sixty men invited to hear the renowned Conservative Party orator Nicholas Flood Davin, whom James had known twenty years earlier as an articling student in Toronto.[22] Women could not vote, or run for office, and hence were not invited. After James became the Conservative senate leader in 1906, Belle entertained a series of distinguished visitors. She hosted in October 1908, for example, a banquet dinner for Lord Milner, who had recently served as the British High Commissioner in South Africa.[23] When Earl Grey, the Governor-General, visited Calgary in 1909, Belle put on

a luncheon reception for Lady Grey at Lougheed House.[24] That same year Lord Grey offered what became known as the Grey Cup for the amateur rugby football championship of Canada.

Few Calgary hostesses rivalled Belle's reputation. Only a year later *The Montreal Star* commented on her special talents at both the family's summer bungalow at Banff and their beautiful Calgary residence: "She is an ideal hostess, full of honest fun and unassuming."[25] Her daughter-in-law, Mary Stringer Lougheed, knew her better than almost anyone else. She remembered her mother-in-law as being "an excellent hostess, a gracious hostess." With great intuition she observed the beneficial effect Belle had on her husband, guiding him socially and culturally into new worlds: "I think she was the driving force behind James."[26]

In Calgary Belle helped many charitable organizations. Liking young people, she also regularly welcomed her children's friends to Lougheed House. As the *Calgary News-Telegram* reported in its "Of Interest to Women" column on 5 October 1911, "Mrs. Lougheed throws open her magnificent home to the many charitable organizations of the city, and her spacious ball room is thronged several times during the season with the many friends of her sons." In early January 1914, Belle held a Saturday afternoon dance at Lougheed House for her fifteen year old daughter Dorothy and twenty year old son Edgar, together with more than sixty of their friends. *The Albertan* commented, "The much talked of tango was the anticipated feature of Mrs. Lougheed's dansant."[27] Fred and Adele Astaire had danced the Argentine dance at the Grand in October 1912, but a year later it still remained "controversial" and too daring for Calgary. Whether or not Ma Trainor and her band actually included the tango among their selection of the latest dance music is unknown.[28] One suspects that Belle would have applauded if they had. The Lougheeds frequently invited Ma Trainor's lively band to play at Lougheed House social functions.[29]

Belle, a woman leader in Calgary, served in 1895 as the first vice-president of the local chapter of the Council of Women, and was elected a vice-president of the national council one year later.[30] In 1909 she became the first president of the board of directors for the Calgary branch of the Victorian Order of Nurses.[31] That same year Mrs. Lougheed opened up Lougheed House for the organizational meeting of the Colonel Macleod chapter of the Independent Order of Daughters of the Empire (IODE). This patriotic association aimed to build a strong empire by building a strong British-Canadian nation.[32] The IODE had a reverence for all things British. Its motto was "one flag (the Union Jack), one throne (the British Monarchy), and one Empire (the British Empire)."[33] Belle became vice-regent, with her friend, Jean Pinkham, the Anglican bishop's wife, as the chapter's regent.[34]

The visit in February 1911 of Minnie Wheeler Parlow, a dear old friend of Belle's from early Calgary days, and her daughter Kathleen, proved a very special occasion. Fifteen years had elapsed since they left Calgary in 1896. In the interim Kathleen had become a world-renowned violinist.

Minnie Wheeler had moved to Calgary from New Brunswick in the late 1880s to teach school in Calgary. She met the Lougheeds through her future husband, Charlie

Parlow, formerly with the HBC. He had acted as one of the two witnesses at Belle and James's wedding in 1884.[35] In early September 1889, Charlie and Minnie themselves married in Calgary. As their wedding present the Lougheeds gave the newlyweds a complete set of the works of Shakespeare.[36] The Parlow's first and only child, Kathleen, was born exactly one year later in September 1890. The Parlows attended the gala house-warming ball at Lougheed House in February 1892.[37]

The Parlows' marriage did not work. It only lasted six years. Apparently Charlie had several extramarital affairs and drank heavily. To ease the torture of living with him, Minnie learned how to play the violin, but the musical instrument proved insufficient solace for her unhappy union. In early 1896 she left Calgary with their five-year old daughter for San Francisco.[38] In California Kathleen told Minnie on a childish whim that she wanted to play the violin, just like her mother.[39] Kathleen began lessons. On account of the young girl's extraordinary talent, Henry Holmes, a former violin teacher at the Royal College of Music in London, accepted her as a student. Through Holmes's connections fifteen year-old Kathleen gave concerts in England. What happened to Charlie? Shortly after their departure for California he returned to his home in eastern Ontario where he died in 1897. Minnie believed he died from tuberculosis caught from a First Nations woman.[40]

Belle's uncle, Donald A. Smith, now Lord Strathcona, the Canadian High Commissioner in London, financially assisted Kathleen. In 1905 she performed with the London Symphony Orchestra and played before Queen Alexandra, the wife of King Edward VII, at Buckingham Palace. Donald Smith funded her studies under Leopold Auer in St. Petersburg, Russia. The legendary violin teacher, "the most celebrated pedagogue in the violin's history,"[41] also taught the child prodigies Jascha Heifetz and Mischa Elman.

While a student at the Imperial Conservatory Kathleen played for the director, the famous Alexander Glazenov. She met the young Russian pianist and composer Sergei Rachmaninoff.[42] On a trip to Helsingfors (now Helsinki), she spoke with Finland's Jean Sibelius. Subsequently, after her professional debut in Berlin in 1907, she began a series of very successful European tours. The king and queen of Norway received her at court. Queen Maud presented her with a diamond necklace.[43] Einar Bjornson, a friend of the recently deceased Norwegian composer Edvard Grieg, gave her one of the finest violins in the world, a Guarnerius, made in 1735 in Cremona by Guarneri del Gesù.

With her fine musical training and life-long interest in classical music, Belle loved to hear Kathleen's and her mother's stories about their travels.[44] Maida Parlow French, Kathleen's cousin and biographer, provides a striking physical description of the youthful violinist at this time: "… a slender girl nearly six feet tall of rather unusual beauty. The heavy curling hair brushed simply from her forehead and hanging about her shoulders, the velvet dress, shirred and gathered from a high lace yoke, gave her the appearance of a figure in a Renaissance painting."[45]

At the reception organized for Kathleen by Belle at Lougheed House on 20 February 1911, Jean Drever Pinkham presented the official welcome. Next to Belle, who was short in stature, the Anglican bishop's wife looked imposingly tall.[46] Jean was very fair in complexion, and Belle was dark, but physical appearances aside, the two women had much in common. First, Jean, like her sisters Mary and Christian, had attended Belle's old school, Miss Davis's in the Red River.[47] Secondly, through their eldest sister Margaret's marriage into the Mackay family, the Drever sisters were linked to the same Western Canadian fur trade aristocracy to which Belle's family, the Hardistys, belonged. Half-a-century earlier Margaret Drever married the Rev. John Alexander Mackay, who later became the Anglican archdeacon of Saskatchewan.[48] Maggie suffered much criticism from racially prejudiced individuals for having married an "Indian," a man of some First Nation ancestry.[49] Bishop Pinkham shared none of these sentiments, and wrote in his autobiography: "Of none can the Church speak more highly than of the Venerable Archdeacon John Mackay, D.D., who married my wife's eldest sister, Margaret Drever."[50] Archdeacon Mackay, a member of an old Hudson's Bay Company family, who was familiar with Cree since childhood, had just revised the first translation of the entire Bible into the Cree language.[51]

Belle and Jean Pinkham also shared social prominence in turn-of-the-century Calgary. Jean's husband, Bishop Cyprian Pinkham, had served for a quarter-of-a-century as the Anglican bishop of Calgary. Jean's two sisters were also married to prominent Albertans. Jean's younger sister, Mary, had married the late Colonel James Macleod of the North West Mounted Police, who had in 1876 suggested the name of Calgary for the police post at the junction of the Bow and the Elbow.[52] Her youngest sister, Christian, had married well-known Calgary lawyer Jermy Jephson.

Born and raised in the Red River by her Scottish-born parents, this iron-willed woman[53] and her sisters had lived through what the Canadians called the first Riel Rebellion, a period Jean referred to as "a reign of terror."[54] As her father opposed Riel's government in the Red River, the Metis leader briefly arrested him. During the troubles, she later recalled, his troops regularly appeared at the Drever house at any hour of the day or night looking for anyone suspected of having taken up arms against them.[55] Jean had come to Calgary with her husband in 1889. She had headed the volunteer team which built Calgary's first hospital. Belle was one of her helpers.[56]

At Lougheed House Jean officially welcomed Kathleen on behalf of the local Colonel James Macleod chapter of the IODE: "Whatever conceptions you may have formed of our growth during your absence, however materialistic we may have been called, we should like you at least to know that we do prize the gift of a musical and artistic soul far more highly than our critics dream. We rejoice therefore with you as we learn of each new triumph won, and with you look forward to still greater conquests in your chosen world of music."[57]

From Calgary Kathleen continued her first North American concert tour. In those last weeks she fulfilled Calgary's wish for "still greater conquests in your chosen world of music." In one of her final engagements she played as soloist with the Philharmonic Society of New York, under the visiting conductor and famous composer, Gustav Mahler.[58] Her repertoire was enormous, her technique effortless.[59] The critics placed her in the same rank as Jan Kubelik and Auer's other "genius pupil," Mischa Elman. As the *New York Herald* wrote at the end of her tour: "Kathleen Parlow the young Canadian violinist is now a world celebrity... The gifts of this young girl are extraordinary... After hearing her marvellous performances of Beethoven, Brahms, Wieniawski and Tschaikovsky concertos, the men in the profession have declared that she is today one of the phenomena of the musical world."[60]

Minnie and Kathleen warmly enjoyed their three-day stay with Belle and her family, apart from the senator, again absent in Ottawa.[61] At Lougheed House Kathleen wrote in her line-a-day diary just two words: "At home."[62]

Fifteen years had brought many changes to Calgary. The town had grown twenty-fold since Minnie and Kathleen's left in 1896. It had become quite a modern urban centre. One could, for example, now buy fresh-cut flowers in February. With her fine eye for colour, Belle Lougheed placed carnations on the tea table at the reception for Minnie and Kathleen.[63] The greening of Calgary owed much to the arrival of Alfred Terrill, an experienced florist from Ontario. His greenhouses actually stood on the very parcel of land at the corner of 6th Avenue and 1st Street W. identified by James Lougheed as the ideal site for his new theatre and office building.

Kathleen, raised in California, and resident for a number of years in Europe, returned to Calgary with a secret wish to see First Nations people. Her biographer, Maida Parlow French, writes that Kathleen's father had enthralled her as a tiny girl in Calgary with bedtime stories of Native lore. These tales "kept recurring to her at crucial times in later life." Her mother had told Kathleen that her father had "gone Indian," and been "intimate" with several Native women. More than once Kathleen confided to Maida: "It was the custom for the Indians to have several wives. I probably have six or seven Indian half-brothers and -sisters."[64]

In 1911, all non-Aboriginal Calgarians, even the Rev. John McDougall who had arrived in Alberta in the mid-1860s, were recent immigrants when compared with the First Nations. For thousands of years the First Nations came to what we now call Calgary for the shelter provided in winter by the high banks of the Bow and Elbow, the smaller river which joined the Bow at this location. The Bow obtained its name from the fact the First Nations found good wood for making bows here.[65] Near the junction of the Elbow and the Bow was one of the best river crossings for miles around. The western breezes in summer kept the mosquitoes and black flies to a minimum.[66]

Millions of buffalo once roamed over southern Alberta. The disappearance of the herds on the Canadian side of the border completely reversed the fortunes of the First Nations within two years. After the demise of the buffalo on the Canadian prairies in 1879 both the plains First Nations and the Metis lost their economic independence. Their impoverishment forced the First Nations onto their reserves to obtain government rations. After the suppression of what the settlers called the Second Riel Rebellion in 1885, and the completion of the CPR that same year, their political independence vanished as well. Overnight they went from power to powerlessness. Diseases such as smallpox and tuberculosis ravaged their communities. By the 1890s the First Nations and the Metis no longer constituted the majority of the population of southern Alberta. The First Nation population of Alberta fell from 18,000 in the 1870s to less than 6,000

"The Coming of the White Man." This bas-relief reflects the image of the First Nations in the early twentieth century in Western Canada. It presents the First Nations as a "broken" people, marching off to oblivion, unable to adjust to the new age, represented by the young farmer and his plough. T.J.S. Skinner presented the work to the Southern Alberta Pioneers. Reproduced with the permission of the descendants of T.J.S. Skinner. Photography by Mel Gray.

by the 1920s.[67] By 1911, the year of Kathleen Parlow's visit, the Native peoples constituted only a tiny percentage of the total population of the Bow River Valley.

Kathleen's openness to First Nation people was quite remarkable at the time. In the early years of the twentieth century racial theory enjoyed widespread support in North America. Many scientists and social scientists endorsed the view that races varied greatly in innate intelligence and temperament.[68] Only in the 1930s, as their disciplines further developed, did North American biologists and anthropologists come to reject race theories as explanations of the character of peoples. By the mid-twentieth century scholars realized that social, political, economic and geographical factors better explained human difference than biology.[69]

Many individuals in early twentieth century Alberta accepted as self-evident the existence of "superior" and "inferior" races.[70] Canadian immigration law placed British and Americans first, followed in descending order by Northwestern Europeans, Central and Eastern Europeans, Jews, Asians, and those of African descent.[71] R. B. Bennett, Senator Lougheed's law partner, explained in a 1914 address why "we" ruled over countries like India and Egypt: "We are there because under the providence of God we are a Christian people that have given the subject races of the world the only kind of decent government they have ever known … and you and I must carry our portion of that responsibility if we are to be the true Imperialists we should be... An Imperialist, to me, means a man who accepts gladly and bears proudly the responsibilities of his race and breed."[72]

As "lesser races" those of Asian and African descent faced real obstacles. In 1911, the Calgary Board of Trade (now the Chamber of Commerce) spoke out against allowing African Americans as immigrants to Western Canada.[73] That same year *The Albertan* bluntly expressed its opinion of non-Whites: "We do not want a colored Alberta … shut out all colored people from homeland rights. Close out the yellow man, the red man and the black man. They are not good settlers. They cannot become good Canadians."[74]

Even the independently minded Bob Edwards of the *Calgary Eye Opener*, who believed in social justice, remained a prisoner of the prejudices of the day. In the *Eye Opener* on 6 December 1913, for example, he railed against Canada "allowing anyone to enter in, irrespective of color, race, creed, or ideals. It is permitting races to enter which cannot assimilate with the white race, and in so doing is retrograding." As *The Albertan* wrote in its editorial, "The Western Humorist," published 16 November 1922, two days after Bob Edwards's death: "He interpreted the rough and ready, unconventional and original thoughts and emotions of the first generation of white men on these plains." In effect, he voiced the racial thoughts of "the first generation of white men on these plains."

Racial preferences were openly stated. The brand-new King George Hotel proudly advertised its "white-only" policy in the city's promotional pamphlet, *Calgary: Sunny Alberta, The Industrial Prodigy of the Great West*. The hotel made known that "their service is first class in every particular, none but the most skilled and experienced white help being employed in all departments."[75] Resentment against discrimination

ran deep amongst its victims. Louie (or Luey) Kheong, a well-respected merchant who established Calgary's first Chinese grocery store in the mid-1890s,[76] spoke out against all racial slurs in a letter to *The Calgary Herald* in October 1910: "You send missionaries to our homes in China, and we use them good; also English business men. If my people are no good to live here, what good trying to make them go to heaven? Perhaps there will be only my people there."[77]

The First Nations that so interested Kathleen Parlow occupied a curious slot in the racial pecking order. Although they had preceded the newcomers into the Calgary area by roughly twelve thousand years the newcomers did not assimilate into their society.[78] On the contrary the Canadians expected the Native peoples to join their society.

First Nations visitors were seen regularly on Calgary streets, but in 1911 they lived on their neighbouring reserves, the Sarcee (Tsuu T'ina) at Fish Creek immediately south of Calgary, the Blackfoot (Siksika) a hundred kilometres to the east, and the Stoney (Nakoda) at Morley fifty kilometres to the west. Conventional wisdom held that in the near future the larger society would absorb them.[79] As one *Calgary Herald* reporter stated a decade later: "It is a general belief that in the next two generations the inhabitants of the Indian reservations will be merely colonies of civilized people, principally farmers."[80] Keir Hardie, a visiting British socialist and labour leader, provided this assessment after a trip out from Calgary to the Tsuu T'ina Reservation in 1907: "At present it looks as though, in a few generations, the hero of our boyhood will have become as extinct as the buffalo."[81]

Probably the most significant event in early race relations in Calgary after the 1885 Rebellion occurred the same year of the Parlow's wedding, 1889. The final sentencing of William "Jumbo" Fisk, a blacksmith and veteran of the Alberta Field Force in the Rebellion of 1885,[82] who brutally killed and mutilated a Cree girl named Rosalie New Grass[83] in a room above a seedy low-life bar, was made only a few months before the Parlows' marriage. *The Calgary Tribune* provided the most graphic description of the murder of the Native prostitute: "The atrocities of Jack the Ripper seem mild in comparison. Jack, in most cases, cut his victims' throat first and did the mutilation with a knife afterwards. But this brute, who ever he is, perpetuated his atrocities with his hand, while his victim was still alive, while an idea of the agony this victim experienced while she was yet alive, may be gleaned from the fact that in the lips were marks where her teeth had cut almost through."[84]

Memory of the grotesque "Jack-the-Ripper" murder lived on for several decades as one of the few local stories in Calgary's collective imagination. Bob Edwards recalled the incident years later in the *Calgary Eye Opener*: "The curious part about this murder," he wrote, the awful details of which were known to all, was that the jury at the trial returned a verdict of not guilty. Enraged by such an outrageous verdict Judge Rouleau sent the jury back. As Eye Opener Bob summarized: "On his second trial Fisk got off with 14 years, but he should have been hanged."[85]

Minnie Parlow definitely recalled the Rosalie murder, Fisk being an acquaintance of her husband's. Half a year before their marriage in early September 1889, Charlie Parlow, who knew Fisk in Calgary and back in his hometown in Ontario, came forward as a character witness at his first trial. He testified that Fisk back in the town of Iroquois "was always considered an unusually good natured and quiet man."[86]

In 1911 a small number of Metis people resided in the city. Those of French and Native background had helped to build the original North West Mounted police fort in 1875. But many of the French Metis still remained culturally separate. In contrast, a number of those of British and Aboriginal parentage had adopted European values. Belle Lougheed herself identified herself as "white," although she had North American Indian and British ancestry on both her mother's and father's sides. Her own mother, and several other family members then living in Manitoba, applied for Metis scrip, a cash or land payment given to descendants of European and First Nation unions. In their applications they identified themselves as "Half Breeds" or Metis.[87]

Given the heightened racial prejudice of the day, other individuals of Native ancestry who lived prominent lives in Calgary chose to identify with their European heritage. Edmund Taylor, Senator Lougheed's chief investment partner, who joined him in 1911 to form the brokerage firm of Lougheed and Taylor, was part North American Indian. Edmund's parents, like Belle's, both belonged to well-known "Hudson Bay Company families," to use what was then the polite description of English-speaking Metis. The financier once told William Pearce, for instance, that "for at least three generations," his ancestors were "intimately connected with the Hudson's Bay and Northwest Companies."[88] In a text he prepared in 1924 Taylor stated his admiration for his ancestors, "those Argonauts of the fur-trade," who lived "in a practical wilderness where the great preponderance of the inhabitants were savages constantly engaged in fierce tribal wars." They prepared "the way for civilization and to make the path easier for those who were to come after them."[89]

Belle knew Edmund Taylor well. After receiving a good education, he entered the Hudson's Bay Company, worked his way up the ranks to become the manager of Calgary store in the 1890s, and later the general manager of the company's stores department in Winnipeg. He left the HBC in 1906 for five years in Toronto's financial world. The offer of a business partnership with Senator Lougheed in April 1911 brought him back west.[90] Much of the mortgage, insurance and financial business once completed by the Lougheed and Bennett law firm now moved over to Lougheed and Taylor.[91]

To repeat, a small number of those of British and Aboriginal parentage, particularly those who belonged to old elite fur trade families, fully adopted European values. As English traveler Elizabeth B. Mitchell noted in her overview of the Prairie Provinces, *In Western Canada before the War* (1915), "in old-timer settlements, important citizens have often much Indian blood."[92] Belle Hardisty Lougheed belonged to this group. At the Wesleyan Ladies' College in Hamilton, fellow students believed that Belle was "the daughter of an Indian chief."[93] In Calgary, Belle's Native background was well-known. In fact, the popular writer, Chief Buffalo Child Long Lance, who had lived in Calgary in the early 1920s, included her in a list he prepared of prominent Western Canadians of North American Indian ancestry: "Some of Western Canada's best citizens are of Scotch and Indian descent. Lady Lougheed, wife of Sir James Lougheed, minister of the interior, is a half-breed."[94] Yet, Belle, like Edmund Taylor, identified publicly with the European, not the Native, side of her ancestry.

Almost all members of the dominant society in Canada a century ago believed in a racial hierarchy. The 1901 census was quite clear about how federal enumerators should record racial background. Skin-colour determined it. The "Instructions to Officers" noted that: "The races of men will be designated by the use of '*w*' for white, '*r*' for red, '*b*' for black, and '*y*' for yellow." The instructions expanded upon this point:

> The whites are, of course, the Caucasian race, the reds are the American Indian, the blacks are the African or Negro, and the yellows are the Mongolian (Japanese and Chinese). But only pure whites will be classed as whites; the children begotten of marriages between whites and any one of the other races will be classed as red, black, or yellow, as the case may be, irrespective of the degree of colour.[95]

No doubt here about who occupies the highest rank. White comes first. The adjective "pure" only describes the "white race."

Belle listed herself in the 1901 census as "white,"[96] the group she identified with. Understandably this influential and powerful woman who stood at the top of the social hierarchy in Calgary did not request inclusion under the fifth category: "Persons of mixed white and red blood—commonly known as 'breeds'—will be described by the addition of the initial letters 'f.b.' for French breed, 'e.b.' for English breed, 's.b.' for Scotch breed, 'i.b.' for Irish breed... Other mixtures of Indians besides the four above specified are rare, and may be described by the letters 'o.b.' for other breed."[97]

Note that the census taker paid no attention to the usage favoured by those of European and First Nations' descent. As early as the late 1850s English-speaking people in the Red River of European and First Nations ancestry objected to the use in English of the term, "half breed." They preferred the term "Native," but the designation "breed" went into the 1901 census.[98]

In her lifetime Belle had seen the high-ranking fur trade families of mixed First Nations and European ancestry plummet in status. Many descendants of Western Canada's old fur trading elite now kept silent about their Aboriginal ancestry. A colour-coded society now racially classified everyone. Belle decided to have no part of it. Obviously she knew many Calgarians knew of her mixed ancestry;[99] but in conversation with writer Elizabeth Bailey Price, Belle did not mention it, nor did Price. Culturally Belle belonged to "white" society, and this is how she defined herself.[100] Yet, if asked if she knew the steps of the "Red River Jig," the dance so closely associated with the fur trade and the Metis people, she replied that she did.[101]

At times racial references must have been difficult for her. The newcomers' ignorance of all aspects of Native history and culture seemed total. She and the senator, for instance, sent their sons Norman and Edgar to Western Canada College,[102] a new private school established in Calgary in 1903. The Rev. Archibald MacRae, the school principal and Presbyterian minister, published his *History of the Province of Alberta* in 1912. Like so many other newcomers the educator had no understanding of, or respect for, the First Nations. In his book this assessment of Native character appears: "The Red Man of the West has always been a difficult individual, he does not care to work, to beg he is not ashamed. In consequence he tends to become shiftless and vagrant."[103]

Whatever aggravation comments like MacRae's caused Belle remains unknown. She enjoyed her growing family, her community work and the fine arts. Once the Sherman Grand Theatre opened, with or without her husband, it was she, with family and friends, who occupied the prestigious family box. It became her great delight to welcome noted artists, musicians, players and playwrights to Beaulieu.[104] She did not wish to be "white," "Indian" or "half breed"; she just wanted to be herself.

In southern Alberta during the early 1920s there lived a very successful Canadian writer named Winnifred Eaton Reeve. Her English father and Chinese mother had met in China. They married in Shanghai before moving to Britain, then to the United States, and finally to Montreal, where Winnifred was born in 1875.[105] Her ancestry normally would have made her life a trial in southern Alberta—Calgary was far from McLuhan's "global village" in the early twentieth century.[105] For example, on 16 January 1918, a *Calgary Herald* editorial entitled "Yellow Labor" pronounced: "So far as the Yellow races are concerned it is not desirable that there should be intermarrying, the effect being usually demoralizing." But Mrs. Reeve, who with her husband had moved to Alberta from New York City in 1917 to buy the Bow View Ranch about sixty kilometres west of Calgary, enjoyed special status. The author of over a dozen novels, mostly on Japanese themes, and scores of short stories and non-fiction pieces in mass market North American magazines like *Ladies' Home Journal*, and *Harper's Monthly* had the aura of success about her. *A Japanese Nightingale* (1901) sold hundreds of thousands of copies and was adapted for both Broadway and film.[107] Like Belle, Winnifred escaped racial classification. After she completed her novel *Cattle* in 1923—under her pen name of Onoto Watanna—Winnifred presented a copy to Belle, inscribed with these words:

> To Lady Lougheed—a picturesque and delightful personality with the regard of the author.
> Onoto Watanna
> Calgary, December 1923
> The world is just as a person's heart makes it.[108]

Belle's love of life was too great to allow racial slurs to hurt her. "The world is just as a person's heart makes it." She had the luxury of being exactly who she wanted to be; after all, who in early twentieth century British Calgary stood higher on the social pyramid than she? No one. Had she not enjoyed the ultimate imperial honour? In early September 1912 Belle welcomed a son of Queen Victoria, the late King Edward VII's brother, to her home. Belle received at Lougheed House the Duke of Connaught, the Governor-General of Canada, who came for the first Calgary Stampede. His Royal Highness travelled with his wife, the Duchess of Connaught, the daughter of a German prince, and their own beautiful young daughter, Princess Patricia, as well as their royal entourage of aides and security personnel.[109] The duke had just officially opened Alberta's Legislature

Building in Edmonton, which stood directly beside Fort Edmonton, Belle's uncle's old Hudson's Bay Company fort. Belle became a great favourite of the duke and duchess.

Whereas James worked constantly to transform himself, to develop the persona of an ultra-British Canadian in speech, manners and dress—Belle simply remained herself. James constantly attempted to improve his diction, tone of voice and delivery. General Griesbach once recalled how the senator struggled to acquire a rich vocabulary and an accent. "Some Senators," he wrote, "probably a bit spitefully," started the story that Senator Lougheed memorized "twenty big words a day and had done so for the past twenty years."[110] *The Canadian Liberal Monthly* magazine savaged him on at least one occasion for his "rich, crusted, old English Stilton accent": "No peer of the realm has anything on Senator Lougheed of Calgary when it comes to the broad 'a' and the slight-ed 'r'."[111] *The Eye Opener* criticized him for his "affected style of grandiose speech."[112] According to Senator Griesbach, Bob Edwards loved to tell stories about Lougheed that turned on his pronunciation of the word "juncture," as "junctchaw." "Apparently at this 'junctchaw' it was suitable to do things which Lougheed approved of. On the other hand at another 'junctchaw' it was inadvisable to proceed."[113]

Belle had no time, desire, or need to transform herself. Her positive outlook, her artistic sense, pleased her vice-regal guests. In her husband's and her joint diary, the Duchess of Connaught observed that Beaulieu was a "very nice comfortable house with a little garden round."[114] The chatelaine of Lougheed House had attended to every detail of their visit. Shortly before the arrival of the duke and duchess, for instance, she contacted florist A. M. Terrill.

At the time of Kathleen Parlow's visit in February 1911, Alfred Terrill had greenhouses on the site of what would become the Lougheed Building. By September 1912, the same month as the duke's visit to Calgary, the office building was completed. It contained Alfred Terrill's new modern flower store on the main floor, 1st Street West side.[115] The city's leading florist supplied Belle all the necessary flowers from his new greenhouses in East Calgary, including his signature mauve orchids. The paneled oak dining room received American beauty roses. Sunset roses were placed in vases on tables in the neighbouring room. For the duke's suite at Lougheed House, furnished with curved mahogany and rich oriental rugs, the florist provided huge bowls of crimson ros-es. The woodwork in the duchess's suite was of white enamel and the furniture of skil-fully carved black walnut. Cut glass jars contained mauve sweet peas and gypsophilia, small fragrant white and pink flowers. In Princess Patricia's rooms, full of furniture of Circassian walnut, he placed masses of dainty pink Killarney roses. Outside, the mag-nificent gardens contained hedges of sweet peas and banks of shaded asters, brilliant flashes of colour against the bright green lawns and the bay trees that bordered them.[116] As a gift for her kindness in welcoming them to stay at her home, the Duchess of Connaught, Princess Louise, daughter of Prince Frederick Charles and Princess Marie Anne of Prussia,[117] gave Belle a broach of diamonds and pearls.[118]

How prosperous, well-known and influential James Lougheed had become. From humble origins in East Toronto he had reached the top echelons of Alberta soci-ety. Unlike the duke and his family he enjoyed no privileged birth, family palaces and

estates, and lacked influential family contacts. He left Cabbagetown three decades earlier with few material possessions and no powerful friends. Now the former Orange Lodge "Young Briton" had become a Western Canadian plutocrat, a social leader and political powerbroker. He even sent his older daughter Dorothy away to Bishop Strachan's School, one of Toronto's most exclusive private girls' schools.[119] Then, in early September, he and Belle hosted in their sandstone mansion Arthur, the Duke of Connaught, the third and only living son of Queen Victoria, a royal prince whose godfather was the Duke of Wellington himself, the victorious commander at the Battle of Waterloo. The province of Alberta took its title from the third name of one of the duke's older sisters, Her Royal Highness Princess Louise Caroline Alberta. The princess also gave her first name to the most beautiful of lakes in the Canadian Rockies.[120]

By September 1912 James Lougheed neared the highest altitudes of worldly success. Belle played an invaluable role in his ascent. Her joie de vivre softened the outlook of her workaholic husband, with his myriad of activities. She guided him through the intricacies of his new social responsibilities. Belle, a lover of music, drama and dance, led him ever more deeply into the world of the fine arts. She reinforced his determination to give Calgary a magnificent performing arts centre attached to his planned state-of-the-art office building.

Chapter Four

NEIGHBOURS

ALFRED TERRILL AND PADDY NOLAN

To build his majestic theatre and showcase office building James Lougheed purchased Alfred Terrill's land at the southeast corner of 1st Street and 6th Avenue West. Alfred and Margaret Terrill belonged to the advance guard of thousands of Ontarians who migrated to Calgary in the early twentieth century. On initial arrival to the prairies many eastern Canadians found the stark treeless country depressing. They proceeded to reshape the short grass country into the image of the lands they had left behind. In trying to make their gardens they faced a short growing season, alkaline soils, and deep-freeze temperatures.[1] The chinook, the dry warm wind that often blows off the Rockies in winter, caused havoc for some plants in the midst of sub-Arctic weather. But the Terrills sensed a great business opportunity in such conditions when they arrived in 1903. They knew they could supply palms and ferns, and particularly flowering plants such as roses, carnations, even orchids, to a Calgary market. Greenhouses meet all the environmental challenges. Alfred Marmaduke Terrill, forty-one years old the year of his arrival in Calgary, was a florist and gardener from Picton, Prince Edward County in Ontario.[2]

The Bow River rose in a glacier-fed lake in the Rockies northwest of Banff. The city occupied a deep, flat-bottomed valley, intersected by the Elbow River. The Elbow joined the Bow at the junction where the North West Mounted Police built their fort. At the beginning of the century Calgary occupied an area of less than one square mile.[3] The frontier settlement still had a small town atmosphere. Hitching posts stood everywhere downtown, but congestion downtown was increasing. About 1905 cowboys abandoned the practice of hitching ponies on Stephen (Eighth Avenue), and left them at livery stables.[4] Soon the herders of milk cows ceased their drives along the streets on their way to, and from pasture.[5]

The growing, ever faster-growing settlement had a vitality and power about it. When Alberta became a province on 1 September 1905, *The Calgary Herald* editorialized: "Today, wherever a Briton lives, he remembers that the empire is being given a new strength in the western world by this development."

Although only three decades old in 1905, Calgary already had its own social hierarchy. At the top, in the male world, stood the Ranchmen's Club, formed in 1891 by prominent Alberta ranchers and members of the city's new professional and business elite. The social prestige and business advantages of membership in this British gentleman's club were immeasurable.[6]

In 1905 lawyer Jermy Jephson occupied the president's chair.[7] From 1892 to 1919 he practised with James Muir, in the well-known law firm of Jephson, Muir and Adams.[8] Jermy and his wife Christian Drever,[9] and their three sons and daughter lived in a rambling red frame two-story dwelling, known as "Out-At-Elbow," as it stood on the banks of the Elbow River. The surrounding village was called Rouleauville, as a substantial number of French-speaking people lived there around the homes of the two Rouleau brothers: Charles, the late territorial judge from Quebec, and his brother, Edouard, the North West Mounted Police doctor. Calgary annexed Rouleauville the following year, and it became Mission.

The Jephsons had a large comfortable home. They paneled their spacious rooms in dark oak. The dining room, furnished with rich mahogany sideboards, a dining suite and chests of drawers, had a large red brick fireplace. A focal point in the hall was a solid oak desk with innumerable drawers within drawers. It had come from Christian's parents' home in Winnipeg; she was of the Red River Drevers. Within this desk Christian's father had hid revolvers and other valuables when Riel's men called during the troubles of 1869–1870. The substantial grounds of the Jephson's property stretched from the banks of the river north to what is now 18th Avenue S.W. They had a stable and many horses. The three Jephson boys and their friends cleared a polo field, which became a centre of fun for the young people of the area.[10]

Few Calgarians were more intensely upper crust British than Jermy Jephson. The Cambridge University graduate and noted scholar in Greek and Latin liked to quote before the local bench English judgements from the original Latin.[11] Often he argued that no one could properly speak the English language without a firm grounding in Latin and Greek.[12] While he highly regarded scholarship, this friendly and kindly gentleman also valued sports. As a young man he had been a keen cricketer, and as his obituary added, he was "an admirer of all form of manly sport."[13] *The Calgary Herald* wrote a special editorial in Jephson's honour after his death in 1923. The paper recalled: "He was keen to have our education in Canada inculcate in our young people a taste for all that was good in reading, a truly 'sporting' observance of sports, and a just knowledge of the great place the Mother Country has occupied in the world."[14]

Alfred Terrill never belonged to the Ranchmen's Club, but did join and actively participated in both the Masons and the Independent Order of Odd Fellows (IOOF). Energetic and capable he soon became treasurer of the Bow River Masonic Lodge. He also served as Noble Grand in the local IOOF.[15] Through these benefit organizations, which helped their members and their families in times of need, and through his church, Knox Presbyterian, he came to know a wide cross-section of people, acquiring good business contacts in the process. Within four years of living in Calgary he ran successfully for the City Council and served a one-year term as alderman for Ward 2 in 1908.

The Terrills came to a city whose smells, particularly in the summer, made a strong impression. One immigrant later commented: "The thing I remember most about my arrival in Calgary was the smell. It was the horse-smellingest town I could ever remember."[16] From the numerous livery stables issued forth the mingled odours of

horse manure and urine, as well as harness oil and hay. A stench often arose throughout the city from numerous cesspools and outdoor privies. A flood of wastes from downtown buildings emptied into an inadequate sewer system, sometimes into downtown cesspools or open street drains.[17] By 1905, the year that Alberta became a province, Terrill-supplied scented flowers helped to fight indoor odours. Terrill shrubs and bedding plants added green and lively colours to homeowners' front yards. Their business thrived, becoming the "first florist enterprise of any magnitude"[18] in the "new" province.

A number of elegant sandstone buildings stood in the city in 1903.[19] When quarried the soft and easily carved local sandstone turned hard with age. The sandstone buildings added to their neighbourhoods a note of solidity and permanence. But apart from these fireproof structures, erected after the disastrous fire of 1886, the rest of the frontier city looked quite temporary and unfinished. The streets were dirt. The city's board sidewalks heaved and teetered.

Alfred chose Calgary in 1903 because he knew that it stood on the cusp of an incredible economic boom. The depression of the 1890s had lifted. With the lack of good, cheap farmland in the American West Canada's prairies became "The Last Best West." Thousands of immigrants from Eastern Canada and the United States and Europe had already arrived in Alberta by the CPR to take up homesteads. Tens of thousands followed. The large ranches retreated before the fence and the plough. Calgary, the service centre of the Bow River Valley, grew again and then again in size. The city's central location on the mainline of the CPR made Calgary the metropolis of southern Alberta.

Thanks to his lifelong experience in the floristry business, Alfred knew how to operate greenhouses effectively and efficiently. Despite the city's high elevation, chinook winds, temperature extremes and low rainfall,[20] he experimented and prospered with his greenhouses on the future sites of the Lougheed Building and Grand Theatre.

The CPR originally controlled the entire Section 15, the square mile section around the train station. In 1889 Messrs. Richard Angus, Donald A. Smith, Edmund Boyd Osler and William Scarth, all closely connected to the CPR, collectively purchased several large blocks of Section 15, including the tract where the florist built his greenhouses some fifteen years later. Four of Calgary's streets bore the names of this foursome. Then in 1892 these close CPR associates re-sold the eight lots that Alfred Terrill later purchased. Four lots went to local banker Samuel Barber, manager of the local Imperial Bank of Canada branch.[21] He had come to Calgary from Ontario several years earlier. The other four went in 1893 to Peter Willoughby King, Calgary's Sheriff, whose name remains an honoured one in Calgary over a century later. In his will in 1921 the Scottish-born bachelor left a quarter-of-a-million dollars, his whole estate, to erect, furnish and maintain "a home for deserving poor, both women and children."[22] In 2003 the Sheriff King Home provided emergency shelter for nearly eight hundred women and children fleeing domestic violence.[23]

On 25 June 1903, Roland Winter, then the southern Alberta register of land titles, recorded Alfred Terrill's certificate of title to the late Samuel Barber's four blocks at the southeastern corner of Angus and Scarth. His executor, lawyer Jermy Jephson, made the arrangements with the florist. Calgary originally named its major streets after CPR officials, but in March 1904 the city introduced numbers for the downtown streets that ran north and south, and for the avenues extending from east and west. The CPR station on Centre Street divided the downtown area into East and West Calgary. Angus became 6th Avenue West, and Scarth became 1st Street West. On 2 March 1904, Registrar Winter issued a certificate of title for Sheriff King's four lots at the same location.[24] Alfred believed that he paid a "big" price—$2,500—for all eight lots, but within a decade, at the height of the land boom, he sold them for a tremendous profit.[25]

As soon as he acquired the land Alfred energetically worked to make his business succeed. Within a few years he even grew orchids in his greenhouses.[26] The flowers used for decoration in the gardens surrounding Lougheed House, including the mauve orchids, came from A. M. Terrill.[27] The newcomer from Ontario soon had five modern greenhouses on his property at the southeastern corner of 6th Avenue and 1st Street West. Horse-drawn wagons made deliveries.[28] On the site his greenhouses, offices and salesrooms completely covered the property.[29] The Terrills lived on the east side of their business, at 127 6th Avenue West.

Rich and poor lived side by side in the neighbourhood. Christina McLaughlin, later Mrs. Bob Brown, Sr., lived in the same district near the Terrills. (Half-a-century later her son, Bobby Brown of Home Oil, would be one of the leading tenants of the Lougheed Building located on the site of Terrill's original Calgary greenhouses.) Originally from Grey County, Ontario, Christina's father, worked as a teamster for the Fire Department, The McLaughlins owned their own home at 124 6th Avenue East, just two blocks from the Terrills. Next to them on one side lived Dr. George Macdonald, a medical doctor from Ontario, and his family. Dr. Macdonald, like a number of the early professionals in town, had a varied employment record. Before entering medicine at McGill he worked as a CPR station agent, and then as a locomotive engineer.[30] On the other side of the McLaughlins lived the family of Jacob Eshleman, a piano tuner. Just one block further east, the Rev. John McDougall and his family resided at 230 6th Avenue East. Beside the McDougalls' house still stood the old Parlow home at 236.[31]

On the southeast corner of Centre Street and 6th Avenue rose Hull's Opera House, an imposing brick building constructed in 1893. Calgary's first theatre hosted all kinds of early social and cultural events, including touring plays, lectures, dances and concerts. For thirteen years it was the focus of culture in the city. Arts-minded Calgarians like Mrs. Lydia Winter and the Irish lawyer Paddy Nolan organized amateur theatricals at Hull's Opera House.[32] Minnie Parlow once appeared in one of Paddy's "Dramatic and Musical Entertainments."[33] In 1906 it became an apartment building with retail units at the street level.[34]

The Terrills' neighbourhood, like the city itself, was still young. Christina McLaughlin later recalled childhood winters skating on the Bow and the Elbow rivers, sleigh rides, church concerts and home parties. In summer there were family, church and lodge picnics, with "the excitement of the foot races and the tugs-of-war and the ball games and the horseshoe contests." In those days, everyone, old and young, enjoyed "the now-forgotten pastime of sitting on their wide, cool verandas." Christina left the neighbourhood after her marriage in 1907 to Bob Brown, a young engineer.[35]

The Terrills' most interesting neighbours, the Nolans—Paddy and his wife Mary Lee Nolan, and young son Harry—lived immediately next to them at 113 6th Avenue. Mary, or Minnie as her friends called her, arrived in Calgary in 1884 at age fourteen with her family from Ontario. Minnie recalled wonderful stories of early Calgary. She vividly remembered that troubled year, 1885, when Calgary feared an attack by the First Nations. There was much rejoicing after the Riel Rebellion of 1885 ended.

Minnie had an independent mind. Unlike many newcomers to Calgary she had a positive image of the Native people. At Father Lacombe's church she knew several Metis parishioners, including the Metis elder Cuthbert McGillis. The old man sang the Mass without music. "He was a very stout man and sang quite lustily, so that his stomach was a sort of bellows which blew in and out." Below his stomach he wore a Metis sash.[36] Minnie employed Metis girls as maids after she married in 1894. She gave them a good training, taught them to wear caps and uniforms, "and they did very well."[37]

Paddy, a handsome, big man, one who weighed nearly three hundred pounds, had a courtroom lawyer's voice, deep and strong. The well-read Nolan came to Calgary from Ireland in 1889 with the best academic credentials: early training at Sacred Heart College in his native Limerick; a B.A. with honours in classics at Trinity College, Dublin, with a gold medal for oratory; a law degree from London University. Called to the bar in Ireland he practiced for four years in Dublin before leaving for North America. The fact that distant Limerick relatives, the Costello family, lived in Calgary brought him to Western Canada. Full of humorous Irish stories, the good-natured Paddy quickly became a favourite after-dinner speaker. In the words of his biographer, Grant MacEwan, his speeches were as welcome as "a chinook arch in a winter month."[38] In this land of new beginning the popular raconteur did exactly what Bob Edwards did: he reduced his age. Bob cut off four years off his birth date;[39] Paddy, just two. Paddy also altered the exact date of his birth by two weeks from March 3 to 17, St. Patrick's Day.[40]

The popular member of the Ranchmen's Club, and founding member of the Knights of Columbus in Calgary, took on cases that interested him, not necessarily those that would advance him financially or professionally. Amongst other clients Paddy defended drunks, prostitutes and disorderly persons. Regularly the criminal lawyer represented Calgary's leading lady—in respect of notoriety—Caroline ("Mother") Fulham. [41] Also known as the Irish pig-lady, Fulham lived a few blocks west of the Terrills and Nolans on Angus (6th Avenue)—a short distance west of the present site of Knox United Church.[42] She kept pigs in her back yard, and to feed her porkers she set off daily with her horse and democrat with a large barrel for kitchen swill. Mrs. Fulham collected kitchen waste from the garbage containers of Calgary's best hotels and restaurants. Whenever anyone challenged her about taking the garbage she verbally abused, and/or physically fought back, considering it her property. Frequently the police prosecuted the "Queen of Garbage Row" for disorderly conduct.

Senator James Lougheed, in one 1891 courtroom exchange, called Mrs. Fulham a "moral leper." He regretted "the liberty or rather the licenses granted to such a woman

Paddy Nolan, with son Harry, at their home 113 6th Ave. West, about 1900. Glenbow Archives/NA-1371-3.

Paddy Nolan, one of the founders of the Knights of Columbus in Calgary, appears in the centre of this photo. Photo courtesy of the Knights of Columbus (Ken Beckie).

who made herself a notorious nuisance."[43] In a 1901 statement to the Calgary City Council the senator again brought forward his own and other property-owners' concerns: "I for instance, have a number of lots in the vicinity of Mrs. Fulham's place and certainly no one would buy them when her pig ranch is taken into consideration."[44] But Paddy, who, in his biographer's words, was "attracted to uninhibited people,"[45] defended her, without fee, until the day she finally left Calgary in mid-September 1904.

Funny tales about Paddy circulated throughout Calgary at the turn of the century. A favourite concerned Shorty McLaughlin from High River, who once made a special trip to Calgary to enlist Paddy's help against the CPR. The railway recently ran over, and killed over twenty of his horses. The criminal lawyer asked the rancher what he wanted him to do. Shorty replied, fight for "double, maybe triple value for every cayuse those blankety-blanks have slaughtered!" But after listening to Shorty's bitter thrusts at the railway Paddy replied, "I'm sorry, but I can't take your case." Shorty protested; he knew Nolan's reputation as a champion of the underdog. "You can't! Why not? Ain't my money as good—" Paddy then held up his hand to explain: "It's nothing like that, Shorty. You see, the railroad men are right. Any horse that can't outrun the C.P.R. deserves to die."[46]

Even James Lougheed, not renowned for his sense of humour, told an amusing tale about Paddy. This one concerned Arthur Sifton, a later chief justice of Alberta and premier of the province. Apparently Paddy offered to help his fellow Liberal in a territorial by-election around 1900.[47] In order to reach voters the introverted Sifton really needed help. He was delighted when Paddy offered to be his campaign manager. A special challenge in his Banff area riding was Canmore, a hard-drinking mining town. As an abstainer Sifton stood at a distinct disadvantage. To win the town Paddy dreamed up an ingenious scheme to convince "the boys" that Arthur was one of them. As the senator told the tale Paddy arranged a political meeting at Canmore. But immediately after the speech he sent Arthur to his hotel room while he went himself to the bar. The miners then asked where "the little fellow was." When Paddy said he had gone upstairs the miners insisted: "Bring him down and let's have a drink with him." Paddy explained the candidate was tired. Louder than before the men insisted that he appear. Finally, in a confidential tone Paddy told them the secret. To be sure of getting him to a meeting the next night at Banff, Paddy had to lock him in his room. "Truth is," he added, "he's one of the worst drinkers in the country." If Arthur joined them, well, "there'd be no holding him, and the only chance to win the election is to keep him under cover, between meetings." The miners were impressed. Sifton won Canmore and the election.[48]

Many Paddy Nolan stories enjoyed a long life in legal circles. One concerned a court encounter Paddy had with R. B. Bennett around 1908. Usually the Irish lawyer arrived in court with the minimum of legal references, depending instead on his knowledge of procedure, his oratorical skills and his knowledge of human nature. In contrast, Bennett, the opposing counsel in this Supreme Court of Alberta case, came with his assistant loaded down with books to give the impression of profundity. Once in the courtroom Bennett laid it on even more strongly when he asked his student: "Boy, give

me Phipson on Evidence; Boy, give me Kenny on Crimes." Paddy broke up the court when he said to his clerk: "Boy, get me Bennett on Baloney."[49]

Bob Edwards and Paddy got along famously. Frequently Paddy wrote for his paper and provided legal counsel whenever the *Eye Opener* became involved in a libel case.[50] Bachelor Bob often came over to the Nolan's small house just beside the Terrills.[51] Bob later wrote of Paddy: "His faculty of keeping a crowd in a sustained roar of laughter for hours at a stretch was a constant source of wonderment. He never repeated himself. Paddy's well of fun never ran dry for an instant and the rapidity with which he could drive away the blues from the mind of a worried friend was not the least endearing of his qualities."[52]

As a staunch Liberal party supporter Paddy had little contact with Conservative Calgary powerbrokers Lougheed and Bennett. But, when he learned that the senator would build a totally up-to-date office building in Calgary, he made plans to become an early tenant. He and many other professionals and businesspeople counted the days until the new structure's completion. Lougheed was greatly influenced by the new and innovative style of construction in Chicago. The need for taller fireproof buildings, the availability of electricity in the place of gas and the introduction of modern passenger safety elevators all helped to allow for the construction of steel framed and reinforced concrete buildings. The use of steel and concrete together allowed for larger windows than ever before, as walls no longer had to be load bearing. Chicago also pioneered the combination of theatres and commercial buildings.[53] From a business point of view features like this greatly appealed to the senator. Terrill's property, with its frontage of 130 feet on 1st Street and 200 feet on 6th Avenue would be just perfect for his project. The emerging importance of 1st Street West, the first north-south thoroughfare to achieve commercial prominence, attracted him to this location.[54]

James Lougheed entrusted Edmund Taylor to make the real estate transactions. On his behalf Taylor made an offer Alfred Terrill could not refuse. The florist sold his eight lots on 2 March 1911 to Edna Taylor, Edmund's wife, for a tremendous profit.[55] The lots sold for $100,000.[56] James Lougheed purchased them from her on 5 June 1911.[57] With his excellent cash reserves at the height of the urban real estate boom, the senator had no difficulty in making the purchase. That same year he transferred ten lots on 6th Avenue to the HBC for $250,000, lots which he had acquired for $13,500 in two purchases, the first in 1902, and the second in 1905.[58] In 1911 the senator also sold another property on 8th Avenue to the English politician, William Dudley Ward, for $150,000.[59]

With the property secured the senator could proceed. He initially favoured the idea of building a theatre and a hotel, but by August 1911 he had decided instead to build a six-story business block to be called the Lougheed Building.[60] He planned on having retail spaces on the ground floor, offices on the second, third and fourth floors, and apartments on the upper two floors. This diversified his sources of income and diminished his risk. The building could not exceed six stories because the city's water pressure in 1911 could not pump water any higher.[61]

The City of Calgary Building Register, January 1910 to December 1913, contains the initial estimated cost of Grand Theatre. The entry under June 1911 records the McNeil and Trainer firm as the contractors of the theatre for an estimated cost of $100,000.[62] Later the assessed value of the completed theatre indicated it cost $229,000,[63] or over twice as much as first estimated. As regards the office building, its assessed value, upon completion, was $277,500.[64] Together the price tag of both the building and theatre came in at over half a million dollars. At the height of Calgary's economic boom again this posed no problem for the Calgary real estate magnate. In the fall of 1911 James Lougheed's challenge was lack of time, not money.

With his cabinet appointment that September as minister without portfolio in Prime Minister Borden's newly elected government, Senator Lougheed needed Edmund Taylor to run his real estate empire. As the sole senator who could speak for the cabinet in the upper chamber, he had to master the full range of government legislation, a task required of no other cabinet member.[65]

American architect Lanier Rumel (Len) Wardrop designed both the office building and the theatre. Most likely the senator heard about him through Bill Sherman, manager in 1911 of the Lyric Theatre on 8th Avenue, which was on the Seattle-based Sullivan and Considine Vaudeville circuit.[66] John Considine had built his first theatre in Seattle in 1889.[67] Now with financier Tim Sullivan the two men in 1911–1912 controlled a chain of theatres across the West known as the Empress Theatres.

Utah-based Wardrop had just designed with his partner, D. C. Dart, the new Empress Theatre in Salt Lake City, which opened in November 1911.[68] Photos reveal that the Grand was a twin of the Empress in Salt Lake. During the construction period Wardrop had his office in the Clarence Block, which housed the Lougheed and Bennett law office at 122 8th Avenue.[69] The Lyric was located next door in the adjoining Norman Block. Wardrop's design followed the popular Chicago Commercial Style, a term used at the turn of the century to describe multi-story buildings in Chicago. Its construction was sound. The commercial style emphasized the skeletal framework of the structure, which included reinforced concrete floors with steel beams and columns. McNeil and Trainer, the same contractors who built the theatre, also obtained the contract for the office building.[70]

The plans showed the L-shaped office building enclosing the shoebox shaped theatre, located behind the retail storefronts, offices and apartments. A shared wall would join the two structures. The pipes for the theatre's water and sewerage were connected to the Lougheed Building under the theatre's floor.[71] Access to the theatre from 1st Street West was through a long, narrow hallway or theatre lobby in the Lougheed Building. This hallway contained the box office. An exit lobby through the Lougheed also connected the theatre with 6th Avenue. The office building itself included a deluxe restaurant in the basement; a row of fifteen retail stores with large display windows on the ground level; offices on the second, third and fourth floors; residential apartments on the fifth and sixth floors; and a small penthouse suite on top overlooking the city.[72] The two passenger elevators stood directly in front of the main entrance on 1st Street. Both the north and south sides of the building had an outside fire escape.

The builders used red brick for the exterior. On the 1st Street side, to make the most of the natural light, the architect placed forty windows, eight for each of the five upper floors, and sixty-five on the 6th Avenue side, thirteen for each floor. Each window had its own sandstone sill and lintel. The retail ground floor contained large commercial display windows. Inside the building the windows looked toward the Sherman Grand Theatre; these took advantage of the two light wells placed between the office building and the theatre.[73] The tungsten filament incandescent light bulb was still a year or two away from commercial development.

Work rushed forward on the theatre. The installation of the heating and ventilating system for the theatre came at the end. In the basement a great fan drove warm, moist air though the auditorium through several openings in the floor. In the ceiling big ventilators then expelled the bad air, completely changing the air in the theatre every fifteen minutes.[74] The completed interior of the Sherman Grand awaited Forbes-Robertson, who opened the theatre on 5 February 1912. Hanging above the theatre entrance at 608 on 1st Street was a two-stories-high sign, with the letters SHERMAN running vertically, and the letters GRAND horizontally.

Construction workers now completed the handsome six-story office building itself.[75] An impressive overhanging cornice made out of painted sheet metal crowned the structure. Ten supporting pillars, or pilasters, projected somewhat from the façade; six were located on the 6th Avenue side, and four on the 1st Street side. Along with the three corner columns, these pillars held up the ornate cornice. Over the building entrances the architect placed glass and metal canopies with the main entrance at 604, 1st Street West.[76] The completed office building awaited its first tenants in early September 1912.

Meanwhile, once the sale of his property went through, Alfred Terrill opened his new greenhouses in East Calgary. He also arranged with Lougheed and Taylor, who handled rental arrangements, to operate a florist's shop in the city's most up-to-date business block.[77] Paddy Nolan also rented several offices for his law firm in the Lougheed Building.[78] He moved in October 1912.[79] But while Alfred would enjoy a decade in the new building before he retired, Paddy was only there a few months. He died on 10 February 1913. Alfred and Margaret Terrill attended their friend's funeral at St. Mary's Catholic Church, as did former Orange Order member James Lougheed and Belle. Within the church, the *Calgary News-Telegram* reported, were "practically all the prominent citizens" and also "a large number of poor people, many of whom had doubtless been befriended by Mr. Nolan during his lifetime." Many of the over fifty floral tributes, which included "some magnificent creations," were purchased at Terrill's new store in the newly-opened Lougheed Building.[80]

Chapter Five

CONSTRUCTION OF THE
LOUGHEED AND SHERMAN GRAND

O N 16 FEBRUARY 1912, LESS THAN TWO WEEKS AFTER THE SHERMAN Grand opened, *The Albertan* carried a story about a most unusual individual, Honoré Jaxon. This intense little man with an incredibly powerful voice was the complete antithesis of James Lougheed and the other members of Calgary's emerging plutocracy. Jaxon, a ferocious anti-imperialist in Chicago, had just launched a campaign to save Persia from division by Britain and other European colonial powers. As *The Albertan* article "Honore Jaxon Out For Persians" stated: "Mr. Jaxon fought as a rebel in the Riel rebellion, being in full sympathy with what he describes as the downtrodden half breeds. After the rebellion he drifted into the U.S., where he advocated the cause of the people against oppressive combinations." His interest then shifted to defending the oppressed "Spanish Indian insurrectos" against a corrupt government in Mexico. Several years earlier, *The Albertan* added, he "made his headquarters in Calgary ... when interesting himself in the case of the striking miners of Western Canada."

Jaxon, a short, rotund man with greying hair and a receding hairline, visited Calgary in the middle of March 1909. He stayed at the Kerr home on the north side of 6th Avenue West, directly opposite the Nolans and the Terrills.[1] Jessie Kerr, whose husband John, a tailor, had died a few years earlier, lived there with her three children. Her younger son was a student, the older son a clerk and her daughter a stenographer.[2] Honoré gave "130 6th Av. West" as his mailing address during his visit to the city. Quickly he became a sought-after speaker in Calgary's small left-wing community.[3] While in southern Alberta he travelled as well to the coal mining towns in the Bow River Valley and the Crow's Nest Pass to help the workers fight for union recognition and better pay.

Honoré was known in his hometown of Chicago as a "French Indian."[4] In 1907, *The Saturday Evening Post* described his colourful background in this way: "Jaxon's father was a Metis Indian, and Jaxon was born in a buffalo camp so near to the forty-ninth parallel, in sight of Woods Mountain, and between Montana and the Northwest Territory, that Jaxon has never been able to figure out whether he was born a British subject or an American citizen."[5] His French-sounding name appeared to confirm his story. Appearances can be deceiving.

Belle Lougheed and Edmund Taylor presented themselves as white North Americans. In contrast, Jaxon proudly advertised his Metis ancestry, which is all the more astounding when one realizes he had none. Will Jackson, to use his real name, was born in Ontario, the son of English immigrant parents. His family moved from the Toronto area when he was quite young to Wingham, about 150 kilometres to the northwest, where his father opened a store. A good student, Will completed high school before studying classics for three years at the University of Toronto. But his father's sudden bankruptcy prevented him from completing his final year. In 1881, Will, aged twenty, followed his family to Prince Albert in the North West Territories where his father began a farm implement business.

During the troubles of 1884–1885, the young idealist sided with Louis Riel and the Metis. He became Riel's English-language secretary. As he wrote: "The oppression of the aboriginal has been the crying sin of the white race in America and they have at last found a voice."[6] 1885 was the turning point of his life. After Canadian troops defeated the insurgent Metis they immediately put Will under custody as Riel's secretary. The Canadians sent him under armed guard to the NWMP barracks in Regina chained to a Cree warrior. A Regina court tried Will for treason-felony, but found him not guilty on the grounds of insanity. It committed the longhaired prisoner wearing a Metis headband to the lunatic asylum at Lower Fort Garry, immediately north of Winnipeg. Escaping from the asylum on 2 November of that same year, he walked to the American border. Riel's execution on 16 November led Jackson to renounce his race. In Chicago, where he made his home for the next twenty years, he identified himself as a Metis and changed his name to the French-sounding Honoré Jaxon. He became a local labour leader.

In Calgary Honoré immediately applied himself to the task at hand—educating the working class about their true condition at local Socialist Party meetings.[7] In his mind no room existed for race theory—the then current belief that "superior" and "inferior" races existed in the world. Only two groups existed in his universe: the exploiters and the exploited.[8]

Between 1907 and 1909 in his travels across Western Canada Honoré wrote notes and took photographs for a proposed history of the Rebellion of 1885. Riel's former secretary looked up old participants in the troubles, but Honoré made no attempt to seek out William Pearce at Bow Bend Shack, his fine sandstone house just east of the city on the south bank of the Bow. As the federal government's superintendent of mines and chief advisor on the development of the North West, Pearce had prepared the official report on the causes of the Riel Rebellion. His summary exonerated the Canadian government from all responsibility. In a document he wrote immediately after the rebellion, Pearce described Jackson's assistance to Riel in this way: "Such men as Jackson—and fortunately they are very few—joined this agitation to advance their own ends and if nothing else is accomplished, their vanity is flattered by being brought into prominence."[9]

Other doors remained closed in Calgary. Riel's secretary would not be welcomed at Lougheed House. Belle Lougheed had lost her beloved brother Richard, a Canadian soldier at the Battle of Batoche.[10] Nor did Jean Drever Pinkham and Christian Drever Jephson have any use for a friend of Louis Riel. On 5 April 1905 *The Calgary*

Honoré Jaxon, 1907. Photographer
Chicago Daily News. Chicago
Historical Society.

Herald declared: "Riel died by the hangman's hand and may all imitators of his reckless career so perish."

Honoré did meet W. M. Davidson, the founder and influential publisher of *The Albertan*, who had the reputation of being "a little left of centre."[11] The Ontario-born Davidson, a graduate of the University of Toronto, came to the city in 1902 after working for Toronto newspapers and editing *The London News*. In 1905, *The Voice*, a Winnipeg labour newspaper, referred to him as "belonging to what is becoming known as the Canadian radical school."[12] With letterhead generously supplied by *The Albertan*'s editor, Honoré wrote a number of letters to his wife and family back in the Prince Albert area.[13] *The Albertan* later described the newspaper's visitor "as a rebel in the Riel rebellion, being in full sympathy with what he describes as the downtrodden half breeds." The paper continued: "After the rebellion, he drifted into the U.S., where he advocated the cause of the people against oppressive combinations."[14]

Either through W. M. Davidson, or R. C. Owens, a fraternal delegate from the Alberta branch of the American Society of Equity, a farmer's organization, Honoré met farm leader William Tregillus. The wealthy English dairy farmer lived at his home, Roscarrock, just west of the city. Only two months earlier Tregillus and Owens had worked hard to unite the two rival Alberta farm organizations, the Society of Equity and the Alberta Farmers' Union into a strong new union—the United Farmers of Alberta (UFA). Over half-a-century later Will's son Cyril still remembered the visit to their home of Louis Riel's secretary, whom he described as an "interesting personality."[15]

Honoré Jaxon made few inroads with his socialist ideas in Calgary, even though great social inequalities existed. In *The Limits of Labour: Class Formation and the Labour Movement in Calgary, 1883–1929* (1998), Canadian historian David Bright states: "Just as in other Canadian cities undergoing industrialization, a single wage was inadequate to support the average working-class family."[16] Driven by the necessity to augment family incomes, second and third incomes, the taking in of boarders and the keeping of pigs and cows became necessities for many. Every able-bodied individual over the age of fourteen was expected to work. Hours of employment extended from eight in the morning to six at night. The working week extended either five and a half or six days a week. At the job few government regulations existed to protect the workers' health and safety.[17] Historian Max Foran adds of their home conditions: "Overcrowded conditions and high rents forced many to live in dismal surroundings. The infant mortality rate was distressingly high among children of poor families. Although the city boasted a splendid hospital, many could not afford its services."[18]

But in Calgary the Socialists made no advances at all. Their cry that "all our people shall be properly clothed, housed and fed" attracted limited support.[19] Before the economic crash of 1913 the prairie working class believed that imagination, sacrifice and hard work would give all who tried a new start. S. J. Ferns, a bricklayer recently arrived from Ontario, remembered the Calgary of the period as a "magic place" full of energy and opportunity: "Calgary was then a young people's city. You never saw any old people in Calgary."[20] As a Calgarian told visiting writer Arthur Stringer, who quoted

Photo of 6th Avenue West, opposite Terrill's greenhouses. On his visit to Calgary Honoré Jaxon stayed about halfway down the block, on the north side of the street, shown on the left of this photo. Glenbow Archives/NA-4375-2.

Big business ran Calgary in the early twentieth century. Photo shows a joint meeting of the Board of Trade (later the Chamber of Commerce), and city officials in 1909, the year Honoré Jaxon visited Calgary. Glenbow Archives/NA-3496-23.

him in a story in the magazine *Canada West* in May 1909: "You can't help being an optimist, in a country like this."[21]

The year of Honoré's stay in Calgary the transport system greatly improved. On 5 July 1909, the City of Calgary inaugurated its street railway system just in time for the Alberta Fair. The corner of 8th Avenue and 1st Street West became the focal point of streetcar convergence, and subsequently the centre of retail activity. Streetcars operated under newly-erected overhead wiring from the convergence to the fair grounds at Victoria Park, and soon elsewhere in the city as well. New trackage proceeded at a rapid pace and soon additional lines were built throughout the downtown area and then expanded to residential areas to the east, west and south. [22]

In Calgary the barriers against social and economic advancement seemed low. Any male, for instance, regardless of class background, could be nominated to join a fraternal organization like the Independent Order of Odd Fellows (IOOF). Calgary's first mayor, George Murdoch, a harness and saddle maker, founded Calgary's first IOOF lodge in 1884. In 1911–1912 Calgary's current mayor, John W. Mitchell, also belonged.[23] He rose to become Grand Master of the Grand Lodge of Alberta. According to the constitution in use in 1904, candidates for admission to the IOOF "must be free white males of not less than 21 years of age, of good moral character."[24] R. B. Bennett of Lougheed and Bennett became a member of the Calgary lodge and remained so all his life.[25] Calgary's leading florist, Alfred Terrill, occupied a high office in the order, Past Noble Grand.[26] Prominent business figures like T. J. S. Skinner who later bought the Yale Hotel,[27] and Dave Black, diamond merchant and manufacturing jeweller,[28] belonged to the Odd Fellows. Those of more modest means did as well; for instance, the elected officers of Lodge I in 1902 included: a cemetery caretaker, a school janitor, a CPR clerk, an employee of Massey-Harris, one labourer and two teamsters.[29] So popular did the IOOF become that in 1910 they decided to build a permanent temple at the corner of Centre Street and 6th Avenue, very close to Widow Kerr's house (the hall was completed at the beginning of 1913).

The life of Richard Brocklebank, the contractor who built the IOOF Temple, provides a textbook example of how a working class person could rise socially and economically in early twentieth century Calgary.[30] The Ontario-born farm boy left school at fourteen, farmed for seven years until the age of twenty-three when he became a carpenter. Having obtained his papers he came west at age thirty-two to work for the CPR.[31] After his 1901 arrival in Calgary, Brocklebank obtained a job as foreman in a contracting business and then established himself as a contractor. In 1907, he rose to the office of vice-president of the Brick and Sewer Company. Elected to city council he served several terms as an alderman.

The self-made Richard Brocklebank became for some workers a man to emulate, and for others, those who believed in working class solidarity, a man to despise. As he rose in social status he cast off his working class viewpoints. In 1906 he attacked the idea of accepting money donated by steel giant Andrew Carnegie to build a Calgary Public Library. He told a labour audience that Carnegie would be better advised to spend his profits to "help support the widows and orphans of the men who were killed every year" in his steel works, "than to donate the money for free libraries." Three years later the vice-president of the Brick and Sewer Company reversed himself and bid, successfully, to build the same Carnegie Library.[32]

Defections like Brocklebank's hurt the unity of the labour movement in the city. Various internal divisions also prevented the development of a working-class consciousness. The local Trades and Labour Council was dominated by construction workers, bricklayers, stonemasons and carpenters, all anxious to advance their own trade's interests. They often quarrelled with each other.[33] Other problems included those of gender and ethnicity.

In Calgary many women worked outside the home in semi- and unskilled occupations such as stenographers, dressmakers, milliners, waitresses, cashiers and domestics. Barred from entering many occupations they found themselves concentrated, and to some extent isolated, in a far narrower range of positions. As historian David Bright has pointed out, as "men and women experienced the daily routine of work in different ways and within different environments," the workplace failed to create strong bonds between men and women wage earners.[34]

Ethnicity also limited the growth of an idea of a single working class in Calgary. While Honoré Jaxon might have been colour-blind, the general population of Calgary was not. Although the Asian population remained miniscule in numbers, the Calgary Trades and Labour Council advocated anti-Chinese discrimination. It said of the city's Chinese population: "No one deserves them for neighbours."[35] Other examples of labour racial prejudice can be cited. In 1907 carpenters refused to work on a Calgary building site with an African Canadian. The Calgary Trades and Labour Council in early 1914 passed a resolution opposing the employment of white girls in any restaurant run by either a Chinese or African Canadian proprietor.[36]

In 1909, Honoré returned to Chicago disappointed by Western Canada's lack of class-consciousness. It took several years for the seeds he helped to plant to germinate. In November 1911 a small awakening occurred among the fifty carpenters[37] working on Senator Lougheed's new theatre opposite Mrs. Kerr's. For six months construction workers toiled away until the contractors lowered carpenters' wages from 50 to 45 and then 40 cents an hour. Immediately the carpenters stopped work.[38]

Naturally, as one of the city's largest property owners and commercial figures, Senator Lougheed had a strong pro-business orientation. Fifteen years earlier he objected to a Parliamentary bill to create a federally recognized Victoria Day holiday on the ground that a day of business would be lost.[39] In Parliament he supported anti-union legislation. As he believed that outsiders caused much of the labour trouble in Canada, in 1903 he proposed an amendment to the Criminal Code "to prevent alien agitators from coming into Canada and organizing strikes."[40] According to Bob Edwards in the *Calgary Eye Opener*: "Not only is he an offensively aggressive promoter of corporation interests to the detriment of the people, but he is the only public man we know of in Canada who has openly shown himself to be the direct enemy of the laboring classes."[41]

On the outbreak of labour trouble on his own construction site, the senator, once a carpenter himself, kept silent and simply waited for the agitation to cool.[42] On account of his inaction the left-leaning *Albertan* ran a column, "Our Political Graveyard: Canadian Labor Papers Become Frolicsome in Which the Senator from Calgary Gets Some Jolts." It offered a recent assessment of the senator by the *B.C. Federationist* tarring him as a complete reactionary: "Lougheed is a benighted fossil that has been elected by nobody and represents nothing, and whose main object in life is apparently to knock labor. He's the fellow who wanted to make it a criminal offence for officials of international unions, with headquarters in the United States, to come to Canada to confer with or advise members of their Canadian locals."[43]

But the strike ended quickly. The construction boom offered workers other opportunities. Tall buildings sprouted up everywhere in Calgary in 1911: work began on a new CPR station, a luxurious CPR hotel, the Odd Fellows Temple, First Baptist Church, Knox Presbyterian Church, the Calgary Herald Building, the Burns Building, the Carnegie Public Library and a host of smaller structures.[44] Then the CPR announced more good news in early October 1911: it would build its railway car repair shops for the area between Winnipeg and Vancouver in Calgary at Ogden.[45] As Senator Lougheed reported on 3 November 1911 to good friend William Pearce, then away on a year-long European tour, "the locating of the railway shops here has given a fresh incentive to development."[46] In this boom time atmosphere the discontented carpenters simply moved to other sites. Within a few days the interior work recommenced with new carpenters prepared to accept the lower wage.[47] The workers completed the theatre for opening night, 5 February 1912. Six months later, in September, they finished the business block itself.

If the opening of the Sherman Grand Theatre become one of the most publicized stories in Bow River Valley history, that of the Lougheed Building proper went practically unnoticed. The first Calgary Stampede, a mega-event, monopolized the news media the first week of September 1912. A four part series of articles appeared in *The Calgary Herald* in late September and early October, but the first tenants had already located to the new building by the beginning of the Stampede. A close reading of the press reveals the arrival date of one of the first tenants, Matt Sheedy, harnessmaker.

Optimism dominated on Labour Day, 2 September 1912, the day of the first Calgary Stampede. In the early morning Milward Marcell set up his large camera in the Burns Building, soon to be the new headquarters of Pat Burns's business empire. From the uncompleted building's second floor the Stampede's official photographer had a full view westward down 8th (Stephen) Avenue to the one-year old Dominion Bank Building (now Teatro's Restaurant) at the corner of 1st Street East and beyond. To the east the American photographer could see the symbol of the new Calgary, its one-year old City Hall, "the most modern city hall west of Toronto."[48]

Pat Burns, the building's namesake, rose from humble beginnings in Ontario to become the owner and manager of one of North America's largest packing and provisioning businesses. Earlier that year Burns and three other Alberta cattle barons, A. E. Cross, George Lane and A. J. Maclean, all intimately involved in the open range phase of the cattle industry, bankrolled the first Calgary Stampede. The "Big Four" simply told organizer Guy Weadick: "Make it the best thing of its kind in the world."[49]

Weadick had worked hard to "sell" the idea of a stampede in Calgary against great resistance. As Calgary Stampede historians Robert and Tamara Seiler have written: "City officials argued that the day of the cowboy was a thing of the past; they claimed that, in fact, farming was more important to the area than ranching."[50] By 1912 wheat dominated the Alberta economy, and the open range was enclosed.[51] The American promoter persisted. The Stampede would keep alive memories of the early frontier in southern Alberta. Once the "Big Four" promised financial support, opposition faded. Early in the planning stages Weadick selected Milward Marcell as the official Stampede photographer.

Marcell was an interesting fellow. By 1912 he had changed his name several times. First he worked as a journalist under his real name, Milward Belmont Davis, but when he entered show business he adopted the new title of Marcus Belmont Marcell. A later alteration transformed him into "Doc" Marcus B. Marcell. On another occasion he went by "Davier de Marseilles."[52] When he left show business for rodeo photography, he adopted a combination of his earlier titles: Milward Marcell.

From his second floor vantage point in the Burns Building the American rodeo photographer awaited the cavalcade.[53] It was a beautiful sunny day. Finally the roar of the crowd below announced the sighting of the parade slowly advancing from the west. Six hundred First Nations people dressed in their finest costumes and horse gear came first. In the centre of the Stoneys, Siksika (Blackfoot), Bloods, Peigans, Tsuu T'ina (Sarcee) and Cree rode grey-haired Rev. John McDougall, the veteran Methodist missionary beside his wife Elizabeth. HBC traders with Red River carts followed along with representatives of the North West Mounted Police. Belle Lougheed and other pioneer Calgary women rode in a vintage six-horse stagecoach, Belle sitting right up on the box with the driver. Cowboys in horse wranglers and cowpunchers outfits followed. The rodeo contestants included brightly dressed Mexican *vaqueros*, each with an enormous sombrero.

An estimated forty thousand people from outside of Calgary viewed the Stampede Parade, some having travelled by train from as far away as Winnipeg.[54] Visitors included twenty-nine year old Jack Calgary Costello, "the first white boy born in Calgary," who came up from Everett, Washington.[55] In total, an estimated eighty thousand people lined the streets.[56] To mark Labour Day trade unionists marched with floats showing Alberta's industrial progress. Boys and girls—the adults of the future—concluded the grand parade of the first Calgary Stampede. That afternoon the excitement of the six-day rodeo began, organized by Guy Weadick as a nostalgic celebration of the ranchers' skills, games and way of life.

Nearly eighty years later two of Milward Marcell's postcards were blown up 1,500 times by computer to the size of ten by twenty feet billboards. Kodak printed them on superflex, or all weather plasticised canvas, with huge laser printers. Used by the Southern Alberta Pioneers in their 1990 Stampede Parade float, one of Marcell's 1912 photographs now hangs in the Stampede Casino on the Stampede grounds. The image shows tough, lean bronco-twisters, ropers and bull-doggers. Just behind the stagecoach in the giant billboard version appear the Texans on horseback, carrying the flag of the Lone Star State, followed by the Oklahomans. Marcell's photo of the crowded street scene includes the stores on the north side of 8th Avenue (now levelled to make way for Olympic Plaza) festooned with ribbon and bunting. Right in the centre of the row of shops on the north side of 8th Avenue appears the sign of "M. J. Sheedy Harness Saddles." But "buyer beware": the location of Sheedy's saddle shop merits further study. On 2 September Matt Sheedy's harness shop no longer stood where his sign appears in the photo. On 3 September the *Calgary News-Telegram* printed his new advertisement, arranged at least one day earlier: "M. J. Sheedy Has Removed to His New Store 129 Sixth Avenue West Lougheed Block and invites customers to inspect his stock of harness, saddlery, trunks, valises and all kinds of leather goods." The smell of leather already permeated Matt Sheedy's shop in the city's newest office complex, 6th Avenue side, by the first day of the Stampede Parade.

The senator's building manager welcomed Matt Sheedy and the first tenants. The retail store interiors were long and narrow in order to provide as many shops as possible with street front exposure. Ceramic tile decorated the floors.[57] Renters on the ground level on the 1st Street side, beginning at the south end, included Terrill's Florists, which proudly advertised, "Having vacated the original location of the pioneer florist… we are glad to announce to the flower buyers of Calgary that we have secured permanent quarters on the old corner."[58] Immediately beside Terrill's, on the south side of the Sherman Grand's lobby, was the Grand Shoe Store.[59] On the north side of the Grand Theatre's entrance, Abraham Kadish opened the Grand Cigar Shop with a stock of over fifty varieties of cigars, and all known brands of tobacco and cigarettes, "to meet the requirements of those who indulge in the sweets of my lady nicotine." The proprietor also stocked a variety of chocolates; "It is only right that the gentlemen should remember their wives or sweethearts when they come out for a smoke between the acts."[60]

W. Doherty Piano and Organ Company, from Clinton, Ontario (just northwest of London), opened its display room in adjacent offices one which faced 1st Street and the other 6th Avenue. This space proved a little too grandiose, which led Doherty to release its rental area on 6th Avenue, leaving the piano company entirely on the 1st Street side of the building. Phil McCrystle, a successful San Francisco tailor, established his modern tailor shop in the vacated space.[61]

On the 6th Avenue side, past McCrystle's, United Agencies rented space. The real estate company leased "a most elaborate set of offices." They had just opened up a large part of the Rosedale subdivision on the north side of the river next to Crescent Heights.[62] Next came Fred Harling, exclusive ladies' tailor. Next to Fred Harling was Matt Sheedy's leather goods store.[63] Strong aromas from the neighbouring livery stables testified to the fact that, although some Calgarians had cars, horses still dominated. Just to the east of the harnessmaker's stood Finch-Fashens, anathema to Fred Harling, as they sold ladies' made-to-order garments, not made-to-measure. Finch-Fashens was particularly proud in its advertisements that it carried a complete stock of Coilene corsets, "the only corset for comfort, style and grace." At the end of the building on 6th two entrepreneurs established a specialty French pastry shop, Parisian Delicacies. When Sarah Bernhardt, the world's most famous actress performed at the Sherman Grand Theatre in

January 1913, she visited the shop and pronounced the "gâteaux" just as tasty as those she bought in Paris.[64]

Architect Wardrop laid out the commercial space on the second, third and fourth floors of the Lougheed as a series of offices with a narrow connecting hallway. Marble installed by the Flesher Marble and Tile Company lined the hallways. They obtained their supply from Italy, Alaska and Vermont. Flesher also did the tile work in the theatre lobby and throughout the office building, using tile from their American factory at Zanesville, Ohio. Fortunately the company took excellent photos of their work. Nearly a century later these shots remain the best interior shots of the building in its early years. Today the company begun in 1910 by Nicholas Flesher of West Virginia and Ohio still exists under its original name.

All Lougheed offices had windows opening either onto the street or a light well. Two reasons explain this. Radiators provided the heat in the building, as air conditioning was not in widespread use at that time. Natural ventilation remained the system. Secondly, electric lighting was fairly new, and the efficiency of the available light bulbs low. Subsequently offices depended on daylight as an additional source of illumination.[65]

A number of those who built the Lougheed opened offices in the building. Flesher did not move into the new building, but others did. H. Kelly and Company, the heating, ventilating and plumbing contractors, located on the third floor.[66] The manufacturers of the lamp standards, elevator enclosures and ornamental stairways in the building, the Alberta Ornamental Iron Company, also chose the third floor for their Calgary office.[67] The general contractors, McNeil and Trainer, now Fyshe, McNeill, Martin, Trainer, took space on the fourth floor.[68] In October Gracey-Crane Electric Co., the building's electrical contractor, set up their show room in a ground floor store on the 1st Street West side, just between The Grand Cigar Store and Doherty Piano.[69]

Over eighty tenants occupied offices on the second, third and fourth floors.[70] On the second floor on the 1st Street side, right at the south end, architect Leo Dowler, originally from Kingston, Ontario, established his office. He had just helped to design St. Barnabas, a new Anglican church on the north side of the river, in the new Hillhurst district. Several years earlier he had married into one of the oldest families in the community, his wife being Mary Livingston, one of the fourteen children of Irish-born Sam Livingston, an original homesteader, and his English Metis wife, Jane Howse Livingston. Mary Dowler's grandfather was the fur trader Joseph Howse, a contemporary of David Thompson's, and her grandmother a Cree woman named Mary.[71]

On the second floor medical doctor Dr. Robert O'Callaghan, whose father had been a prominent surgeon in London, England, set up his office.[72] Hook Construction Company, "one of the prominent contractors and builders of the metropolis,"[73] located on the 1st Street side of the second floor. Harry Finch, a broker from Toronto, occupied space on the 6th Avenue side. He sold stock in the Peace River Land and Investment Company, which owned a hundred thousand acres of agricultural land in the Peace River district.[74] James Farquharson Macleod Pinkham, the bishop's middle son, who had been named after his uncle, the late Colonel Macleod, established his real estate headquarters also on the second floor, 6th Avenue side.[75]

The interior of Phil McCrystal's tailor shop, 1913. Glenbow Archives/NA-5434-8.

Hallway on the 4th floor of the Lougheed Building, September 1912. Photo from the Flesher Marble and Tile Company. Glenbow Archives/NA-1469-32.

Walter Jull, the provincial representative of the Toronto General Trust, an Englishman from Kent, opened his office on the third floor.[76] Also on the third floor Paddy Nolan's law firm took half of the offices on the 1st Street side. Cattanach Advertising from Winnipeg moved into a third floor office on the 6th Avenue side, directly beside the Grain Growers Company, which also had its headquarters in Winnipeg. An excellent photo of the Grain Growers Company office survives.

Canada's largest insurance company, the New York-based Metropolitan Life (now MetLife),[77] took several offices on the fourth floor. Metropolitan entered the Lougheed Building "for the long haul," the *Henderson's Calgary* directories lists them in office 416 until 1956, a tenure of over four decades. A rival firm, the much smaller Winnipeg-based Monarch Life, selected an office on the same floor, but left after ten years.[78] In late 1912 one of the firms located on the 1st Avenue side of the building, between the two insurance companies' offices, was an early driving school. But the economic bust of 1913 swept the Alberta Auto School away, and they do not appear in the city directories' Lougheed Building entries again.

Brown and Vallance, the Montreal architectural firm then erecting the Calgary Herald Building just south of the Lougheed, established their office on the fourth floor.[79] The Lougheed contained hosts of real estate people, one being the Canadian New Town Company Limited, located on the 6th Avenue side on the fourth floor. Fortunately one of their advertising posters survives; they sold businesses lots on the main streets of new railway towns in Western Canada. The poster cites that main street business lots in Red Deer had risen in value from $250 three years earlier to $5,000. In Bassano they had jumped in the same time period from $450 to $10,000.[80]

The fifth and sixth floors contained two and three room suites with separate bathrooms. The management provided continuous night and day elevator service. First-class maid service was available.[81] Each apartment contained a special touch—a stained glass transom over the main door.[82]

Two early apartment dwellers included George Rutley and Herbert Burbidge. Not wishing to live at his place of work, Rutley, the manager of the Alberta Hotel two blocks south, took up quarters in the Lougheed on the fifth floor.[83] Wishing to be close to the building site, HBC Stores Commissioner Herbert Burbidge rented an apartment on the 6th floor of the Lougheed until the new $2.5 million Hudson's Bay Store, four to five times the price tag of the Lougheed Building/Grand Theatre,[84] was completed on 18 August.[85]

In the penthouse or small structure on top of the building lived Matthew Dougherty, who had begun as the janitor of the Grand Theatre. But when it opened, he became the building manager of the Lougheed itself.[86] Later his replacement Grenville K. Jack, who started out as a Lougheed and Taylor's rental agent, lived in the penthouse for a few years in the late 1910s.[87] Probably the foremost tenant the Lougheed's building manager and rental agent dealt with was dairy farmer William T. Tregillus, the same individual who welcomed visiting radicals like Louis Riel's secretary to Calgary. In its first years of operation the newly minted millionaire rented several offices on the fourth floor in "The Lougheed Building; Calgary's Finest and Most Up-to-Date."[88]

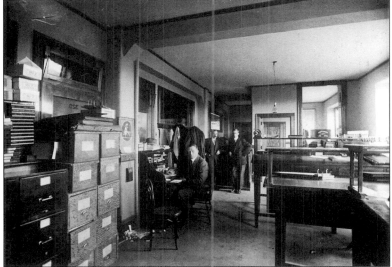

Staff of Flesher Marble and Tile Company, the company that installed the tile and marble in the Sherman Grand Theatre and the Lougheed Building. Glenbow Archives/NA-1469-52.

Grain Growers Grain Company (later United Grain Growers) office in the Lougheed Building, 3rd floor, 1913–1914. Department of Archives and Special Collections, University of Manitoba Libraries/Photo Collection 83, Box 4, Folder 7, Image 8.

The lobby of the Lougheed Building, 1912. The office building's two elevators appear in the centre of the photo. Photo from the Flesher Marble and Tile Company. Glenbow Archives/NA-1469-31.

Chapter Six

W. J. TREGILLUS

THE PRIME TENANT

URING ITS FIRST TWO YEARS OF OPERATION WILL TREGILLUS WAS THE Lougheed Building's single most important tenant. Shortly after it opened in September 1912, the farmer turned manufacturer rented offices on the fourth floor. The Lougheed Building became the corporate headquarters for Tregillus Clay Products, his brick plant built at a cost of one million dollars. Then he took another office on the same floor for Tregillus-Thompson Directory Publishers, his new city directory company. Finally, in 1913, the president of the United Farmers of Alberta (UFA) placed the offices of the brand-new Alberta Farmers' Co-operative Elevator Company, a provincial system of farmers' elevators, on the third floor.[1]

This human dynamo had prodigious energy. As UFA president, in 1914 alone, he made fifty trips to small towns throughout Alberta for the purpose of forming both new Alberta Farmers' Co-operative grain elevators and UFA locals.[2] In his visits he celebrated the farmer's way of life as "the most natural and healthful life we can live; the only one in which we may breathe the air of freedom, and enjoy health, space and sunshine."[3]

Every working day the dedicated farm leader drove his team of high-spirited hackneys to and from his offices in the Lougheed. A public-spirited man, he had many civic obligations. A strong believer in public education Will sat on the West Calgary School Board. In 1912 he ran for alderman on Calgary's City Council on a platform that enlisted the support of "every man, rich or poor, no matter what his color, creed or politics."[4] After his successful election he served on several occasions as acting mayor.[5] In addition he belonged to the Alberta Horticultural Society, as the vice-president in fact.[6] This man of manifold talents was also an early president of the Calgary Choral Society.[7]

Only a decade earlier the well-educated Englishman, with some capital behind him, arrived in Calgary with his family. After two decades as a flour dealer and broker in the English port city of Southampton he wanted a larger stage for his ambitions. Although Calgary was the same latitude as Southampton, he soon learned the harshness of its winters. But he and his family adjusted, and he rose meteor-like to fame and fortune. In Western Canada he reinvented himself as rancher, dairy farmer and finally as southern Alberta's biggest brick manufacturer west of Medicine Hat. One Calgary paper referred to him in 1912 as a "millionaire," one of the city's sixteen, up there with Senator Lougheed himself, the celebrated meat packer and rancher Pat Burns and real estate giant, T. J. S. Skinner, who had just completed a huge mansion in Mount Royal.[8] With his gift in 1912 of a huge land grant for the proposed new University of Calgary, Will instantly became one of Calgary's major philanthropists.

Born near Plymouth, England, in 1858,[9] Will Tregillus had entered his early forties when he left Britain for Western Canada in August 1902. Two of his younger brothers, Fred and Alfred, departed from their native Devon for Western Canada twenty years earlier. Both brothers joined a CPR construction gang at Medicine Hat that helped lay rails westward on the way to Calgary. No fortunes were to be made with CPR pay; labourers earned two dollars a day, and those who laid the steel made twenty-five cents more.[10] The Tregillus brothers continued on through the Rockies to the rugged grandeur of the Rogers Pass. Gold mining drew Fred northward to Barkerville in the Cariboo country, while Alfred stayed a little longer with the CPR. He witnessed Donald A. Smith drive the last spike on 7 November 1885.[11] With the completion of the railway Alfred went south to prospect in the Kootenays. A rich strike by Fred near Barkerville in the late 1890s paid for the brothers' around-the-world holiday in 1900 to China, India, Egypt and England.[12] They visited brother Edwin, a British customs official in Hong Kong, and his Chinese wife. Then they visited their brother Arthur, a missionary in India, and his family. They ended their tour in England, calling upon their father, two brothers and two sisters, all still in Britain.

The family patriarch, John Tregillus—his wife had died twenty years earlier—was a prosperous, hardworking miller with several flour mills in Devon and, for a decade or so, one in Somerset. But in 1900 the elderly manager only operated the most important, the mill at Loughtor, near Plymouth, which provided flour and cattle feed for the immediate district. Fred and Alfred arrived back in Devon in time for their dad's seventieth birthday, the occasion for a grand family reunion. [13]

John Tregillus, a heavily built man, had the look of the British bulldog—strong and self-reliant. He encouraged the greatest independence in his offspring, who had scattered across the British Empire and beyond. In 1900, four of his six sons lived overseas. Of his four daughters, the oldest lived with her husband in France. A younger daughter joined her husband as a missionary in Morocco. Only two of his daughters remained in England: Mary and Bee, the youngest, who married and became Mrs. Beatrice Chapman.[14] But now John needed help; he wanted to retire. Finally he convinced Sydney to move back from Southampton to Loughtor.[15] His youngest son's return in 1902 allowed the old miller to enjoy "a hale, hearty sundown of life in quiet retirement,"[16] before his death in 1909.

Sydney returned to take over the Loughtor operation, but not Will, who had resolved to follow Fred and Alfred to Western Canada to begin a new career as a farmer. Will decided to emigrate, and sold all his assets, departing with his family in August 1902. Some years later he commented on the word "opportunity." He described it as "a passing event," which "if we fail to grasp it," could "pass beyond our reach."[17]

Like James Lougheed, Will came to Western Canada with the advantage of both a good practical and academic education. He had attended grammar schools in Devonshire and Taunton College in neighbouring Somerset. Just after college he leased

John Tregillus and four of his six sons. Left to right: Fred Tregillus, Sydney Tregillus, John Tregillus himself, Will Tregillus, and Alfred Tregillus. Photo taken in 1900 at Loughtor Mills, near Plymouth, Devonshire, during Fred and Alfred's world tour. Photo courtesy of Margaret (Peggy) Tregillus Raymond.

a mill in Devon, but around 1890 he moved to Southampton further east on the English Channel to establish himself as a flour factor, or dealer in flour imported from North America. A decade earlier Will had married Lillian Chapman and they had a family of four: two boys, Harold and Cyril, and two girls, May and Muriel. For a time the newcomer from Devon worked in downtown Southampton in the sales department of Spillers, one of England's largest flour milling firms.[18] Later he operated his own milling and brokerage business from his home. Will enjoyed selling, and was good at it. Around 1900, Southampton and its suburbs had a population of approximately a hundred thousand, twenty or so times Calgary's population at the same time.

A memoir prepared around 1970 by Will's younger son Cyril, then in his late seventies or so, recalls the family's comfortable middle class life in the Southampton area.[19] They had a large house in the residential suburb of Freemantle, nearly two kilometres west of the city. Will had a telephone installed for business; a telephone was then an innovation for a private home.[20] The family had a series of domestic servants. Will rode regularly with the Chilworth and Stoneham harriers, a club that hunted over the land owned by Squire Fleming, a member of an old district family that owned two manors. Will enjoyed visits to Ireland to buy three or four hunters at horse fairs.[21]

Will and his wife Lillie Tregillus enjoyed an active social life in Southampton. Cyril, born in 1890, remembered: "During the winter there were dances and parties which she and Father attended in formal dress. It was all white tie in those days, and in return, they would give a party and dance. For this a hall would be rented, musicians hired, and refreshments—non-alcoholic—provided. Victorian middle class society shunned alcohol; brandy might be found in a sideboard, used strictly as a medicine." The family loved music, and regularly attended concerts and the opera when it came to Southampton.[22] All the family had their bicycles, as did Mrs. Tregillus's helper, Miss Holland, who rode "a jazzy number called a Centaur."[23]

No evidence exists of any political involvement by Will in Southampton, apart from the two years he served on the local Shirley and Freemantle Council, until the suburb merged with the city in 1895.[24] Apart from those two years of public service he apparently had no prior political experience before his election as the second president of the UFA in January 1912, after serving three years as its vice-president.

Will responded fully to the energy, vitality and optimism of his new Alberta home. Although his college education separated him from the average Western Canadian farmer, who as late as the 1930s only had a grade five to eight education, he soon became a prominent farm leader.[25] The UFA selected him in December 1910 as one of their four representatives to join the Canadian Council of Agriculture's delegation to meet Prime Minister Wilfrid Laurier. Nearly a thousand Canadian farmers from across the country marched through Ottawa to Parliament Hill to present their case for reduced tariffs and other pressing farm issues.[26] For the first time farmers across Canada had taken a firm stand for economic and social justice for rural Canada.[27]

Will's geniality and warmth made him a popular individual in Calgary. George Edworthy, a neighbour on the south bank of the Bow, remembered his family as "cultured, charming people."[28] Later the *Grain Growers' Guide,* the Western farmers'

Sydney and Kathleen Tregillus, with
their daughter Joan at Loughtor
Mills, around 1902. In the 1920s Joan
performed in a number of productions
at the Grand Theatre. Photo courtesy
of Margaret (Peggy) Tregillus Raymond.

newspaper, described Will in this way: "His genial disposition, his tolerance of the opinion of others, and his unassuming modesty won him friends in large numbers."[29] Yet, among his children his word was law in no uncertain terms. They called him "the governor."[30]

Cyril Tregillus well remembered the small community of about five thousand that the family reached in the fall of 1902: "Calgary was a typical cow town then. The sidewalks were wood with hitching posts in front with rails joining them."[31] Most people came from Eastern Canada, Britain or the United States, although the city adjacent had a small Chinese population, engaged chiefly in laundries and domestic service; "most of them wore queues, long braids of hair hanging behind." Groups of First Nations people lived just out of town, chiefly on the west side. Jack Butlin, the son of Joe Butlin, one of the original Mounties on the march west in 1874, and his Metis wife, Angélique Rosselle, later broke horses for the Tregilluses once they established their ranch.[32]

In Calgary Will first leased a quarter section of land just west of the city and south of the Bow River, very close to the Edworthy farm along the river. He then expanded his general farm operation, buying from the CPR three adjacent quarter sections of unbroken prairie next to the quarter section he rented. The tract occupied the districts now known as Wildwood, Westgate and Rosscarrock. Later he extended his holdings by buying immediately to the west two more quarter sections from the Hudson's Bay Company.[33] For several years he also leased twenty-five hundred acres of land immediately opposite on the north bank of the Bow River, in what became known as Bowness.[34] Son Cyril later recalled: "It was a choice property with several hundred acres of river bottom including an island, and hillside rising with two flood plains providing pasture and meadow." Will finally bought another three hundred acres adjoining the leased land. He now owned outright over a thousand acres.[35]

On the eastern portion of their farm the Tregilluses built a spacious two-story brick house, with a stable and barns. They named their new home on the vast treeless flatland above Spruce Cliff "Roscarrock," after the Cornish place of origin of distant Tregillus ancestors.[36] Will had his own library there.[37] The outgoing family welcomed visitors from the surrounding ranching country and from Calgary. The huge living room doubled as a ballroom for festive occasions. The family loved to give parties.

The *Calgary News-Telegram* reported a Tregillus party on 7 January 1914: "The house throughout was aglow with Christmas decorations, wreaths of holly and mistletoe." William and daughter Muriel, then a student at the University of Calgary, received in "the flower decked drawing room… supper was served in the dining room at prettily decorated tables." Perhaps Will had picked up the floral decorations from Terrills, Calgary's leading florist, whose uptown store was on the main floor of the Lougheed Building. To the party the Tregilluses invited their houseguests as well as the "faculty and students of Calgary university." That weekend their houseguests included two of Will's nieces, Phyllis Chapman, daughter of his sister Bee; and Joan Tregillus, his brother Sydney's daughter.[38] The Chapmans with brother Sydney and his family had recently arrived from England. Bee's husband, A. S. "Jack" Chapman, helped briefly at Tregillus Clay Products until he began work as Calgary's city engineer in the spring of that year.[39]

The Tregillus family at Roscarrock, about 1908. Left to right: Will Tregillus, daughter Muriel, son Cyril, wife Lillian, daughter May, and cousin Howard Chapman from Victoria. Miss Holland, lady's companion, is shown reclining on the hammock. Photo courtesy of Robert Tregillus.

"Roscarrock," the home of Will Tregillus and family. Photo taken around 1913, Will Tregillus on the left and his brother Sydney on the right. Glenbow Archives/NA-4377-1.

Sydney, in Canada now for half-a-year, worked as Will's chief assistant at Tregillus Clay Products' Lougheed Building headquarters.

At Roscarrock Miss Susannah Holland, a woman in her early thirties, assisted Lillie Tregillus and her two daughters with domestic chores. She had accompanied the Tregilluses from England, and for years afterwards she stayed with the family. Miss Holland had an exotic background. The Tregillus family believed that her maternal grandfather was a prince of the ruling family of Montenegro, who killed his father and then fled to England where he married and remained for the rest of his days. They also brought with them from Southampton an outside man named Hooper, a former jockey, who took care of the horses and the garden before striking out on his own shortly after their arrival in Calgary. Additional members of their party included two wirehaired fox terriers, a male called Pinkie (an abbreviation for ping pong, then the rage in England), and Patsy, a pregnant female. In Alberta they paid their keep by protecting Roscarrock's vegetable garden from raids by gophers and rabbits.[40]

A balanced, self-confident man with capital behind him, Will did extraordinarily well in Alberta. He loved the entrepreneurial atmosphere. At first the experienced horse trader bought and sold horses from British Columbia; a tremendous demand existed for them before the full mechanization of Western Canadian agriculture. A number of young Englishmen who came out to Alberta to become farmers and ranchers obtained basic training at his ranch. At any time there might be half-a-dozen trainees at Roscarrock as well as the experienced hands.[41] Next Will became interested in the dairy business, and founded the first pasteurized bottled milk business in the city. For several years he also supplied milk and cream to the CPR trains. He next transformed his operation into a centre for the breeding of thoroughbred Holstein cattle to supply dairy herds throughout Alberta.[42] During the great Calgary real estate boom the value of his property soared.

In 1911 the family left on a Grand Tour of Europe. While abroad Will wrote a series of articles of general interest for *The Albertan* in Calgary. His letters reveal the depth of his cultural and intellectual interests. He loved Rome, "with its paintings, sculpture, mosaics, columns and ruins of historic importance." A lover of opera, he described the performance of "Don Pasquale" in Rome's Opera House as "one of the richest musical treats of our lives." Of Florence he commented, "[it] must be a paradise for artists and scholars… I would have lengthened our stay if it had been possible." In Venice he sought out Titian's masterpiece, "The Ascension." In his opinion, the world-renowned garden of Villa Carlotta, south of the Italian Alps, exceeded the beauty of "the best gardens in England, Ireland and Wales." Once in Northern Europe his enthusiasm declined somewhat, but he commented on the beauty of the Rhine Valley near Cologne. In Denmark his practical side reasserted itself over the romantic. He wrote about the skilled Danish farmers, "unquestionably masters in the art of dairying."[43]

The Tregilluses arrived in London in time to view King George V's coronation procession on 22 June. Fellow Calgarians Dr. Blow and his wife and T. J. S. Skinner and his family stayed at the same hotel, the Metropole.[44] Mr. Skinner had come to England as the Calgary Board of Trade's official representative at the coronation.[45] As a representative of the Canadian Senate, James Lougheed also attended the coronation at Westminster Abbey. He and Belle were presented to Their Royal Majesties at the splendid reception for the representatives of the overseas dominions at Buckingham Palace.[46]

While not a guest at the coronation or invited to Buckingham Palace, Will thoroughly enjoyed his return visit to England. On the sea voyage back to Canada he met James Cameron, agricultural editor of the *Glasgow Herald*, who left this word picture of the new Calgarian returning home from his Grand Tour: "… on board he was one of the most charming of companions—optimistic, humorous, broad in outlook, happy in reminiscences, and for ever seeking the good of others."[47]

Just after his return Will made the biggest gamble of his career: the construction of a modern one million dollar brick plant to employ 250 workers on completion, 500 after six months of operation, and eventually 1000.[48] Always the optimist, he had his eyes on the rainbow. The rapidly growing city of Calgary and surrounding district badly needed building materials. Will knew he could meet the demand, not just of bricks, but also of high quality tiles and sewer pipes. On its northern edge, across the river from today's junction of Sarcee Trail and the TransCanada Highway, his property contained high-grade clay deposits. As most of Calgary's quarries had been exhausted by this time, bricks had replaced sandstone.

Enthusiastically the *Calgary News-Telegram* described early in 1913 the Tregillus operation, which produced the finished product "for just about one-half the cost of imported brick of the same quantity." The plant, located at the foot of the cliff on the south side of the CPR track, included a laboratory and test-kiln. Nearly ten million bricks were used in the construction of the kilns.[49] Immediately to the east, the existing Crandell brick plant at Brickburn stood dwarfed by the huge new operation. Ingeniously, Tregillus Clay Products used the gravity of the cliff behind the plant to their advantage. As the *News-Telegram* explained: "The shale banks are located on a higher level than the works and the raw material is loaded into cars which run down the incline to the mill, and at the same time by their added weight draw empty cars up the grade."[50]

Will only used family money to build his brick plant, although several other individuals expressed a desire to invest in it.[51] Free of obligations to others the newly minted millionaire need cater to no one. He openly endorsed the radical taxation and social theories of American economist Henry George, who argued that rent should be paid to the state rather than to private landowners. Will also supported George's campaign for widespread public education. As the UFA president stated in one of his forceful addresses: "We are beginning to see that Henry George was right when he said 'Under all forms of government the ultimate power lies with the masses.' It is not kings, nor aristocracies, nor landlords nor capitalists that really enslave the people. It is their own ignorance."[52] He told the Annual UFA convention the previous year: "Knowledge is power, gives light, independence, and freedom; while lack of knowledge—ignorance—is weakness, darkness, dependence, and bondage."[53]

At what is now Strathcona Park, just south of Coach Hill, beyond the city's western boundary, Will donated a large tract of prime undeveloped land for a university. *The Preliminary Announcement of the University of Calgary*, published in July 1912, described the future campus in these terms: "The site donated for the University, consisting of one hundred and sixty acres four and a half miles west of the Calgary Post Office, is truly a magnificent one, and it may be doubted whether any other college in Canada has its equal. At an eminence of 550 ft. above the central portion of the city, or an altitude of about 4,000 ft.—on a level with the crater of Mount Vesuvius—the view in every direction is one not easily surpassed. To the west the snowcapped peaks of the Rockies are in plain sight. To the east the eye has a splendid range of vision over the city and the valley of the Bow River, while in all directions is a commanding view of the country round about."[54]

An extremely generous man Tregillus left the university free to sell the land and locate the campus elsewhere in Calgary if they wished. He once told his minister, Rev. J. C. Sycamore of First Baptist Church, why he made the gift. As Rev. Sycamore later recalled, "[Tregillus] said that his land had advanced in price since he bought it. The coming of so many people to Calgary had helped toward this. Therefore, he said, it was the duty of others, to do something for these people."[55]

In addition to providing prime real estate, worth an estimated $150,000 in late 1912, Will Tregillus did more.[56] He promised a cash donation of $50,000.[57] Then, he went further, he gave something even more precious than land or money—his time. The already overextended farm leader and Calgary manufacturer became the first secretary of what the organizers hoped would become "the outstanding private University of Western Canada."[58] From Tregillus Clay Products headquarters in the Lougheed Building he worked to put both the new university as well as his brick plant on their feet.

Will had considerable business acumen, but he had one serious shortcoming. Unlike older Calgary residents, he had not lived in the city during the economically-depressed 1890s. He only knew the golden years of the early twentieth century leading up to the crescendo of 1911–1912. On account of this blind spot he vastly overestimated the value of his Roscarrock farm, needed as security to obtain investment money for his brick plant. With great enthusiasm he wrote Thomas Crerar, the Manitoba farm leader, on 1 November 1912. He used "University of Calgary" stationery: "I have my home farm consisting of 430 odd acres, we subdivided some 40 acres of this & am selling it at from $250 to $300 per lot say $2500 to $3000 per acre so those remaining 430 odd acres are worth & can be sold in a block at $2000, at a short notice say at least $862,000." His home and outbuildings, he believed, were worth another $15,000. Will added that soon the value of his land "will be over one million in the spring as the University building will be commenced then & the site is to the West of this property, so that it stands between the University & the city."[59]

Many influential Calgarians believed the largest city between Winnipeg and Vancouver deserved its own university. In the words of *The Albertan*: "Calgary cannot become a great city without a university. There is no other city in Canada or, as far as we know, in the United States, of the size of Calgary without a university."[60] After

Tregillus Clay Products, looking
north toward Bowness,1913–1914.
Glenbow Archives/PA-3590-1.

The faculty and student body of
Calgary's first university standing on the
steps of the Carnegie (now the Memorial
Park) Library, 4 October 1912, the first
day of classes. The young Eric Harvie,
the future founder of Calgary's Glenbow
Museum appears at the back, at the
left side of the library door, immediately
to his right in the back row is Ernest
Pinkham, later killed in Flanders in the
War. Glenbow Archives/NA-713-1.

Edmonton was named the provincial capital in 1905 Calgary expected to receive the provincial university. In neighbouring Saskatchewan had not Saskatoon obtained the provincial university after Regina became the capital? But political patronage intervened. When the provincial cabinet chose a site in 1907, it selected land on the south bank of the Saskatchewan in Strathcona (which only five years later was incorporated into Edmonton), Liberal Premier Alexander Rutherford's own riding.

Although Will Tregillus described himself as having been a Liberal in England,[61] he joined Dr. Thomas Blow, one of the city's most prominent Conservatives, to fight for a Calgary university. Dr. Blow, the leader of the Calgary University Committee, had an interesting background. He came from a poor family, but never relinquished his boyhood dream to one day obtain a good education. After working for years as a carriage-maker in the small village of South Mountain, fifty kilometres south of Ottawa, he decided, at age twenty-eight, to become a medical doctor. He proved an outstanding student, one who completed all the grades of high school in one year.

After graduating in medicine at McGill, Dr. Blow undertook post-graduate work in Edinburgh. He, his wife and their four children came to Calgary in 1903. To the amusement of many, on account of his name, Dr. Blow practiced as a nose specialist (ear, eyes and throat as well). As did Senator Lougheed, T. J. S. Skinner and Will Tregillus, the medical specialist had an excellent idea of land values, and quickly made a fortune in real estate.[62] In 1912 the doctor built an impressive mansion with ornate Italianate and Queen Anne features in Mount Royal. Some years later the Blow family became allied to the Lougheeds when the doctor's daughter Marion Irene married Douglas Lougheed, the senator's youngest son.[63]

The promoters of a privately financed university in Calgary had several shared motives. They first believed that a university would improve business. It would drive up land values, increase trade and generally help the town to grow. Secondly, they saw the obvious need of scientific and technical experts to exploit fully the province's natural resources, its forests, minerals and agriculture. Finally, a university would allow Calgarians to attend university in their home city. Proudly, the *Preliminary Announcement of the University of Calgary*, published in July 1912, stated: "Nothing could be more necessary to our highest welfare, to the maintenance of our relations with the Empire, and to our contribution to Anglo-Saxon civilization, than that the opportunities for higher education in every considerable centre of population, should be such that the nation will be assured of a continual supply of qualified and educated leaders."[64] The pillars of Calgary's establishment lined up behind Dr. Blow: Senator Lougheed attended the committee's organizational meeting, and R. B. Bennett joined chairman Blow, secretary Tregillus and four other prominent Calgarians as members of the first Board of Governors.[65]

Will's ascent into the higher altitudes of Calgary's ruling elite had no effect on his political views. Despite his new friendships in the University of Calgary committee he kept his previous political beliefs intact. In a fiery 1914 public address at the Calgary Library, for instance, he directly attacked Canada's three great trusts: the banks, railways and manufacturers. "Although I say three trusts, they function for all intents and purposes as one, so far as skinning the people are concerned. By means of interlocking directorates and centralized ownership, they are enabled to filch from the great mass of the people practically everything they possess over and above the food and clothing they need to maintain a painful and miserable existence."[66] In contrast, Will Tregillus's landlord, Senator James Lougheed, in a public address the previous year had ranked the Bank of Montreal as the greatest institution in the history of the Dominion, followed closely by the Canadian Pacific Railway.[67] The senator and the agrarian radical could agree on the need for a university in Calgary, but little else. With such different perspectives, the two men stood at opposite ends of the Calgary elite's political spectrum.

Perhaps more than any other date, 5 May 1913 marked the high-water mark of Will Tregillus' prominence in Calgary. The Hudson's Bay Company building, the Canada Life Building and the new CPR hotel, all three under construction, used his face brick.[68] That day the *Calgary News-Telegram*'s front page carried a drawing of him riding one of his beloved hackneys in front of the Tregillus Clay Products plant. The paper praised his contributions to the city, including his role as "the organizer and head of Tregillus Clay Products Company, one of the city's greatest industries." His old routine existence in England seemed so remote now. Just six weeks earlier he wrote his brother Sydney, who after their father's death had decided to join him in Calgary: "I am looking forward to your coming & trust you will enjoy the move as much as I do. Honestly I don't know how I should feel now to have to go back to the old life."[69]

Will Tregillus's fortunes looked rosy on 5 May 1913. He had two excellent assistants. Although only twenty-three his son Cyril had become his right hand man for his farming operations. And now Sydney joined Tregillus Clay Products as the new manager. On that very same day the *News-Telegram*'s "People You Know" column contained the announcement: "Mr. and Mrs. Sydney O. Tregillus and two daughters, from England, have arrived in the city, where they will in future reside." Almost ninety years later Peggy Tregillus remembered her uncle, a "great big man with a moustache," arriving with his prancing hackneys to greet them at the CPR Station.[70]

Will, Cyril and Sydney Tregillus, and the central office staff, worked at headquarters in the Lougheed, fourth floor, 6th Avenue side.[71] The building boom, it is true, had subsided by early 1913, but as Will told city council's railway and new industries committee in mid-March: "There never was a better time for a man or the city to buy land for investment than at the present time. There were bargains that would never be seen again, for the money tightness was only a passing phase...."[72] As he had written brother Sydney six weeks earlier, "If the money market loosens up, the building will break all records, Calgary is destined to become a great city & we shall always have a big demand as far as we need it."[73]

With Sydney now helping with Tregillus Clay Products, Will could finally devote himself full time to his political reform and volunteer work. He told Sydney, "I don't want to be doing any thing more in the way of business as there is more than enough in public matters if one could take it up."[74] The University of Calgary, only half a year old, remained very close to his heart.

On 5 May 1913, the very day that he appeared on the front page of the *News-Telegram*, the university held its closing exercises in the auditorium of First Baptist Church, an imposing Gothic structure. Only three years earlier the old First Baptist church stood immediately south of what was now the Lougheed Building/Grand Theatre. But the flood of newcomers led local Baptists to build the new, much larger church about ten blocks away at 13th Avenue and 4th Street S.W.

Will spoke that afternoon to the hundreds of people, strong supporters of a degree granting university in their city. Hope still existed. In 1911 the province provided a charter for the university, but then refused to allow Calgary to grant anything more than diplomas and certificates. In early 1912, the very week that the Grand Theatre opened, the legislature came very close to granting the University of Calgary degree-granting status. But the final vote was seventeen votes to fifteen against.[75]

Strong opposition to Calgary granting degrees came from Henry Marshall Tory, the founding president of the existing University of Alberta. A brilliant student at McGill, he later joined the university's faculty and proved himself a skilled university administrator. Before accepting his Alberta post, Tory helped establish what later became the University of British Columbia. One central principle guided all of Tory's actions: Alberta needed only one university. No proliferation of colleges could be allowed. Tory loathed Will Tregillus, the Calgary university's secretary with whom he clashed over the university question at a UFA annual meeting.[76]

In early 1912 Tory lobbied furiously among the members of the legislature to defeat the proposed bill, one that would allow Calgary University to grant degrees. The province, he told politicians and all Albertans, could support only one university capable of first-rate research and teaching. The bill failed, not because of Tory, but rather on account of Calgary's limited rural support. Many rural legislators believed that primary schools, not university education, needed the new province's attention.

Despite the defeats of 1911 and 1912, Calgarians fought on to secure their own university. The newly appointed dean, Edward Braithwaite, who had both his M.A. and Ph.D. from Harvard, began work in the spring of 1912.[77] He hired the initial three-member faculty, all Protestant and Ontario-born like himself. Classes began on 4 October 1912. The faculty included Frank MacDougall, professor of chemistry and acting professor of mathematics, with his M.A. from Queen's University in Kingston and Ph.D. from the University of Leipzig in Germany.[78] Charles Ward, professor of French, had his M.A. from Toronto and Ph.D. from the University of Chicago.[79] Thanks to a gift of $35,000 from T. J. S. Skinner, the university established a chair in history, the appointment being Mack Eastman, a Toronto graduate then finishing his Ph.D. thesis at Columbia University in New York City.[80] With the help of W. Kent Power, a Calgary lawyer with his law degree from Dalhousie University in Halifax,[81] the university established a law department with lectures prepared by local members of the Law Society of Alberta.[82] In order to attract schoolteachers and office workers, many of the arts and law lectures were given in the late afternoon or early evenings.[83]

One month after classes began in the Carnegie Public Library, now the Memorial Park Library, Dean Braithwaite remained optimistic. He told a British visitor

The drawing of Will Tregillus that
appeared in the Calgary News-Telegram,
5 May 1913. Glenbow Library

CALGARIANS IN CARICATURE

WILLIAM JOHN TREGILLUS

that the future Calgary University one day might well make Oxford and Cambridge sit up and take notice. "It may take fifty years, but it will be done."[84] The Toronto architect H. B. Dunnington-Grubb of Toronto, in consultation with Thomas Mawson, the well-known English landscape architect, drew up the plans for the campus.[85] Everything still seemed possible to the promoters of the university. In an expansive mood Dr. Blow proposed that the university acquire a large part of the Sarcee (Tsuu T'ina) Reserve for future expansion.[86] But the Alberta legislature still refused to confer degree-granting powers, and turned down another request to do so in early March.[87]

Still the perpetual optimist, Will Tregillus strongly believed the institution would survive and prosper. That fall the Board of Governors planned a fourth attempt to obtain degree-granting powers and receive full university status. At First Baptist on 5 May 1913, the *News-Telegram* reported that Will had said, "It was their object to develop this institution, and with the enthusiastic support of the people of Calgary he was confident that in the future the University of Calgary would stand in the front row of universities in the world."[88]

In his address Will Tregillus praised the arts faculty: Dean Braithwaite, professors MacDougall, Ward and Eastman; and the sessional lecturer, Fred Albright. He knew that the professors "frequently worked 18 hours a day during this first difficult year."[89] Will knew Ward and Eastman the best. Both visited Roscarrock in mid-January 1914. The university's secretary welcomed faculty, students and all friends of the university to form a French club. In addition to the student office-holders selected, the meeting named Dr. Ward as honorary president, Dr. Eastman as vice-president and Will's brother, Sydney Tregillus, as secretary.[90] The faculty liked Will. Walter Sage, who came in the fall of 1913 to teach English, described "Mr. Tregillus, the Secretary of our Board of Governors, & the organizer of the United Farmers of Alberta" in this fashion: "Mr. Tregillus is also an alderman, a millionaire and in spite of these defects a really fine fellow."[91]

As a strong opponent of Canadian involvement in any forthcoming European or imperial war, Will liked one of Mack Eastman's speeches so much that he sent a copy to the *Grain Growers' Guide* in Winnipeg.[92] It published the address in their 25 May 1914 issue. In the text the Calgary history professor criticized the militarists in Europe and North America who called for more arms build-up. One of Eastman's most telling lines reads, "one discharge of a big gun costs as much as a four years' university course."[93]

In reality the university lasted just two more years. The collapse of the real estate boom in 1913 hurt it enormously. Dean Braithwaite resigned in August 1913 and obtained a new job shortly afterwards as the president of the University of Western Ontario.[94] Frank MacDougall succeeded him, but faced enormous challenges. The fact that the University of Alberta continued its hostile stance, refusing to move any faculties southward, or to allow any duplication of its operation in Calgary, continued to hurt. The province refused to grant degree-granting powers. The outbreak of World War One in early August 1914 doomed any remaining hopes the University of Calgary might have had of survival.

The first faculty members of the University of Calgary, September 1912. Left to right: Mack Eastman, Edward Braithwaite, Charles Ward, and Frank MacDougall. Glenbow Archives/NA-801-1.

The economic crash brought Will down with it. He had overreached. The depression of 1913 reduced the value of his farmland to a fraction of its former value. With the end of a demand for bricks, his plant could not sell its product. By late 1913, son Cyril later recalled; "Father was busy with many affairs. He had a suite of offices in Calgary and spent most his time there … he was a worried man, and was having a difficult time keeping his ship afloat."[95]

On 13 February 1914 the *News-Telegram* reported that Alderman Tregillus could not pay a bill of $4,550,[96] small change compared to the $165,311 payment that the Bank of Quebec requested the following year.[97] Tregillus-Thompson published only the directory for 1913 before its office closed in the Lougheed. Pressed to wall, Will resigned from the University of Calgary Board of Governors in late July 1914.[98] His empire quickly shrank in the months to follow. On 11 August 1914, Will outlined his financial plight to Thomas Crerar: "Things have gone roughly with me & I am up against it, the war has made it very hard indeed. We were getting some good paying orders & laying out for the busiest time we have had, when all orders except a few insignificant ones have been withdrawn or delayed."[99] The *Tregillus-Thompson Directory* for Calgary listed Tregillus Clay Products in 1913 as occupying several offices on the fourth floor of the Lougheed Building, 6th Avenue side. In 1915, the *Henderson's Calgary Directory* lists just one.

A three-person commission appointed by the provincial government to inquire into the question of degree-granting universities in Alberta sealed the University of Calgary's fate. In its report tabled in the provincial legislature on 25 February 1915, it pronounced the university bankrupt, which indeed it was. Henry Marshall Tory might have been wrong in the flush of the great economic boom of 1909 to 1912, but he was right in 1915: Alberta could only support one university.[100] The last word on the university question went to Bob Edwards, in 1912 a strong supporter of the initiative.[101] In the *Calgary Eye Opener* of 23 October 1915, he wrote: "The Calgary University, so-called, is busted. It is no more. The city had finally to come to its rescue and pay the last salaries of the professors, to enable them to get out of town."

Will Tregillus was dead by the time the University of Calgary closed in the late spring of 1915. He died as a result of a freak accident on a visit to Winnipeg in early November. As the *Grain Growers' Guide* reported in early November, his chair slipped on the edge of the platform at a meeting of the Grain Growers Grain Company, and he suffered an injury as a result of the fall. Apparently "he paid little attention to it at the time, and later in the evening delivered one of the best speeches of his life."[102] On the journey back to Calgary, however, complications set in.

Shortly after his return to Roscarrock on 12 November, Will Tregillus died from typhoid fever.[103] Immediately the City of Calgary dropped its flag at City Hall to half-mast.[104] Letters of condolence arrived at Roscarrock from across Western Canada. Out of respect for the deceased, City Hall closed the afternoon of his funeral, held at First Baptist Church. Many citizens attended. Seldom, the *Calgary News-Telegram* commented, "are so many floral tributes seen at a funeral as were in evidence in the church. There were banks of wreaths." Six City of Calgary mounted policemen escorted his body to Union Cemetery after the service.[105]

Obviously much of what he sought to accomplish came to naught, pulled down by the economic collapse. The brick plant failed, but not all of the evidence of its fine product disappeared The passer-by on 12th Avenue S.W. can still see today, for example, the handsome Tregillus brick on Calgary's recently restored Lorraine Apartments in the 600 block, directly opposite where William Roper Hull's old sandstone mansion once stood.[106] Other evidence of his contribution to his adopted city remains. While his beloved University of Calgary disappeared, the idea survived. It rose again after World War Two, when a second University of Calgary was born in 1966. Finally, part of what Will began in the Lougheed Building lived on sixty-five years after his death. In 1917 the Alberta Farmers Co-operative Elevator Company, for which he worked, amalgamated with the Grain Growers Company of Manitoba to form the United Grain Growers Limited. The UGG maintained its Alberta or western headquarters on the entire third floor and parts of the fourth floor of the Lougheed building to 1979. On the wall of their Calgary office boardroom, Will Tregillus's portrait looked down upon the assembled UGG area managers until the late 1970s.[107]

Chapter Seven

FRED ALBRIGHT
FROM CALGARY TO PASSCHENDAELE

S O FAR NO REMINISCENCE, NO FAMILY STORY, NO NEWSPAPER INTERVIEW, has come to light that gives an insight into Senator Lougheed's thoughts in September 1912—the month of the first Stampede, the visit of the Duke and Duchess of Connaught and the opening of the Lougheed Building. In addition, James's impressions of the Lougheed Building and Grand Theatre remain unknown. Alas, none of the tenants, from harness maker Matt Sheedy to florist A. M. Terrill to UFA President Will Tregillus, left letters with references to the Lougheed Building. Yet, fortunately, hundreds of letters on Calgary survive, written by Fred Albright, a contemporary of theirs, an individual with a connection to both the Lougheed and the Grand Theatre.

Fred Albright admitted to the Alberta Bar just two weeks after the Stampede parade, had worked in a Calgary law office since 1909.[1] Now free of his bar exams he attended the rodeo events of Calgary's first Stampede. On September 18 he sent back this report back to his girlfriend, Evelyn Kelly, in Ontario's Niagara Peninsula: "I thoroughly enjoyed the whole thing although one or two of the contests are more or less brutal. But it was a wonderfully realistic indication of the life of the early days. You couldn't help but admire the wonderful daring and steady nerve of the cowboys and cowgirls and you are seized with an intense admiration for the qualities that have made pioneering possible. The Stampede was interesting too as marking the passing of the old and the swift incoming of the new regime in the prairie west."[2]

While Fred Albright did not have an office in the Lougheed Building he visited it, and frequently went to the Grand Theatre. In late October 1912 the new University of Calgary hired him to teach an economics course.[3] Will Tregillus, the university's secretary, had his offices in the Lougheed, on the fourth floor on the 6th Avenue side, three floors above Matt Sheedy's shop. From the letterhead Fred Albright used on 1 June 1913, we know that he frequented the "University Club of Calgary," as "University Club of Calgary" is printed at the top of the covering page.[4] This support group for the university had a suite on the sixth floor of the Lougheed.[5]

John "Jack" Brownlee and Fred Albright, best friends at Victoria College at the University of Toronto, visited Calgary together in the summer of 1908 to look for possible positions in law.[6] Both men, then in their mid-twenties, came from small towns in Ontario, and had briefly taught school. At university they did well academically in their political science honours program, with perhaps the edge going to Fred, who had a stronger finish in his final year.[7] Both men participated fully in extra-curricular activities at Victoria, a Methodist college.

In terms of physical height, at nearly 6' 4", Jack towered over Fred, almost a foot shorter at 5' 6",[8] but the smaller man had more friends. At university Fred's friends called him "Sox," short-form for "Socrates," the ancient Greek philosopher—high praise for a country boy from Beamsville.[9] In their senior year the cool, business-like Jack served as the college magazine's business manager under Fred, whom the student body elected as the magazine's president. The students chose Jack as "Critic" in the Union Literary Society, but Fred won the more prestigious office of "Leader of the Government." Jack, a future premier of Alberta, learned a great deal from Fred. As Franklin Foster, Brownlee's biographer, has noted: "Through Fred Albright, Brownlee discovered a most fulfilling role: the trusted confident and counselor of a strong and admirable leader respected for his ability, integrity and high sense of purpose."[10] At this stage in the lives of the two men Albright, rather than Brownlee, seemed the one destined for distinction.

During their two final years at Victoria the two college students roomed to-gether at the same Toronto boarding house. Upon graduation they decided to travel across Canada. Over half-a-century later John Brownlee recalled that summer in an interview in Calgary just several months before his death: "We took a line of samples, each of us representing a different organization and selling a different commodity, and travelled west, starting at Cobalt, then at the very beginning of the Great Cobalt boom, and then working our way across Canada as far as Vancouver, our object being to look over western Canada." Both men still intended to enter law. In the end it proved a toss-up between Vancouver and Calgary. They both chose Calgary, "for one particular reason, mainly that in Vancouver there were too many young Englishmen, financed from home, in the legal profession and the opportunity for young men without money to start up in law was not as good there as in Calgary."[11]

After their Vancouver visit Fred returned to Calgary and began work in one of the major law firms in the city, Walsh, McCarthy and Carson. He and Clinton Ford, an-other Victoria College graduate, also then an articling student, lived in the same room-ing house.[12] For three years Fred articled under Maitland McCarthy, nephew of Dalton McCarthy, the famous federal Conservative politician.[13] Maitland, himself a seasoned Conservative Party politician, served two terms as Calgary's Member of Parliament in the Ottawa. At times their association must have had its trying moments, as Fred was an abstainer, and Calgary's MP a notorious drinker. But, despite any personal differences they might have had on the prohibition question, Maitland prepared him well for his law examinations. In his final exams, taken in the summer of 1912, Fred stood second amongst all the candidates across Alberta.[14] William Walsh, the firm's senior partner, later to be named the fourth Lieutenant-Governor of Alberta, praised Albright as the best law student Walsh, McCarthy and Carson had ever trained.[15]

A year after Fred began articling in a law office in Calgary, Jack arrived in the city. The fact that Florence Edy, a tall attractive young woman he knew in Toronto, had

Fred Albright. Fred and Evelyn
Albright Fonds, University of
Western Ontario Archives.

Partners and staff of Walsh, McCarthy,
Carson and Macleod, Calgary, around
1912. William Walsh, the firm's senior
partner appears in the centre of the
photo, seated in the second row. Fred
Albright is shown seated on the far
left in the front row. Leo H. Miller
Collection, photo no. 68-G-2. The
Legal Archives Society of Alberta.

moved with her sister and her widowed mother to Calgary confirmed his decision to come to Alberta. At first, Fred, Jack and Clinton Ford all roomed together, their rooming house strategically located only two blocks from where the Edys rented a home.[16] Almost immediately Jack obtained an articling job with Lougheed and Bennett, Allison, and McLaws, the most powerful firm in the city, with a clientele reading like the Who's Who of the Western Canadian business world. At Lougheed and Bennett, he articled under R. B. Bennett himself, who took an interest in the intense articling student. But Jack, who wanted to practice in commercial law, later decided to change his articles to Muir, Jephson and Adams, which he did. James Muir and Jermy Jephson were two of the province's most senior and respected lawyers.[17] After intense preparation Jack passed his final exams in the late fall of 1912, gaining entrance to the Alberta Bar.

John Brownlee, as the newly minted lawyer preferred to be known, worked as a lawyer with Muir, Jephson and Adams. They entrusted him with work for the UFA and the legal aspects of the creation of a province wide farmer-owned elevator company. In late 1913, John was appointed the solicitor of the newly organized Alberta Farmers Co-operative Elevator Company, headed by UFA President Will Tregillus. Four years later Brownlee helped bring about the amalgamation of the co-operative with the Grain Growers Grain Company, a farmer-owned elevator company from Manitoba, one of the first tenants in the Lougheed. The two elevator companies formed the United Grain Growers Limited (UGG) with headquarters in Winnipeg and a Western Divisional office for Alberta and British Columbia in Calgary.[18] With amalgamation on 1 September 1917, the new company occupied nearly two whole floors in the building with a show room on the ground floor for implements and farm machinery sold by the company's big-co-operative department.[19] The UGG occupied the third and much of the fourth floors in the Lougheed Building until 1979, more than sixty years.

Fred remained good friends with John and Florence. All three shared a similar spirit of idealism and optimism for the future. They and their circle in Calgary sought out and recommended to each other morally educating and inspiring books.[20] Fred and John both taught Sunday School. As good Methodists they believed in the Social Gospel—the need to apply Christian teachings to an urban, industrialized society.

Two years after the Brownlees, Fred married. The collection of over 550 letters between him and his fiancée, later wife, Evelyn Kelly, is a rich source for Calgary history in the early and mid-1910s.[21] Fred and Evelyn spoke of their feelings for each other, told of their activities, fears and uncertainties. In the words of Lorna Brooke, the transcriber of the letters: "The collection has the added advantage of being a two-way dialogue between a well-educated, articulate couple at a time of immense change."[22] They discussed religion, literature and relationships between men and women. They expressed their opinions on varied topics from popular entertainers, to racial concerns, to political events and personalities of the day.

The correspondence between the twenty-seven-year-old articling student in Calgary and his twenty-year-old girlfriend, a student at Victoria College at the University of Toronto, consists of only one or two letters a month between 1910 and the summer of 1913. He first met her when she was a young school girl, years before she left to attend

Evelyn Kelly, on her graduation from
Victoria College, University of Toronto,
in 1912. Fred and Evelyn Albright Fonds,
University of Western Ontario Archives.

Victoria College.[23] Shortly before her graduation, she and Fred came in touch again. They began a correspondence, which led to a growing romance. After their engagement in the summer of 1913 the exchange speeded up dramatically. They wrote daily, sometimes twice daily, until their June 1914 marriage in Ontario. While the newspapers of the time allow for a good exterior view of life in Calgary immediately before the First World War, the Albright/Kelly letters provide an intimate look at the interior.

As a Victoria College graduate of 1912, just beginning a teaching career, Evelyn had pronounced ideas about women's rights. She was perfectly frank in her letters to her male friend; "What makes me mad, just hot, fighting mad, is for a man or boy to claim that because he is a man he should vote, because I am a woman, I should not." Then to underline the point she continued in her letter of 27 April 1913: "That he has any more interest in government than I have I resent and deny, what is implied in that contention, that is the superiority of the man over the woman." Fred replied on 4 May that he supported her viewpoint entirely.

If Fred wanted to win her hand he had to exercise great caution, as Evelyn believed marriage meant quite different things for a woman than for a man. As she wrote on 22 June 1913: "It would be very good for you to get married, because you're a man. But how would you like to be a woman, and to think of having to get breakfast every morning? That's the thing that keeps me from even thinking about it." In an age when married women simply were known by the title "Mrs." added to their husband's name, Evelyn protested. Shortly before their marriage she wrote Fred on 6 April 1914: "One thing I don't like about getting married, is that I'll have to take your name, and I like my own better. I don't want to be a "Mrs." either but I suppose I 'gotta' do both." Nor, she added, would that be the only infringement on her freedom: "Sometimes I wonder if I really want to be married to live in a place I certainly should not choose for myself, to make another person's friends my friends. It seems so, so lamblike a course that it makes me mad." Even after she agreed to marry she kept a spirited independent mind. Evelyn totally dismissed the Pauline doctrine that "Wives be submissive unto your husbands." As she later wrote Fred after their marriage: "Such rot, and St. Paul was never married. Such a doctrine tends to make a man tyrannical and selfish."[24]

In his letters Fred spoke at length about his adopted city. Even though the pace of construction greatly declined in 1913, work continued on several large structures, including the new ten-story Herald Building beside the Lougheed, and the new CPR luxury hotel, later named the Palliser, by the CPR station. The new Hudson's Bay Company store opened at the end of the summer.[25] On 16 September 1913, Fred reported on its opening: "Many people have said and I believe it that there is no finer store in Canada." After lunch in its new restaurant he went up on the observation tower on the roof: "Speaking of the view—you surely don't labor under the misapprehension that Calgary is flat. The older part of the city is on the flat in a bow of the river but the city crowds out and upward on all sides on to the surrounding hills and river banks." To those that suggested Edmonton had more to offer, he replied on 10 April 1914: "Calgary as a city is much ahead of Edmonton. It is more compact, more business-like, cleaner, better paved and less raw and crude generally."

Although she studied English literature at university, Evelyn, the daughter of a Methodist minister, had never attended a play or an opera. The culturally liberated Fred wanted to introduce her to both in Calgary. On 17 March 1914 he wrote: "I hope you'll wait and see your first play in a theatre, and hear your first opera with me." Calgary offered many cultural possibilities: "Calgary may not be a centre of culture but we're certainly better off than the average small Ontario city."[26]

On the evening of 11 March 1914, Fred attended "The Only Way," the dramatization of *A Tale of Two Cities*. Dickens's novel of the French Revolution tells the story of English lawyer Sydney Carton, who goes to the guillotine in the place of a French aristocrat. He sacrifices his life, until then one marked by debauchery, to save that of his rival for the hand of Lucie Manette. Unfortunately the demure beauty loved the correct and successful aristocrat, not him. Of all the plays that he saw at the Sherman Grand, Fred liked this one best. It starred the celebrated English actor-manager, John Martin-Harvey, and his English company. "The Only Way" had established Martin-Harvey's reputation. During his stage career he performed the play with his company over two thousand times.[27]

Fred wrote Evelyn after the long evening performance, which ended at 11:15: "We have just returned and while I know it is easy to speak in superlatives, I can only say that I never enjoyed any play more than this—not even 'The Passing of the Third Floor Back' which the great Forbes-Robertson opened the Sherman theatre more than two years ago." Every seat was taken. "Oh it was wonderful—and then the final tableau on the Guillotine platform when Carton says, 'It is a far, far better thing that I do than I have done. It is a far, far better rest that I go to than I have known!'" Women in the audience wept openly at several dramatic moments.

At the Grand Fred saw Margaret Anglin, a Canadian actress of international renown. She appeared in an outstanding performance of Shakespeare's "As You Like It." Fred loved the evening. How appropriate that she chose that Shakespearean play, as a famous quote from "As You Like It" appeared on the drop curtain immediately below the proscenium arch: "All the World's a Stage and All the Men and Women Merely Players" (Act 2, Scene 7, lines 139 to 143).[28] Equally at home in Greek tragedy, Shakespeare or the comedies of Oscar Wilde, Margaret Anglin toured with her company throughout North America. She had red-golden hair, long, slender hands and a magnificent cello-voice that filled the performing hall.[29] The *Montreal Star* theatre critic, Samuel Morgan-Powell, once wrote of her in "As You Like It": "Her Rosalind was the very spirit of Romance walking in the Arden forest paths, pure woman, and pure fascination all through."[30] Fred emphasized to Evelyn the dramatic power of the Canadian actress, and tossed a bouquet to his fiancée as well: "I enjoyed the whole play very much. The cast was very well balanced and of course Margaret Anglin needs no words of praise. You were actually present to me in the flesh last night in the person of Margaret Anglin as Rosalind. She was just an adorable woman with a woman's sweet caprice, delightful variability and dazzling contradiction and yet withal an intensity and constancy of devotion that always wins a true man's homage."[31]

Perhaps as interesting as the names of the actors and actresses he mentions are those he omits. To a number of Protestants, particularly Presbyterians, Baptists and Methodists, the theatre retained a lingering air of scandal about it. William Aberhart, for example, a Calgary school principal who preached regularly at Trinity Methodist Church in Inglewood—often sharing the assignment with fellow lay preacher John Brownlee—denounced the theatre as "worldly."[32] A famous actress who performed at the Grand in early 1913, the legendary Sarah Bernhardt, certainly had that reputation. The famous French actress, then in her late sixties, had lived an "evil" life with scores of lovers.

But feelings about the theatre were changing. When the Presbyterians awaited the completion of their new church, having vacated their old one, they met for several months in the Grand Theatre.[33] The congregation of First Baptist Church also held their services at the Grand in 1912 while their new church was under construction.[34] Similarly, after a disastrous fire four years later reduced the neighbouring Central Methodist Church to a smouldering shell, the Methodists rented the Grand Theatre for Sunday services for over a year until the church was rebuilt.[35] But Fred took no chances. In his letters to Evelyn in mid-January 1913 the Calgary lawyer made no mention of the performances of "The Divine Sarah." His avoidance of a single reference to her is extraordinary, as the French actress virtually conquered Alberta during her short visit. The *Edmonton Bulletin* described her in this fashion: "Rather small of stature, by her flowing garments and statuesque poses, she gave the impression of height. Her hair is tawny, falling over forehead and eyes. Her eyes are large, tragic, filled with fires of all emotions. Her little fingers, vibrating, full of life, scatter lightnings. The whole Bernhardt is a thing beyond comprehension, a wonder woman, a goddess."[36]

Fred loved theatre, and certainly knew of Sarah Bernhardt's visit as the Calgary papers gave it such prominence, but the Calgary lawyer's mention of a performance by the French actress might antagonize Evelyn. Any reference to the French actress's views on the possibility of male and female political equality would infuriate his bride-to-be. The great actress always performed in French, but gave interviews through an interpreter. When asked in Calgary of her opinion of women running for political office, Bernhardt told the inquiring *Calgary Herald* reporter: "Men are the natural leaders and lawmakers, and it is the height of folly for women to aspire to such positions."[37]

In his correspondence Fred played it totally safe. He mentioned neither Bernhardt nor the appearance at the Grand in mid-December 1912 of Lillie Langtry, once one of the most glamorous women of her time.[38] The conquests of the "Jersey Lily" included, many years earlier, the Prince of Wales, later King Edward VII. In his letters to Evelyn, Fred made no reference to a third female star, Olga Nethersole, the well-known English actress who performed at the Grand in mid-February 1914. *The Albertan* called her the "Bernhardt of the English speaking stage."[39] In New York she made her reputation for her role in "Sapho," one of the first "sex dramas"—plays which presented "truthful pictures of contemporary life,"[40] While the "sex drama" had since gained widespread acceptance, Nethersole's initial appearances in "Sapho" had led to several court appearances in the United States as a public nuisance.[41] Fred made no references to Bernhardt, Langtry or Nethersole.

Both Evelyn and Fred ardently supported social reform. In distant Ontario Evelyn had somehow learned that Calgary faced a serious prostitution problem. "What are you doing to bring Christ's Kingdom in?" she asked Fred in her letter of 25 May 1913. Wisely, Fred replied immediately. Yes, a red-light district had existed, outside the city limits. In his letter of 1 June 1913, he mentioned that he and two friends made a fact-finding visit to the area the previous summer. "You speak of the great social curse of today. Evelyn it's simply appalling. You can have no idea of the extent or terrible degradation of this thing… I'm not very emotional but I could scarcely keep the tears from my eyes at the sight. I never saw such pitiable human beings in all my life. To think of girls, somebody's daughters, born with all the high and noble impulses that are the part of every woman—sold and degraded and killed, body and soul to satisfy the cravings of bestial lust!" The Mounted Police, he added, had since raided the district; but this had only spread the houses of prostitution throughout the entire city: "The trouble is now that men who are known to live impure lives are received in fine houses and their sins are overlooked. I don't think lasting reform can come until people ostracize men as much as they do women for impurity."

The earnest Calgary lawyer took a leading role in the campaign to make the Province of Alberta dry. In a note to Evelyn on 4 February 1914, he confessed his concern that progress was slow, "because there are so many foreign born who have to be educated away from the use of liquor." The following summer Fred attended a large meeting that featured an American anti-temperance speaker. During the American's lecture the Calgary lawyer jumped up onto his seat in the centre of the house. He then pummelled the guest with a series of sharp, probing questions, revealing the weakness of his arguments. On account of this intervention Fred Albright overnight became known to thousands of Calgarians. The following year he helped to frame the Alberta Temperance Act.[42]

Evelyn herself felt so strongly about alcohol's pernicious effects she felt obliged to tell Fred about her ancestry in case they had children. She wanted Fred to know her immediate family was "clear." She wrote on 14 May 1914: "On my father's side, on the Kelly side, the line is clear of alcohol. I don't know about my grandmother's father. Grandpa's uncles, some of them drank, but I don't think his father did. My grandmother's sister, oh, that is a sad story, but my grandmother of course was clear. And on my mother's side it is the same, so far as I know."

Fred's demanding job with his law firm gave him precious little time for social reform work. As he wrote Evelyn on 14 March 1913: "It's a case of working hard all day and a good part of the night if one would make a success of law…" From the fall of 1912 to the spring of 1913 he also taught his university economics course and the Methodist Sunday School class. He also led a Bible Study class.[43] The following fall and winter he stopped teaching his university economics class to make more time for plays and musical events.

The Calgary Symphony, formed in late 1913, played in the Sherman Grand the entire 1913–1914 season. Proudly Fred wrote Evelyn on 6 November 1913: "An orchestra of fifty pieces giving a program of 6 concerts during the winter betokens some desire on the part of Calgarians other than a passion for making more money." On 11

Two exterior shots of the Lougheed Building in 1914, showing the signs for Cronn's Rathskeller and the Sherman Grand. The City of Calgary Archives/3-Mc-8 file.

November he returned to the same theme: "That the 'cow town' of Canada is the only one of all her cities to support a purely professional symphony orchestra is worth proclaiming from the housetops."

On the evening of Monday, 9 March 1914, Fred attended the Calgary Symphony's fifth concert. All winter they had provided the city and southern Alberta with a "feast of good things,"[44] works from the great composers of orchestral music. That evening the program included Mendelssohn's "Scotch Symphony" and Wagner's "Traume" from his opera, "Tristan and Isolde." Fred judged "Traume" "one of the sweetest and most melodious numbers the orchestra has given all winter."

After the performance those in his party invited Fred to Cronn's Restaurant in the basement of the Lougheed Building. On 9 March 1914, he described for Evelyn Cronn's new tango tearoom fitted out in cabaret style: "There is an orchestra and several girls who sing and in the afternoons—and sometimes at night—there are exhibitions of tango dancing." For the conservative Fred who had never stepped in the nightclub before, with all the majestic rhythms of the symphony's performance still in his mind, the evening proved quite an adventure. He continued: "The tables are arranged around the outside of the room and there is a green wooden lattice work around the walls, while the ceilings are pretty festooned with some green stuff too. The whole give a very pretty effect." Overall he had fun: "The singing was good, but mostly popular songs, and after the classic renditions of the symphony, both songs and orchestra ragtime jarred a good deal. But in spite of that we had some nice refreshments and as our company was congenial I enjoyed myself."

The sensuous tango had first been introduced to Calgary by two young American dancers, Fred and his sister Adele Astaire. They danced it in a vaudeville act at the Grand in early October 1912.[45] A little over a year later "the wild dance of the Argentine,"[46] now sweeping North America, hit Calgary with full force. Instruction was provided at Cronn's up-to-date Tango tearoom. In late January *The Albertan* reported: "Almost any afternoon now, Calgarians may be seen practicing the dance at a popular tea-room on First street west, and there is said to be no dearth of men available even at the busy hour of five o'clock."[47] At a "dansant" organized by Belle Lougheed for her daughter Dorothy at Lougheed House on 1 January 1914, rumour ran that the tango had been danced. Afterwards no one seemed to want to affirm or deny it.[48] After all, a number of clergy in Calgary had censured the dance as indecent.[49] The University of Calgary's administration informally forbade the students to dance it at their big college dance on February 2nd. After the party President Jim Nicoll of the University of Calgary Athletic Association made the following statement to take the heat off the student body: "The students' executive decided not to have the 'tango' or 'ragging' at the 'prom' and there was nothing of this kind at any time during the evening, as all who were present know."[50]

Fred made known to Evelyn his negative impression of modern dances like the tango, which he regarded as indecent. On 6 February 1914, he explained to his fiancée why he never learned to dance. "I've never been able to rid myself of an aversion to dancing as it is generally done, because it seemed to me immodest, and to tend to arouse the sexual passions."

Evelyn enjoyed political topics, so did Fred. A note of 1 February 1914 on Canadian nationalism reveals the high tone of much of their correspondence. "One thing is certain," Fred wrote, "Canada has advanced beyond the colonial state of development and no status is tolerable that does not recognize her absolute local autonomy and her equality with other portions of the Empire—the British Isles included."

Fred's letters reveal his certitude about the superiority of English Canadians over Americans. To Evelyn he openly expressed a strong dislike for a certain type of American. When Art Smith, a colleague in his law firm, had a criminal trial that brought ten American witnesses to Calgary from Missouri, including a district attorney, a sheriff and a town constable, Fred commented on the visitors. In a letter to Evelyn on 29 November 1913, he wrote: "The whole bunch looked like a lot of ignorant bloated Yankees of the typical Yankee type. One couldn't help comparing these minions of the American law with our judges, court officials and the Northwest Mounted Police." When an American preacher spoke at Central Methodist Church Fred confessed to Evelyn, on 1 March 1914, "the American style of preacher grates upon me." Fred believed all newcomers to Canada must assimilate into Anglo-Canadian society, including Americans.

Like most of his contemporaries Fred was a prisoner of the racial and class attitudes of the day. His opinions come out most clearly in his comments about the great Shakespearian Robert B. Mantell's production of "King Lear" in early February 1914. He had taken a balcony seat. On February 4th he mentioned to Evelyn, "last night I noticed in one seat, two Greeks, 2 Canadian girls of very good family, a mulatto, and a couple Italians. Many other races were represented within a very small radius." The Calgary lawyer did not approve of this "indiscriminate assembly of extremely diverse classes." He went on to add: "This is one disadvantage in taking seats anywhere but in the best part of the house. I wouldn't want to take any lady unless I could afford the better seats for this reason."

Non-Whites fared poorly in his assessment. His attitude toward the Chinese, largely confined to the laundry and restaurant business, seemed contradictory. He mentioned in a letter to Evelyn on 7 September 1913 of helping once a week with the Methodist mission to the Chinese in the city. It worked to teach the Asians English and to introduce them to Christianity. Yet, in another note he rejoiced that he had found the Empress cafeteria did not employ Chinese labour: "The dishes are clean the food well cooked and reasonable in price—and there is only white help in the kitchen."[51] As for the First Nations he hardly recognized them at all. Certainly he overlooked the fact that Treaty Seven recognized Indian reserves as First Nation property. With several friends he went trespassing on the neighbouring Sarcee (Tsuu T'ina) Reserve hoping to stake an oil claim on their land. He and his friends also took their guns with them to do some game hunting. As he frankly admitted to Evelyn on 18 October 1913, "Now we were violating the law in 2 particulars—We had no license and shooting on the Indian Reserve is forbidden. I hope you don't think we were terribly wicked."

Throughout his correspondence with Evelyn, John Brownlee's name appears regularly. 1913 proved a tough year for many in Western Canada as the crisis in the

Balkans ended British investment in Calgary and other cities. Apart from the major construction projects already underway, Calgary's boom came to a halt. Thousands lost their jobs. The economic downturn of 1913 and early 1914 made things difficult for many, but the Brownlees faced other challenges as well. Jack's wife Florence suffered a miscarriage brought on by appendix operation in September 1913. Then just four months later Jack had an emergency tonsil operation with complications. On account of excessive bleeding he almost died. The doctor's fees for both operations took a huge slice of his income.[52] As Fred summarized on 1 March 1914: "They've had pretty hard luck financially this past year. Jack was only getting $1,500 a year and they built their house and had so much sickness besides. Their doctor and hospital bills alone were almost $600." Yet, on the positive side, they had a happy marriage. Fred then made a very revealing comment about his best friend at college: "Jack has thawed out a good deal since marriage and Mrs. B. improves greatly upon acquaintance. She's a good home maker and has cultured and literary tastes."

John's firm link with the Alberta Farmers' Co-operative Elevator Company, which joined with the Grain Growers Grain Company to form the United Grain Growers (UGG) in 1917, allowed him to shore up his finances. Shortly after the UGG invited John to become their general solicitor at a salary of $6,000 per year, a raise to $7,500 per year soon followed. Upon his UGG appointment he left Muir, Jephson and Adams. He now had his office in suite 320 in the Lougheed.[53]

John Brownlee's fortunes rose as a corporate lawyer: he joined a golf club, Calgary St. Andrews, west of the downtown and north of the Bow. He became a member of its board of directors.[54] Fred had clubs, and perhaps the two friends occasionally played a round or two together.[55] The St. Andrews Golf Club, Calgary's second, was formed in the spring of 1912, named after the Royal and Ancient, the most famous course in the entire world at St. Andrews, Scotland. [56] By the Parkdale streetcar it took only twenty minutes to ride there from the Lougheed Building and 1st Street West.[57] A photo taken on 4 September 1914, the day that St. Andrews hosted the amateur golf championship of Alberta, shows men in golfing jackets and ties and women in straw hats, billowing blouses and skirts. Several Brits, led by Tait White, a Scot who worked as an irrigation engineer with the CPR, and who had played the Old Course in Scotland, belonged to the organizing group. Tait White had suggested the name chosen for the club. Within weeks of its establishment St. Andrews had 200 male and 50 female members. By early 1914 it had 326 members. The club had some strange rules, such as Rule Three: "A ball played into a gopher hole may be lifted and dropped behind without penalty."[58]

Members of the club in its first three seasons included Rev. Andrew MacWilliams, the Registrar of the University of Calgary;[59] Will's nephew, Art Tregillus;[60] and "Eye Opener Bob" Edwards.[61] Alfred Terrill, the florist who had his major shop in the Lougheed building, was a shareholder.[62] Two of Senator Lougheed's sons belonged. In the spring of 1914 member Clarence Lougheed, the oldest of the four sons of James and Belle, proposed his younger brother Edgar, then a student at the University of Calgary, as a junior member. During the Alberta championship that September Belle Lougheed motored up to the links overlooking the city in what is now the suburb of St. Andrews Heights.[63] The course commanded magnificent views with the city lying at its feet on the east and the Rockies towering along the western skyline.

The economic depression forced many of the original tenants from the Lougheed, but Alfred Terrill's store and harnessmaker Matt Sheedy's shop (until 1920 horses outnumbered people in Alberta)[64] weathered the storm. Alfred Terrill astutely established a successful flowers-by-wire service; his ad in the first programme of the Calgary Symphony Orchestra states: "We are members of the Florist's Telegraph Delivery and can deliver flowers for you any place in Canada or the United States a few hours after we receive your order."[65]

Wealthy Metropolitan Life Insurance, with more business in force in Canada than any other company, remained unaffected by the economic downturn. They operated their Calgary office on the fourth floor of the Lougheed for over four decades.[66] Others were not so fortunate. The Doherty Piano and Organ Company located on the ground floor was out by 1915.[67] Into half the vacated space came tailor Phil McCrystle from San Francisco, where he operated two tailoring shops; he too had a short life in the building—just two years.[68] The specialty French bakery, Parisian Delicacies, vanished. The real estate firm of Jim Pinkham, the Anglican Bishop's middle son, went bust despite his excellent family connections. Jim's fortune, all in land, lost its value in the bust, forcing him to return to banking, first in Victoria, and later in Vancouver.[69] In December 1914, just below Jim Pinkham's old real estate office on the 6th Avenue side, James Cleave opened up his insurance, investment and real estate business. The recently arrived Cornish immigrant was in for the long run, he remained there for over half-a-century.[70]

At the time of this economic disaster two individuals made big gains: Stewart Herron and Archibald Dingman. In 1914 they took office space for their Calgary Petroleum Products Company, formed two years earlier, in a suite very close to Metropolitan Life's offices on the fourth floor, 6th Avenue side. The original backers of their consortium included James Lougheed, R. B. Bennett, T. J. S. Skinner and rancher A. E. Cross. The group acquired a majority interest in thousands of acres of surface and mineral rights in the Turner Valley to the southwest of Calgary. In late 1913 Fred Albright became one of the many small shareholders in the company, which began drilling that January. The Calgary lawyer bought twelve shares in the "Dingman Company." As he informed Evelyn in his letter of October 22nd: "This is no wildcat company but one that owns about 2,000 acres of surface rights and 11,000 acres of oil rights, besides having done actual development work."

On May 14th head driller Dingman struck oil at the well he named after himself in the Turner Valley approximately seventy kilometres southwest of Calgary. Locally called "Dingman No. 1," the Calgary Petroleum Products No. 1 Well immediately went into production. The strike attracted attention across the country. On May 30th *The Canadian Courier* noted the Turner Valley strike "is making more stir in Calgary now than the discovery of gold in the Yukon made in Edmonton in 1897." As oil and gas historians David Finch and Gordon Jaremko write in *Fields of Fire: An Illustrated History of Canadian Petroleum,* a short, intense period of speculation followed: "Every nook and

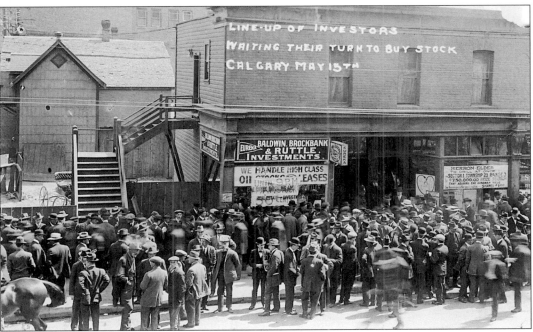

cranny in downtown Calgary became an office for some oil company. Likely as not, the company had no land, drilling rig or even a board of directors."[71]

At least three companies leased space in the Lougheed, two on the same fourth floor as the Calgary Petroleum Products Company. In their ad in the *Calgary Herald* on 25 May 1914, the Clark-Mitchell Oil Wells Ltd. (with their general offices in rooms 433–435) predicted: "It is most likely that the Calgary oil fields will be the greatest in the world. Orders for stock by mail, wire or phone may be made to the general offices of the company." On June 18th, in the *Calgary Herald*, the Pioneer Oil Company Ltd., office 413 Lougheed Building, assured its potential shareholders: "Among the one hundred and ten oil companies hurriedly organized during the past week there is one that is conspicuously SOUND, and thoroughly equipped." Clark-Mitchell remained listed in the city directory in 1915 only to vanish in 1916. Pioneer lived as long as a firefly; it never even made the directory. Moose Mountain Oil Company, whose board of directors consisted largely of Calgary and Banff doctors who tested the Moose Mountain structure west of Bragg Creek, opened offices on the third floor in 1914 (334) and on the fourth in 1917 (417).[72]

When Fred and Evelyn married on 12 June 1914, the Turner Valley oil frenzy continued. Momentarily the sun shone again on Calgary. Yet, as war in Europe appeared likely, interest in Turner Valley plummeted. On 4 August 1914, the Great War began. On their second wedding anniversary, 12 June 1916, Fred recalled in a short, separate diary account the now very distant atmosphere of their wedding day: "The second anniversary of our wedding day! What a change from 2 years ago. Then Calgary with her sporadic oil boom seemed the centre of the universe. Today the very mention of oil causes a smile or a shrug. Then the world was sleeping on the edge of the volcano. Today the volcano is thundering and roaring destruction and desolation to nearly all the civilized world."

After their marriage, letters between each other became limited to periods of absence, as in 1915 when Evelyn returned to Ontario to see her family. From the letters written in 1915 it is clear that Fred's genius for making friends continued. A new acquaintance was Leonard Brockington, a tall red-haired Welshman, just a year younger than Fred who had just moved to Calgary to work as a clerk at the land titles office. He had graduated *magna cum laude* in Latin and Greek from the University College of South Wales, where he edited the college magazine and served as president of the drama club. After several years as an English and Classics master at an English grammar school, "Brock" arrived in Alberta in 1912. He first lived in Edmonton, where he worked briefly as a journalist and then in an administrative job at the Edmonton city hall before obtaining his new job in Calgary. His father, a Cardiff headmaster, had taught him poetry and enunciation from an early age, and he could quote readily from Shakespeare, Milton and Donne, as well as from the Bible. His mother was a native Welsh speaker. "Brock's" magnificent voice, his wide breadth of knowledge in many areas and his fund of stories made him ideal company.[73] As Fred told Evelyn in a letter: "I like and respect him."[74] Fred's good friend, George Coutts, became a life-long friend of "Brock's."[75]

No letters from 1916 survive, but a large correspondence exists from the moment of Fred's enlistment in the Canadian Army and transfer, first to Eastern Canada,

Fred and Evelyn Kelly Albright on their wedding day, 19 June 1914. Fred and Evelyn Albright Fonds, University of Western Ontario Archives.

and then to England and France. During Fred's absence Evelyn began articling at Fred's law firm in preparation to becoming one of the first female lawyers in the province. She also became a much closer friend of Florence Brownlee, who continued to suffer from poor health. Despite her physical weakness Florence now had two baby sons to look after: John, born in December 1915, and Alan, born in September 1917.[76]

As one of the leaders of the congregation of Central Methodist Church, Fred served as the chair of the special finance committee to raise money to rebuild after the fire of February 1916.[77] Strongly conscious of the sacrifices of those who had enlisted for overseas service, he himself wanted to enlist. In late 1915 he joined the local militia, as he explained on October 22nd to Evelyn, then absent with her family in Ontario: "I have never told you that I have felt for some years that I was a coward once. I think I should have entered the ministry, I believe now it was my duty but there seemed so many plausible and valid reasons why I should not. Well I didn't but I have had to confess to myself since that the reason was that I was selfish and didn't want to make the sacrifice, and I made up my mind that if ever God gave me a second chance to make good—and I felt it would come some day though in what way I could not guess—I would answer 'Ready, aye, ready'." Once the church re-building campaign was underway, he took the next step and enlisted in June 1916 as a private for active service.[78]

After over half a year as a recruiting sergeant Fred left with his unit for England. He bore all physical hardships without complaint. Wishing to serve at the earliest opportunity in France he reverted to the rank of private in the 50th Battalion. In a letter to his Calgary friend George Coutts, he mentioned on August 20th that "I may be leaving for France any day. I'm available for draft now having shot my musketry, thrown live bombs, gone through gas etc. etc." He thanked George and his wife for their kindnesses to Evelyn. In addition he asked George to mention him to a special friend, David, the Coutts's young son: "Remember me to David and give him an extra good night hug and kiss for me."[79] Fred left England for the front in Flanders in September 1917. In his letter of 20 October 1917 he spoke of the terrific bombardment the previous evening. In a postscript he added that he carried a Belgian coin given by a friend of theirs "for luck."

Evelyn continued her work in Fred's law office five and half days a week, with Saturday afternoon and Sunday free. She wrote regularly. Saturday, November 10th, she told Fred about her visit that day to Lougheed Building, where the Board of Trade had established its office and new restaurant.[80] "To-day we had lunch at the Board of Trade. You must join when you come home; they get excellent meals there for 50 cents, and the members may take their wives on Wednesdays and Saturdays." The next day, Sunday, she wrote of the church service at Central Methodist, to which she had taken young David Coutts that morning.[81] She ended her note: "You seem far away tonight dearest. I wonder why. You are ever uppermost in my thoughts." Fred never received her last letters. His life had already ended when she wrote them.

On Monday, November 12th Evelyn received a terse telegram from Ottawa.[82] Her life changed forever. It read: "Deeply regret to inform you 895173 Pte Frederick Stanley Albright Infantry Officially Reported Killed In Action between Oct 23 and 26 1917, Director of Records."

Just after he wrote his last letter to Evelyn, Fred moved with the 50th Battalion into a front line position in the Ypres area, and to a village called Passchendaele. This would be Fred's first battle. Victor Wheeler, a signaller in the 50th Battalion who survived the engagement, later recalled the Canadian Expeditionary Force's struggle for a couple of square miles of Passchendaele mud and deep shell holes filled with water: "Unmitigated hell reigned."[83] No trenches existed as the whole area was simply a mass of mud. Later Evelyn heard from the lieutenant in charge of his platoon. They had held "a badly exposed position without trenches to call by that name, under heavy fire. There were only three or four in the platoon who came out alive."[84]

Jack Brownlee learned the news that same day as the *Calgary Herald* reported Fred Albright's death in their evening paper. Two days later the *Herald* included an editorial on the well-respected Calgary lawyer: "A rising barrister, who gave promise of going far in his chosen calling, popular with a legion of friends and esteemed by the members of his profession, an energetic and zealous church worker, a loving and devoted husband, above all a good Canadian citizen, his death leaves a void that will truly be felt in this community."[85] Jack had lost his best male friend. In an interview over forty years later Brownlee made a special reference to Fred Albright, "unfortunately killed overseas in the first war."[86] In the interview the former premier of Alberta mentioned no one else by name as a friend from his university and early Calgary days.

The news of Fred's death profoundly saddened his good friend, Clinton Ford, now the City of Calgary solicitor. Both farm boys from southern Ontario knew each other at Victoria College. Like Fred, Clinton had considered the ministry but eventually selected law. In Calgary both men participated fully in Central Methodist Church. Before they married the two men with several other lawyers lived in the same rooming house in Calgary.[87] Fred thought "Clint," "a fine fellow and excellent company."[88] Evelyn liked him immensely as well. As she wrote Fred, then in the Canadian Army and training in England, how she appreciated his treating her as an equal: "I like Mr. Ford in many ways. He doesn't seem to stoop down to be on a par with a woman's intelligence."[89]

So touched he was by Fred's death, Clinton wrote a memoir about him, "A True Soldier of Jesus Christ—A Tribute," for the national Methodist newspaper in Toronto, the *Christian Guardian*. He began: "Among the many heroes of the great war there is one whose memory will always be an inspiration. The life of F. S. Albright must always be distinguished by the nobility of its sacrifice. He regarded it as wrong that others should be permitted to do the fighting for him, and therefore he had to go. What he did proved he was truly great, and because he was great and true to his convictions the course he followed was 'the only way'."[90]

In 1919, after two more years of legal study in Calgary, Evelyn gained entry into the Alberta Bar, becoming the second female lawyer in the province, but she did not practice. The young war widow decided instead to return to Ontario, where she obtained a position teaching English at the University of Western Ontario in London. She was the first female instructor in the department. In 1926, thanks to several summers work at the University of Chicago, Evelyn obtained her M.A. in English. She never remarried, retiring in 1951. She died in London in 1979 at the age of eighty-nine. Upon her death Frances Gage, Professor Albright's literary executor, donated her and Fred's letters to the University of Western Ontario Archives.[91]

Jeff Lydiatt, mid-1920s. Photo
courtesy of Jeff Lydiatt, Jr.

Chapter Eight

JEFF LYDIATT
THE GRAND IN THE GREAT WAR

JEFF LYDIATT, THE GRAND'S NEW THEATRE MANAGER, WELCOMED FORBES-Robertson on his North American farewell tour in early February 1915. The previous summer Senator Lougheed, provoked at last by several poor management decisions, sacked Bill Sherman.[1] With the flamboyant impresario's departure the Sherman Grand lost the first half of its two-barrelled name. It simply became "the Grand." Unlike his colourful predecessor Jeff Lydiatt did not wear black and white checked suits, smoke large cigars or wear a diamond on his ring finger. The new manager was slim and nearly six feet tall,[2] not corpulent and wide. Unlike Bill Sherman, he looked like a gentleman and acted like one.[3]

Bill Sherman was a flamboyant promoter. In the elegant auditorium he installed local merchants' advertising on the asbestos fire curtain. The press complained. Veteran journalist Andrew King later recalled how the fiery theatre manager responded. One evening during the first intermission he barged forward and marched onstage to defend his curtain. Wearing a rented full dress suit, a poor fit on his ungainly body, he began: "Ladies and gentlemen. Youse have no doubt seen in the papers somthin' about this here curtain." Then pointing toward it, asked: "I ask youse what is the matter with that there curtain?" The contrast between Bill's low-brow English and the actors' perfect speech put the audience into convulsions as he slipped backstage.[4]

In the *Calgary Eye Opener* of 23 March 1912, Bob Edwards had a field day with the incident. Tongue in cheek he praised Sherman's "plea of surpassing eloquence on behalf of his ad curtain." He judged that its quality "has only been equalled by one public speaker since the world began, and that is Mark Antony. Perhaps Mark's address to the Roman mob with regard to the assassination of J. Caesar was a little more brilliant and scholarly, but not so pathetic and rugged as Bill's." Keep up the advertising on the curtain, Bob recommended, for such "a noble and thrilling" address "deserves our thanks rather than our censure."

Such press comment embarrassed the senator, but as a theatre owner he tolerated Sherman for good reason—he turned a profit. In just two and half months the advertising on the fire curtain brought in over $5,100, which helped enormously.[5] Everything connected with the theatre seemed to cost so much. In winter the coal bill ran to $500 a month,[6] electricity roughly $2000 a year.[7] On top of these regular expenses, advances for the top road shows similarly cost huge sums.[8]

Bill had a good financial sense. Quickly he solved the booking problem by signing an agreement to co-operate with theatre magnates C. P. Walker of Winnipeg, and John Cort of Seattle.[9] All three now joined together for the scheduling of road shows across the Canadian Prairies and the Pacific Northwest. Road attractions played the Grand from Monday to Wednesday, and from Thursday to Saturday the theatres welcomed the big-name Orpheum Circuit.[10] Vaudeville, or British Music Hall, a marvellous pot pourri of individual acts with mixed numbers of singing, dancing and gymnastic exhibits, brought in large crowds during the 1910s and 1920s. A bill must have variety, and change of pace. It normally consisted of eight star acts, each approximately twenty minutes long.[11] The Chicago-based Orpheum organization brought some of the world's top performers to Calgary, including Lillie Langtry in December 1912,[12] and Sarah Bernhardt in January 1913.[13] Two young Orpheum dancers who later became big stars, Fred and Adele Astaire, visited the Grand in October 1912.[14]

On account of his financial success Bill initially enjoyed the senator's trust. But, by the end of the summer of 1913, rumours of financial problems surfaced.[15] James Lougheed's admiration for Sherman's managerial skills plummeted further early in February 1914 over an ugly incident of bad judgement and poor taste.

The discrimination suit launched by Charles Daniels caused the final break between the owner and his theatre manager.[16] Daniels, chief inspector in Calgary of CPR porters, had bought a reserved seat on the Sherman Grand's ground floor for "King Lear" starring noted Shakespearian actor Robert Mantell. When the African Canadian arrived the box office refused him entry to the main floor on account of his colour. He was told that he could exchange his ticket for one upstairs in the balcony.[17] Daniels immediately hired Barney Collison, who had started practice with the late Paddy Nolan.[18] The criminal lawyer filed a discrimination suit against the manager and the theatre owner. In turn *The Albertan* asked the management of the Grand for an interview about the incident. Perhaps finally recognizing his difficulty in articulately expressing himself, Bill Sherman asked Jimmie Leatherby, the Grand's treasurer, to respond.

Leatherby had come to Calgary from South Africa after service with Remington's Scouts in the South African War fifteen years earlier. Born in England in 1883, he was the son of a labourer in a brickyard.[19] James had a trade; his military enlistment form prepared on 9 September 1914 lists his own occupation as "plumber." In terms of physical appearance the Grand's thirty year chief ticket taker was short, 5' 4" tall, with fresh complexion, blue eyes and brown hair.[20] According to the *Calgary News-Telegram* he "was a genial chap, with a sunny smile and a bright word for everybody, and was highly popular."[21]

James Leatherby did speak to *The Albertan*. The paper reported him as saying white people objected to African Canadians sitting on the theatre's main floor: "Negroes are not excluded from the theatre, provided they take the seats in the section of the house assigned to them." The management, having received "numerous complaints from white people who occupied high priced seats that the negroes were offensive to them, decided to refuse negroes admittance to the ground floor."[22]

James Lougheed lacked many of his contemporaries' racial prejudices. During his first winter in Calgary in February 1884, for example, he defended Jesse Williams, an African Canadian accused of murder.[23] He lost the case and Williams was judged

Jimmie Leatherby, photo from
the Calgary News-Telegram, 12
March 1915. Glenbow Library.

Jeff Lydiatt and Clara Fooks, at Jeff's
parents' 25th Wedding Anniversary.
Clara appears on the extreme right,
and Jeff is at front on the right.
Jeff's mother Annie Lydiatt appears
third from the left, and his father,
James Lydiatt, fourth from the left.
Photo courtesy of David Ogden.

guilty by the magistrate and hanged. But James Lougheed's defence of Williams, in a community with a lawless element anxious to lynch him, showed courage. The senator also supported Black entertainers. In 1905, Lougheed financed a travelling show of thirty-five African American performers, "a combination of all the best and most popular features of farce, travesty, vaudeville and opera". The company included "funny comedians, brilliant ensembles, pretty girls."[24] In Calgary at this time the leading hotels refused rooms to those of African descent.[25] Finally, far from a policy of "white help only," the senator in the 1910s employed an African American couple, Owen and Alice Stone, as the caretakers of the Grand Theatre.[26]

Calgary's small African Canadian community of approximately one hundred people included a number of railway porters.[27] Sleeping car porters worked the long trip from Toronto, or Montreal, to Calgary and Vancouver, sometimes with only three hours sleep a night, for up to four successive nights.[28] They were responsible for all aspects of the sleeping car journey, apart from collecting tickets, the train conductor's task. Wages remained low, hours long and job security a distant dream. No chance existed of joining the union, the Canadian Brotherhood of Railway Employees, as only white men could become members.[29] Yet in the African Canadian community in the early twentieth century this was an elite job; porters were "the aristocrats of African-Canadian communities."[30]

One newspaper in Calgary openly criticized the Sherman Grand's management's decision. Although *The Albertan* and *Calgary Herald* editorial boards apparently made no comment on the incident, the *News-Telegram* soundly condemned the Grand's management. In their editorial, "Calgary Resents Race and Color Distinction," the paper wrote on February 7: "This is a free country, and whether a man be black or white, a British subject or an alien, no one has the right to draw the color or any other line to subject him either to indignity or inconvenience."

The incident embarrassed Senator Lougheed. Financially the subsequent legal case hurt as well, as Charles Daniels won his suit of $1,000 damages in late March.[31] In early June 1914 the senator replaced Sherman,[32] and turned booking for the Grand over to C. P. Walker, the Winnipeg theatre magnate and impresario with whom he already was associated. [33] At the same time the senator hired Jeff Lydiatt as his "personal representative" in his "theatrical enterprises."[34] He delegated the Grand's business dealings with Walker to him. Then, in late December 1914, Senator Lougheed named Lydiatt the permanent manager.[35]

Both James Lougheed and Jeff Lydiatt shared a Toronto Methodist background. At Yonge Street Methodist Church in Yorkville Jeff had met his future wife, the English-born Clara Fooks. Born in Kent she had come to Canada with her parents at a young age. All her life she still retained a soft slight English accent.[36] Both Jeff and Clara sang in the church choir.[37] Although he had never taken a music lesson in his life, Jeff taught himself to read sheet music, to sing, to play the piano and later to conduct choirs.[38] At Yonge Street Methodist he also volunteered as the church's librarian, and Clara worked as the church's associate secretary.[39] From a young age Jeff acquired the Methodist commitment to the ethic of hard work. On the way to their elementary school, Jesse Ketchum, Jeff and his older brother, Will, had to wait at a railway crossing. To discipline their minds the two young boys memorized the numbers on passing freight cars.[40]

A photo survives of the young Jeff and his betrothed at Jeff's parents' twenty-fifth wedding anniversary.[41] After finishing high school he worked as a clerk for several years at Fudgers, the big Toronto wholesale grocery firm, which later amalgamated with Simpsons.[42] At age twenty-one he switched jobs, successfully obtaining a clerk's position with the Operating Department of the CPR. Posted to Owen Sound, Ontario, Jeff's absence from Toronto confirmed both Clara's and his love for each other. Their relationship deepened following his transfer back to Toronto. They married on 26 June 1902.[43]

Marriage liberated them both. Under their parents' and relatives' strict Methodist regime neither could dance, play cards, go to the theatre or even read a newspaper on Sunday. After their wedding Jeff said; "Now things are going to change."[44] Ready for adventure the young couple went off to Jeff's next posting in Fort William, Ontario. While still faithful churchgoers their Methodism became more relaxed. Not that all Methodist traits were harmful; particularly in business, respect for hard work and punctuality both constitute big assets. All his life Jeff strove to be always on time. He taught the same virtue to his children.[45]

Off Jeff and Clara went to the head of Lake Superior. His talent for administrative work, and likeable personality led to quick advancement. At the lake head he briefly worked for Alfred Price, superintendent of the Fort William division, before his transfer to the Winnipeg office. Here Dorothy, the oldest of the Lydiatts' six children, was born just one day after their first wedding anniversary. After Price himself moved to Winnipeg in 1904 to become superintendent of CPR's western lines, Jeff became his private secretary and chief clerk.[46] Although Alfred was almost twice Jeff's age the two men got along splendidly and became life-long friends. The son of an impoverished Irish-born shoemaker and Cornish-born mother, Alfred entered the work force at age fourteen as a telegram messenger, later becoming a railway telegraph operator.[47] After joining the CPR in 1882 as a dispatcher, he successfully worked his way up through the system to reach the top administrative level.[48]

The Lydiatts' second child, son Ellis, was born in Winnipeg in 1906, just before the family moved to Calgary. After Alfred Price's appointment as general superintendent of the CPR's Alberta division the following year, he again made Jeff his chief clerk. By 1912 the CPR had over 2,500 kilometres (1,400 miles) of track in the province.[49] It was largest employer in Calgary itself. In the spring of 1912 the company broke ground for the Ogden Shops, a heavy repair and rebuilding facility, the largest between Vancouver and Winnipeg.[50] That same year the railway also completed the third and last stage of its new sandstone station downtown. The new station became the railway's Calgary headquarters until it was demolished in 1966 to make way for the Calgary Tower. Befitting his position Alfred Price built for himself and family a substantial two-and-a-half-story home in Mount Royal, but he left the city before being able to enjoy living in it.[51] In July 1913 the CPR called him to Montreal to become assistant general manager of the entire CPR system in Eastern Canada.[52] This time Jeff Lydiatt did not travel with him, as he had left the CPR service almost a year earlier.

Through his CPR position and his involvement as the choir director at Calgary's Wesley Methodist Church, Jeff came to know many people.[53] He served as an important CPR spokesperson. After a railway accident, for instance, in which Senator Lougheed as a passenger in the Pullman car suffered a strained tendon, Jeff made the public statement. The *Calgary News-Telegram* of 2 February 1911 reads: "R.J. Lydiatt, of the general superintendent's department, Calgary, stated yesterday that the accident was being investigated by the company. He did not believe that any blame could be attached to the train crew." In 1912 Jeff was elected to the Calgary Y.M.C.A Board of Directors.[54] He also volunteered in 1912 as the secretary for subscription classic concerts in the city.[55]

William Pearce, now one of the most senior CPR officials in the Calgary office, knew Jeff Lydiatt well. In 1904 Pearce left government service to work for the CPR. The railway assigned him the responsibility of making an inventory of all its land and mineral assets in Western Canada. As CPR Chief Statistician, he was also assigned to keep a record of the extent of freight and passenger traffic in Western Canada, and to monitor the profitability of branch lines.[56] Very impressed by Jeff Lydiatt, he knew Alfred Price's chief clerk's telephone number by heart, "C.P.R. 6641."[57]

A dutiful father, William Pearce saved his enormous family correspondence. In 1909 his communication with his offspring was particularly prolific. We know that in the spring of that year his oldest son, Seabury, was off completing his third year in Engineering at McGill,[58] and his two younger sons attended private schools in Ontario.[59] One daughter travelled in Germany.[60] The other left on a European trip in 1912.[61] The family employed a maid.[62] William had sufficient capital to give each of his three sons a gift of $1,000 when they turned twenty-one.[63] The long-time federal turned CPR senior employee believed in opportunity for all in the West. In March 1909 he wrote a letter to Seabury with this optimistic comment: "In a new and developing country as is the west, any young man who is well grounded and has his health and exercises due economy in his living, need not fear but that he will making a fair liv[e]lihood and in the end probably a very good one."[64]

In May 1912 William also provided his youngest son Harry, then seventeen,[65] some career advice: "If I were a young man commencing life I think I would fit myself thoroughly as a stenographer and typewriter, read up current works so as to keep abreast of the times in all matters, particularly in business and mechanical development, and try to get a position with a railway divisional superintendent, say like Mr. Price at this point, as private secretary to him." An individual in this position, he continued, "if he shows himself competent more and more responsibility will be thrown on him, and in time he becomes really assistant superintendent...."[66] In effect, without naming him, William Pearce had just proposed Jeff Lydiatt as a role model for his son.

As he got along so well with his supervisor, and had a secure job, Jeff's decision to leave the CPR proved a difficult one. But the city's economic boom reached its peak in late 1912. Most believed that the great prosperity would continue for a long time to come. Years later he spoke to his young daughter Grace about change. He said to her

William Pearce in his CPR office, January 1914. Glenbow Archives/NA-325-1.

Clara Lydiatt with her children, about 1915 in Calgary. From left to right: Dorothy, Kathleen, Ellis, Grace (on her mother's lap), and Margaret. Photo courtesy of Jeff Lydiatt, Jr.

that people, even from a young age, must learn to move. The earlier you discover this the better. People, he added, are like plants in a little pot, if you don't transplant plants they wither and die.[67] Jeff and Clara voted for change. He had reached the limits of his job with the CPR. It no longer creatively challenged him.

Jeff accepted the offer of Dr. Blow, founder and chair of the board of governors of Calgary's new university, to become his private secretary. On 4 October 1912, *The Albertan* explained: "During his residence in Calgary, Mr. Lydiatt has been in close touch with many civic movements and has been keenly interested in the musical development of the city. As secretary to Dr. Blow, he will establish an even wider personal connection with public affairs." In addition to his responsibilities to promote the new university, Jeff would also help with the doctor's real estate holdings. The medical specialist owned a warehouse, several business blocks and, with his brother, speculated in large blocks of farmland around the city.[68] Very successful with his investments he had just moved from his large home on 7th Avenue West, one block away from the newly constructed Lougheed Building, to an impressive-looking mansion in Mount Royal.

Jeff attended the World Series in New York just before taking up his new responsibilities. He adored baseball.[69] Upon his return his colleagues held an all-male banquet in his honour at the newly opened Cronn's Rathskeller in the basement of the Lougheed Building. Eighty railroaders attended. An orchestra played during the meal. Once the men lit their cigars after dinner, the business of the evening began.[70] The toastmaster Alfred Price "spoke of the many years of his association with Mr. Lydiatt, of his sterling worth and trustworthiness."[71]

Initially, for the first month at least, all went well for Jeff in his new position. He established his office in Dr. Blow's office building on 7th Avenue, where the 1913 directories list him as secretary to Dr. Blow, as well as being involved in real estate.[72] That Christmas Jeff's parents came out from Toronto to spend the holidays with Jeff and Clara and their four children.[73] These included the two oldest, Dorothy and Ellis, and the two youngest, Margaret and Kathleen, both born in Calgary. Clara, then three months pregnant, would give birth to Grace the following July. Jeff, Jr., the last child, was born in Calgary in 1915. Just before Jeff left the CPR the Lydiatts had settled into a comfortable new home on the northern boundary of Mount Royal, at 1720 11th Street West.[74]

That spring Jeff assisted Dr. Blow with his business and political ventures. In order to defend Calgary University against the University of Alberta in the provincial legislature, the doctor ran as a Conservative candidate for South Calgary in the election of April 1913. Jeff acted as his official agent.[75] The doctor won, but his victory constituted the only good news he received that spring as the real estate market in Calgary continued to collapse. The bust took with it all hopes for a university in Calgary. Although the exact timing remains unknown, Dr. Blow must have indicated to Jeff sometime in the late spring of 1913 that he no longer had work for him. Fortunately Jim Davidson, Jeff's friend and fellow director of the Calgary Symphony Orchestra, intervened. He told James Lougheed about Jeff.[76]

Elected as secretary of the symphony's board of directors in the spring of 1913, while he still worked with Dr. Blow, Jeff served on the same blue chip organizing committee as Jim Davidson.[77] Many in the city wanted both a university and a symphony. Judge Winter, husband of Lydia Winter, explained the point of view in an interview in the spring of 1914: "I have often said that we do not want Calgary to become a Reno as a divorce center, nor do we want it to become a prize-fighting town; but no better name could be attached to a city than to have it regarded as an intellectual center."[78] The board sponsored the first concert of the fifty-five-member orchestra in the Grand Theatre on 13 November 1913, after nearly a year of organizational work.[79] The season lasted until the end of March. Six more evening concerts and three children's matinees followed in the Grand Theatre, until the economic depression and the outbreak of World War One carried away both Calgary's first symphony and its first university.

The question of when exactly Jeff began working for James Lougheed is unknown.[80] In June 1913, Maude Adams, the popular American actress who introduced James Barrie's "Peter Pan" to the North American stage, appeared at the Grand.[81] From her first performance of the role in 1904 her name had become inseparable from the part. Years later the Lydiatts' eldest child, Dorothy, recalled her joy as a girl of almost ten in seeing the performance. Had Jeff already made a connection with the Sherman Grand at this point? Dorothy remembered that her father began at the Grand as a part-time bookkeeper.[82] In any event Jeff definitely worked at the theatre by 1914.

The first reference to Jeff Lydiatt and the Lougheed Building relates to Rotary, a new service club organization organized in 1905 among business and professional men in Chicago. They called it Rotary as the members met, in rotation, at their various places of business. This practice continued until the membership became too large to make this practical. Rapidly the club with the motto, "Service Above Self" expanded internationally, first to Britain and then Canada. In late 1913, a group of individuals met at Cronn's to plan the formation of a Calgary club.[83] Other meetings followed at Cronn's, leading up to the gathering of sixty men on Monday, 16 February 1914, at which forty of those present decided to proceed.[84]

The original Calgary group included Lougheed retail tenants Phil McCrystle the tailor and women's clothing storeowner Fred Harling. Once the Rotary Club of Calgary incorporated on 9 April 1914, Jeff Lydiatt became a member and soon one of its driving forces. In Rotary only one member could be selected from each recognized business or professional activity in the community. In Jeff's case he represented "Theatres," which indicates that his connection with the Sherman Grand had already begun. Rotary opened its first office in the Lougheed in room 303 in 1914. Jeff went far in Rotary in Western Canada, serving as president of the Calgary club from 1917 to 1918 as well as governor of the Western Canadian District. In 1922-1923 he was a director of Rotary International.[85]

Sir Johnston Forbes-Robertson's visit to Calgary in early 1915 proved Jeff's first mega-event as theatre manager. The Calgary Herald termed Sir Johnston's four-day engagement at the Grand, "the supreme event of the local theatrical season."[86] In addition to "The Passing of the Third Floor Back," he and his company presented

Shakespeare's "Hamlet" and "The Light That Failed," a melodrama adapted from the novel by Rudyard Kipling. They always performed to packed houses.[87]

The Great War had changed Calgary almost beyond recognition from the time of Forbes-Robertson's first visit at the height of the city's economic boom. As part of the British Empire with no control over its foreign affairs, Canada entered the conflict the instant Britain did. The morning of 4 August 1914, German troops crossed the border into Belgium. Under an 1839 treaty Britain, France and Prussia had agreed to protect Belgian neutrality. Immediately upon the invasion of Belgium, Britain issued Germany an ultimatum to withdraw. Twenty minutes after it expired, at eleven p.m., August 4th, London time, the British Empire entered the war on the side of the Allies—France, Russia, Serbia and Belgium—against the Central Powers, Germany and Austro-Hungary.

Just after seven p.m. that same evening, news of Britain's declaration of war on Germany reached Calgary. The night staff in the Herald Building hastily updated all the latest bulletins on its news board located in the alleyway between their building and the Lougheed Building/Grand Theatre. Simultaneously the paper sent out its newsboys to distribute pink "extras" throughout the city. As a round, blood-red summer moon rose on the southeastern sky, masses of people, the patriotic and the curious, assembled along 9th Avenue between Centre and 1st Streets. A Scots piper marched up and down in front of the CPR Station and the brand new Palliser Hotel, opened just two months earlier. Shouts of "Vive la France!" and "God Save the King!" greeted the impromptu processions of flag draped motorcars.[88]

Legions of eager volunteers came forward as everyone on the Allied side initially expected the war to be over by Christmas 1914. But the unexpected German thrust through Belgium into France took the Allies by surprise. Only in October did the Allies check the German advance at Ypres in the tiny corner of western Belgium that remained under their control. The German front lines as the crow flies were now about the same distance from Dover, England, as Calgary was from Banff—approximately a hundred kilometres. Both sides built a series of trenches from the Swiss border to the North Sea. Only two months after Forbes-Robertson's visit, the Canadians entered into their first major battle at Ypres, where they endured the world's first large-scale use of poison gas.

A martial atmosphere dominated in the city in early 1915. Sir Johnston visited the city's parade ground where the 31st Battalion marched before him. He later wrote of the experience: "Deeply moved at the honour shown me, I stood erect with bared head as the battalion swung past me in perfect alignment on the hard and slippery snow."[89] Forbes-Robertson felt the war's intensity. He described the German emperor to a Calgary reporter as a "monster," an "incarnation of iniquity."[90]

Jeff Lydiatt's office in 1914 was in room 205 on the second floor of the Lougheed Building,[91] which was itself transformed by wartime developments. Dr. Robert O'Callaghan retained his office nearby in room 210 but, in addition to his practice, the McGill-trained surgeon now served as a recruiting officer for the Princess Patricia's Canadian Light Infantry, the military unit named after the Duke of Connaught's

The first Calgary Symphony Orchestra, 1913. Glenbow Archives/NA-2039-1.

Declaration of war, 4 August 1914. A great crowd gathered at the CPR train station the evening that war was declared. The Palliser Hotel, only two months old, appears in the background. The Calgary Herald/ "World War I (Hist. File)." Reprinted with permission of The Calgary Herald.

daughter.[92] In early 1916 he himself enlisted in the British Royal Army Medical Corps and spent over a year in several hospitals in England and France.[93]

Other military related activities occurred in the building. As soon as the war broke out Calgary's naval volunteer headquarters opened an office in the Lougheed's fourth floor.[94] In late October 1915, Senator Lougheed and his business partner Edmund Taylor donated two vacant retail spaces on the building's ground floor for a soldiers' club open to all ranks of enlisted men every evening from 4:30 to 10:30. The four Calgary chapters of the Imperial Order of the Daughters of the Empire operated the club.[95] The Calgary office of the Patriotic Fund moved into room 300 of the Lougheed in late 1916.[96] The following April the recruiting office for the Army Medical Corps opened in the building as well.[97]

Senator Lougheed, President of the Alberta Boy Scouts Association, provided two rooms rent-free for the duration of the war in the Lougheed Building for the association's headquarters.[98] Founded in Britain by Robert Baden-Powell in 1908, the Boy Scout movement reached Calgary in 1910 with the establishment of the St. Stephen's Church Scout troop later designated as "the 1st Alberta Troop." Chief Scout Baden-Powell himself visited Calgary on 21 August 1910.[99] As Robert H. MacDonald has argued in *Sons of the Empire: The Frontier and the Boy Scout Movement, 1890-1918*: "Scouting came to mean King and Country, Duty and Self-Sacrifice."[100] From the outset in Britain, Boy Scouts were thought of as little soldiers with an honorary connection to the military. It trained boys to do their duty.[101] During the Great War a total of 222 Calgary leaders and Scouts or former Scouts enlisted, of whom 24 died in action.[102]

No information survives on the stand taken on Canada's war involvement by the Lougheed's major fourth floor tenant, Will Tregillus. Before the outbreak of hostilities he determinedly opposed any involvement for Canada in a European war. But now preoccupied by his failed brickworks, he made no statement. The German invasion of neutral Belgium, however, did reverse the earlier stance taken by University of Calgary professor Mack Eastman, who just half-a-year earlier attacked the piling up of arms by the world powers at the expense of the farmers and working class. Horrified by the German invasion of a small neutral country, the history professor now endorsed the war against Germany. "Autocratic government in Germany will yield only to force," he told a Calgary interviewer in mid-October 1914.[103] Mack tried to enlist, but the historian failed the stringent physical test.[104] Robert Maclean, Calgary's classics professor, had enlisted successfully immediately after the outbreak of war.[105]

Anxious to help the Allied cause Mack devoted long hours that winter to raise money throughout southern Alberta for the Belgian relief fund.[106] During his last months in Calgary he boarded with George Coutts, Fred Albright's great friend.[107] Fred had taught the university's first economics course, now taken over by Walter Sage, a University of Toronto graduate with further training at Oxford University. Sage, who also taught English and history, was also a great friend of George Coutts.[108]

After Will Tregillus's death in late 1914 and the collapse of the University Club, Mack had no reason to visit the Lougheed Building. That winter he completed his Ph.D. for Columbia University in New York. It won high praise from the head of the

history department at the University of Toronto, as well as from the Canadian history specialist at Harvard.[109] The study of the early Roman Catholic Church in the French Regime appeared in print as *Church and State in Early Canada* just before his departure for the University of British Columbia in May 1915.[110] In Vancouver he taught for several months at the UBC as the university's first professor of history before successfully enlisting for overseas service under the more relaxed recruiting standards of 1916.[111]

Walter Sage was the last instructor to leave the city.[112] On 4 September 1915, he married a Calgarian, Nelda MacKinnon, at her parent's home. He wanted to stay. In one of his early letters from Calgary he explained that, "here one has to be a teacher, a preacher, an organizer and (to use a Western phrase) a 'mixer'." This made for a great deal of work but, he added, "One good thing about it is that the students are beginning to ask questions & have difficulties which shows that they are trying to think for themselves."[113] The closure of Calgary University in late spring 1915 forced Walter to look for university work elsewhere. Shortly after the wedding he began teaching at Queen's University in Kingston, Ontario.[114]

Calgary became an armed camp over the next four years. Nearly forty thousand men enlisted for overseas service here.[115] Jeff Lydiatt continued the Grand's policy of welcoming soldiers to performances. As guests of the house he invited the entire 50th Battalion to attend the production of "Baby Mine."[116] In late February 1915 it was the turn of the 31st Battalion, 1100 strong, to see the play, "The Private Secretary."[117] The *News-Telegram* on 6 March 1915 congratulated Jeff Lydiatt and his counterpart at the Lyric, now called the Pantages Theatre,[118] for doing "all in their power to make life pleasant for the men who will soon be on the firing line." In late April, nine hundred members of the 50th Battalion returned for the last performance of "My Tango Maid." The men in khaki joined in singing the chorus lines.[119]

Information survives on one Lougheed apartment resident in the war years: Millicent McElroy, "the lady who played the cornet." She played the send off for each outgoing train carrying soldiers from the CPR Station in Calgary to England and France. Born in England in 1869, she immigrated to Canada with her husband in 1911. George McElroy had been the band master of the Salvation Army Belfast Citadel, and Millicent was a well-known Salvation Army musician in northern England.[120] After the war ended she returned to the CPR platform and played rousing tunes as the men disembarked.[121] She had moved into the Lougheed apartment with her daughter and family while her daughter's husband was overseas in the war. Her own husband, a painter, was employed with the decoration of the new Vancouver CPR railway station.[122]

Fortunately correspondence from a Lougheed tenant in the years 1915 to 1916 survives. In 1915 Seabury Pearce, William's oldest son, moved into offices on the fourth floor, 6th Avenue side, just opposite where the headquarters of the ill-fated Tregillus Clay Products had once been.[123] Unlike his two younger brothers William and Harry, both in the Canadian Army, Seabury could not enlist, even under the more relaxed recruiting standards of the second and third years of the war, as he had lost the sight in his right eye as a young boy.[124] In fact, he wore a glass eye.[125]

Members of the 50th Battalion,
to become known as the "Suicide
Battalion," parade through
Calgary before leaving for Britain.
Glenbow Archives/NA-3419-3.

Although trained as an engineer and a surveyor, Seabury managed his father's company, "Pearce's Limited." Its letterhead read, "Loans negotiated, estates managed."[126] In 1916 both of Seabury's brothers were in Europe. Bill, who had arrived at the front in charge of a machine gun unit during the early spring of 1915, had been badly wounded in May, hit in the back of the neck by a piece of shrapnel.[127] After hospitalization in England, he returned to the trenches. Younger brother Harry left for England with his Calgary unit in March 1916. Within less than five months he too was wounded in a bomb accident in France with exploded shrapnel wounds to his head, neck and both thighs.[128] For two days the surgeons considered the amputation of his right arm at the elbow, but fortunately, by day three, he began to recover.[129] Once he had recuperated he returned to the front, also in a machine gun battalion like his brother.

Seabury Pearce, the trusted agent of his father, knew the Lougheed Building well, particularly the Cronn's Rathskeller portion. As president of the Calgary Planning Commission in 1913, his dad chaired executive meetings at Cronn's.[130] There, on 21 May 1913, the robust-looking Pearce, about six feet tall, a man with broad powerful shoulders, introduced Thomas Mawson.[131] In short order the thin, professorial-looking Englishman won over the City of Calgary aldermen, city commissioners and chairs of the various committees of the city planning commission. The urban planner and architect spoke with authority and conviction, urging them to develop a plan to control Calgary's urban sprawl and provide for additional green spaces.[132] Council later hired him to prepare one. Seabury helped to show Mawson the city and surrounding area.[133] Amongst the Englishman's photos is a shot of the Lougheed Building and entrance to the Grand Theatre with the emerging Herald Building in the background.[134] In his completed 1914 report, which was not acted upon, Mawson quoted William Pearce extensively.[135]

Since opening in late 1912 Cronn's Rathskeller had been the spot to dine in the city. Jeff Lydiatt's friends hosted his retirement party from the CPR there. When the Royal Architectural Institute of Canada held its sixth general annual assembly at Calgary in September 1913, the City of Calgary welcomed the delegates at a luncheon at Cronn's.[136] The Rotary Club of Calgary had been planned around one of Cronn's restaurant tables in the winter of 1913–1914. William Pearce and the Calgary Planning Committee Executive scheduled their meetings there. But with the outbreak of war in August 1914 things changed. Now any establishment with a German name became suspect.

As the war continued anti-German feelings rose. As early as late August 1914, *The Calgary Herald* endorsed the dismissal by the City of Calgary of German and Austrian employees.[137] That same month James Lougheed urged public calm. On August 19th he mentioned to his fellow senators, "at such a time when all the national impulses are stirred it is peculiarly an occasion for dispassionate deliberation...."[138] But hysteria mounted as the war, with no end in sight, took more and more victims. One of the first Calgarians to die in active service was Jimmie Leatherby, the Grand's first treasurer. He died of cerebral spinal meningitis in France on 5 March 1915 while serving with the Princess Patricias.[139]

Grand Theatre
The Show Place of Alberta

PLAYING

Orpheum Supreme Vaudeville

Every Monday, Tuesday and Wednesday, at 8.15
Matinees Tuesday and Wednesday, at 2.30

and

First Class Road Attractions

Every Thursday, Friday and Saturday, at 8.15
Regular Matinee Saturday, at 2.30

Seating Capacity 1,500

THE THEATRE BEAUTIFUL

Perhaps more than any other Albertan in the summer of 1915, James Lougheed knew the high casualty rate suffered by Canadian troops on the Western front. In July and August 1915 he served as acting minister of the militia.[140] His personal and emotional involvement increased with the enlistment that fall of Clarence, his oldest son,[141] followed by Edgar, his third son.[142] Understandably the senator lost his footing and alarmingly emphasized the danger posed by Germans within Canada itself. In the senate on 16 January 1916, he stated that Germany had embarked on "a war for world power, of territorial conquest," Canada being one of its principal objectives. "Germany," he added, "through its system of espionage, has a more thorough knowledge of Canada in the pigeon-holes of its foreign office than would be found in the departments of our own Government."[143]

Long-standing resentment against the enemy surfaced in Calgary in mid-February. Seabury was a tenant in the Lougheed at the time. His father learned from his son and the newspapers what had occurred. In a note to his daughter Frances, then in Victoria, B.C., William summarized what happened: "The soldiers in garrison, aided to a large extent by civilians, have given vent to their anti-German and anti-Austrian feelings in wrecking several Buildings."[144] They trashed two restaurants on February 10th and a hotel the next night.[145] William Pearce was appalled, and added: "It is a deplorable state of affairs, and the saddest part of the whole thing is that public sentiment seems to be largely in support of that class of work, perhaps not to the extent of wrecking buildings, but there is a most insane anti-German and anti-Austrian feeling."[146]

Nor was that all. On the evening of the 11th a rumour spread that rioters had targeted Cronn's Rathskeller. Twenty-five quickly assembled defenders of the restaurant blocked the doorway, and an armed guard stood across the road in case of trouble.[147] The defenders prevented an attempt to rush it. Long-time Calgarian Leishman McNeill later recorded what Edgar Lougheed told him about the aftermath. Immediately after the mob dispersed, Jimmy Hunter, the Lougheed Building's Scottish-born superintendent, called a truck to cut the wires leading to the large outside sign, "Cronn's Rathskeller." After the sign was carted away, he turned out all the lights and had the doors locked. The mob did not return. McNeill concludes: "Mr. Lougheed tells me that Mr. and Mrs. Cronn disappeared that night and he never afterwards heard of their whereabouts."[148]

Cronn's Rathskeller suddenly became Cronn's Restaurant,[149] then, by April 1st, Cronn's Café.[150] After that it had a new name entirely: the Cabaret Garden.[151] It took its new designation from the bandstand framed in latticework and hung with baskets of flowers.[152] For a new image the management hired an African American quartet. In the basement of the Lougheed Building, in February 1917, jazz was first played in Calgary. The Cabaret Garden later changed its name to the Plaza,[153] but it retained its popular African American jazz bands until 1920.[154]

The Grand Theatre faced a problem with booking shows during the war. The Orpheum Vaudeville Circuit, which came to the Grand three days of every week, stopped its visits to Calgary and all Western Canadian cities with the exception of Winnipeg in late 1914. Attendance had fallen after the war's outbreak, but a year later Jeff Lydiatt successfully convinced the Orpheum circuit to return to Calgary.[155] By keeping the Grand full of life Jeff Lydiatt kept it alive, and helped enormously to maintain Calgary's wartime spirits.

1916 proved a terrible year for Calgary, as Canadian casualties in France and Belgium increased. Calgary's 31st Battalion lost more than half its strength, with 130 killed, nearly 500 wounded and 4 missing in a six-month period. The 50th Battalion, which had also visited the Grand earlier that year, lost 230 men in a fight by the Regina Trench. Of the 260 officers and men went who went "over the top" to attack the German lines, only one officer and 30 men returned without a wound.[156]

By the summer of 1916 Calgary's daily newspapers carried long lists of casualties. Amongst the heavy losses that June was Dick Brocklebank, former alderman, killed in action.[157] That September twenty-five year old Ernest Pinkham, the Pinkham's beloved youngest son, died at the Battle of Courcelette.[158] In some fashion or another, the impact of the mounting casualties was felt in thousands of Calgary homes.

Jeff Lydiatt worked very hard throughout the war to lighten the city's spirits. The *News-Telegram* knew him as "the popular manager of the Grand theatre."[159] The hard-to-please Bob Edwards also praised him. Writing in the *Eye Opener* on 2 December 1916, he tossed this bouquet: "Manager Lydiatt, of the Grand theatre, is to be congratulated on the high quality of theatrical fare he has been feeding his patrons upon of late. There has been quite an epidemic of good things." Bertha Hart, Bob's secretary in the 1910s,[160] also appreciated what Jeff Lydiatt did: "He used to bring in some grand shows."[161]

Through his work for the Rotary Club of Calgary Jeff Lydiatt contributed much to the community. He also generously devoted his time to the Victory Loan campaign.[162] Later in the war he chaired the publicity committee to raise funds for the Y.M.C.A. and its overseas work on the war front in Europe.[163] Next he chaired the Red Shield campaign to collect money for the Salvation Army's war work.[164] On account of all these responsibilities Jeff reluctantly resigned in early 1915 as leader of the Wesley Methodist Church choir.[165]

Jeff's job was full of minefields. He had to deal with such difficult personalities as Patrick Harcourt-O'Reilly, the Grand's solicitor. In early 1916 the lawyer saved the theatre $3,000 by reducing in court its original assessment of $12,000 to $9,000.[166] But, as a consequence, Harcourt-O'Reilly expected complimentary tickets to all performances. He appeared in full evening dress for big stage shows, without a ticket, and expected to be taken to the best seats. Operating under an extremely tight budget, Jeff repeatedly had to explain that there were no free tickets.[167]

Politically the Grand's manager must appear totally neutral as the theatre hosted both the Conservative and Liberal political leaders. Wisely he identified himself as an independent.[168] In the war years the leading provincial Conservative R. B. Bennett spoke several times there,[169] but Alberta's Liberal Premier Arthur Sifton also addressed a large gathering at the Grand.[170] In late 1916 Conservative Prime Minister Robert Borden held a massive rally in the theatre,[171] as did Wilfrid Laurier, the former Liberal prime minister turned leader of the opposition, in late 1917.[172]

Even with the selection of movies, now an essential component of the Grand's program, problems could arise. In February 1915, just after Jeff had taken over as manager, "Neptune's Daughter" caused some comment. Nearly seventy years after the showing of the five-reel silent film, Frances Coulson[173] remembered the controversy. The feature starred Australian synchronized swimmer Annette Kellerman. She had invented the one-piece bathing suit, which she wore instead of the cumbersome dress and pantaloon combinations women were then expected to wear. As Mrs. Coulson recalled: "The actress was a noted swimmer and audiences were thrilled (and shocked) when she was shown in the distance clad in white tights. Although she was covered from neck to ankles, this was considered to be extremely daring!"[174] She must have been quite a sight as *The Calgary Herald* described her in these terms on February 12th: "Miss Kellerman is the world's greatest woman swimmer, diver and natatorial expert, besides being credited with possessing the most truly classical figure known to the modern world—a figure even surpassing the lovely lines of the ancient Greek goddesses."[175]

Be that as it may, Jeff faced heated comment from one member of the clergy for not only the film, but also for the pictures advertising "Neptune's Daughter" in the Grand's lobby. In his Sunday sermon Rev. Alex Esler of Grace Presbyterian Church criticized the "theatre pictures of a woman that were even more suggestive than if they had represented the nude. These wrought the greatest evil."[176] The Rev. Esler had strong opinions about many subjects. It seems that the pressures of the war had affected the Presbyterian minister's mental stability. That July the he shared with his congregation his personal opinion that the pope had caused the Great War.[177]

D. W. Griffith's "The Birth of a Nation," a sensational box-office success throughout North America, also caused discussion. Beginning with its first showing in 1915 African American and African Canadian organizations protested against its romantic treatment of the Ku Klux Klan and the film's disparaging images of African American people. In Calgary the controversy arose in June 1918 on the occasion of its third repeat showing at the Grand. After the film's first presentation at the Grand in mid-December 1915, *The Calgary Herald* praised it as "one of the finest films produced for the modern stage."[178] It returned to Calgary in October and in December 1916.[179] But when it was announced as coming back to the Grand a fourth time, in early June 1918, the African Canadian community acted. A delegation went to City Hall and asked that the film be prohibited. As the *News-Telegram* reported the objection on 31 May 1918: "The delegates argue that the play holds the Negro up to ridicule... It was claimed that the picture had been disallowed in many of the leading cities of the United States and Canada...." The city did not act, nor did the provincial censor. Albertans in the late 1910s were as culture-bound as any people of their own time or ours. The Grand proceeded and showed the picture as advertised for three days in the second week of June.[180]

At the end of that same month an event occurred at the Grand that harkened back to the theatre's origins, to a moment of distant innocence. Forbes-Robertson appeared again in the Grand in "The Passing of the Third Floor Back," but this time on the silver screen rather than the stage.[181]

The Victory Parade, 11 November 1918. During the flu epidemic facemasks were common. Glenbow Archives/NA-431-5.

The hanging of the Kaiser in effigy in front of City Hall, where Olympic Plaza is today, after the Victory Parade of 11 November 1918. Glenbow Archives/NA-3965-6.

Finally in August 1918 the war took a turn for the better, with great Allied advances on the Western Front. But just as the end of Great War finally seemed imminent the deadly and highly contagious Spanish Flu epidemic struck. World wide the virus claimed twenty million lives. In Canada perhaps fifty thousand died, approximately the same number of Canadian service personnel lost in World War One. From mid-October and mid-November all churches, schools and theatres in Calgary remained closed.

The signing of the November 11th armistice in Europe allowed for a slight relaxation of the strict rules against public assemblies.[182] The news reached City Solicitor Clinton Ford when he was arguing a case before the Appeal Court. He and H. P. O. Savary, the opposing counsel, had to wear cotton masks on account of the epidemic. All the members of the court wore them. Nearly half a century later, Ford recalled that during his presentation Savary suddenly stepped out into the corridor. He returned a short time later waving a newspaper. Shouting incoherently through his mask he interrupted the city solicitor. When Clinton read the headline he understood. "ARMISTICE AGREED ON." "It meant the war was over. I will never forget the great feeling I had at that moment."[183]

Once news of the armistice reached the mayor he temporarily relaxed the anti-contagion rules and declared a half-day holiday, even allowing a victory parade. It began that afternoon at the Central Fire Hall on 6th Avenue, just two blocks from the Lougheed Building, and proceeded around the central part of the city, ending at City Hall at 3:30. The parade ended with the hanging of two effigies of the Kaiser and the German Crown Prince opposite City Hall, in what today is Olympic Plaza. Five hours later the effigies were removed from the scaffold and burned. Calgarians crowded the streets in every direction.[184]

The Grand Theatre's Opera Festival in late January marked Jeff Lydiatt's gift to Calgary to celebrate the war's end. The visiting San Carlo Opera Company enjoyed a worldwide reputation.[185] Calgary choir leader Percy Lynn "P. L." Newcombe publicly thanked Jeff Lydiatt in an article in *The Albertan*: "Manager Lydiatt of the Grand, is to be congratulated on his efforts, culminating in success to give Calgary the privilege of witnessing a real debut into grand opera."[186]

The checking of the influenza epidemic, which took 341 Calgarians' lives in late 1918, added to the joy of the five operas.[187] Influenza cases dropped from 938 in December to thirteen in January.[188] No one had to wear "flu" masks anymore. With great anticipation the public came to see and hear *Aida, Rigoletto, Tales of Hoffman, Il Trovatore* and *Madame Butterfly*, the San Carlo Opera Company's pièce de résistance. In honour of the Grand Opera Festival the Palliser Hotel hosted a special supper dance on Thursday, Friday and Saturday after each evening performance.[189]

On the evening of Friday January 24th Haru Onuki, the Japanese prima donna, captivated her audience in *Madame Butterfly*, the tragic tale of Cio Cio San and her ill-fated love for an American naval officer. Jeff and Clara and family sat in their loge in the centre of the first balcony overlooking the stage, the younger children in jump seats beside their parents and older siblings seated in chairs. Jeff and Clara both believed it important for the children's education that they attend theatrical events whenever possible.

Over the years the six children saw everything: musical comedy, stock company repertoire and tours of the "Greats" as well as opera. [190]

Madame Butterfly, Puccini's masterpiece, has wonderful music, especially the magnificent love duet closing the first act, and Cio Cio San's celebrated aria, "One Fine Day," at the beginning of the second. But it was Jeff and Clara's little Grace, age four, who stole the show at the very end of the performance. Grace played "Trouble," Cio Cio San's and Lieutenant Pinkerton's child. The San Carlo Opera travelled without any children. When asked, Jeff and Clara agreed that their youngest daughter could take the role if she wished. She did.

In the opera, to review the story, Lieutenant Pinkerton had left several years before, promising to return when cherry blossoms are in bloom. [191] The faith of Cio Cio San (whom everyone called Butterfly) in her husband, whom she married in a Christian ceremony—which ostracized herself from her own people—remained unshaken. For years she waited. Finally she viewed an American ship in Nagasaki harbour. The joy of Cio Cio San was complete when she saw him. But then she noticed beside him walked a foreign woman—his American bride. She saw that they were approaching from the harbour. Forsaken she placed a small American flag in their child's hand to wave.

At this point, as the opera moved to its powerful and tragic conclusion, Haru Onuki, who played Madame Butterfly, sat Grace in front of the headlights. The child was supposed to be a boy, but Grace had Dutch-cut hair, and so passed. [192] The betrayed Cio Cio San pulls out her father's sword on which she reads the inscription: "To die with honour when one can no longer live with honour." She then steps behind a folding screen, takes the blade and mortally wounds herself.

As her final contribution to the play approached Grace was totally exhausted. It was at least eleven at night when the sword fell clattering to ground and her "mother" hit the floor behind her. She yawned. [193] The child's yawn, so understandable in light of the hour, brought the house down. [194] In his review of the opera that evening, P. L. Newcombe wrote: "The part of Cho Cho San's child was charmingly taken by Mr. Lydiatt's little daughter." [195]

Jeff Lydiatt took the Grand through the upheaval of the Great War. An outstanding and imaginative administrator, he selected an effective management team, one which remained in place into the 1920s after he left the theatre. In late 1919 he assumed the vice-presidency of Trans-Canada Theatres Limited, a national theatre circuit, with his office in the Lougheed Building. James Lougheed, who was knighted Sir James Lougheed in 1916 in recognition of his senate and federal cabinet work, had a major financial interest in Trans-Canada. [196] The senator knew well his employee's true worth. When Jeff left Trans-Canada in 1923 to manage the Orpheum Theatre in Vancouver, James Lougheed wrote: "I could not wish from anyone who has been associated with me in business any greater satisfaction in that association than you have given me." [197]

Chapter Nine

AN ALBERTAN POLITICAL
REVOLUTION, 1921

The *Calgary Herald* OF 27 JULY 1921 REPORTED THE EXCITEMENT OF that morning: "It was only towards mid-day that there appeared any animation within the room, so closely guarded, wherein the farmers were holding their deliberations. It began with mild applause. This increased as time wore on until there was a deafening roar which appeared to shake the girders of the Lougheed Building itself."

Immediately after the Great War the United Farmers of Alberta (UFA) formed a political party to fight the provincial election of 1921. They put 40 candidates in the field for the election of July 12th and won all but one of the ridings. With 39 out of the 61 seats in the Alberta legislature the UFA held a decisive majority. Its victory was so unexpected by the public, as well as by the farmers themselves, that they came to power without a premier designate. Hastily called together from across the province the UFA MLAs-elect met in secret session at UFA headquarters in the Lougheed Building to pick a premier. Only one woman, Irene Parlby from Alix, attended amidst nearly forty males.

After the deafening noise from the second floor died down the UFA office door opened with a swing. The farmer politicians stepped out to announce the name of their new leader: Herbert Greenfield. The popular "dirt farmer" from Westlock had served as the chief organizer of the successful membership drive of the previous fall in which the UFA canvassed literally every farm in Alberta—quite a task in an age of only few gravelled roads, when travel was mainly by buckboards and horses.[1] The new premier, now fifty-two years old, who had come to Canada from England in his early twenties, told those assembled: "I will do my best for the farmers and every class in the province of Alberta." Deafening cheers followed.[2]

In 1921, two-thirds of all Albertans lived on farms. The province then had a population of only 600,000. Saskatchewan, with a population of 750,000, had 150,000 more people than Alberta. Agriculture remained the economic mainstay of both the "new provinces," created only in 1905.

Convinced that political involvement could better rural Alberta's depressed economic situation, the UFA entered the provincial election.[3] The UFA, born in 1909, and its women's section, the United Farm Women of Alberta, established in 1915–1916, had successfully pressured the provincial Liberal administration, in office since 1905, to pass favourable legislation for Alberta farmers. In this moment of rural crisis, however, the farmers deemed this insufficient with the costs of running a farm prohibitively high. The farmers blamed the old-line parties, the Liberals in power in Edmonton, and the Conservatives in Ottawa, for failing to safeguard their interests and control the "exploiters."

Many challenges confronted Alberta's farmers immediately after World War One. In 1917 a drought began in southeastern Alberta, where one-quarter of the province's farm population lived. The lack of rain over several years ruined many. Farm costs continued to rise at a faster rate than agricultural prices. UFA members called for immediate relief for farmers. The farmers had heavily mortgaged their land and overextended their lines of credit. The federal government's disbanding of the Wheat Board, established to provide minimum wheat prices, added to the rural unrest.

The grassroots-controlled UFA consisted of locals, a central office and a board of directors. The pressure from the membership for the organization to enter both provincial and federal politics increased after the end of World War One. UFA President Will Tregillus first made the call for a farmers' party shortly before his death in late 1914.[4] But then it was too early. Now the dire economic conditions of post-war Western Canada led farmers toward a political solution to their problems. Under intense pressure UFA President Henry Wise Wood bowed to the members' will. The UFA entered and won a provincial by-election at Cochrane in 1919. When the provincial Liberals called a snap election in mid-1921, the local UFA and farm women's groups mobilized again. By the final months of 1921 the provincial farm organization had grown to nearly forty thousand members, which meant that almost forty percent of Alberta's male farmers belonged.[5]

The UFA's membership controlled the organization from the bottom up. Every year the UFA held its annual convention, usually in January, and alternated regularly between Calgary and Edmonton. Vigorous and democratic, the UFA became known in Alberta as the "farmers' parliament."[6] At the Edmonton meeting in 1916, a number of candidates ran for the office of president. Each nominee addressed the convention, the last being "a tall, slim man dressed in a plain brown suit with a black shirt open at the neck devoid of tie." He spoke in "a deep, clear voice, which could be heard distinctly in every corner of the auditorium… He spoke slowly and briefly and when he had finished, the thunderous applause left no doubt that Henry Wise Wood, the man with the much weathered face and deep voice, was to be the new president of the United Farmers of Alberta."[7] For the next two decades Wood became the dominant personality in Alberta's agrarian movement.

Henry Wise Wood, an American cattle breeder and farmer born and raised in Missouri, came north to Western Canada, "The Last Best West," in 1905. He was forty-five years old. The availability of good cheap land attracted him, as it allowed him to provide land to all of his four sons. He chose the Carstairs district, north of Calgary, due to the beauty of the area. To the west rose the foothills of the Rockies, and beyond stood the high snowy peaks of the mountains themselves. Often he told his friend Len Nesbitt "of his pleasure in gazing at the beauties of the sunsets over the Rockies, particularly in the autumn season."[8]

Calgary Herald staff photographer W.J. Oliver's photo of the newly elected UFA MLAs who chose Herbert Greenfield as the new provincial premier, 27 July 1921, on the second floor of the Lougheed Building. Provincial Archives of Alberta/ A482.

The newly elected UFA MLAs outside the Lougheed Building, 6th Avenue West side. 27 July 1921. Irene Parlby who became Alberta's first female cabinet minister appears in the centre. Photo by W.J. Oliver. Glenbow Archives/NA-2204-4.

Born just one year before the outbreak of the American Civil War, the Alberta farm leader came from a Confederate family. His father, a slave owner, migrated to Missouri from South Carolina, where he had married. True southerners, the Woods named their fifth child after Governor Henry Wise of Virginia who, in 1860, signed the death warrant of abolitionist John Brown. During the U.S. Civil War Henry Wise Wood's father fought for the Confederacy.

Young Henry had a good education for the times, first at local schools and then for two years at Christian University, Canton, Missouri, where he met Leora Cook, whom he married at the end of his second year. He became a successful cattle breeder and farmer. While in Missouri he took an interest in the state farm movement. During his twenties and thirties he witnessed the rise and fall of numerous campaigns: "Free Silver," the Grange and the Farmers' Alliance,[9] all of which failed to better the farmer's lot. Henry came to distrust professional politicians who, he felt, often took advantage of the tillers of the soil.

Instead of agrarian political action, Henry favoured the ideal of co-operation and unity amongst farmers. A deeply religious man and a great reader of the Bible, his speeches frequently included biblical references and phraseology. He enjoyed particularly the Gospel according to St. John and the Book of Revelations. "John," he often said, "taught social reconstruction, and I am a disciple of John."[10]

Historian Brad Rennie refers to Wood as "the greatest UFA leader of all, whose sincerity and homely charisma attracted mass loyalty."[11] He had platform presence. In the 1920s newspapers often referred to the well-respected farm leader with such titles as the "Uncrowned King of Alberta" or "the Moses of Alberta." He worked to establish a more co-operative and less competitive society. In the words of historian W. L. Morton: "Out of the farmers' movement Wood saw a new society arising, more democratic, juster, and more civilized than the fiercely exploitative and competitive society he had known."[12]

During his first years in Alberta the Carstairs farmer evolved his own political philosophy. Night after night on returning home his neighbours saw a light burning in the Wood home.[13] He read voraciously the literature of economic and social reform. Wood came to believe in group co-operation. He felt that economic interest was the only way of achieving democracy. Political parties should be abolished and group representatives rule. Idealistically he believed that when all groups had a say and input into law making—when all groups were organized equally—mutual respect and inter-class concord would follow.

The agrarian philosopher believed that a small group of well-organized "plutocrats" governed the country. Unashamedly they did so to their own economic advantage at the expense of the unorganized masses, particularly the farmers. As he told a journalist after the initial UFA victory: "Five percent of the citizens of Canada organized into stable, efficient social groups are ruling absolutely over ninety-five per cent, who have been acting as individuals. We are now trying to build up democratic efficient groups as a counter-force to those already built by Plutocracy." Asked if the farmers sought to

UFA Board of Directors, 1918. Henry Wise Wood appears in the centre of the first row. Irene Parlby, at that time the President of the United Farm Women of Alberta, appears immediately to the left of him. Photo by A.L. Hess. Glenbow Archives/NA-447-1.

"The Milch Cow," probably the most famous of Arch Dale's cartoons in The Grain Growers' Guide, the voice of the Western Canadian farm movement, 15 December 1915. Glenbow Archives/NA-3055-24.

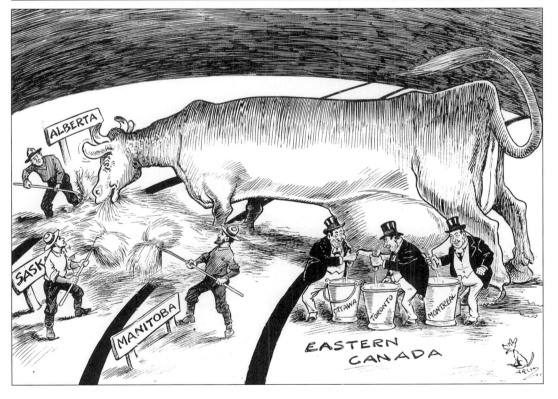

destroy the manufacturers, Wood replied: "No, the United Farmers Movement has no idea of destroying manufacturing industry, but we are going to bring the manufacturing group into servitude to humanity instead of humanity being in servitude to it."[14]

Several years previously the UFA chose the *Grain Growers' Guide* of Winnipeg as one of their official publications.[15] The *Guide* fully shared Wood's fears of the "plutocracy" and its allies. In its editorial page cartoons the *Guide*, as Canadian historian Gerald Friesen has pointed out, constantly drove home the message that farm families (clean lines, straight jaws, plain overalls) were locked in a deadly battle for survival against the vested interests (portly men, business suits, watch chains, and cigars).[16]

The UFA had moved into the Lougheed Building in late 1913,[17] with the United Farm Women of Alberta arriving in 1919.[18] By 1920 Henry Wise Wood's devotion to his job had become so all encompassing that he lived as well as worked in the Lougheed. He took an apartment on the sixth (later moving to the fifth floor) and left the running of his farm to his sons and wife, only returning home to Carstairs on weekends.[19] His office on the second floor of the Lougheed on the 1st Street side exhibited Wood's basic simplicity: a few books on a shelf, a hat rack, a couple of chairs, a desk for writing and a noisy telephone. A visitor commented on the noises on his floor in the lively, vibrant building, with "the sound of honking horns on the street, clattering feet in the hall ways, purr of voices in the outer offices, snatches of song and softly whistled tunes from corridor and street and office."[20]

While friendly and approachable, Henry Wise Wood proved the terror of the Lougheed Building manager. As he loved to smoke his straight-stemmed pipe the smell of fragrant tobacco filled his office. This was not the problem. Apparently, the agrarian leader did his best thinking with his straight-stemmed pipe in one hand and a burnt match in the other. More often than not his lighted match went out before it made contact with the tobacco. More seriously, on at least two occasions, he threw a still flaming match into the wastepaper basket after successfully lighting his pipe. Fortunately, on both occasions, the blaze was smothered before it got out of hand.[21]

In Wood's struggle for a more cooperative and less competitive society, Irene Parlby, the first president of the United Farm Women, became a close associate. Born in 1868 in London, England, Irene (Marryat) Parlby belonged to an English military family. Her father was a colonel in the Royal Engineers; and her mother was the daughter of a British Army major general. She was a grand-niece of Captain Frederick Marryat, the English author known for his children's sea stories. Her great-grandfather Joseph Marryat had served for fifteen years in the British House of Commons. Privately educated, she had a series of governesses. As a young woman Irene lived all over the world, including four years in India. There her father served as manager of the Bengal and North Western Railway running from Lahore to Peshawar with headquarters at Rawalpindi. Upon the family's return to England Irene spent half a year in Germany studying German and music. She became an accomplished pianist.[22] Visits to Ireland and to Switzerland followed.

A chance meeting with a woman from Western Canada led Irene to visit Alberta. Alix Westhead, a friend from Rawalpindi days, stayed in England with the

Marryats. She and her husband had settled in Alberta. When Mrs. Westhead invited Irene to visit Western Canada the adventurous young English woman enthusiastically accepted. In the Buffalo Lake area Irene met Walter Parlby, an Oxford graduate with an M.A. in classics and a rowing blue to his credit. After leaving Oxford, Walter had gone to Assam in India for two years as manager of a tea plantation before joining his brother in central Alberta.[23] Irene and Walter fell in love; they married and she became a rancher's wife.

The well-born Englishwoman adjusted quickly to her new way of life at Dartmoor Ranch, named after the famous moor in her husband's native Devon. Despite the newness of the tasks Irene adjusted well to her new life. An extremely efficient and immaculate housekeeper, she soon had made a comfortable home for herself and Walter. She was also a superlative cook and gardener. Despite the challenge of the tasks at hand, she remained very positive in outlook. She had a rich imagination. Quite easily she could transport herself to distant times and worlds, as the poem she later wrote in her future daughter-in-law's autograph album testifies. The poem entitled "Housework—an Art, or Drudgery," reveals her life philosophy:

> While sweeping up the oriental rungs
> > I'm walking through the woods and kissing trees;
> While smoothing eiderdowns upon the beds
> > I'm lying in the clover watching bees.
> Arranging flowers in a relic vase
> > To colourings Egyptian I awake,
> And as I wash and wipe the willow ware
> > A little talk with Emerson I make.
> While polishing the glasses till they gleam
> > To dazzling dreams my home I dedicate,
> And as I get the meals three times a day
> > My conscious mind no drudgery doth hate.[24]

It is hard to imagine two greater opposites: the well-groomed and well-spoken daughter of an English army colonel, and the tall, gaunt and slow-speaking son of a Missouri slave-owner almost a decade her senior. A friend of Irene's later described her as "always cool, collected and quiet with a good measure of dignity and reserve."[25] Truly she was a cultured English gentlewoman in every sense, who shared with husband a deep love of literature and drama. In contrast the very serious Wood had quite simple tastes. At the Lougheed Building his apartment was as sparse and austere as his office. As regards his clothes, Henry literally waited until his existing suit had worn out before going to his tailor to ask for an identical replacement.[26] His favourite restaurant in the neighbour of the Lougheed Building was the Buffalo Café at 112 7th Avenue, one block away, where the house specialty was hot turkey sandwiches with cranberry sauce.[27] He never drank. To relax he enjoyed playing rummy and going to the movies, most frequently to see a "western."[28]

But appearances can deceive. Henry shared with Irene a passion for literature, and had an equally vibrant imagination. He had read deeply the works of both British and American authors, particularly Dickens, Burns, Poe and Emerson. As did his refined English-born ally, he found inspiration in poetry, especially lyric poetry, of Walt Whitman and Sidney Lanier, along with the lyric passages of Tennyson.[29] The agrarian idealist loved to quote lines from John Addington Symonds' "The Days That Are To Be":[30]

> These things shall be—a loftier race
> Than e'er the world has known shall rise,
> The light of freedom in their souls,
> The light of knowledge in their eyes.

Both reluctant politicians, but natural born leaders, they each entered politics with a vision of what the world one day might become.

Years later Irene Parlby shared with Barbara Villy Cormack, her biographer, her impressions of Henry Wise Wood. Although the meetings at the Lougheed Building took place decades earlier, her recall was total and warm: "I remember him so well at board meetings, sitting up at the end of the table, sometimes with his eyes shut, apparently taking no notice of what was going on or being said by the various members. Then he would suddenly look up and very slowly and clearly sum up all the discussion, clarifying all the wordy speeches and bringing wisdom and logic to bear."[31] In turn, the UFA president held her in the highest regard. When Irene retired as president of the United Farm Women of Alberta in 1920, he made a presentation on behalf of both men's and women's sections of the movement. Henry presented her with a little velvet box, which within contained an exquisite ring set with one single clear blue diamond.[32] Ten years later when Irene asked to retire from cabinet and the legislature, the veteran UFA president himself earnestly asked her to reconsider: "No one else could have made the contribution you have; no one else can fill your place."[33] At his urging she remained.

Henry Wise Wood and the UFA supported what Irene Parlby and the United Farm Women of Alberta fought for: equality between male and female. During Will Tregillus's presidency the UFA had welcomed women as members. Accepting women as economic and physical helpmates the UFA endorsed voting rights and a minimum wage for all women, and property rights for married women. It helped Alberta women to obtain the provincial franchise in 1916, the year Henry Wise Wood became UFA president. With the UFA victory in 1921 Premier Greenfield appointed Irene Parlby to cabinet. She became minister without portfolio, the first female cabinet minister in the history of the province. In office she campaigned for women's property rights, education and improved rural health care. She became in 1929 a member of the "Famous Five," the five women who contested and won their case before the Judicial Committee of the Privy Council, then the Supreme Court of Law in the British Empire, to have women

Irene Parlby. Glenbow Archives/NA-273-1.

This cover of the 23 November 1921 issue of The Grain Growers' Guide shows its fierce animosity to the protective tariff. Glenbow Library.

A MODERN DAVID AND GOLIATH

recognized as "persons" at all levels of law and government in Canadian law. Alberta's UFA government was the only one in Canada to support their appeal.[34]

When invited to run for premier, Wood declined. From his Lougheed Building office he masterminded the landslide that ended the Liberal regime, but he did not want the position. He considered the UFA presidency a far more important job.

Personally Henry Wise Wood had long opposed the farmers' entrance into politics. In the early 1920s he devoted a tremendous amount of time to help form the Alberta Wheat Pool, a voluntary co-operative. The Pool would reduce the role of the middlepersons in the grain trade and provide farmers with bargaining power as a union of many sellers delivering a product to a small number of buyers. Each farmer would receive the same price per bushel for the same grade of wheat. On 29 October 1923, the Wheat Pool opened its head office on the second floor of the Lougheed Building in one-half of a large room; within six years it grew to occupy two-and-a-half floors.[35]

John Brownlee worked in 1921 on the Lougheed's third floor, the headquarters of the United Grain Growers (UGG). Henry Wise Wood had heartily endorsed the 1917 amalgamation of the Alberta Co-operative Elevator Company, which Will Tregillus had headed before his death in late 1914, and the Grain Growers Grain Company, the large Manitoba-based wheat co-operative. Wood looked upon the UGG's lawyer, who had helped the UFA with legal advice, as the logical choice for premier. Some of the farmer members-elect supported him, but due to his profession, which he felt would not sit well with the UFA rank and file, Brownlee turned down the nomination. With Henry Wise Wood and John Brownlee out of the race, the MLAs-elect unanimously selected Herbert Greenfield who, in turn, appointed Brownlee his attorney general.

In retrospect, it is extraordinary that the UFA MLAs chose the province's next premier in a building named after a key figure in the "enemy's" camp. Sir James Lougheed, who had been knighted in June 1916 in recognition of his wartime cabinet work,[36] served in 1921 as both the leader of the Conservative Party in the senate and Minister of the Interior in Prime Minister Arthur Meighen's cabinet. As a member of cabinet the senator endorsed the hated tariff that forced farmers to buy expensive eastern manufactured goods in a protected market at the same time they had to sell their wheat in an unprotected one. In 1921 the Conservatives raised the tariff again.[37] While the farmers called for withdrawal of the high tariff, the election of senators through senate reform and the elimination of titles like the one given their landlord ("tin-pot titles have no place in a democratic country" (*Grain Growers' Guide*, 1918)),[38] they loved Sir James's building. By 1921 the UFA occupied almost the entire second floor.

Political power proved a challenge for the farmers' government. Only one of the newly elected UFA members had ever before sat in the legislature. In terms of his administrative ability the hale-fellow-well-met Premier Greenfield proved ineffective. The government needed someone skilled in law, competent in administration and self-confident in dealings with non-farmer groups. Virtually every issue before the government necessitated Brownlee's legal advice. A flow of correspondence from the premier's office regularly arrived at the attorney general's with a simple memo attached: "Kindly let Mr. Greenfield know what to reply to this."[39] In 1925 the UFA caucus acted upon

Henry Wise Wood's initial advice and made corporate lawyer John Brownlee, the most competent UFA member both within and outside the assembly, premier of Alberta.

As attorney general and then premier, John Brownlee pushed himself to the limits with work. Fortunately three of the study books for his Sunday School classes have survived. Francis Greenwood Peabody, professor of Christian Morals at Harvard University, wrote the series, entitled *Mornings in the College Chapel*. He prepared the volumes to help those who gave informal and brief religious instruction. Of all his essays, one in particular received John Brownlee's undivided attention, as he freely marked in the margins of it. The third volume of the series, published in 1911, contains Professor Peabody's essay, "Work and Revelation," inspired by the passage from John II: 9—"But the servants which drew the water knew." Brownlee put a double line in the margin beside Peabody's comment: "the chief source of self-respect, self-discipline, intellectual power, and moral growth is to be found in the work one has to do."[40]

The intense-looking man, hair parted in the middle, with the rimless glasses, high, tight-winged collar and dark bulky suit, worked constantly.[41] As attorney general the number of issues he had to attend to was mind-boggling. Yet at the same time he held his cabinet post he continued, until he became premier, as chief counsel for the UGG.[42] He also maintained ties with his law firm, John E. Brownlee and Company, with offices in the Lougheed Building. The firm operated under retainer for both the UGG and UFA. True, he received assistance from T. C. Rankine, and later Bill Hall and Marsh Porter, as staff and then partners, but his firm in Calgary still demanded his time.[43] Only in 1932 did the premier sell his law practice to Marsh Porter.[44] Chester Bloom of *The Calgary Herald* commented of John Brownlee in 1927 shortly after he had become premier: "He is a prodigious worker, so much so, in fact, that during the exhausting night and day sessions of the concluding weeks of a legislative session the nervous energy sometimes drains his physical endurance to the limit and he passes sleepless nights."[45]

Brownlee led the UFA to victory in the 1926 provincial election, helped by the economic upswing of the mid-1920s. His success in gaining provincial control from the federal government over Alberta's land and natural resources in 1930 led to another electoral victory that year. But the Great Depression hit the UFA badly, with record-low grain prices and rising urban unemployment. In 1933 personal scandals also hurt the party, namely a suit against Premier Brownlee for the seduction of a young woman named Vivian MacMillan. The statement of claim alleged that the premier had arranged for the teenaged girl to move from her hometown of Edson to Edmonton to take a provincial government clerical job. He seduced her when she was eighteen years old in 1930 and had ongoing sexual relations with her over a three-year period in various locations, including his office, home and car.[46]

The jury in the first trial found that Brownlee had indeed seduced the young woman, but William C. Ives, the judge, disagreed. In his formal judgment on 2 July 1934, Acting Chief Justice Ives overturned the jury's verdict and overruled the damage awards.[47] But the mere fact that the jury had unanimously sided with Vivian MacMillan ended Brownlee's political career, and the premier knew it. He immediately announced that he would resign as soon as the UFA chose his successor.

Were the charges true, or was it character assassination of the first order? The Appeal Court of Alberta upheld Judge Ives. But a subsequent appeal of their decision to the Supreme Court of Canada succeeded in 1937. Rejecting Judge Ives's ruling, the Supreme Court awarded damages to Vivian MacMillan. Now it was Brownlee's turn. He pursued his final option and appealed to the Judicial Committee of the Privy Council in London, then the supreme court of law in the British Commonwealth. In their judgment, rendered 4 June 1940, the top court dismissed Brownlee's appeal. The case closed with the awarding of damages of $10,000 to Vivian MacMillan.

Was he guilty of seduction? Brownlee's biographer, Franklin Foster, provides this summary: "In general, those who knew Brownlee least were readiest to accept the charges at face value, while those closest to him found it most difficult to believe he had been living a double life."[48] To those in his closest circle the charge was totally ridiculous. Foster continues: "The idea of passionless, remote, cautious and calculating John Brownlee behaving like a love torn teenager discovering sex was ludicrous. That the man who lived in his briefcase, who virtually was the Government of Alberta, with all the work load that that entailed, went out two or three nights a week for quickie sex on district backroads seemed, to say the least, improbable."[49] Irene Parlby put absolutely no stock at all in the charges. She knew him well: "I have the greatest admiration for him, both as a political leader and as a person."[50] Nor did Henry Wise Wood and his wife believe the "slander." On the wall of their guest room at Carstairs they kept on display a large photo of John Brownlee.[51]

Once he retired and returned to his law practice in Edmonton, the UGG appointed the former premier once again as their general counsel. In 1942 the company that he helped to form a quarter-of-a-century earlier named him their first vice-president. He returned to the same office on the third floor of the Lougheed Building he had occupied before the provincial election of 1921.[52] Upon the retirement of UGG President R. S. Law in 1948, John Brownlee obtained the top job. As president he spent about forty percent of his time in the Winnipeg headquarters, and the remainder in Calgary.[53] Although always busy, in summer he always remembered to ask rural visitors the key question: "How are the crops?"[54]

Even before the Brownlee sex scandal hit the press, the UFA had been losing membership. After Henry Wise Wood's retirement as UFA president in 1930 many in the UFA executive moved toward socialism. This cost members. The sex scandal accelerated the exodus. Many disaffected UFA members found a much more acceptable home in the Social Credit study groups soon to be organized across the province. In 1934, Richard Reid, the chair of the UFA meeting in 1921, which chose Herbert Greenfield as leader, became the third UFA premier. A year later William Aberhart and his Social Credit movement swept Reid and the UFA away to political oblivion in the provincial election of 1935. The results in the 1935 election revealed that some ninety percent of UFA members transferred their allegiance to Social Credit.[55] The UFA left

the political sphere to concentrate on service and agricultural products for farmers. The United Farmers of Alberta Co-Operative Limited remains an active business operation today.

Aberhart himself provides another link with the historic Lougheed Building/ Grand Theatre. In the early 1920s, some years prior to the future Social Credit premier's entry into politics, the high school principal and freelance evangelist used the Grand for his Sunday afternoon Bible Conferences—Biblical prophecy being his central theme. Shunning mainstream churches, the unordained lay preacher branched out on his own. As stated in a 4 March 1922 *Calgary Herald* summary of the weekly series, "The Prophetic Bible Conference, holding meetings in the Grand theatre for the past 20 or 25 consecutive Sundays is … one of the unique home productions of the city."[56] In his prophetic lectures Aberhart introduced the Appearing of Christ (the Rapture) and the Second Coming, separated by a seven-year parenthesis. "True" Christians would mysteriously go to heaven at the Rapture only to return seven years later with Christ to begin the Battle of Armageddon, which would begin the Millennium, a thousand-year reign of peace on earth.[57] His preaching electrified audiences. At his talk on 7 October 1923, the Grand filled to capacity one hour before it began.[58] After the Grand the evangelist moved over the Palace Theatre, where, in November 1925, he began broadcasting his biblical sermons over CFCN radio from the theatre's stage.[59]

The handsome old Lougheed Building could claim an association with both the vanquished UFA and the victorious Social Credit, as well as with the socialists. In 1933 Amelia Turner, who worked in UFA offices on the second floor,[60] ran in a Calgary provincial by-election as the first Co-operative Commonwealth Federation (CCF) candidate in Canada.[61] Already she had served as a Labour Party Calgary School Board trustee.[62] The previous year she attended the founding convention of the CCF in Regina. In the provincial election she lost, but only by a narrow margin.

Social Credit's political opponents immediately before the provincial election of 1940 also had a connection with the Lougheed. Just after the provincial election of 1935, a People's League, later called the Unity Council, was formed. This non-partisan coalition united Liberals, Conservatives and many others without party affiliation opposed to Aberhart. Just before the outbreak of the Second World War the Unity Council of Alberta took over offices 430 to 432 in the Lougheed Building. It worked to have independent, anti-Aberhart candidates nominated for the next provincial election without regard to their normal party affiliations. Changing their name once again to the Independent Movement, they did very well in the provincial election of 21 March 1940, almost defeating Aberhart.[63] Yet the coalition had no uniform platform, little organization and no leader. Dissension soon surfaced among the elected members. After the election the Independent Movement declined as their MLAs returned to their old parties. Apparently the Unity Council, later the Independent Movement, left the Lougheed in 1940.[64]

Nor was that the Lougheed's last link with provincial politics. Almost half-a-century to the month from the momentous UFA meeting of July 1921, the venerable old building participated in an urban, not a rural revolution. In the late 1960s and early

William Aberhart at the first anniversary picnic of the Social Credit electoral victory, St. George's Island, Calgary, September 1936. Ernest Manning appears seated second from the right. Glenbow Archives/NB-17-207.

Election poster for Amelia Turner, candidate for the CCF, January 1933. Glenbow Archives/Smith Fonds, file 215.

Calgary Candidate of

THE CO-OPERATIVE COMMONWEALTH FEDERATION

AMELIA TURNER

(Nominated by Canadian Labor Party, with endorsement of all other Calgary Units of the Co-operative Commonwealth Federation as follows: Calgary National Labor Club, Calgary U. F. A. branches and Co-operative Commonwealth Club.)

THE CANDIDATE

MISS TURNER, the Labor-C.C.F. Candidate, was born in Ontario, and brought up on a farm in Southern Alberta. She has lived in Calgary since 1913, and has had extensive experience in the publishing and advertising business. At present she is employed in an important executive position as advertising manager of *The U.F.A.* Miss Turner has been an active member of the Labor Party for fifteen years. She was first elected to the School Board in the school book recall election in the spring of 1925, when she defeated the then chairman of the Board by a very large majority. She was re-elected in 1927, 1929 and 1931, heading the polls on the last two occasions. For several years she has been Vice-chairman of the Board.

WORK AND VOTE for AMELIA TURNER
The Labor-C. C. F. Candidate in the Provincial By-election

COMMITTEE ROOMS, Labor Temple, 229 - 11th Avenue East
Telephones M4201, M3401 and M1759

1970s the penthouse on the seventh floor housed the provincial headquarters of Peter Lougheed's Progressive Conservative party. On 30 August 1971, the grandson of the building's namesake, Sir James Lougheed, won the provincial election and ended thirty-six years of Social Credit rule.

Chapter Ten

Sir James at the Top
and After

J AMES LOUGHEED REACHED THE PINNACLE OF HIS POLITICAL CAREER immediately after the Great War. On 27 May 1921, journalist Tom King provided a vivid physical description of Senator Lougheed in the *Toronto Star Weekly*. An energetic-looking man approached the senate chamber; "... a well built athletic man with buoyant steps comes down the corridor. He nods to one, speaks to another, and stops by a third to exchange a word of greeting. You would say that he was an English visitor, probably an army officer, or a hunter of big game, probably under 40." After he removes his hat closer scrutiny reveals that his black hair is thinning, and his closely cropped moustache contains some silver. "You begin to think that after all he must be 45." Not so. "You will be surprised to learn that he is 67, and that the man you took for a English visitor has lived all his life in Canada, being no less a personage than Sir James Lougheed, minister of the interior, and the leader of the Dominion Senate."[1]

During World War One, Minister without Portfolio and Senate Government Leader Lougheed gained several important assignments. Prime Minister Borden made him acting minister of the militia in the summer of 1915, a two-month posting in which he acquitted himself well despite having no military background. More importantly, Borden appointed him chair of the Military Hospitals Commission in June 1915, a post in which his vast administrative experience prepared him well. The provision of hospital accommodation and convalescent homes proved an ever-increasing challenge as Canadian casualties soared. Although a somewhat authoritarian administrator, he had the knack of choosing efficient, capable civil servants to run the commission.[2] The commission appointment was one of the most significant moments of his public career.[3] In recognition of his increasing government responsibilities James Lougheed was knighted in June 1916, the only Albertan ever to receive this honour.

When the prime minister established the Department of Soldiers' Civil Re-establishment in early 1918 he selected Sir James as its head. His new position required that he oversee the general outreach to sick and wounded veterans, and assist the dependents of the sixty thousand Canadian armed services personnel who died in the war. This was an enormous responsibility. More than seventy thousand Canadians returned to Canada with disabilities. The war dead left behind more than thirty thousand widows and children dependent on federal government help for their survival. By the end of June 1920 the department had a staff of ten thousand employees.[4] As minister the senator did a first-rate job.[5] Upon his departure from the department, his staff presented the senate with his portrait, painted by J. W. L. Forster, the well-known Canadian artist. The inscription below the painting thanks Sir James for his "untiring efforts and support on behalf of disabled ex-soldiers of the Great War 1914-1918."[6]

In July 1920 the senator rose still higher in cabinet ranking. He had proved himself during the war. After Borden's resignation, Arthur Meighen, the new prime minister, appointed him minister of the interior, one of the most senior cabinet posts. Meighen also made Lougheed superintendent of Indian affairs and minister of mines. The new prime minister had such faith in Sir James that he also named him acting prime minister during a two-week absence in November 1920, and again for several weeks in October 1921.[7]

The senator's work with the Military Hospitals Commission and his role in cabinet as minister of Soldiers' Civil Re-establishment won over one of his harshest critics in Alberta. Fifteen years earlier Bob Edwards in the *Calgary Eye Opener* termed him "a CPR solicitor of no particular note" (5 May 1906). In a later issue that same year he referred to the newly appointed Conservative senate leader as "an offensively aggressive promoter of corporation interests to the detriment of the people" (6 October 1906). Yet, during Lougheed's tour of duty as minister of Soldiers' Civil Re-establishment, Eye Opener Bob changed his tune. Of his handling of the department the unusually severe critic wrote: "He is a great administrator, shrewd as the devil and full of the milk of human kindness" (23 August 1919). When he learned of Sir James's appointment as minister of the interior in July 1920 Edwards rejoiced: "Sir James Lougheed's appointment meets with universal approbation." (17 July 1920).

Bob Edwards' compliments about Sir James did not extend to the institution he continued to head, and to which he had already devoted three decades of his life. Over the years Eye Opener Bob directed many vitriolic political attacks against the Canadian senate,[8] such as this earlier tirade: "It is the hypocrisy, the bogus prestige and the spirit of make-believe which pervades the red chamber, making it redolent of pompous humbug and aristocratic mystery, that irritates the people so much" (22 December 1906). In the pages of the *Calgary Eye Opener* its fiery editor advocated abolition of the senate or, at least the reform of "that important relic."[9] Yet, Bob Edwards came to like, even to admire, "the Senator."

Over the course of his long parliamentary career, as Minister of the Interior, Superintendent of Indian Affairs, and Minister of Mines, Lougheed had learned to deal simultaneously with a myriad of complex and involved issues. He was very time efficient. Later the *Ottawa Citizen* recalled: "When Minister of the Interior his desk would be cleared in an hour for his mind was keen and his decision quick."[10] In addition to his cabinet duties he also had his responsibilities as senate government leader. In 1920 and 1921, for example, he contributed to senate debates on such varied topics as the Bulgarian Peace Treaty, First Nations land rights in British Columbia and Canada's entry into the Court of International Justice.[11]

Without knowing it as the time, the new minister of the interior gained lasting commemoration of the Lougheed name in the High Arctic. In early 1921 both Vilhjalmur Stefansson, the Canadian Arctic explorer, and Sir Ernest Shackleton, the

The Lougheeds with family and friends at their cottage in Banff in the early 1920s. Senator Lougheed appears in the centre at the front, Belle is second from the left. Glenbow Archives/PD 132, vol. 20, #510.50.

great explorer of Antarctica, vied to obtain the cabinet's appointment to lead a major Canadian Arctic expedition. Stefansson had already traveled through the High Arctic on the Canadian government's behalf in the mid-1910s. In an attempt to curry favour with the senior politicians the imaginative self-promoter suggested appropriate names for two islands he had located; Meighen for one and Lougheed for another. The Arctic veteran did not obtain the appointment, nor did Shackleton, but the island Stefansson named after the interior minister was later recognized as Lougheed Island. Today it lies within the new territory of Nunavut.[12]

All the knowledge the senator amassed over his long political career now served him well as a member of the Meighen cabinet. Senator William Benjamin Ross, a Conservative from Prince Edward Island, later recalled how knowledgeable he was in so many different areas: "In all the years which I was thrown very often in his company I never spent a dull five minutes: it did not matter where one was going, or what one was doing. If travelling in the cars through the country, and interested in the landscape, Sir James Lougheed was also interested in the scenery, the farms, and everything that was going on. He took great interest in railways, and there was no subject that could be mentioned on which he did not know at least something, and on many he was thoroughly well informed."[13]

At last Sir James relaxed a little with the press. For once the senator talked about himself and his early life. The new candour revealed a self-made man with a justifiable pride in his success. To a *Toronto Star Weekly* columnist he confided: "I'm talking freely about things I haven't discussed with anybody for I don't know how long." He spoke of his youth in Cabbagetown, a section of Toronto that then had "one-story houses, on humble streets." He continued: "Though I was born in Brampton, we moved when I was a child, and my boyhood and earlier manhood were spent in Toronto. We used to have great times around the Don ... I can't visit my old home, as so many of my old friends visit theirs. It used to stand—I wonder if you know the place—right where there are a couple of horse troughs between the Queen and King approaches to the Don station bridge ... I had worked as a carpenter for a while, but managed to get through Osgoode Hall." Then, a new beginning, he left for the west and within a year or so in Winnipeg moved to Calgary—"the C.P.R. wasn't up to the foothills then." Soon he became "one of the busiest lawyers in a town of two thousand people." He married "a Hardisty of Lady Strathcona's family ... my father-in-law having been chief factor of the company ... I came to the Senate in 1889, in Sir John Macdonald's time. I was the junior member of the house—only 35."

Hidden beneath his stolid "British" exterior one interviewer discovered Sir James had a sense of humour. When he first entered the upper house over thirty years earlier, an old man, "who had the idea that at thirty-five a western lawyer was a mere boy, and might be rude to the elder statesmen among whom he was to sit," took him aside. He "reminded me of Mark Twain's advice to little girls—'don't sass old people, unless they sass you first'."[14]

James Lougheed had good reason to be proud of his accomplishments during the Great War. His appearance at the "Great Public Testimonial" in Toronto, organized to honour Canadian soldiers blinded in the war, proved a special moment. On the evening of 7 January 1919, he spoke to three to four thousand people crowded into Massey Hall. The other speakers included Sir Arthur Pearson, the Englishman who had done so much to help rehabilitate blinded veterans; Sir William Hearst, the premier of Ontario; and Captain Edward Baker, one of the founders of the newly formed Canadian National Institute for the Blind (CNIB). Blinded by a sniper's bullet in 1915, Captain Baker had benefited greatly from his training at Sir Arthur's Dunstan's Hostel in London. After his return to Canada Captain Baker was appointed by Sir James to head his ministry's training and after-care program for Canada's 150 war blind. At the Massey Hall meeting Sir James promised support for the CNIB "that will not be disappointing."[15]

To the city of his youth Sir James returned a federal cabinet minister, and a knight. "He doesn't talk quite like the old Cabbagetowner he is," one Toronto journalist later commented.[16] He returned with what some people chose to regard as an English accent. But as he freely admitted his Toronto origins, it is clear that he regarded his "British" way of speaking—his vocabulary and inflections—as simply those of a well-educated individual. His model of correct behaviour always came from Britain, the imperial centre.

Jim Lougheed's Toronto had been transformed in his lifetime from a small city of 50,000 people to a metropolitan centre of 500,000. When he left the city in 1882 it had not a single tall building; now the city had nearly thirty buildings over six stories high. The tallest, the Royal Bank Building, was twenty stories.[17] In Toronto, one strong personal link to his boyhood remained: "Emerson," as he called him, his life-long friend, the benchmark against which he could compare his own accomplishments. In many ways Emerson Coatsworth,[18] then a York County judge, and living in Rosedale, remained identifiably the same. In the words of the *Toronto Star*, he was known for his "Methodism, his Orangeism and his Conservatism … a Coatsworthian Trinity of which he never needed to be ashamed."[19] The "Coatsworthian Trinity" proved a winning combination in Toronto. Lougheed's boyhood friend from Cabbagetown had served as mayor of Toronto from 1906 to 1908.[20]

In addition to his political successes immediately after the Great War, the senator's business interests prospered in 1920 and 1921. As a beneficial consequence of his parents' modest economic status, he remained careful with his money. As one journalist reported: "'Waste not, want not,' is still a golden rule for the senator."[21] But, as every good rule has its exception, Sir James had one extravagance, one greatly promoted by his wife. He loved theatres and spent a great deal of money on them. In December 1920 he attended with Lady Lougheed and the Lydiatts the opening of the New Empire, in Edmonton, a theatre in the Montreal-based Trans-Canada Theatres chain, in which he made a substantial investment.[22]

To guarantee his investment in Trans-Canada, Sir James insisted that Jeff Lydiatt become one of the three vice-presidents.[23] In 1920 the chain began well, with a circuit of eighty theatres across Canada. By the summer of 1921 this number increased to 125.[24] Trans-Canada brought to Canada big box office draws from London and New York. The first Trans-Canada production at the Grand featured well-known English-born actor Tyrone Power, Sr., in "The Servant in the House" and "The Little Brother" in April 1920.[25] That November one of the biggest shows of all arrived—"Chu Chin Chow." The spectacular three-hour musical based on Ali Baba and the Forty Thieves had played to capacity in London for five straight seasons. The company sponsored by Trans-Canada came direct from the Century Theatre in New York. It included three hundred people.[26] "The Wanderer," a New York production based on the biblical story of the prodigal son, travelled with a cast of 100. It followed in December.[27] From his office on the fifth floor of the Lougheed Building Jeff Lydiatt directed the company's operations throughout Western Canada.[28]

Revenue also came to the senator from his law firm. Although he no longer actively participated in Lougheed and Bennett, he automatically received $3,000 from the annual net income of the firm. Swamped with legal work, Lougheed and Bennett had grown into Alberta's largest law office.[29] It spilled across two floors of the Clarence Block on 8th Avenue West. Although it was seldom used, James retained an elegantly furnished office there with oriental rugs and imported drapes. [30] The firm's clients included four chartered banks, the CPR, the HBC, Imperial Oil and Burns and Company.[31] In September 1921 Lougheed and Bennett achieved a rare distinction when R. B. Bennett joined Sir James in Meighen's cabinet as minister of justice. Few law firms in Canadian history have ever had two lawyers from the same firm in the federal cabinet at the same time.

Over the years the senator had moved his investment business out of Lougheed and Bennett. His brokerage firm, Lougheed and Taylor, formed in 1911, now handled his mortgage and loan and insurance business.[32] No problem existed when Sir James wished to find his two top business associates: Jeff Lydiatt had his office in the Lougheed Building in the early 1920s, and Edmund Taylor and his family lived in the Lougheed's Penthouse (1920–1922), until they moved to their new home on Frontenac Avenue in Mount Royal.[33] The Western Canadian financier ran the senator's investment portfolio and looked after his many real estate holdings.

Senator Lougheed narrowly escaped one major investment loss. Along with R. B. Bennett, Thomas Skinner, rancher A. E. Cross and several others he was an original shareholder in Bill Herron's and Archibald Dingman's Calgary Petroleum Products Limited, the syndicate that drilled the successful Dingman well in Turner Valley in May 1914. By late 1920 it had produced 50,000 barrels before a fire in October 1920 destroyed its extraction plant, forcing it to shut down operations. As the plant, built at a cost of $70,000, was not covered by insurance, it looked as if Calgary Petroleum Products was finished.[34] But then Imperial Oil, anxious to intensify its search for oil in Alberta, stepped in and agreed to acquire its properties. Calgary Petroleum Products had its offices on the fourth floor of the Lougheed Building, where one of the early agreements for the transfer of properties to Imperial was signed.[35]

In Sir James's final settlement with Imperial, instead of losing his investment in Calgary Petroleum Products, he obtained two thousand twenty-five dollar par shares of the new Royalite Company.[36] The bonanza came three years later. The second Turner Valley oil strike began on the night of 14 October 1924, when Imperial's Royalite No. 4

well blew in with a measured daily flow of six hundred barrels of light crude. By 1925, Royalite No. 4 had increased annual production in the Turner Valley a thousand per cent over 1922 levels. [37] In that year the twenty-five dollar par value Royalite shares were quoted at three hundred dollars per share, a twelve-fold mark-up.[38]

Even after the creation of Imperial's Royalite, Archibald Dingman kept his Calgary Petroleum Products office in the Lougheed Building. It was maintained superbly by Jim Hunter, the Lougheed Building's manager. Calgary Petroleum Products remained in the Lougheed Building until Dingman's death in 1936.[39] The senator had a talent for hiring good employees. Jim Hunter, a Scot from Perthshire, Scotland, proved one of the best. He and his wife Agnes and baby daughter came to Calgary in 1911, just before the Lougheed Building opened. Jim belonged to a large family of seven children. In Perthshire his dad had a small farm and worked as a road toll collector. Family members today remember being told that Jim's mother cooked meals in a large iron pot over an open fire. Once out of school he apprenticed as a carpenter and stonemason. As the senator had a carpentry background himself, one can understand how the two men would get along. Sir James later made James Hunter his building superintendent for all his properties. The Scot, who spoke with a soft Scottish burr, liked to quote Robbie Burns. He loved sports, soccer and, in Canada, hockey. But his greatest passion was fly-fishing at Sheep Creek, up the Highwood and in the Kananaskis, his good fishing partner being Alf Shackleford, who looked after all the boilers for the Lougheed properties. Jim served the senator, and later the Lougheed Estate, for forty-three years.[40]

Politically and economically the senator stood in the top echelon of Alberta's power elite. For three decades James and Belle also headed Calgary's society circles. The visit of Edward, Prince of Wales, to Calgary in mid-September 1919 confirms their importance. The prince's late summer tour of Canada succeeded wonderfully. Analyzing the success of it several years later, journalist Fred Griffin wrote that the future King Emperor stepped "auspiciously into a moment and a mood. Thousands of the youth of Canada had been sacrificed in Europe for reasons which were already less certain than they seemed. People sought something clean, honest, hopeful." And then across the North Atlantic came the handsome young prince, "shy, smiling, unspoilt, magnetic, in appearance and spirit young as the morning."[41] Calgary's leading couple welcomed His Royal Highness with open arms.

On Sunday morning September 14th, the Royal train arrived in Calgary. Late that afternoon, the Lougheeds entertained Edward at a garden party at Beaulieu. From outside the grounds a crowd of thousands awaited to cheer the prince, who reached the Lougheed House at five. The weather co-operated brilliantly with warm sunshine, allowing the hundred carefully selected guests to circulate on the lawns then "at the very best of season." A string orchestra played in a marquee situated in the centre of the west lawn, where staff served tea. *The Albertan* provided a word picture for its readers: "Masses of vivid flowers against the borders of green trees and foliage were a effective background for pretty light colored summer frocks worn by the women." The guests included the Anglican bishop and Mrs. Pinkham, the Catholic bishop, the editors and their wives of both *The Calgary Herald* and *The Albertan*, as well as many from

James's professional world and Belle's wide social circle. The guest list included their two sons, Norman and Edgar, just out of uniform; their twenty-three-year-old daughter Dorothy and some of her friends; business and political associates like R. B. Bennett and Lieutenant-Governor Brett were present, as were the Winters and Lydiatts from the arts world; General McDonald, the military commander of southern Alberta and his wife attended, as did Pat Bergeron, the president of the Ranchmen's Club; George Walker, the CPR's solicitor in Calgary, was also there.[42] Belle knew how to make a good party by inviting guests from a variety of backgrounds.

That same evening the prince met the senator again. Sir James sat on the Prince Edward's immediate right at the eight o'clock dinner held at the Ranchmen's Club.[43] Club President Pat Bergeron possibly made arrangements to help convey the prince and his entourage from the Palliser to the club, as he lived near the Palliser in the Lougheed Building.[44] No problem existed for the senator to make it on time, as he lived across the street from the club. The Ranchmen's Club was located on the very spot where his former partner Peter McCarthy's house once stood. At the dinner Sir James proposed the toast to the King, to which the Prince responded.

During dinner Edward and Sir James undoubtedly discussed contemporary world and imperial issues. No doubt one name popped up, that of the only individual they both knew who belonged to both the British House of Commons and the Ranchmen's Club: William Dudley Ward. The prince knew Dudley Ward as Britain's vice-chamberlain, the member of the House of Commons responsible for writing a summary of parliamentary proceedings for the monarch every day the House of Commons sat. Such reports were composed before dinner. He discussed the proceedings up to that point, along with a note of any happenings of importance from the previous day after the last report was written. Vice-Chamberlain Dudley Ward also had some residual responsibility for the running of the royal household—he was summoned for duty at garden parties at Buckingham Palace.[45] A more onerous duty for Dudley Ward involved his work as the Liberal Party's whip. This necessitated regular communication with Prime Minister Lloyd George.[46]

William Dudley Ward had just the right credentials to act as the liaison between the Royal Family and the House of Commons. Coming from an ancient English family, he was a nephew of Lord Esher and a cousin to Lord Dudley.[47] A graduate of Eton, and Trinity College, Cambridge, he was called to the bar in 1904. An excellent athlete, Dudley Ward rowed for three years with the Cambridge eight and later became a member of the English Olympic rowing team. Since 1906 he had represented Southampton in the House of Commons.[48] In Parliament he knew well the rising Liberal politician Winston Churchill, to whom he sent a congratulatory letter after his marriage in 1908.[49] Before his own 1913 marriage to Winifred Birkin in London, Dudley Ward regularly visited Canada.[50] Senator Lougheed knew him as he had purchased in 1911 one of his properties on 8th Avenue, the building now known as the Ward Block.[51] The Ranchmen's Club elected him a non-resident privileged member in May 1912.[52]

It turned out to be a raucous evening at the club. Colonel H. G. Henderson, Military Secretary to the governor general of Canada, the Canadian official responsible for making sure the tour ran smoothly, later gave a full report to the Duke of

Edward, Prince of Wales waving to crowds on 7th Avenue near lst St. East, mid-September 1919. Glenbow Archives/NB-16-10.

Pat Bergeron, who as president of the Ranchmen's Club hosted the prince at a dinner at the club, 14 September 1919. Glenbow Archives/NA-813-10.

William Dudley Ward. Photo courtesy of Larry Winter.

Devonshire. Although prohibition had been in force for three years the Alberta government had seen fit to allow liquor at the function. "The Ranchmen rose to the occasion, and at one moment during the evening a judge of the Provincial Supreme Court saw fit to rise and sing a little song, the chorus of which runs: 'Another little drink won't do us any harm'." At this point Pat Bergeron became concerned and asked if he should end the boisterous concert. The colonel advised no, as the "guest on his right," the heir to the throne, was "by no means the least vociferous of those who were singing."[53]

The evening concluded with an incredible display of high spirits. The immediate past president of the Ranchmen's, George Peet, led the pack.[54] Peet had come to Canada from Ireland at age twenty-one in the early 1890s. After a few false starts (prospecting, coal and insurance, CPR work) he began a real estate business in Calgary with William Toole.[55] The firm, Toole Peet, remains in operation over a century later. George made a big impression on the prince. A real character, he loved to wear white spats and all the other accoutrements of Victorian Ireland.[56] Claude Smith, assistant manager at the Grand in the 1920s, remembered that the eccentric realtor wore a monocle to the theatre. He attended regularly every Monday night, the evening the Ranchmen's Club reserved the front row.[57] Possibly George told Prince Edward that he had known the man after whom his Calgary hotel was named—Captain John Palliser—who had lived a couple of kilometres from George's boyhood home at Tramore, County Watford.[58]

The prince never forgot what followed the formal dinner. Thirty-five years later he described the "war dance" in a letter sent 13 April 1954 to his friend Alick Newton in Calgary. Alick had mentioned that George Peet had passed away in December: "I was sorry to hear about poor old George Peet; he was a great character and the Ranchmens' Club won't be the same without him. I will never forget his lighting a fire on the floor in one of the rooms after the dinner the Club gave me in 1919, around which we all stumbled painlessly in an Indian war dance!"[59]

Nor did the festivities end with the war dance. Signatures of those involved in the grand finale survive. Bob Newbolt, an original member of the club, who ranched at Indus, east of Calgary, near where the Bow meets the Highwood, attended the dinner.[60] Unusual dress for him, he came in white tie. At the height of the post-dinner festivities he made a request. Bob asked everyone still present to sign his white shirt. He took it off and etched his brand on the fabric with a scratchy pen, "DIO," the abbreviated form of "Dammit I'm Off." The others followed. Nearly forty years later Bob's widow donated the treasured object, never worn or cleaned again, to the Glenbow Museum.[61] Many of the signatures remain quite legible. "James A. Lougheed" does not appear but the honoured guest's does, "Edward P." Other identifiable signatures include: George Peet; Pat Bergeron; cattleman Joseph "7-U" Brown;[62] rancher A. E. Cross; CPR solicitor George Walker;[63] Laurence J. Clarke, clerk of the Alberta Superior Court in Calgary;[64] Captain Lord Claud Hamilton, younger son of the Duke of Abercorn, Great War Grenadier Guards veteran, and equerry to the Prince of Wales.[65]

What did the prince think of the evening? A letter he wrote immediately upon his return to his third-floor suite at the Palliser tells all.[66] Appearances can be deceiving. No paragon of virtue, the young man already had a mistress, the woman he termed

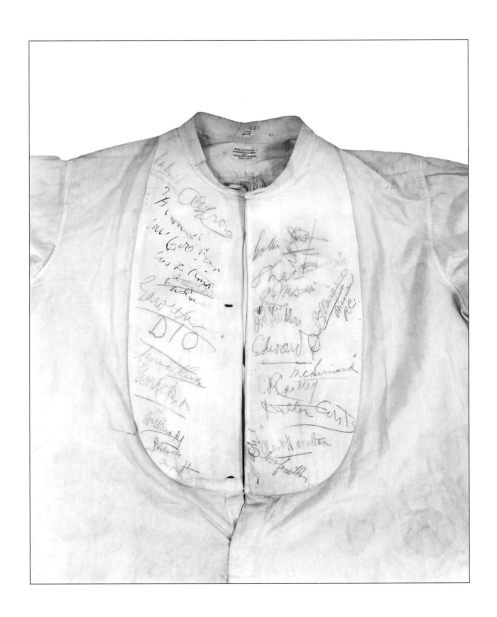

Bob Newbolt's shirt, with autographs, including that of Edward, Prince of Wales, "Edward P.," in the centre, right hand side. Glenbow Archives/C-4384.

"his precious beloved little Madonna."[67] His letters to her were published in 1998. In his 12:30 a.m. note of September 15th, Edward reviewed the evening behind him: "I've just got away from a vewy [very] wet & noisy dinner at the Ranchman's [Ranchmen's] club, though I think the title implies tight men, doesn't it darling? They are a fine crowd of Westerners, but God they drink & they don't let dryness worry them much; it was stiff cocktails & Scotch tonight followed by dirty songs & guess I was lucky to be able to escape before midnight...."[68] He ended the note affectionately, then addressed it to "Mrs. Freda Dudley Ward"—the wife of William Dudley Ward.

The Prince of Wales returned to the fray the next day. Earnestly the heir of the British Empire declared at a citizens' lunch at the Palliser Hotel: "This city, one of the great centers of Western Canada, will wield a great influence in the destinies of the Empire, and I know well that you will always guard your British institutions and allegiance as faithfully as you have done in the past."[69] His public loved it. In retrospect Calgary's British enthusiasms of the 1910s seem so at odds with the modern city's public memory of its roots.

Many activities followed, including a trip after his civic reception to the Bar U Ranch south of Calgary. He fell in love with the foothills country, so much so that he himself later purchased an attractive ranch beside the Bar U, to be known as the "E.P." (Edward Prince). The next evening the royal visitor was rushed back to Calgary for the last grand occasion of the Calgary visit, a huge event held at the Mewata Armouries, the newly completed red brick fortress at the end of 8th Avenue West. Here Brigadier General H. F. McDonald and the officers of southern Alberta's Military District 13 gave a military ball in his honour. Maynard Joiner, the Grand Theatre's musical director, had been requested by General McDonald to organize and conduct a special orchestra for the ball.[70] He chose the best professional musicians available; all the theatre managers had been contacted.

Prior to the dinner the royal visitor danced first a waltz with Mrs. McDonald; then, to Belle Lougheed's delight, he asked her spirited daughter Dorothy to be his second dance partner of the evening. The band played a one step, "In the Land of Beginning Again."[71] The prince and Dorothy took the floor. *The Albertan* commented, "They danced beautifully together, the center of concentrated attention." Later the prince returned and asked Dorothy for the fifth selection on his dance card, a two-step, "K-K-Katy."[72] At the supper that followed the eighth dance Belle Lougheed herself sat beside His Royal Highness.[73] After the refreshments the dancing resumed. In fact, the prince so enjoyed the party he kept his train waiting with full steam up for three hours. The guest of honour left the 1200 guests only at 2:40 a.m., with the party still in full swing. Shortly before 3 a.m. Edward, Prince of Wales, boarded his train headed westward to Banff.[74]

By coincidence, Vilhjalmur Stefansson, Canada's best-known northern explorer, departed from Banff for Calgary the very same day that the prince left Calgary for Banff. The next evening he lectured at the Grand Theatre on his Arctic explorations.[75] The senator might have heard him if he stayed over one more day before returning to Ottawa. Sir James remembered warmly the royal visitor who left Calgary that day.

The programme for the Military Ball
given in honour of H.R.H. The Prince of
Wales, Mewata Barracks, 16 September
1919. Photo courtesy of Bill Joiner.

Dorothy Lougheed. Glenbow
Archives/PD 132, vol. 20, R510.42.

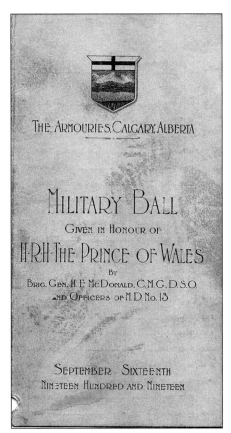

Programme

	Extra Commencing	9.00		ENGAGEMENTS	RENDEZVOUS
1	WALTZ	"Cecile"	1		
2	ONE STEP	"In The Land of Beginning Again"	2		
3	FOX TROT	"Hindustan"	3		
4	WALTZ	"I'm Sorry I Made You Cry"	4		
5	TWO STEP	"K-K-K-Katy"	5		
6	WALTZ	"I'm Forever Blowing Bubbles"	6		
7	FOX TROT	"Oh So Pretty"	7		
8	ONE STEP	"How Ya Gonna Keep 'Em Down on the Farm"	8		
9	WALTZ	"Till We Meet Again"	9		
10	FOX TROT	"Allah's Holiday"	10		
11	TWO STEP	"Where Do We Go From Here"	11		
12	WALTZ	"Destiny"	12		
13	ONE STEP	"Mammy O'Mine"	13		
14	FOX TROT	"Chong"	14		
15	WALTZ	"Flora Bella"	15		
16	ONE STEP	"Me-Ow"	16		
17	FOX TROT	"I'm Always Chasing Rainbows"	17		
18	WALTZ	"Mighty Lak' a Rose"	18		
19	TWO STEP	"Jim, Jim I Always Knew That You'd Win"	19		
20	ONE STEP	"Come On Papa"	20		
21	WALTZ	"Maytime"	21		
22	ONE STEP	"My Barney Lies Over The Ocean"	22		
23	FOX TROT	"Jump Jim Crow"	23		
24	WALTZ	"Missouri"	24		

Three years later he recalled Edward's visit: "So strongly marked is his personality that he is to-day acclaimed as the most popular personage in the Empire to which we belong."[76]

In early July 1921 only one dark cloud appeared on the senator's visible horizon, the forthcoming Alberta provincial election. The UFA had just shown great strength in the federal by-election in Medicine Hat in late June—the UFA's Robert Gardiner polled nearly ten thousand more votes than his only opponent.[77] As Sir James told a journalist: "Medicine Hat was a blow, and to be frank, it looks as if the Alberta provincial election means a blow-out for both the old parties on the prairies."[78] Prime Minister Arthur Meighen already feared the impact on his party of the western farmers' political revolt. Allegedly he called the UFA's Henry Wise Wood and Thomas Crerar, UGG president, "Bolsheviks" and "enemies of the state."[79]

Strangely the nudge that contributed to toppling the senator from the pinnacle of power came from the very office building that bore his name. On July 18th the UFA swept into power in the Alberta provincial election. Nine days later they had picked Herbert Greenfield as the new provincial premier in their central UFA offices in the Lougheed Building. Foreseeing the upcoming federal election later that year, Meighen shuffled his cabinet in mid-September, bringing in the senator's law partner as minister of justice, and making other adjustments. But another Albertan who supported the high protective tariff was not what the farmers wanted. The election of December 1921 was, in part, a replay of that of 1911, the battle of the protective tariff against free trade, with the Liberals this time replaced in Alberta by the UFA, which had entered into a loose alliance with other farmers' groups across Canada to form the Progressive Party.

On the evening of Tuesday, December 6th, Trans-Canada Theatres presented the famous English actress Marie Lohr at the Grand in "The Voice from the Minaret," one of her most recent London successes. During the intermissions the management of the Grand arranged to give bulletins on the election returns from the stage.[80] In the disastrous vote Meighen and eight of his cabinet ministers, including R. B. Bennett, lost their seats. The Conservatives came third in number of seats, behind the farmers of the Progressive Party. Mackenzie King and the Liberals formed a minority government.[81] In Alberta the voters returned not a single Conservative, electing instead ten UFA members and two Labour members from Calgary elected with the UFA's endorsement.

Politically Sir James lost enormously with the Liberal victory. The senate government leader became the opposition leader without access to patronage. The Liberals quickly struck down at least one measure he fully endorsed and believed in. As Superintendent General of Indian Affairs, Senator Lougheed sought to enforce compulsory enfranchisement, the ending of the legal Indian status of any individual deemed capable of entering the larger society. He wanted them immediately "enfranchised," removed from band lists and made citizens, no longer under the Indian Act. The new legislation granted the superintendent general the authority to end "Indianness." Without application a three-member inspection boards would recommend to the superintendent general individuals for enfranchisement.[82] The First Nations vigorously opposed this. The Liberals withdrew compulsory enfranchisement after they took office.

From Senator Lougheed's vantage point assimilation, or "full British citizenship," to use the words of Duncan Campbell Scott, his deputy minister, remained the goal.[83] Assimilation into the larger society seemed totally natural to the senator. While he did defend the First Nations' right to appear at the Calgary Stampede in their old costumes, and to tell their ancient stories,[84] in the long run he opposed their retention of their cultures and separate ways. He advocated assimilation of the First Nations to the British Canadian model.

As superintendent of Indian Affairs and a Calgarian, he must have been aware of the accomplished Sylvester Long Lance, a First Nations person from the American side, well known in the community. A graduate of the Carlisle Indian School in Pennsylvania, a war hero, a wonderful athlete and a polished writer for *The Calgary Herald*, he functioned with ease in the larger society. During the spring and summer of 1921 he wrote an excellent series of articles on the First Nations in southern Alberta.[85] He was a perfect model of what the senator wanted First Nations people to become.

Long Lance certainly knew the Calgary office building that bore the senator's name, as his good friend Hugh Dann had his apartment there, and he visited often.[86] The *Calgary Herald* reporter would see the senator's photo in the lobby of the office building ever time he called upon his friend.[87] In the early 1920s Long Lance also visited the Board of Trade (Chamber of Commerce) restaurant in the Lougheed Building's basement. George F. G. Stanley, later to become a well-known Canadian historian, recalled seeing him there when taken to lunch by his father. John Stanley pointed out to his son the "tall dark man, well built, wearing a tweed jacket and plus fours. I did not know who he was, but he was interesting to look at." John took George over to Long Lance's table to introduce him. "Of course this was very exciting to me. I understood that he was a Blackfoot chief who had served with the Canadians during the First World War."[88]

In Calgary Sir James knew a number of successful people in the larger society who had some Native ancestry. They included, in addition to Belle and her Hardisty relatives, his business associate Edmund Taylor, Brigadier General H. F. McDonald, commander of Military District 13,[89] and the scholarly lawyer Laurence Clarke, clerk of the Alberta Supreme Court in Calgary.[90] The senator believed in the bill endorsing forced assimilation, but the Liberals killed it.

In addition to his political woes, the senator also lost economic ground in 1922. Trans-Canada Theatres proved a financial disaster, and he had to withdraw from the venture. Bob Edwards sounded the alarm in the *Eye Opener* back on 25 December 1920. In his review of "The Wanderer" he wrote: "We don't know what goes wrong with some of these big, pretentious, topheavy, spectacular productions which come to Calgary, but they rarely give us the quality which must been originally existent in order to have attained such long runs in sophisticated cities like New York and Chicago. 'Chu Chin Chow,' as given in Canada, was a glaring example of this 'missing vital spark'." The chain continued to lose money: $100,000 in 1921–1922 and $40,000 in 1922–1923.[91] Challenges came from the soaring travel and production costs of Trans-Canada's large shows, the unions' demands for more money for actors and technicians and competition from the new medium of radio. But, above all else the major competition came from the movies, still silent, but increasingly the preferred form of popular entertainment.[92]

After Trans-Canada's failure all Sir James could do for Jeff Lydiatt was to re-appoint him manager of the Grand. Jeff returned to the Grand at the time of Bob Edwards' death in November 1922. Immediately he sent this message of sympathy to the *Eye Opener*: "The Grand Theatre is pleased to add its tribute to the memory of BOB EDWARDS, whose never-failing courtesies and kindly constructive criticism were always appreciated. R. J. Lydiatt, Manager."[93] As always Jeff participated fully in community life. In May 1923 he travelled to Los Angeles on behalf of the Calgary Exhibition Board. As an indication of how popular interest was shifting in Calgary to Hollywood's direction he carried letters warmly inviting the "King and Queen of Movieland," Douglas Fairbanks and Mary Pickford, to the 1923 Calgary Exhibition and Stampede. Unfortunately tight filming schedules prevented them from accepting.[94]

It was Senator Lougheed's loss that he could not keep his treasured associate in Calgary. Jeff Lydiatt left the Grand in July 1923. Sir James wrote him a letter expressing his regret at his departure. All bottled up in his "British" persona, James found it difficult to express his emotions. The last two lines read: "I wish you every success in the new sphere of activity you are about to enter upon, and bespeak for you the largest measure of prosperity and happiness. Believe me, with every good wish, Yours sincerely, James A. Lougheed."[95] Edmund Taylor also sent a letter to describe his own sense of loss, and to underline the contribution Jeff had made. In contrast to the senator he did this entirely naturally: "For ten years you have been closely identified with interests in which I also have been concerned. The personal contact has been most pleasant, and the results in a business way highly satisfactory." He concluded: "With every good wish for success in your new field, and for the health and happiness of yourself and all the members of your family. Sincerely yours, Edmund Taylor."[96]

The Orpheum Circuit had hired Jeff to run their theatre in Vancouver. They quickly realized his potential. Only a year after he joined their organization they promoted him general manager of the Western Vaudeville Managers' Association in Chicago. From Orpheum's headquarters in Chicago Jeff supervised the operation of all their existing theatres in Western Canada and the United States. He also oversaw the construction of new theatres, including Vancouver's new Orpheum Theatre, at a cost of more than one million dollars.[97] Tragically he did not live to see it completed. He became seriously ill and could not, as planned, attend its public opening. He died the day after it opened. To this day his children know the beautiful theatre, now the home of the Vancouver Symphony, as "Father's Theatre."[98]

Politically, economically and socially, Sir James lost ground in 1922 and 1923. He also faced the consequences of a political decision he had made as minister of the interior about ranching leases. A. E. Cross, for one, was furious at him for introducing a two-year cancellation clause on grazing land leases to allow for the expansion of the farming frontier. The Conservative Party had committed itself to the agricultural settlement of the West. Some evidence exists of initial bad feelings between the senator and the ranchers. This very prominent resident of Calgary was only elected a member

Long Lance, late 1920s. Glenbow
Archives/NA-1811-81.

The Board of Trade Rooms in the
basement of the Lougheed Building,
included a lounge, dining hall, and
billiard parlor, 1919. Calgary Year
Book, 1919. Glenbow Library,

of the Ranchmen's Club in 1909, eighteen years after its founding.[99] To judge from one surviving letter his relationship with rancher A. E. Cross, whom he had known for over thirty years, was glacial in its formality. His long time Toronto friend Emerson Coatsworth was "Emerson" in correspondence, but he addressed A. E. Cross in 1921 as, "Mr. Cross."[100] The ranchers were delighted when the Liberals struck down Lougheed's leasing proposals when they came to power in 1922.[101]

The senator's phenomenal blow-up with R. B. Bennett, his law partner of twenty-five years standing, added to his woes in 1922 and 1923. Bennett saw their law firm formed in 1897 as a partnership between themselves alone. In contrast, Lougheed regarded the firm as one between both of them and the new associates who had since joined them. Bennett had a very short-fused temper. After Sir James suggested that their partnership consisted of more individuals than just the two of them, R. B. replied that the others were not partners, just employees serving under a profit-sharing arrangement.[102]

If the senator acted too hastily in the summer of 1922 in trying to wind up the firm of Lougheed and Bennett, R. B. acted too quickly in his hot-tempered response to the initiative. He alleged that Sir James's messages to him about the dissolution of their legal partnership were full of "incompleteness, inaccuracy, insincerity."[103] Acting harshly, but within his legal rights, Bennett had the receiver of the old firm's assets take physical possession of everything from Lougheed and Bennett's old offices in the Clarence Block. The seizure included all the office files, furniture, office equipment, fixtures, fittings, law books, stationary and even all the paper clips. Bennett also advised the receiver that the senator's new firm, Lougheed, McLaws, Sinclair and Redman, had already taken some of the old Lougheed and Bennett's property to the Regent Theatre Building and the Lougheed Building, both owned by James Lougheed.[104] These items must now also be seized and held in receivership. The receiver obtained storage space on a vacant floor in the Southam or Herald Building, next to the Lougheed Building and Grand Theatre.[105] To obtain access to a client's files it was necessary for a sheriff's deputy to retrieve the material from storage.[106]

R. B. started his own firm, Bennett, Hannah, and Sanford. They rented space on the vacant sixth floor of the Lancaster Building on 8th Avenue. Most of the office staff and secretaries opted to go with the Bennett firm, which prospered. The overwhelming majority of the old Lougheed and Bennett clientele similarly followed Bennett.[107] Just to add to Sir James's aggravation, R. B. himself moved into the Ranchmen's Club, next to Lougheed House, for the remainder of the year and into 1923, at which point he rented a suite on the seventh floor of the Palliser Hotel. Members of their two rival firms passed each other on the street without speaking; one wonders if R. B. and Sir James acknowledged each other's presence when their paths crossed.[108]

During this explosive time Belle and Dorothy took the opportunity to take a winter European tour. If his model country was England it was not hers. Instead of London, Belle and her daughter headed directly for Paris followed by Rome, with a number of other French, Swiss and Italian stops in between. They loved Paris, as *The Albertan* reported on 3 May 1923, on their return: "The weather was bright during their stay and the cheery spirit of the Parisians added greatly to their enjoyment." For Belle nothing surpassed the Eternal City: "Rome is perfectly wonderful. I would like to live there the rest of my life."[109]

Upon their return to Calgary, as Belle expected, they found the sky had not fallen in. The sun still shone in fact throughout 1923 and 1924. Jeff Lydiatt did leave the senator's employ in the summer of 1923, but he left in place an excellent management team under Maynard Joiner. Edmund Taylor continued to fill the Lougheed Building with tenants, even attracting two new important ones: Canada Cement and Calgary Power. The farmers loved their space and continued to take more of it. The United Grain Growers held onto the third floor, and the newly formed Alberta Wheat Pool prepared to expand from the UFA offices on the second floor onto the sixth floor, formerly reserved for apartments.[110] Also, more good news, Sir James's Royalite stocks soared in value in late 1924 after Royalite No. 4 blew in. The senator also remained a director of several important companies: Canadian General Electric, Canada Life Assurance Company and the Calgary Natural Gas Company.[111] His net worth in 1925 was a very healthy $1.5 million, consisting mainly of real estate in Calgary.[112]

Suddenly, it appears, the senator became easier to live with. His rants in the senate against high taxes continued, for example, with the following contribution while Belle and Dorothy were away in Europe: "We are imposing taxation to such an extent as to throttle business prevent development and progress, and bring about final collapse."[113] Paying the federal income tax did indeed hurt. For those years that his income reached $100,000 or more he had to pay the highest rate, twenty-five percent.[114] Yet, after Belle and Dorothy's return, he seems to have accepted the new taxes, including the federal income tax, which had become permanent. It was introduced initially in 1917 only for the duration of the war. Apparently he made no further major interventions on the tax issue in the Red Chamber. As an astute staff writer on the *Winnipeg Tribune* noted on 16 June 1923: "He has the rare gift of knowing when to press a point, and also the much rarer gift of knowing when to retreat. He is one of few parliamentarians who know when criticism is worthless and when it is worth while."[115]

Finally Sir James had more time for his passion—the theatre—and for the Lougheed's family cottage in Banff. He seems to have accepted his own mortality for, on 16 August 1923, at the age of 69, he executed his last will. He chose as executors his sons Clarence and Edgar, business associate Edmund Taylor and the Royal Trust Company.[116] At last he had time to enjoy his beautiful home, Lougheed House. After long decades of constant work the senator's enormous drive to succeed, to advance himself, diminished.

In early 1925 Sir James became seriously ill for several months, but seemed to have recovered well, as he returned to his senate duties in May.[117] In addition to his responsibilities as opposition leader in the upper house, he chaired the important Senate Committee on Divorce.[118] The Parliament of Canada retained jurisdiction for divorce in Ontario and Quebec, which had no divorce courts—divorce bills for these two provinces still had to be initiated in the upper house.[119] This process began in the senate committee.

By early summer Sir James had returned to Calgary where Conservative leader Arthur Meighen wrote him on July 13th.[120] He asked Lougheed to return to Ottawa to assist with party organization, in Canadian historian David Hall's words, "a task, along with handling patronage, at which he had always excelled."[121] Apparently, by the time of his departure for Ottawa, the senator had more or less patched up relations with his Ranchmen's Club associates, for he appears in a group photo taken on the veranda at the rear of the club on July 27th.

Senator Lougheed did return to Ottawa in the fall, but he contracted bronchitis in mid-October and later pneumonia set in. He died in the Ottawa Civic Hospital on November 2nd, with Belle and son Clarence at his side in the hospital room.[122]

In Calgary, thousands paid their last respects to Sir James; hundreds of individuals crowded into the Anglican Pro-Cathedral, the Church of the Redeemer, for the funeral service on November 8th. Bishop Pinkham and the Dean Paget of the Pro-Cathedral conducted the Church of England burial service. The family member who had known him the longest of all, the senator's brother Sam, also attended. He had lived for a number of years in Winnipeg, working as a CPR carpenter, but later moved to Vancouver.[123] Packed to the doors inside, hundreds stood outside the church, unable to gain admittance. Later hundreds gathered with the Lougheed family for Sir James's burial in the Lougheed family plot at Union Cemetery.[124] Nellie McClung, who had moved with her family to Calgary several years before, in a letter to Mackenzie King noted: "We regret the passing of Senator Sir James Lougheed. He was well respected in his own city." [125]

One of the finest tributes to Senator Lougheed came at the Grand Theatre on the day of his death. At the beginning of the program, manager Maynard Joiner stepped to the front of the stage. Eloquently he paid tribute to the theatre's founder and owner. The Lougheed family's box on the right hand side had been beautifully decorated with flowers. The Grand's manager began by recalling the senator's gift to the city: "… it was due to his confidence in Calgary and his love for the best in music and entertainment that in 1912 the Grand Theatre was opened to the citizens of our city. Since its inception it has enabled us to spend many happy hours enjoying some of the greatest talent the stage and art has produced. Since February of 1912 the box on your right has been kept for his private use and whenever in the city one of his greatest delights was to be present at our performances." In his honour Maynard Joiner requested the observance of a few moments of silence in his memory.[126]

Thirty-five years later, memory of Sir James and the Grand remained, although by that date, the days of live theatre in the Grand had ended. The Canadian Players from Stratford, Ontario, performed the last two productions in the early spring of 1957: Shaw's "Man and Superman" and Shakespeare's "Othello."[127] The Grand by the early 1960s had become exclusively a movie house, with only very rare local events, such as a "Twist" dance contest in early 1962, taking place on its stage.[128] Yet, memory of powerful and moving live performances lived on. *Herald* reporter Tom Primrose discovered as much in researching in 1960 his feature article, "Old Grand Theatre Holds Memories." From several older members of the community he learned: "There is an old legend that after a top performance at the Grand, Sir James Lougheed appears briefly on stage to acknowledge the applause of the patrons."[129]

Members of the Ranchmen's Club, 27 July 1925. James Lougheed appears seated on the far right, George Peet appears seated to the left of him in this photo. Edmund Taylor, the Senator's business partner appears seated on the far left, at the end of the first row. Glenbow Archives/ND-8-368.

Maurice Colbourne filming a scene from "Arms and the Man," one of the first Shaw films (1932). He embraces Angela Baddeley, renowned later in her career as Mrs. Bridges, the cook in BBC's "Upstairs Downstairs." National Film and Television Archives, London, England/124572.

Chapter Eleven

THE GRAND TRANSITION

O N LATE FRIDAY AFTERNOON, 6 DECEMBER 1929, NELLIE MCCLUNG and the local branch of the Canadian Women's Press Club welcomed Maurice Colbourne and his English theatre company to Calgary.[1] Their guest, a versatile Shakespearian actor and great admirer of the works of George Bernard Shaw, introduced Shaw to Canadian theatre audiences in the late 1920s. Colbourne's players in the 1929 tour included leading British actors Barry Jones and Margaret Rawlings. Leonard Brockington, the City of Calgary's solicitor and part time *Calgary Herald* drama critic, wrote enthusiastically of their performances at the Grand: "There is a tradition abroad that Bernard Shaw's plays are designed to fascinate young men and intense young women and are otherwise 'caviare to the general.' As a matter of fact they are the best possible fun for the average man and woman. They stimulate, and above all they amuse."[2]

Nellie and her husband Wes lived on the southwest corner of 15th Avenue and 7th Street West.[3] Quite advanced for the times, the twenty-year-old Tudor-style home incorporated a number of new design features, including fireplaces inspired by the arts and crafts movement.[4] One authority has termed similar houses to this, built in Calgary immediately before World War One, as "Edwardian eclectic."[5] The McClungs arrived in 1923.

As the sun was now setting, and temperature well below freezing, it felt good to step inside from the porch.[6] The large square entrance hall had a fine carved staircase with polished wooden floors. Once coats were taken the guests entered the carpeted living room, on the left, dominated by the large, open brick arts-and-crafts style fireplace. With books and pictures on the walls the large room contained an inviting chesterfield and various comfortable chairs placed to enjoy the blaze.[7] Over the mantel hung a landscape of the Baltic Sea coast of Finland, a gift from the government of Finland in appreciation for Mrs. McClung's study of a Finnish immigrant girl in Manitoba.[8] The idea of writing the novel about the Canadianization of "Hemli," a fictional Finnish woman, came from her close observation of a young Finnish domestic who worked for the McClungs for three years.

A guest from an earlier visit provided this impression of the room: "a place of light, space, warmth, and homelike hospitality."[9] For her reception that early winter afternoon Nellie purchased golden chrysanthemum and rose carnations to give a note of colour. She placed lavender blooms, with their fragrant smell, on the tea table.[10] The hostess served tea, not sherry, as she and her husband Wes were ardent prohibitionists, staunch members of the nearby Wesley United Church.

Two prominent Calgary theatre people attended the gathering: Mrs. Lydia Winter, grande dame of the city's Little Theatre; who herself performed on the London stage over thirty years earlier, and Florence Piercy, formerly Florence McHugh, then on honeymoon in Canada with her husband, Dr. John Piercy, a London surgeon. Florence had become a noted actress on the British stage. Three years earlier she appeared with the already legendary Sybil Thorndike in "Granite."[11] A chance to perform the challenging role of Hilda Wangel in Ibsen's "Master Builder" followed. Earlier in 1929 she played the part of "Magnolia," the showboat owner's daughter, in Jerome Kern's and Oscar Hammerstein's musical, "Showboat," then on tour throughout Britain.[12] *The Glasgow Citizen* praised her performance to the skies: "She can sing, she can dance, and what is more important, she can act, infusing her work with real pathos and passion."[13] Previous to her departure to study vocal music and piano at the Royal College of Music in London in 1921, the St. Mary's High School graduate performed at the Grand. This young member of an old Calgary family appeared in "The Highwood Trail," a play written by the man responsible for the first Calgary Stampede in 1912, Guy Weadick.[14]

Many topics arose at the reception. An excellent conversationalist, Maurice Colbourne talked about Shaw with ease and insight. The Irish playwright, he explained, wanted to see depth in contemporary theatre. He detested scripts with heroes being "nothing but heroic and the villains nothing but villainous." He wanted three-dimensional characters. As he would say: "Show me in real life a villain who has not some finer moments or a hero without his weak spot…"[15] Colbourne, a past president of the Oxford University Dramatic Society (OUDS),[16] had just finished writing a short biography of Shaw.[17]

Only the previous year, "The Apple Cart," Shaw's latest play, reached the London stage. The Piercys must have seen it. The new play joined a long series of witty and incisive works by Shaw, a list that included "Arms and the Man" (1894), "Caesar and Cleopatra" (1899), "Man and Superman" (1905), "Pygmalion" (1913) and "St. Joan" (1923). What were some secrets of the famous playwright's approach to writing? "Shaw is serious," Colbourne explained, "but he is never solemn… He combines philosophy with propaganda, and his wit only serves to camouflage his seriousness."[18] Often he used characters regarded as "mad" to do so. "In your perusal of the plays, when you meet a character who is considered mad by all the other characters, make a note of him or her; he or she is worth watching. Ten to one the real Shaw is lurking in the very words which caused their speaker to be thought mad. You will find the epithet 'Mad' applied to any character in the play who drops bombs of shattering common sense…"[19]

Nellie had met Maurice Colbourne on his previous visit to Calgary in 1928.[20] The engaging conversationalist talked and wrote about more than his own line of work. In fact, the versatile actor-manager had just published a popular book on economic theory. In 1932, three years later, a local Calgary high school principal read his *Unemployment or War*, a simplified treatise on Major C. H. Douglas's intricate theories of Social Credit[21]—the book changed William Aberhart's life.[22]

In the absence of a university, the city had a limited number of meeting places where one could exchange ideas. After the collapse of the University of Calgary in 1915,

Alexander Calhoun, the city librarian, did his best to encourage intellectual discussion. As his biographers Donna Lohnes and Barbara Nicholson point out, he organized a wide variety of programs and lectures at the library. He made rooms available to community groups like the Canadian Authors Association for their meetings.[23] In a more private way Nellie McClung made her own home available for the same purpose. Calgarian writer Elaine Catley, a decade after the McClungs left Calgary, gratefully remembered Nellie's gift to the literary community: "For years she made her home in Calgary, where many delightful literary gatherings were held, and famous writers entertained."[24]

Nellie remained incredibly busy although all five of her children had left home. From 1921 to 1926 she served as a Liberal MLA in the Alberta legislature. Now fifty-six, Mrs. McClung continued to write books and numerous articles. In the late 1920s her schedule of club work remained as hectic as ever, with active membership in the Women's Press Club, Canadian Authors Association, Local Council of Women, Women's Canadian Club and the Woman's Missionary Society. She had a large Bible class at Wesley United (in 1925 with church union Wesley Methodist had become Wesley United) and helped run a girls' club there.[25] Within the United Church she campaigned for women ministers. In her opinion the "heavy weight of prejudice" was the only reason against the ordination of women by the churches.[26] On account of the enormous demands on Nellie's time, the McClungs employed a maid at home to help with the domestic work. She also had in husband Wes an extremely understanding and devoted life partner.

By 1929 Nellie McClung had become one of the best-known public personalities in Western Canada. She enjoyed a national readership for her books and articles, and her skill as an orator was legendary.[27] Even the hard-to-please Bob Edwards was impressed by her debating skills.[28] After one of her talks in the Grand, Eye Opener Bob wrote: "Did you ever hear Nellie McClung when in good form? If not, you have missed the treat of your life. Woe betide the poor fish who interpolates a silly question. He gets his so quick that his head swims for about a week."[29]

In many ways Wes and Nellie were complete opposites. Physically, for example, Wes was tall (roughly six feet), whereas Nellie was short (five foot).[30] Wes loved sports, particularly curling and golf.[31] In contrast Nellie kept busy with writing, lecturing and outreach to others. Politics was her all-consuming interest. When she picked up the morning paper, Mark McClung, her youngest son, recalled: "It was always politics. She never paid any attention to the sport pages, or the social pages that had to do with women, as they often did."[32] Despite their different interests, the McClungs had a strong marriage based on mutual respect and great affection.[33]

As in any partnership, quarrels sometimes arose, but as Nellie said: "... I would rather quarrel with my husband than agree with any other man, because he was a good straight debater, with a sense of justice and fair play that has always held my admiration."[34] Implicitly trusting her life partner's opinion, she read every word of her manuscripts and drafts of articles to him. Wes stretched out on the chesterfield as his wife read to him,[35] and he frankly gave his opinions of the text.[36] Their youngest son Mark

Nellie McClung, on the right, appears in this photo with the famous British suffragist, Emmeline Pankhurst, at Edmonton's Macdonald Hotel, 17 June 1916. Glenbow Archives/NC-6-1746.

"At the Great Divide, August 1932." Nellie and Wes McClung at the point of division between Alberta and British Columbia – on the BC side the water flows to the Pacific, on the Alberta side to Hudson Bay. The photo was taken en route to Victoria from Calgary. British Columbia Archives/BA-23456.

later recalled how his father would say to her: "Well, you now, I'd tone that down, or I'd build this up," and so on.[37]

At the moment of the Colbourne Players' visit to her home, Nellie McClung and four other prominent Alberta women—Emily Murphy, Irene Parlby, Henrietta Muir Edwards and Louise McKinley—had just finished an exhausting but successful legal battle. They fought first in the Supreme Court of Canada in Ottawa (unsuccessfully), and then in the Judicial Committee of the Privy Council in London (successfully), to obtain legal recognition of women as "persons." Today they are known as "The Famous Five."

Only the day before the Colbourne reception Nellie spoke on the "Persons Case" at a luncheon of the Calgary Business and Professional Women's Association, held in the Alhambra Room of the new Eaton's store.[38] Before 1929 women had gained the franchise and could now run and hold office both federally and provincially, but they could not be named to the senate. Only "persons" could sit in the senate, and women under the British North America Act of 1867 did not qualify. Yet, that very October, the Privy Council in London, the final court of appeal of the British Empire, reversed the Supreme Court of Canada's verdict. It ruled that the word "persons," in section 24 of the British North America Act, contrary to what the Supreme Court of Canada had said, included women. This meant that Canadian law now recognized women as "persons," eligible to be summoned to, and to become members of, the Canadian Senate.

The McClungs had moved to Calgary in May 1923 from Edmonton,[39] where they lived for nearly nine years after leaving Winnipeg. Wes worked as the manager of the northern Alberta office of Manufacturers Life until his transfer to Calgary to head the company's southern Alberta office on the fifth floor of the Lougheed Building. He had a very successful career with Manufacturers. Although he trained as a pharmacist, and worked as one for over fifteen years, Wes later switched to insurance and went straight to the managerial top. As his Winnipeg co-workers said of him upon his departure for Edmonton in late 1914, he had "pluck, and energy, and spunk."[40] In Calgary his office won the company's "President's Trophy" in 1926, awarded to the branch that showed the greatest general development in the past year. For the first time the cup travelled to Western Canada, where it remained in the branch's Lougheed Building office throughout 1927.[41]

As the reception began at 4:30 p.m., it is quite conceivable that Mr. McClung, the other half of the famous couple, returned home before it ended. Manufacturers Life left the Lougheed that fall, but their office remained downtown in the Dominion Bank Building (now home to Teatro Restaurant).[42] He probably walked home, only fifteen minutes or so, to keep in shape for the next bonspiel. The out-going and good-natured Wes, a man used to dealing with the public in his business, would have been a great asset at the party.[43] In the first volume of her autobiography, *Clearing in the West*, Nellie writes of him as one whom "loved fun and company."[44] Agnes MacPhail, Canada's first woman MP (elected in 1921), met him in 1931 and had this to say: "He is a man of substance, financially, mentally and physically." Then she went on to add: "He is unique in that he is very proud of his wife's achievement."[45]

Wes's successful business career allowed Nellie an economic independence few women of her generation enjoyed. Her publishing revenues alone could not possibly pay for the large house, the servant or the expenditures that came from her active involvement in so many different clubs and causes. Son Mark later recalled how his dad provided his mother with housekeeping money. Sometimes the figures did not balance out. His dad would then say to his mother, "Nellie, you must look after these things more carefully." To which she replied, "It just bores me. Why don't you do it, or get somebody else to do it?"[46] Finances were not Nellie's strong suit.

Wes had a very responsible job, first to run the Calgary office in the Lougheed Building, but also to supervise the sub-agents of the company in the small outlying towns in southern Alberta. Manufacturers Life invested in loans to farmers, but also city businesses. The company also participated in the financing of schools and municipal governments in southern Alberta.[47] Wes made a good living and enjoyed job stability. Manufacturers eventually felt the impact of the Wall Street Crash in late October 1929, but not immediately. 1930, in fact, proved a good year for the company, and they weathered 1931 well. Only in 1932 and 1933 did Manufacturers report net losses.[48]

Maurice Colbourne could talk economics with Wes. After the crash of late October the markets continued to decline in November and December. The Colbourne Players' first experience of the crash came in Toronto. Only a few days after Black Thursday, October 24th, people there who had previously booked their tickets for performances at the Royal Alexandra begged to have their money back.[49] The Colbourne Players's 1929 tour of Canada proved a critical success, but a financial failure.[50]

The McClungs put on wonderful receptions. One guest recalled from a visit to 1501 7th Street West the previous year: "Nobody wanted to leave, if pressing evening engagements had not been recalled, there was apparent likelihood that the guests for the tea-hour would prolong their visitation until midnight supper!"[51] But the party must end, as the actors and actresses had to return to the Grand for their evening performance.

In hindsight the Colbourne Company's visit to Calgary in early December 1929 marked the end of almost two decades of regular road attractions at the Grand. Two weeks after their Calgary performances the consequences of the economic crash registered. On December 27th, for instance, Irene Gardiner of *The Calgary Herald* wrote that those who understand the local theatrical situation believe that "within a few weeks the present vaudeville schedule will be cancelled and that, already, there is very little hope that many of the companies booked at the opening of the season will fulfill their contracts."[52] In fact, vaudeville at the Grand lasted only until the end of January 1930.[53]

The stock market crash accentuated the rapid decline in touring shows in Canada. Other factors contributed as well. The advent of sound movies in the late 1920s proved catastrophic. Now you could see a talkie for fifty cents, or one-quarter the price of a ticket for a good play. It also was becoming difficult to find performance space. The movie chains in Canada excluded road shows in their theatres. If Famous Players, the largest, existed to show movies, which made money, why would they want to rent their premises to low-paying touring companies? The film chains wanted to shut down live theatres or, if they left them standing, to convert them into movie houses, which they did. [54]

Road attractions became rare at the Grand during the Great Depression. Already by 1933 nostalgia for the great days of live theatre had surfaced. A *Calgary Herald* story on 18 November 1933, "Many Famous Actors Have Trod the Boards in Calgary's Theatres", emphasized that "Hundreds of companies have toured Canada in the days 'before the depression' and no official record of their visits to Calgary kept. Omissions are inevitable in a list supplied by memory."

Already to Calgary theatregoers the 1910s and 1920s had become a lost Golden Age. Maurice Colbourne and his colleague Barry Jones did return several times to Western Canada in the early 1930s.[55] Only a relatively few professional theatre groups did so. The professional performers who played the Grand in the early 1930s included, in addition to Colbourne and Jones, Sir Barry Jackson and his company from London. In late 1931 (28 December to 2 January 1932) they presented three plays, one being Rudolf Besier's smash hit of 1930, "The Barretts of Wimpole Street," a popular dramatization of Elizabeth Barrett's and Robert Browning's love story. Leonard Brockington liked it so much he compared it to George Arliss's production of "Old English," performed at the Grand seven years earlier.[56] Sir Barry and the Jackson Players also returned to the Grand two months later (22–24 February 1932). Other international visitors included Ireland's national theatre company, the famous Abbey Theatre Irish Players of Dublin, who brought to Calgary "Playboy of the Western World" and "The Whiteheaded Boy" (12–19 January 1932). They played to packed houses. The beloved Sir John Martin-Harvey made his last visit to Calgary (21–26 March 1932). Colbourne and Jones returned in early 1933 (3–4 February 1933), then came a break of several years before the appearance of another international company at the Grand. A sea change had occurred since the mid-1920s in the Grand's live theatre offerings.

Maynard Joiner, manager of the Grand from late 1919 to 1921, and again from 1923 to 1929, followed Bill Sherman and Jeff Lydiatt as the theatre's third great manager. In the early years at least, the Grand continued as one of the outstanding centres of live entertainment in Western Canada. An incredibly energetic man, Maynard likened life to a violin: "The tighter the strings the better it plays." As the pianist and orchestra leader at the Grand in the late 1910s he had the ability to pay the piano with one hand while conducting with the other, all the while keeping an eye on the stage.[57] In the mid-1920s the talented musician wrote the music for Calgary's community song, "C-A-L-G-A-R-Y and that Spells Calgary," widely used for the next three decades.[58]

In order to support his wife and young family in the late 1910s, Maynard's day's schedule went something like this: 9:15 to 11:30, orchestra rehearsal; 12 to 2, play at a local restaurant; 2 to 5:30, matinee performance at the vaudeville show; 6 to 8, restaurant engagement; 8:30 to 10:30, evening show; 11 p.m. to 1 a.m., restaurant program."[59] After Jeff Lydiatt asked Maynard to succeed him in late 1919, this brutal schedule ended, but now new responsibilities descended on his shoulders.[60] As manager he had responsibilities for office work, the preparation of publicity, the checking up on

The main offices of Manufacturers Life on the 5th floor of the Lougheed Building, late 1910s. From the Manulife Financial Corporate Archives. 1919 Agent's Newsletter, p. 97. Courtesy of Manulife Financial.

Maynard Joiner, as a young man, Calgary. Photo courtesy of Bill Joiner.

the box-office receipts, as well as the supervision of personnel—ushers, ticket-sellers and other theatre attendants. Even the dress code for employees remained in his job description.

Another issue was security. In the early days there had been robberies from the dressing rooms.[61] Once a car was stolen right in front of the Lougheed Building.[62] At all times vigilance was necessary. At the end of the summer in 1927 two boys broke into Maynard's office.[63] Another incident occurred the following summer when thieves ransacked it one night.[64] Maynard's hours remained long.[65]

Probably the most demanding aspect of his job involved the bookings. In the list of artists that played the fifteen-hundred-seat theatre from late 1919 to late 1929 appear the names of many major (and soon to be major) Canadian and international performers of the day: Harry Lauder (18–20 December 1919; 12–14 September 1929); Tyrone Power, Sr. (22–24 April 1920); Mrs. Minnie Fiske (22–24 July 1920); Kathleen Parlow (11 April 1921 and 7 March 1922); Marie Lohr (7–8 November 1921 and 5–7 December 1921); the Marx Brothers (12–14 January 1922); Dame Clara Butt (4 February 1922 and 31 October 1923); Percy Grainger (23 March 1922); Ethel Barrymore (24–26 April 1922); Margaret Anglin (6–8 September 1923); Edward Johnson (9 January 1924); Jack Benny (11–12 January 1926 and 9–11 February 1928), Julia Arthur (28–30 January 1926), and George Burns and Gracie Allen (18–20 October 1928). In addition to visiting entertainers the Grand in the 1920s welcomed well-known public figures: including Helen Keller (22–24 September 1921); Lowell Thomas (1 October 1926), Captain Roald Amundsen, explorer of the Arctic regions (18 May 1927).

In the mid-1920s Maynard also brought in popular travelling musical shows, such as "The Merry Widow," by Franz Lehar (26–28 February 1923); "No, No, Nanette" (7–9 June 1926)—the musical comedy hit which included one of the most famous show-tunes ever, "Tea for Two"—the D'Oyly Carte Opera Company with its fabulous Gilbert and Sullivan repertoire (28 February to 3 March, 4–9 April and 26–28 November 1927) and "The Student Prince" (18–20 November 1926), Sigmund Romberg's operetta about a romantic German prince and his university days at the University of Heidelberg. The booking of the big road shows in New York required a year lead time.[66] Of all the New York shows, "Blossom Time," Romberg's adaptation of Franz Schubert's melodies, eclipsed all others by far in terms of popularity. It came four times to Calgary (17–19 March 1924; 5–7 February 1925; 12 November 1925; 2–5 February 1927). The Grand's doorman and the head usher typically wore tuxedos. If the show had a special theme the ushers dressed in costume, be it Japanese, Quaker, Spanish or whatever the program called for.[67]

When gaps emerged in the offerings in the mid-1920s the energetic Maynard invited a stock company to Calgary. In the 1922–1923 season the Royal Collins Players spent eight months in the city.[68] Of all the troupe members Ray Collins, the company's leading man, probably had the longest stage career, as he later entered the movies and performed on television. In the late 1950s he appeared as Lieutenant Arthur Tragg in the Perry Mason television series. Subsequent stock companies included the Grand Players in the summer and fall of 1923, and the Belmont Players in the late spring and summer of 1925. They also returned in the spring and early summer of 1926, as well as late for a final engagement in 1926.

Sir John Martin-Harvey, who was knighted by King George V in 1919, made an enormous contribution to the enjoyment of Grand audiences.[59] He and his English company came back again and again in the 1920s and always obtained an extremely warm reception, even for his old warhorse, "The Only Way."[70] A generous spirit, he always made a point of thanking each member of the Grand's stage crew after every performance.[71] In his outreach to others the famous actor-manager made a rather unusual gesture. Having heard that a community of First Nations people lived south of the city, he invited their chiefs to the Grand. On 15 and 16 April 1924, he and his company performed Sophocles's "Oedipus Rex," one of the greatest tragedies of the ancient Greek theatre. In his memoirs Sir John recalled what followed: "All was speedily arranged with their superintendent, Dr. Murray, and it was a memorable sight to see Big Plume and his chiefs in their great blankets, sitting immovable in the boxes of the theatre. Never a muscle moved. Never a word escaped their lips."[72]

Whatever the Tsuu T'ina (Sarcee) chiefs thought of Sophocles's tragedy of a man who killed his father and married his mother remains unrecorded. In any event they liked this friendly Englishman who had reached out to them. Shortly after the performance they gave him a Tsuu T'ina name—"Ta-dicaszi"—as reported in Sir John's autobiography: "the name is quite beyond any European tongue to pronounce. So I hasten to add that being interpreted it means 'Red Feather'." They also gave him a headdress. Sir John reciprocated by presenting Big Plume the sword he used as Oedipus in the play. They remained in touch: "Since that Oedipus night we have always received a visit from Big Plume and a group of his people to see our plays at Calgary."[73]

Elaine Catley and her husband Syd, both from London, witnessed the glories of the Grand in the 1920s. Years later Elaine recalled: "There were traveling opera companies, and good plays. I recall seeing George Arliss in 'Old English,' Sir Martin Harvey in 'The Only Way' and Bernard Shaw's 'St. Joan'."[74] Both the John Galsworthy play "Old English"[75] and "The Only Way," based on Charles Dickens' *Tale of Two Cities,* pleased Elaine, but "St Joan" possibly had the greatest impact. Her diary, which usually simply recorded events without comment, hints at this play's impact. On Wednesday, 28 January 1926 she wrote: "Syd & I went to see Shaw's 'St. Joan.' Julia Arthur in the title role—a most memorable evening."[76]

Julia Arthur took the Grand Theatre to one of the highest points reached in its history as a live theatre. In 1926, this celebrated Canadian actress approached the end of her very successful acting career in North America and Britain, one that had begun as a teenager in her native Hamilton, Ontario, forty years earlier. She gave in her performances of St. Joan an amazing spiritual intensity.[77]

Just eight months after her performance, the Grand suffered a major setback to its aspirations to continue as a live theatre. The Lougheed Estate sold the lease of the Grand Theatre to Famous Players, a movie chain linked to Paramount, the American film giant. Their holding of the lease marked the end of the golden era of live entertainment at the Grand. Famous Players initially promised to keep live theatre alive.[78] For two years or so they did, but with the advent of the talkies they altered their policy. The first movie with sound was shown in Calgary in early November 1928.[79] To avoid competition with their other Calgary theatres, Famous Players would not re-wire the Grand for talkies. On 1 January 1930, only two theatres in the city remained silent, the Grand being one of them.[80]

From its early days the Grand had occasionally shown silent movies. In fact, it had played "The Birth of a Nation" several times in the mid- and late 1910s. Other pictures followed, including "Quo Vadis" (17–19 June 1920), on life in ancient Rome in the days of Nero, a film that contained, in the gleeful words of *The Albertan*, "realistic orgies of nobles;"[81] Douglas Fairbanks in "The Three Musketeers" (31 October–2 November 1921); Cecil B. deMille's dramatic spectacle, "The Ten Commandments" (3–6 September 1924); D. W. Griffith's "America" (3–6 December 1924); John Barrymore in the "The Sea Beast" (24–28 February 1926), based on Herman Melville's *Moby Dick*; the blockbuster, "Ben-Hur" (1–3 January 1928), with its cast of thousands headed by Ramon Novarro. The Grand Concert Orchestra accompanied these pictures with special musical settings.[82] Once Maynard booked an "operafilm," "The Bohemian Girl" (28 November–3 December 1927), a silent movie picture with opera singers standing by the side of the screen singing the various arias, with orchestra accompaniment, in as close synchronization as possible with the action on the screen.[83]

But Famous Players had no intention of introducing talkies at the Grand to supplement live theatre bookings. Maynard Joiner re-considered his options. In late summer 1929 he accepted the post of manager of the Orpheum in Vancouver, still primarily a live theatre, but one also adapted to run sound films.[84] With his departure live entertainment at the Grand lost its leading advocate at time when the Great Depression soon reduced travelling road shows to a minimum.

In the early 1930s amateurs from across the depression-plagued prairies came forward to fill the vacuum created by the departure of the touring companies. A network of "Little Theatre" organizations in Alberta, for example, formed to plan an annual dramatic festival. On account of its central location Calgary was chosen for the first Alberta Drama Festival in 1930, which was held at the Grand.[85] In subsequent years it again hosted the festival.[86]

An important moment in the history of Calgary's Little Theatre Association came in September 1932 when it presented two one act plays: "Q," a farce by Stephen Leacock, and "The Drums of Oude," a drama centred around a British garrison in India and directed by the legendary Mrs. Lydia Winter. The visiting Governor General of Canada, the Duke of Bessborough, viewed both performances.[87] He loved theatre. In fact, his castle in Hampshire boasted the best-equipped private playhouse in England. On his arrival to Canada the state of national theatre profoundly depressed him: "When I arrived in 1931," he later wrote, "I found road company activity dead. Theatres had been taken over by film companies. Depression had practically killed touring by professional companies from abroad."[88]

In the intermission between the two performances at the Grand, His Excellency made a short speech to the crowded theatre about the need for a national drama festival.[89]

One month later the annual Dominion Drama Festival was born, the first being held in Ottawa in the week commencing April 23rd.[90]

The re-emergence of a Calgary symphony also strengthened the Grand in the 1930s. The first Calgary symphony organized in 1913–1914; the second existed briefly in 1919–1920; the third emerged in the 1930s. *Calgary Herald* reporter Lou Laverie later recalled the contribution of Maestro Gregori Garbovitsky in the depression: "He had a Russian's passion for music, a contagious enthusiasm, an expressive personality which attracted more than 70 musicians to his re-organized Calgary Symphony Orchestra."[91]

Throughout the 1930s the symphony gave successful concerts.[92] Particularly impressive was violinist Jean de Rimonczy, a graduate of the Royal Hungarian Academy of Music in Budapest, one of whose teachers had been the famous composer Bela Bartok. He moved to Vancouver in 1934 where he later became concertmaster and associate conductor of the Vancouver Symphony.[93] Similarly, concertmaster Jascha Galperin, a refugee from revolutionary Russia, had an excellent musical training in Europe.[94] Decades after he left Calgary immediately following World War Two, the red-haired violinist was remembered for having "captivated us with his music" and for his stories of the Russian Revolution.[95] The symphony's performances brought needed solace to a population living through Calgary's greatest economic collapse since the bust of 1913. The concerts were great social occasions, and the audience attended in their best attire.[96]

The Great West Canadian Folksong-Folkdance and Handicrafts Festival, held at the Grand and the Palliser Hotel from 19–22 March 1930 also enlivened Calgarians. John Murray Gibbon, who later wrote the important book, *Canadian Mosaic: The Making of a Northern Nation* (1938), organized the Festival for the CPR.[97] At the Grand over fifteen national groups of different backgrounds gave evening concerts over the course of four nights.[98] From Mundare, Alberta, came the Ukrainian National Choir. Glyndwyr Jones and Calgary's St. David's Society Choir under the direction of John Rhys Jones represented Wales. Folk dancers from Edmonton and Regina performed the German "Schuhplattler." The Metis dance troupe from St. Paul, Alberta, won particularly warm applause for a "dexterity and grace almost indescribable." The reviewer in *The Albertan* of March 20th continued: "One member of the troupe in particular scarcely touched the stage, so light was her step, and her toe dancing would have put a ballet performer of the professional stage to shame."

Economic conditions continued to deteriorate in Calgary. As early as May 1930 the city commissioners inserted "Stay away from Calgary" notices in daily newspapers across Canada as a response to the ever increasing number of unemployed in the city.[99] Workers clashed with police in late June 1931 at a public meeting place of the unemployed nicknamed "Red Square." Five persons including two police were injured.[100] The lot at the southwest corner of 2nd Street East and 6th Avenue stood only three blocks from the Lougheed, and just north of City Hall. Not even Mount Royal escaped the economic crisis; Larry Winter, grandson of Judge and Lydia Winter, later recalled: "The community began as American Hill and by the thirties it was known as Mortgage Hill."[101] As if the economic crisis was not bad enough, the rebellious Bow River in 1932 overflowed its banks.[102] That spring much of Sunnyside on the north bank of the Bow

Métis dancers at the Great West Festival at Calgary. They performed on the Grand Theatre stage, 19 March 1930. Canadian Geographical Journal, 1,3 (1930):273.

The district of Sunnyside on the north bank of the Bow disappeared under water when the river flooded in June 1932. Glenbow Archives/NA-1044-3.

disappeared under water. Upstream dams eventually provided minimal protection for the city, but the Bow had none at the time.[103]

A handful of outside groups shored up Calgary's spirits, or at least the spirits of those who could afford a ticket. The English Light Opera Company visited the city in late 1931 (16–21 November). Other performances with international stars included the fourth visit to the Grand of Scottish singing comedian Harry Lauder (4–5 November 1932).[104] The famous Canadian road show, "The Dumbells," full of bouncy and peppy music, returned throughout the early 1930s (13–15 and 24–25 November 1930; 26 October 1931; 26–31 December 1932; 4–7 January and 13–15 February 1933). But the troupe that had originally begun among soldiers in the Canadian Expeditionary Force in World War One folded in 1933, which ended their annual cross-Canada tours. Throughout the 1920s Calgarians strongly supported their performances at the Grand.[105] Calgary had to make do with mostly home-grown live theatre entertainment after 1933.

Musically a few international visitors continued to visit, notably two world famous violinists: Fritz Kreisler (2 November 1934) and Jan Kubelik (21 March 1936). Other great artists who came to the Grand in the mid-1930s included pianist and composer Percy Grainger (19 March 1936) and one of the greatest pianists of the decade, Josef Hofmann (6 January 1937).

The Calgary Light Opera Society assisted greatly in this new era of self-help. Organized locally in 1927 it worked to develop musical theatre in Calgary. In spring 1930 (24–26 April), the society performed its fourth production, "San Toy," a musical comedy with a Chinese background.[106] "The Rebel Maid" (11–13 December 1930), based on the 1688 fight of William, Prince of Orange, for the throne of the King of England, followed. It had a cast of sixty-five with orchestra accompaniment. Over a year later the society performed "Miss Hook of Holland" (17–19 November 1932), a musical comedy with a Dutch theme. The following year "The Quaker Girl" (16–18 November 1933) proved so popular it had to be held over an extra night. Public support allowed the society to offer four more productions over the next three years: "The Geisha" (5–7 April 1934), "The Arcadians" (14–17 November 1934), "The Merry Widow" (20–23 November 1935) and its last operetta before it disbanded, "The Chocolate Soldier" (18–21 November 1936), based on Shaw's "Arms and the Man."

As they had regularly done in the 1920s, Calgary's service clubs held several special events at the Grand in the 1930s. The Rotary Club of Calgary on 8 and 9 April 1931 sponsored S. Coleridge Taylor's choral work, "Hiawatha," with an accompanying orchestra of 40 members and a local chorus 150 strong. Taylor, an Anglo-African from Sierra Leone in West Africa who had studied in England, based his combined choral and orchestral performance on Longfellow's famous "Song of Hiawatha."[107] In May 1935 the Rotary Club of Calgary produced its "Grand Slam of Rotary, Sunset Revue," which included cheery songs, dances and skits, with all profits going to the cancer fund. The Alice Murdoch dancers assisted with the performances. The Lions Club of Calgary sponsored the "Grand Theatre Party" the following year (17–18 January 1936). The profits from the play, "The Bachelor Husband," went to help their community projects,

particularly their work with the blind. On 9 May 1937 the Elks Concert Band performed.

A religious group, the Four Square Gospel Church, rented the Grand for a public talk by their leader, noted evangelist Aimee Semple McPherson (8 November 1935). Earlier General Edward J. Higgins, the commander of the Salvation Army throughout the world, made three addresses on one day at the theatre (24 September 1929). Mayor Fred Osborne introduced the important visitor.[108]

Local dance schools held their annual shows at the Grand. Native-born Calgarian Pat Talerico danced on the Grand's big stage in the Alice Murdoch's revue "Golden Days," in late May 1934. Pat's father had come to Calgary from Italy in 1901 as a young man of seventeen. Her mother arrived from Yorkshire, England, in 1914. After their marriage in 1917 they moved to Grand Trunk (now West Hillhurst), a new district southeast of Calgary St. Andrews Golf Club in the northwest. In 1934 Pat was one of the Alice Murdoch students selected for the annual revue at the Grand. The eleven-year-old found the theatre with its large auditorium, upper and lower balconies, and the boxes on each side, extraordinary. "It also had a sunken orchestra pit, which held a large band. The lightening system was exquisite." The dressing rooms and make up rooms were situated below the stage. The beautiful red velvet stage curtain impressed her. She remembers still the "thrill, when you were at the back of that curtain waiting to perform, and a bigger thrill to see it going up."[109] The theatre was packed. The city loved Alice Murdoch's annual revues.[110]

Ralph A. Rogers's locally produced musical review, "Stepping Up," played in early March 1935. By popular demand it played again two weeks later. The cast included 160 young Calgarians, including three of the Kheong sisters.[111] Dorothy Kheong has kept all these years the photo Ralph Rogers took of them on the stage of the Grand. Dorothy, Mabelle and Vivian Kheong danced and sang a Chinese song. Although not included in the photo, Vivian played the Chinese harp for her sisters' duet.[112] It would be hard to find more native Calgarians than the Kheong sisters. Their father, Louie Kheong, came to Calgary in 1895 and opened the city's first Chinese grocery store.[113] Another outstanding local event was the presentation of "The Passion Play" with a cast of 275, all local talent, on 2–4 March 1933.[114]

Lady Lougheed remained a pillar of support for the musical world in Calgary. All her life she loved music. Just after she returned from school in 1876 to rejoin her family in the Mackenzie River Valley, she wrote Aunt Eliza Hardisty at Fort Edmonton: "Oh! I do find it hard when I cannot practise my music. I will be glad when we go out, I am sure I will sit at a piano all day long if I get a chance."[115] Regularly she and her family took their seats in the Lougheed family box, the lower rear box on the south side of the theatre.[116] Over the years Lady Lougheed entertained at Lougheed House "many noted artists, musicians, players, and playwrights" who appeared at the Grand.[117] Throughout the early and mid-1930s she served as one of the honorary patrons of the Calgary Symphony Orchestra.[118]

By the early 1930s Belle's personal fortune was nearly gone. Her father's estate, once considerable, now amounted to a fraction of its former size as a result of large-scale withdrawals in the 1920s by her brothers and sisters in Manitoba.[119] In hindsight, Royal Trust, the executors of the Lougheed Estate, made a mistake in liquidating the Royalite Oil shares to pay succession duties after Sir James's death. They should have sold the family's buildings and kept the oil stock. During the depression rental revenue from the properties plummeted. They now lost rather than made money.[120] In contrast, Royalite Oil stocks skyrocketed in June 1936 with the discovery of Turner Valley Royalite No. 1, which sparked the third Turner Valley oil boom.[121]

R. B. Bennett, despite his differences with James Lougheed, always remained extremely fond of Belle. After her death he wrote her son-in-law, J. A. Hutchison, Dorothy's husband, to express his sadness: "She was a fine character. Few people knew her perhaps as well as I. Thirty-five years ago she was very, very kind to me and I cannot tell you how sorry I was that conditions should have so changed as to make her life miserable at its close."[122] Music at the Grand proved a solace for Belle in her final months. In 1935 she attended the concert of Richard Crooks, renowned Metropolitan Opera tenor in early October,[123] and heard the world famous Moscow Cathedral Choir of Paris perform in mid-November.[124] Four months later she was gone. The woman who helped to convince her husband that business and culture were inseparable died on 13 March 1936.[125]

One individual remained at the Grand throughout the transition from the 1920s to 1930s: Annie Wilson. In the golden days of vaudeville and touring shows during the late 1910s and 1920s, the Grand employed Mrs. Wilson as their full-time treasurer or ticket seller.[126] In the early 1930s Annie branched out to the Stampede and Stampede racing tickets, as well as to the occasional local productions and Calgary Symphony Orchestra performances at the Grand.[127] Her connection with the Stampede dated back to the late 1920s; in 1927 advance tickets for the Stampede could be purchased at the Grand Theatre box office.[128]

Annie and her husband John had come to Calgary from England via Ontario just after the Grand opened in 1912. She was born in Yorkshire, England, the daughter of Frank Lockwood, a well-known English cricketer. A tiny lady, just five feet tall, she ran the Grand box office with stature and style. The Wilsons were the quintessential Lougheed/Grand family. They both worked in the building; from 1918 to 1921 they lived with their daughter Dorothy in an apartment on the sixth floor. Years later, in the 1930s, Dorothy Wilson belonged to the Calgary Symphony, which played in the Grand.[129]

John Wilson worked as the assistant secretary or manager of the Calgary Board of Trade (now the Chamber of Commerce) clubrooms, located from 1917 to 1933 in the basement of the Lougheed Building.[130] There was much to do, as many groups in addition to committees of the board used the rooms. In fact, in 1918, of the 180 meetings held there that year, only 40 were related to the Board of Trade.[131] The Southern Alberta Pioneers and their Descendants, for instance, met there on a regular basis from 1921 to 1923, and then from 1931 to 1933.[132] The Calgary Women's Literary Club celebrated its twentieth anniversary at the Lougheed on 9 February 1926 by holding a reunion luncheon.[133] In 1927, the Calgary St. Andrew's Golf Club held their annual general meeting there.[134] For two years or so in the mid-1920s the Calgary Stock Exchange had its offices next to the Board of Trade, which increased the demand for the board's facilities.[135]

The Board of Trade organized luncheons with speakers who ranged from Princess Catharine Radziwill, a cousin of the wife of the assassinated Archduke Ferdinand of Austria, whose murder in July 1914 precipitated World War One (20 January 1919), to Emily Murphy of Edmonton, the first female magistrate in the British Empire, a future member of the "Famous Five" (18 March 1921), to Guy Weadick, originator of the Calgary Stampede (9 May 1924). The dining room could accommodate 110 guests.[136] John Wilson occasionally livened up Board of Trade events. During their stay in Calgary he invited the company of the "Student Prince" to attend a special luncheon of the Board of Trade (19 November 1926), and entertain those present.[137] During the visit of the D'Oyly Carte Opera Company in early April 1927, the Board of Trade and the Rotary Club, together with the Gyro Club and the Calgary St. David's Society, hosted a reception and informal dance in the Board's rooms on Friday evening, April 8th.[138]

In the basement of the Lougheed, the McClungs said their farewell to Calgary on Friday, 6 July 1932. They left by car for their new home in Victoria the weekend before the 1932 Stampede. In retrospect it was a strange place for the female rights activist to say her farewell, as the Board of Trade only admitted women as members two decades later in 1953.[139] But she made no reference to this in her address. At the conclusion of Nellie's address her very good friend Leonard Brockington wished Wes and her well in their new abode.[140] *The Albertan* recorded his speech, in which he thanked Mrs. McClung for her work over "many years in opening the eyes and clearing the vision of the prairies; now she was to have an opportunity of polishing up the monocles of Victoria." "Brock's" reputation as a speaker came from his sense of fun as well as his mastery of the English language. In his rich Welsh accent he ended by warning the prohibition leader that "in the British Columbia capital the whisky and soda was as sacred as the waters of the Ganges."[141]

Just as the theatre underwent a transition, so too did the office building. Throughout the 1910s and into the 1920s the Lougheed Building had apartments on its fifth and sixth floors, with a special penthouse suite altered from its original function as the building manager's residence. In the early 1920s, Edmund Taylor, Senator Lougheed's business partner, occupied the prestige space. The residents during the late 1920s to the early 1930s were John and Helena Lethbridge—John was the CPR's chief accountant in their divisional headquarters in Calgary. Their daughter Helen was the *Calgary Herald* social columnist in the late 1920s. Helen lived with her parents until she left to take her own apartment for a year or two on the sixth floor.

After the Lethbridges, Irish-born Rose Wilkinson lived in the penthouse with her husband Fred and son Gene from 1933 to 1939. Having trained as a nurse in London, England, she operated a physiotherapy clinic in Calgary. In 1935 she served as the first Social Crediter ever elected to the Calgary City Council.[142] On council this champion of the underdog fought for people on relief and those with housing problems,

Photo of Belle Lougheed, taken by
C. Darts, probably in the mid-1920s,
as the same photo appears in the
Calgary Herald, 25 November 1926, p.
14. Glenbow Archives/NA-4441-I.

especially two or three families living under one roof.[143] Calgary's Irish Rose served on Council for twenty years, and later for five terms as a Social Credit MLA She often said: "Legislative bodies, to be representative, should be composed of men and women."[144]

Renters of apartments on the sixth and fifth floors included an interesting assortment of Calgarians united only by the fact that they could all afford the rent.[145] Just to make some introductions, residents in 1921 included, in suite 638, on the east side, lawyer Pat Bergeron, who had just served as president of the Ranchmen's Club. George Walker, a future chair of the Canadian Pacific Railway, occupied the suite for almost ten years after Bergeron's death in 1921.[146] In room 635 resided James G. Edgar, an accountant and friend of R. B. Bennett.[147] Hugh Dann, the Calgary representative of the John Deere agricultural implements company, lived in 631. Frank Denton of 613 had his real estate business on the second floor of the Lougheed. Fred and Bertha Johnston and their two children resided in apartment 600 next to John and Annie Wilson in 601. Fred Johnston was the founder and proprietor of the Johnston Storage and Cartage Company, and also the owner of the Arctic Ice Company.[148]

Quite early, certainly by the late 1920s, the Alberta Wheat Pool began its dominance on the sixth floor. Originally located in a modest office on the second floor in October 1923, it had gone from strength to strength.[149] *The U.F.A.*, official publication of the United Farmers of Alberta, reproduced a photo of the Lougheed Building in its issue of 15 August 1927 with the caption, "The Home of the Alberta Wheat Pool." The text below the photo explained that the Alberta Wheat Pool now occupied "the greater part of the second and sixth floors of the above building." By 1929 it was expanding onto the fifth floor.

The Wheat Pool held onto all its new space, even when the price of wheat plummeted after the stock market crash. Against tremendous odds the co-operative survived.[150] The re-establishment of the Canadian Wheat Board by the federal government in 1935 helped ensure this. Quickly a Calgary office opened in room 202 in the Lougheed Building.[151] It assisted those Alberta farmers who chose to use it, and each year it guaranteed a minimum price for their wheat. By the late 1930s the Wheat Pool finally started to show a profit again.[152] It repaid all the debt it incurred in the early 1930s in 1947.[153]

The transformation of the fifth floor into offices proved faster than the sixth. In the early 1920s Chautauqua, a non-denominational organization that sent musical performances, lectures and plays across Western Canada, established its headquarters in the Lougheed Building. The brown tents that housed their performances brought culture and drama to isolated communities. It also enjoyed in the 1920s popularity in major towns and cities. Financially and culturally Chautauqua proved a great success. The series of programs generally lasted in a given location from four to six days, the Chautauqua week.[154]

After Chautauqua left the Lougheed in 1922 another commercial tenant replaced them. But one distinguished Calgarian momentarily reversed the trend of apartments being converted into offices. Annie Glen Broder, Calgary's well-known music critic, lived in 538. In her wonderfully flamboyant way, she inserted this "Change of

Address" notice in *The Calgary Herald* on September 18th when she left the building: "Owing to business reconstruction in Lougheed Building, Mrs. Glen Broder has removed to 1111 7th Ave. West (Upper Duplex Suite)." Yet, for all her cool exterior, Mrs. Broder was a brilliant piano teacher. As Muriel Manning, who studied with her in the 1920s, recalled, "she would allow you to interpret a composer the way you saw him. She wanted you to put your own emotion into the piece. In short, while respecting what the composer had written she wanted you to have your own voice."[155]

By 1931 the Wheat Pool occupied the entire sixth floor with the exception of three offices. It also had four offices on the fifth.[156] By the end of the 1920s only one apartment tenant remained on the fifth floor: Henry Wise Wood. His apartment would be the last in the building, held by his family for five years after his death in 1941.[157]

Commercial tenants who replaced the apartment dwellers on the fifth floor included Manufacturers Life Insurance Company, from 1919 to 1929. Dominion Bridge located on the fifth floor in the mid-1920s, and Canada Cement from the mid-1920s to the mid-1930s. Canada Cement, with its large cement plant at Exshaw, Alberta, was hit hard by the depression: in fact, from 1929 to 1932 the value of its stock fell by 93.8 percent.[158] It at least survived. On the fourth floor, the long-established local firm, Binnie Lumber and Coal Company, which shipped lumber and Alberta coal across Western Canada, went bankrupt.[159] By the summer of 1931 they could not pay their rent for office 429, and were evicted. The bailiff sold the firm's three typewriters, two "tilting chairs," three desks, filing cabinet, their adding machine and hall safe on 2 May 1932 to pay the rent claim and costs.[160]

In the late 1920s other tenants on the fifth floor included A. W. Dingman of Calgary Petroleum Products, who kept an office in the building right up until his death in March 1936 at age 35.[161] Another long-term tenant was Sydney Tregillus, brother of William. After his brother's death and the final collapse of Tregillus Clay Products he worked as the assistant UFA secretary until the late 1910s. He then became northern and central Alberta manager for the Farmers' Fire and Hail Insurance Company on the fourth floor of the Lougheed.[162] Other accountancy jobs followed, such as with the Alberta Co-Operative Union. Although Sydney briefly farmed at Shouldice (now Montgomery) in the mid-1920s, he kept a small office in the Lougheed until 1929.[163] He needed it, as he played the cello in a trio during the dinner hour at the Palliser. Occasionally he also joined the theatre orchestras of the Grand and the Palace. The office became his equipment and changing room downtown.[164] His daughter Joan appeared on the stage at the Grand in "The Highwood Trail" and other local productions.[165]

By the late 1930s accountancy firms dominated floor five. Harvey and Morrison, which became one of the city's most renowned firms, arrived first in 1920. Senior partner Frank Harvey, auditor for the City of Calgary, chaired the board of the Calgary Symphony Orchestra, the predecessor of the Calgary Philharmonic, which played in the Grand Theatre in the 1930s.[166] The Kenneth John Morrison Room at the Calgary Chamber of Commerce commemorates Frank Harvey's well-respected partner. The accounting firm of W. Herbert A. Thompson was on the fifth floor from 1926 to

1933. The devoted Rotarian allowed the Rotary Club of Calgary to have their office in his suite in the late 1920s. For nearly forty years George Touche (now Deloitte & Touche) had their Calgary office in the building. They remained until the late 1950s. Accountant J. H. Williams opened his accounting firm on the fourth floor in 1920, but moved upstairs to the fifth in 1929. The Institute of Chartered Accountants of Alberta had their provincial headquarters in J. H. Williams's office during the 1930s.

The law firm of Porter Allen spent three decades in the building. Senior partner Marsh Porter first worked in the Lougheed in the mid-1920s when he joined Premier John Brownlee's firm. When Brownlee withdrew from his firm's active legal work, Porter became the Alberta Wheat Pool's legal counsel.[167] Previous to Porter's joining, partner Bill Hall withdrew from the Brownlee firm and established his office in the Lougheed Building.[168] Hall took with him the United Grain Growers legal work. According to the understanding reached, Marsh Porter became the head of the firm as Brownlee withdrew. Lawyer Gordon Allen joined in 1930, soon becoming Porter's chief associate.[169]

The fourth floor also had many business tenants. Many insurance adjusters located in the Lougheed. Metropolitan Life (now MetLife) retained its fourth floor suite from the building's opening in 1912 to the mid-1950s, over forty years. In the interwar period it did more business in Canada than any other life insurance company, Canadian, British or American.[170] Metropolitan held most of the mortgages on the Lougheed properties.[171]

From the late 1910s to the late 1970s the United Grain Growers occupied the third floor exclusively. In 1923 the UGG helped the Alberta Wheat Pool get established. It provided a loan of $10,000 to cover initial expenses and assisted the new organization in setting up an accounting system. The UGG also immediately agreed to handle the Pool's wheat at its elevators.[172] While the two groups discussed a merger, they opted to remain separate. Over time the Alberta Wheat Pool decided to build its own network of grain elevators and terminals to rival those of the UGG. In the words of the UGG's company history, *The First Fifty Years* (1957), their relationship "can probably best be summed up as keen but friendly rivalry."[173]

The UFA left the second floor after its 1935 electoral disaster, but their twelve-year-old offspring, the Alberta Wheat Pool, remained. As the economy improved, it thrived. Together with the UGG, the Wheat Pool occupied half of the building by the 1940s. In both offices women dominated in the clerical field. When the Lougheed first opened, many of the clerical workers were male. They handled correspondence, took dictation and maintained the files. This changed with the feminization of the office during the First World War. With the entrance of many men into the army young single women entered the secretarial field. Quickly they made the machine-related clerical jobs their own.[174] No statistical information is available for the 1930s and early 1940s, but by 1946 almost one half of the UGG's employees in the Calgary office were female.[175] During the 1920s in Western Canada, once a single woman married it was universally assumed that she would quit work to assume the role of wife and, ultimately, mother. In most large establishments women automatically left their jobs with marriage.[176] The UGG had no such policy in the 1940s.[177]

THE U.F.A.

OFFICIAL ORGAN OF

THE UNITED FARMERS OF ALBERTA :: THE ALBERTA WHEAT POOL

AND OTHER PROVINCIAL MARKETING POOLS

VOL. VI. CALGARY, ALBERTA, AUGUST 15th, 1927 No. 20

The Home of the Alberta Wheat Pool

The Alberta Wheat Pool, Pool Elevators Ltd., and the Western Sales Offices of the Canadian Wheat Pool now occupy the greater part of the second and sixth floors of the above building.

The main offices of the Pool are on the second floor and include: Manager's office, Secretary's office, Growers' Department, Grain Department and Department of Education.

The sixth floor is occupied by Pool Elevators Ltd., and the Western sales force of the Canadian Wheat Pool.

The building is known as the Lougheed Block and is situated on the southeast corner of Sixth Avenue and First Street West.

Pool members are always welcome at the Pool offices.

The retail space on the ground floor of both the 6th Avenue and 1st Street sides of the Lougheed had the same interesting mix of businesses as the office floors. Two tenants had particularly long records of occupancy. Royal Typewriter had its Calgary office from the mid-1920s to mid-1940s on the 6th Avenue side. James Cleave, an insurance broker, investment advisor and real estate agent rented space on the same side for over half-a-century, from 1915 to the late 1960s. The native son of Cornwall came to Canada at the age of thirty with a strong background in England in office procedure and accounting.[178] In 1915 James Cleave became the first to sell auto insurance in Calgary.[179]

Poor Matt Sheedy, also a tenant on the 6th Avenue Side, knew all about the impact of automobiles. In 1920 the harness maker could rest content that horses in Alberta outnumbered people 800,000 to 600,000.[180] Despite this statistic the automobile soon eclipsed the horse. In 1929 the City of Calgary removed a wide section of the existing sidewalk on 6th Avenue by the Lougheed Building to alleviate downtown traffic conditions.[181] All this work occurred outside his old store, but Matt had already left the Lougheed. The *Henderson's Calgary Directory* for 1930 states that he worked at Macklin Motors, the Ford Dealership in the city.

On the 1st Street side of the building Harry Epstein operated the Grand Cigar Store and Tea Rooms. It was a very successful business. His advertisement in the Grand Theatre program for the week commencing 26 November 1934 read: "Some of our specialties: Creamed Chicken on Toast Tea or Coffee 25 cents, Denver Sandwich Tea or Coffee 25 cents… Fresh Fruit Salad Buttered Toast Tea or Coffee 25 cents…" In the late 1920s and 1930s LaFlèche Brothers men's tailors had their store opposite the Herald Building, right where Terrill's Florists had been. They had moved from the Lougheed in 1922. The LaFlèche ads in the early 1930s had a real bounce to them; one which ran in *The Calgary Herald* on 23 June 1930 read: "Order Your Eggs Fried in Toronto! Would You Enjoy Your Breakfast? Why allow the element of CHANCE to enter into the selection of your clothes, by sending East for them?"

By the mid-1930s the Lougheed office building no longer was brand-new, but it remained in good shape. At the height of the depression it still made the A-list of Calgary's top buildings.[182] The big expansion of the Turner Valley oil field in the mid-1930s led by Home Oil, a major tenant in the Lougheed Building, gave it new life. Both the Alberta Wheat Pool and United Grain Growers remained major tenants. As regards the Grand it was struggling in 1937, but with its sale that same year a new era began under the energetic management of J. B. Barron, who renovated the theatre and re-wired it to allow for the showing of talkies.

Chapter Twelve

THE BARRONIAL ERA,
1937-1969

IN EARLY 1942 THE LONG AWAITED BRITISH FEATURE FILM, "49th PARALLEL," premiered in Calgary at the Grand. The all-star cast included three of the silver screen's biggest names: Laurence Olivier, Leslie Howard and Raymond Massey—all familiar to Calgary audiences. The previous year the Grand showed "Wuthering Heights" with Olivier and Merle Oberon (12–13 April 1941), and "Pride and Prejudice" with the matinee idol and Greer Garson (24–25 June 1941). In the summer of 1940 Grand audiences viewed Leslie Howard in "Gone with the Wind" (4–9 July 1940). While "Abe Lincoln in Illinois" had not been shown at the Grand, Calgary filmgoers knew of Canadian Raymond Massey's role as the future president for which he won a 1940 Oscar nomination for best actor. But these "big names" aside, Calgarians appeared as extras in the scenes shot at Banff National Park. The ads for the British blockbuster on six Nazis at large screamed out: "Canada Invaded/ Impossible! Wait Until You Have Seen 49th Parallel," and added, "With a Canadian Cast of Thousands including Residents of Calgary."[1]

The Grand showed the film forty-five times in nine days (30 January to 9 February).[2] As the theatre had a seating capacity of 1500, and only about 90,000 people then lived in the city, potentially over half of Calgary could have seen the film. Tens of thousands did, as well as thousands from communities around the city.

"49th Parallel" was shown at a very difficult time for the Allies. In Eastern Europe the Nazis had attacked Poland in 1939, and conquered it. The following spring the Germans invaded and occupied neutral Denmark, Norway, Holland, Belgium and Luxembourg. France fell in June 1940. They attacked Russia in the summer of 1941. During the winter of 1941–1942 the German Army encircled Leningrad and stood close to Moscow. Then came the 7 December 1941 Japanese surprise attack on Pearl Harbor, which devastated much of the American Pacific fleet. Hong Kong fell on Christmas Day to the Japanese. In late January the Japanese threatened the great British naval port of Singapore. If the Japanese overpowered the American forces in the Philippines, and the Dutch in what is now Indonesia, Australia faced possible invasion. A massive Japanese naval force advanced toward Hawaii. Nor was the campaign in North Africa going well in late January 1942; German Field Marshal Rommel had just launched a new offensive from Libya into Egypt.[3]

In the context of the times, the "49th Parallel" was inspirational. Emeric Pressburger, the script-writer, obtained the 1942 Oscar for best story. In making their film, Pressburger and Michael Powell, one of Britain's top directors, bore in mind the axiom known to all propagandists that "films must be good entertainment if they are to be good propaganda."[4] Conceived in early 1940, the film was seen as a vehicle to help bring the United States into the war on Britain's side. One cannot predict the future. The film was released in Canada and the United States just after America entered the war.

Thanks to initial funding from a newly established British propaganda fund Powell and Pressburger made a quick trip to Canada in early 1940. In Ottawa they met key Canadian officials including former Calgarian Leonard Brockington, then a special advisor to Prime Minister Mackenzie King. "Brock" had left Calgary in 1935 to work in Winnipeg as the general counsel for the North West Grain Dealers Association of Winnipeg. Renowned across Western Canada for his wit, culture and eloquence, Brock was named by Prime Minister Mackenzie King in 1936 to a three-year term as the CBC's first chair. After the outbreak of war the Prime Minister called him to Ottawa to advise him in the preparation of important documents and drafts of speeches.[5]

After hearing the filmmakers' proposal, "Brock" supported it fully. In his memoirs Michael Powell included this word picture of the former Calgarian, soon to be invited to London to head the Empire Division of the British Ministry of Information, responsible at the time for telling the Commonwealth about the war's progress.[6] Michael Powell described "Brock" as "a long, lean, handsome man with reddish curly hair and extraordinary bright eyes." He continued; "He was obviously crippled and tortured by arthritis… He was always in pain and always prepared to help others. He was just the kind of experienced, civilized, knowledgeable man who knows and knew everybody that we needed to meet at the particular moment."[7]

After the Canadian trip Pressburger wrote a rough outline of the script's intricate plot. The locations selected included Wolstenholme in Northern Quebec (the HBC post close to where the Hudson Strait opens into Hudson Bay), a Hutterite colony in Manitoba, Winnipeg, Banff and Lake O'Hara in the Rockies and Niagara Falls. The story centred on the destruction of a Nazi U-Boat in Hudson Bay by the Royal Canadian Air Force. The six Nazi survivors at first attempt to try and reach the neutral United States in a stolen plane. One dies in the capture of the plane. Another perishes in their crash landing, short of fuel, north of Winnipeg. The four Germans still at large then revise their plan. They decide to head for Vancouver and board a ship to Japan. When one of the fugitives, a former baker, sickened by his colleagues' bloodthirsty viciousness, attempts to leave them and live in a pacifist Hutterite community in Manitoba, they murder him. The three remaining Nazis travel from Winnipeg to Banff, which they reach the day of the Grand Parade of Banff Indian Days. With the help of First Nation people the Mounties capture one Nazi after the procession reaches the central courtyard at the main entrance to the Banff Springs Hotel. Another fugitive is later taken at Lake O'Hara, leaving only Lieutenant Hirth, the Nazi leader, at large. He decides to turn east in an attempt to try to cross over into the neutral United States at Niagara Falls.

The film had a very strong cast, with Laurence Olivier bizarrely selected to play a French Canadian trapper, and Leslie Howard as Philip Armstrong Scott, an effete British Canadian author who lived in a teepee at Lake O'Hara in Yoho National

Park while writing his book, *Red Men in the Rockies*. Others involved in the film include Anton Walbrook, a extremely good choice as Peter, the Manitoba Hutterite leader who denounces the Nazis, and Raymond Massey, an AWOL (absent without leave) Canadian Army soldier who captures Lieutenant Hirth at Niagara Falls. Eric Portman contributed an extraordinary performance as the fanatical Nazi leader. Only one of the Alberta extras received mention in the film credits—the Stoney Tatanga Mani, or Walking Buffalo, whose English name was George Maclean.[8] In the credits his name appears as "Tawera Monanna," the way it sounded to the member of the British crew who recorded it. Norman Luxton, "Mr. Banff," then editor of the *Banff Crag and Canyon* newspaper and director of events at "Banff Indian Days," played himself. Unfortunately Powell and Pressburger overlooked him in the credits. Celebrated British conductor Ralph Vaughan Williams wrote the music, played by the London Symphony Orchestra. Responsible for the photography was Freddie Young, who had just worked on "Goodbye Mr. Chips."[9] Film editor David Lean's greatest honour came two decades later as a director with his Oscar for "Lawrence of Arabia."

The film opens with a map of Canada and the voice of Vincent Massey, then Canadian High Commissioner in London.[10] He introduces the 49th Parallel as the "only undefended frontier in the world," making the point very clear to the Americans.[11] The principal actors, Olivier and Howard, as well as Wallbrook, were shot at Denham Studios just after the London Blitz, the savage Nazi air assault on London in the early fall of 1940. Raymond Massey (Vincent's brother), then in the Canadian Army, was filmed in Montreal. The actors who played the Nazi roles crossed the country with Michael Powell to their locations. He returned in the late spring and summer of 1940, backed up by additional British Ministry of Information funding. The filming proved enormously expensive. To obtain the Canadian footage the filmmakers employed a permanent staff of twenty-five who covered over fifty thousand miles.[12] When the ministry funds ran out, the British filmmaker J. Arthur Rank stepped forward with the sixty thousand pounds necessary to complete the film.[13]

Calgarian Bonar Bain belonged to the group of extras hired for the shooting at Banff. What a proud moment the premiere at the Grand was for him. In his last year at Western Canadian High School the nineteen-year-old had invited his girlfriend to witness his movie debut. His name had appeared in the Calgary newspaper ads identifying the Calgary extras. The Banff scenes had been completed a year and a half earlier. The participants were selected by the casting director in interviews held at the Palliser Hotel.[14] Every day for ten days they went back and forth to Banff by train.

Bonar found the shooting of sequences somewhat boring, much like waiting for a bus. Yet, he liked the cash. At Safeway on Saturdays he earned two dollars, but he received ten dollars a day as an extra. Both Bonar and his brother Conrad had acted at Western Canada High School under Calgary drama teacher and director Betty Mitchell. Conrad had the special talent, and many years later, after training at the American Academy of Dramatic Arts and appearances at Stratford and in Broadway productions, he had major roles in the television sitcoms "Maude" and "Diff'rent Strokes." Initially Conrad, not Bonar, had been selected as an extra, but he had an attack of nerves before the shoot and could not do it. Bonar, being an identical twin, stepped in with no problem.

For the first hour and a half of the roughly two-hour film, Bonar sat anxiously with his girlfriend by his side. Tension rose with the sequences showing the sinking of the U-Boat in Hudson Bay, the scene with Laurence Olivier as a French Canadian trapper eventually murdered for speaking back to the Nazis, and then the incredible moment in which Anton Walbrook as the Hutterite leader chillingly denounces the Nazi's ideology: "We are not your brothers... We hate the power of evil which is spreading over the world."[15]

For Bonar this all led up to his Banff appearance. A tremendous disappointment awaited him. As he later said: "Fortunately I didn't sneeze or I wouldn't have seen myself on the screen."[16] In the completed film he only appeared for about ten seconds. As Eric Portman, the head Nazi, made his way through a CPR observation car on the way to Banff, Bonar sat in an aisle seat grinning happily.[17] Other "extras" in the audience experienced a similar disappointment, but Calgary audiences loved the film so much that the Grand announced on February 6th: "For those unable to catch the show during the past week, three more days give desired opportunity."[18]

J. B. "Jack" Barron had carried off a tremendous coup by obtaining the Calgary premiere of "49th Parallel." When the film opened on January 30th, *The Calgary Herald* reported the telegram from London to the Grand Theatre from Laurence Olivier, Leslie Howard, Anton Walbrook, Eric Portman, Emeric Pressburger and director Michael Powell: "GREETINGS CANADA! THIS IS YOUR FILM. YOU MADE IT JUST AS MUCH AS ANY OF US. WE THANK EVERY CANADIAN WHO HELPED US AND ARE PROUD TO BE YOUR PARTNERS IN THIS AND EVERY OTHER UNDERTAKING."

When J. B. Barron took over the Grand in the summer of 1937 he did not have a guaranteed supply of first-run films. Finally came the glorious day, December 17th, when the Grand announced in the *Herald*: "First Run Feature Pictures, at New Low Admission Prices! We are glad to announce that we have been successful in closing contracts with Hollywood producers especially advantageous to us permitting us to show ROAD SHOW Pictures..." On New Year's Eve the Grand presented a double bill featuring the Canadian premiere of "Jericho" starring the famous African American actor and singer, Paul Robeson, along with Gene Autry in "Springtime in the Rockies." In 1941 the Grand's owner linked his theatre with J. Arthur Rank and the Odeon chain, assuring a continual supply of first run pictures. This link gave the Grand the premiere of the "49th Parallel" in Calgary.

J. B. Barron had an incredible flair as a theatre manager. His developed his interest as manager of the Palace Theatre in the mid-1920s. Born in Winnipeg, Jack and his younger brother Abe were the sons of Jewish emigrants from Russia who had arrived in Canada around 1882.[19] They were raised in the city until their early teens, and from 1903 to 1905 they spent two years in Dawson City, where their father opened a clothing store. At the height of the Gold Rush he had come over the White Pass with a stock of merchandise.[20] After graduation from Dawson High School the two brothers

In 1942 the Lougheed Building as shown in the centre of this postcard still remained a prominent landmark on the city's landscape. Postcard collection, Calgary Public Library.

The Banff extras for "The 49th Parallel," at the Banff railway station, July 1940. Bonar Bain appears standing at the back, third from the left. He stands between Calgarians Maureen Tighe, and Magalina Polley. Pauline Mackenzie stands to the right of Magalina Polley. Doran Moore, who saved the print, is in the back row at the extreme right. Other Calgarians appear in the shot kneeling in the front row, from left to right: Blair Colborne, unidentified individual, Bill Quigley, and Peggy McGannon. The train conductor Samuel "Smokey" Shaw was a CPR employee in Medicine Hat. Sgt. Howard Hopper Cronkhite of the Banff RCMP had previous movie experience. According to the Banff *Crag and Canyon* (26 February 1943) he had doubled for Nelson Eddy in the 1936 shooting of "Rosemarie." Photo courtesy of Doran Moore.

attended the University of Chicago. They obtained undergraduate degrees before entering the University of Chicago Law School.[21] Their mother accompanied them to Chicago where she worked as a seamstress to help pay for her sons' education. She made dresses for leading Chicago actresses in vaudeville and the Yiddish theatre who came to her for fittings.[22] In 1911, Charles Bell, the owner of the brand-new King George Hotel (later the Carlton) on 9th Avenue West, invited both his nephews to Calgary, then in the full flush of its first big boom. Their parents later followed, Elizabeth Barron having returned to Dawson and finally convinced her husband Joseph to leave his beloved Yukon.[23]

During their first ten years in Calgary Jack and Abe practised law in the city in the firm of Barron and Barron. They were among the first Jewish lawyers to practise in the city. In 1914 Jack married Amelia Helman, a public school and piano teacher from Winnipeg. They had a family of three boys: Bill, Bob and Dick.[24] Gradually Jack entered the entertainment industry. He acted as the solicitor in Calgary for the Allen family, who had established Canada's national movie chain.[25] Then in the early 1920s the Famous Players chain, just formed by Paramount, stopped the Allens from obtaining Paramount pictures. This pushed the Allens into bankruptcy, forcing them to divest themselves of their showpiece Allen's Palace Theatre in Calgary. In order to save the money they owed him, J. B. Barron entered the theatre business, taking out a second mortgage on Allen's Palace, which subsequently became the Palace. A new career was born for him.

A natural impresario, J. B. brought some of the greatest musical figures to the Palace. These included, for instance, the renowned violinist Jascha Heifitz (1 December 1924). Annie Glen Broder, no doubt writing her review for *The Calgary Herald* in her Lougheed Building apartment, stated that the twenty-four-year-old artist, "whose fame is phenomenal and skill extraordinary," had satisfied Calgarians' "soul-hunger for music."[26] *The Albertan* assigned credit for the visit where it was due, to the management of the Palace: "The cost must have been stupendous and their reward only a sense of a duty well done. For that reason the gratitude of their patrons must be appreciated. Musical Calgary will not soon forget the debt they owe to these progressive citizens, who, at the risk of heavy loss, undertook the work of the concert."[27] Nearly two thousand people, a capacity audience, attended the extraordinary concert. It was indeed a high risk. Heifetz had asked Jack Barron for the enormous sum of $2,250 for that one performance (or eighty percent of the gross profits, whichever figure proved higher).[28]

Only three months after the Heifitz visit, J. B. Barron brought Sergei Rachmaninoff to Calgary (27 February 1925). Calgary was a good show town, particularly for music. Radio eventually allowed Calgarians access to excellent music, but not during its early days in the mid-1920s.[29] The celebrated Russian composer-pianist travelled with three Steinway concert grand pianos; one went to the Palace, one to the Palliser Hotel where he stayed and the third on the train to his next destination.[30] Again Annie Glen Broder's review in the *Herald* was very positive. The caption of her article reads, "Rachmaninoff's Genius Delights Calgary Audience." She threw a bouquet to J. B. as well. The Palace's manager was "much to be commended for his acumen and

On the right of this photo the
Palace Theatre, around 1924.
Glenbow Archives/ NA-2575-43.

Calgary Symphony Orchestra, 1931.
Grigori Garbovitsky, conductor, appears
in the centre. Immediately to the left
of the maestro is Jascha Galperin,
first violinist and concertmaster. On
the left, in the centre, surrounded
by four female members of the
orchestra is Harcourt (Toby) Smith,
who kept the photo for over seventy
years and lent it for reproduction.
Photo courtesy of Harcourt Smith.

CALGARY SYMPHONY ORCHESTRA, 1931   GRIGORI GARBOVITSKY, CONDUCTOR

enterprise." The following year Mrs. Broder again publicly thanked Jack Barron when she learned that he had booked for 6 May 1926 the London String Quartet, one of the most famous in the world:[31] "That the management of the Palace theatre may give again such opportunities for pure pleasure is the prayer of every musician and music lover in Calgary."[32]

Anxious to keep the Palace as busy as possible, Jack Barron organized a full program of silent films and vaudeville. He also enticed William Aberhart away from the Grand. Until he built the Prophetic Bible Institute several years later, the evangelical high school principal held his religious services at the theatre. On November 1925 Aberhart launched his first radio broadcast of "Back to the Bible Hour" from the Palace stage.[33] However, Jack Barron lost control of the theatre three years later in 1928, when the trust company administering the property sold it. Soon afterwards the theatre landed in the hands of Famous Players.[34] Although Jack Barron returned to practising law fulltime, he kept alive his dream of one day returning to the theatre business. A decade later he had his chance.

One of Jack Barron's greatest contributions to Calgary was his invitation to Grigori Garbovitsky to move from Winnipeg to Calgary in 1927. [35] The Russian conductor and violinist had a very interesting background. His talented father, an engineer, loved languages and translated Russian and Hebrew works into Yiddish.[36] Born in the Crimea, Grigori studied violin at the St. Petersburg Conservatory with Leopold Auer at the same time as Kathleen Parlow and Jascha Heifitz. Upon graduation he became the conductor of the Rostov Symphony until the turmoil of the Russian civil war led him to leave Russia for Berlin, where on two occasions he conducted the Berlin Symphony Orchestra. A relative in Winnipeg invited him to that city, where he resided until J. B. Barron brought him to Calgary to conduct the Palace Theatre Orchestra.

Maestro Garbovitsky officially founded the Calgary Symphony Orchestra in the winter of 1929-1930. For its performances he selected the Grand.[37] In the symphony's first year the *Toronto Globe* recognized the Russian musician's contribution: "His residence in Calgary means much for music in Canada."[38] Annie Glen Broder, very pleased with the results, continually congratulated him "for his splendid work."[39] But financial problems plagued the symphony until, after valiant efforts to keep it afloat, the symphony's board of directors resigned on 1 October 1937.[40] A successful fund drive and a board re-organization led to a short-rebirth. The outbreak of World War Two, and Garbovitsky's departure for Vancouver, brought an end to the experiment.[41]

J. B. Barron's opportunity to return to theatre management came in 1937. That February Jack and Edgar Lougheed made an agreement leading to the sale of the Grand Theatre. It was a complicated arrangement, but it worked. The Lougheed family desperately wanted to sell. They were absolutely broke. From the lofty heights of the early 1920s their fortunes—socially and economically—had plummeted.

After Sir James's death in 1925 a series of tragedies befell the family—the first blow, psychological rather than financial, came shortly after the senator's death. It illustrated how quickly his memory faded. In 1926 the Liberal administration named a mountain in the Rockies after him, but in an isolated area west of Banff.[42] In its place

Clarence Lougheed, the eldest son, recommended "the very handsome and imposing peak bearing the name of 'Wind Mountain'."[43] Overlooking his father's acrimonious split with R. B. Bennett, Clarence contacted him early in 1928 for help.[44] The newly elected leader of the federal Conservatives wrote back: "I have gone to the Department and I think you will find matters will work out to your entire satisfaction."[45] The old Wind Mountain became Mount Lougheed, the peak that dominates the view to the south from Dead Man Flat, and is visible approaching the Rockies from Calgary.[46]

Clarence Lougheed looked after the Lougheed Estate. The Great Depression led to a real financial crisis for the family, now dependent on rental revenue, at a time when tenants could not always pay. The oldest of the Lougheed children died from heart failure in early 1933.[47] Clarence was only forty-five years old. The weight of handling the estate fell on Edgar's shoulders. The younger brother was forced to devote all his attention to estate matters and, in effect, leave the practice of law.

A court case in the mid-1930s revealed just how far the family had economically fallen. In 1938 the city seized Lougheed House for non-payment of taxes.[48] Just before the mansion's contents went to public auction in late August 1938, Edgar's younger son, ten-year-old Peter, with his friend Alan Johnson, secretly explored the old house from top to bottom. At the two-day-long auction the contents of the house went for ridiculously low amounts, another moment of humiliation for the proud family.[49]

Despite all the financial pressures he endured, Edgar tried to do the right thing in difficult circumstances. Toward the end of the 1930s he saved from eviction Albert Calman, a Lougheed tenant who owned a fur salon located by the entrance to the Grand Theatre. Edgar provided extra time for Calman's payment of his monthly rent. Hy Calman, Albert's son, recalls he "saved many businesses from going bankrupt, a wonderful gentleman in the true sense of the word."[50] Fortunately with the end of the depression the Lougheed properties gradually fared better, enjoying greater occupancy and steadier rents in the last few years before Edgar's death in 1951.[51]

The Grand Theatre became one of Edgar's biggest financial problems in the late 1930s. In 1931 Famous Players ended their five-year lease of the Grand. The Lougheeds ran it alone from late 1931 to early 1933, but they lacked the necessary show business background to do it successfully. Aware that they needed help, they signed a lease on 31 October 1933 with Ken Leach, an experienced theatre operator and an associate of the Famous Players chain.[52] The agreement entered into effect on 1 January 1934.[53]

Ken Leach attracted a stock company to the Grand that February. Ernest Willis, who briefly, twenty-five years earlier, had run Senator Lougheed's old Lyric Theatre for him,[54] assembled the company. The British Guild really was an outstanding group. They played in Calgary almost every week over a four-month period.[55] Two guild members went on to big accomplishments in Hollywood. Gaby Fay, who changed her stage name to Fay Holden, became Mickey Rooney's mum in the Andy Hardy series. Fellow actor Basil Radford obtained in London a supporting role in one of Alfred Hitchcock's early films, and later appeared in other mystery comedies.[56]

A successful beginning but, after the British Guild left, Ken Leach seemed out of ideas. Road shows were almost impossible to obtain. He attracted a few additional shows, including a stock company for about six weeks in 1935, but the Grand remained dark most of the remainder of that year.[57] As he owned two other theatres in Calgary, Leach had no desire to increase the competition by wiring the Grand for sound. His inactivity hurt the Lougheeds enormously as the deal struck in the lease agreement of 1933 set the rental at fifty percent of the net profits made by the lessee in the operation of the theatre. All the estate received was $100 a month. With this tiny amount it tried to pay the heating costs, up-keep, taxes and insurance. In 1936 the theatre operated for only thirty-three days.[58] J. B. Barron proposed a solution: if the Lougheed Estate sold the theatre, they could then break their lease with Ken Leach. In his ruling Judge Sheppard of the Supreme Court of Alberta agreed that the sale of the building cancelled the lease.[59]

With J. B. Barron's purchase of the theatre the Grand returned to life. With the help of Clarence Dowsley, a fellow entrepreneur with a background in electricity, they renovated the Grand that summer. They installed a new, larger projection booth—triple the size of the old one—along with modern stage lighting and wiring for sound.[60] On September 3, *The Calgary Herald* reported that twenty-five workers had been involved on the project for six weeks.[61] Jack's youngest son, Dick, then sixteen, helped first with the replacement of old lights with florescent fixtures, and then with the entire renovation. They painted the auditorium and lobby. The placing of the seating was left intact, and the boxes were not changed at this point. The Barrons worked from eight in the morning until midnight, day after day, until the theatre was ready. Jack put every penny he had into the project. Fred Lepper, a local plumber, lent money to the Barrons to complete it.[62]

The new owners gave special attention to the acoustics. Designed for stage productions, the acoustics had always been good. Mrs. Lydia Winter, for example, commented on this quality years earlier: "Being adventurous, I have wandered upstairs and down and heard equally well in front or back seat."[63] But for musical performances problems existed. As Annie Glen Broder once commented: "Though rejoicing that this city has so fine a theatre it must be admitted that it is a difficult one in which to sing, every first venture, in whatever language, British or foreign, and for whatever range of voice being obviously discomfited till an adjustment to somewhat ungraceful conditions is accomplished."[64] In a special ad for the September 1st *Herald,* Clarence Dowsley explained the improvements made in preparation for talkies at the Grand: "In accordance with the best modern sound engineering practice the walls, ceiling, arches and curves have been remade and acoustically treated to accentuate and emphasize the finer sound shadings and vibrations of the modern sound equipment in the projection room."

With the introduction of a huge exhaust fan in the ceiling, the renovations allowed for smoking in the balcony. The main floor still remained smoke free. One of the ads for "49th Parallel" reads, "700 Balcony and Loge seats for Smokers."[65] At the time of the Grand's opening in 1912 smoking was almost completely a male custom. The Grand made provision for this by providing a "gentleman's smoking room" in the basement of the theatre.[66] By the 1930s the cigarette habit had now taken hold among women as well as men. Under their new smoking policy, the Barrons soon found that instead of the balcony being the last area of the theatre to fill, it now became the first.[67]

The re-opening was dramatic. On 3 September 1937, renowned bandmaster Giuseppe Creatore, who Jack had first brought to Calgary to perform at the Palace in 1927,[68] directed a thirty-five-piece orchestra in a programme of popular classical music.[69] He was a marvellous conductor. Years later Dick Barron could still hear Creatore and the orchestra's "triumphant march from Aida ringing in his ears."[70] Elvira Helal, a coloratura soprano from the opera stage, accompanied the orchestra. She began with a soprano solo from *La Traviata*.[71] Two films followed the orchestra and singer. Creatore remained at the Grand throughout September.

For year or so after the opening J. B. tried to line up vaudeville shows for the Grand, but this proved very difficult. By the early 1940s the Grand had become primarily a movie house, but one which welcomed a number of live performances each year. One of the old favourite groups came back. Jack Barron first tried for a return of Sir John Martin-Harvey in November 1938.[72] No luck. Now in his mid-70s the English actor was on the point of retiring, which he did in 1939.[73] The Grand did succeed in booking the popular San Carlo Opera, so popular in the 1920s, which returned three times (4–6 April 1938; 31 January–2 February 1944; 26–28 February 1945).

In 1938 the San Carlo Opera closed with *Carmen*, always a hit with Calgary audiences.[74] All four operas brought out capacity crowds.[75] Eleanor Dyke, a local violinist, took her son Christopher. She was becoming concerned about her twelve-year's growing attraction to the cowboy songs of Wilf Carter, and wanted to introduce him to Grand Opera. It worked. Over sixty years later Christopher remembered the outstanding performance. "I sat spellbound throughout all four acts. In the final scene, on hearing the triumphant march of the victorious Toreador approaching, Carmen flaunts her fickle affections in the face of the jilted Don Jose, who enraged opens a long flashing knife with teeth and stabs her fatally right through the beast! Paralyzed by fright over this dastardly deed, my quick witted mother grabbed me just in time as I nearly fell over the balcony rail."[76]

Following the example of the Grand in earlier days, Jack Barron brought animals back to the Grand stage. In the early days six Kentucky thoroughbreds once trod the boards of the newly-built Grand Theatre in the production, "Old Kentucky."[77] The musical "Chu Chin Chow" in 1920 had included an old camel and a donkey. That same year, in the biblical play "The Wanderer," a herd of sheep moved across the Grand's stage.[78] During Maynard Joiner's tenure in the mid-1920s the Grand had welcomed "Powers' Dancing Elephants" who travelled with the Orpheum Circuit. Lena, the oldest of the four at age forty, weighed five tons. Little Roxie weighed two tons. The most famous of the former stars of the New York Hippodrome was Jennie, "whose shimmy dance and fox trot are the most difficult feats ever mastered by a performing animal."[79] In late May 1938, Jack Barron introduced the Polack Circus, which had a week-long run. As *The Calgary Herald* reported on May 30: "Jumbo, the elephant, is the star animal performer, leading a routine in which a Great Dane dog, a camel and a pony take part." It was a commercial success, but the circus left such a mess and stench in the theatre that the Barrons vowed never to have animal acts again.[80]

Always ready to try a new idea, J. B. Barron introduced a dance band to the Grand. Over a two-year period, February 1940 to May 1941, Jerry Fuller and his orchestra played regularly on Sunday nights beginning at 9:15. As there could be no admission charged on a Sunday, the Grand management asked the audience to make a voluntary cash contribution to the "silver collection." To tap a new market the Grand also began a talent night with radio announcer and future Calgary mayor Don Mackay as host. The talent nights ran from September 1940 to mid-1941.

In early 1943, 120 local Calgary performers participated in a special three-hour gala variety show at the Grand in honour of Canada's armed forces, "Salute to Arms" (14 January 1943). Mayor Andrew Davison introduced the program. Officers of the army, navy and air force stations in the Calgary district also spoke briefly.[81] Two smash hits followed: the Canadian Army and Royal Canadian Navy shows, both staged entirely by service people. The "Army Show" (7–9 June 1943), written by comedians Johnny Wayne and Frank Shuster, included the big army band and a huge cast. As *The Calgary Herald* wrote on June 8th: "The Army Show has everything it takes to win an audience—pretty girls, singable tunes and clever comedy." The next year the Grand hosted the "Navy Show" (17–22 April 1944), then on its cross-Canada tour. Different from the army's variety show approach, it was more like a Hollywood musical.[82]

Throughout the war, and immediately after it, the Grand welcomed a series of celebrated visiting artists. One of the first was the acclaimed African American singer Marian Anderson, who obtained an outstanding reception (15 March 1940). The audience of fifteen hundred called her back for five encores.[83] Lauritz Melchior, Danish tenor of the Metropolitan Opera Company, also brought out a capacity audience (21 October 1940). His program extended from Scandinavian folk songs to Wagnerian opera. Another favourite was violinist Yehudi Menuhin (4 November 1943).

Artur Rubinstein came twice. He first played at the Grand on 17 March 1942. An outstanding success it was, as indicated in Margaret Steven's review for *The Calgary Herald* the next day: "Never a Dull Moment in Rubinstein's Brilliant Playing." An eyewitness account by Alexandra Munn of his second Calgary visit two years later also indicates the tremendous power of the great Polish pianist. Alexandra's uncle took her to hear Rubinstein when he returned to the Grand on 7 February 1944. She knew well the neighbouring Lougheed Building as her dad, a chartered accountant, worked in the office of George A. Touche and Company on the fifth floor.[84] It was a late evening for a nine-year-old, as the recital began at 8:15 p.m. But Rubenstein's playing swept her away and over half-a-century later she still remembered his electric performance of Manuel de Falla's "Ritual Fire Dance." Alexandra later became pianist with the Calgary Philharmonic, a professor of music at the University of Alberta and subsequently an instructor at Alberta (Grant MacEwan) College Conservatory of Music, as well as the choral director of the Edmonton Opera Association. For one month after the Rubinstein recital she practised at the family piano to imitate his style of playing of the "Ritual Fire Dance," her hands flying furiously up and down.[85]

Lobby of the Grand Theatre, January 1944. The poster for the San Carlo Opera Company, Monday, January 31 – Tuesday, February 1 – Wednesday, February 2, 1944, allows the photo to be dated. Photo by Joseph L. Rosettis. Courtesy of Robert H. Barron.

The theatre underwent physical change in the mid-1940s. Possibly in March 1944 the Barrons removed the boxes in the theatre's auditorium.[86] Additional engineering work in the auditorium during the mid-1940s allowed for the removal of two of the four columns supporting the balcony. This greatly improved the view for those at the back on the main floor.[87] A set of photographs taken before and after these renovations provides an intimate view of the theatre in the mid-1940s. Other changes came in early 1947 with major modifications to the lobby and the foyer. The Barrons doubled the width of the entrance lobby. They installed a multi-coloured terrazzo floor and eight sturdy glass entrance doors, four of which were full vision doors controlled by photo-electric cells to make them self-opening when the approach of a person cut the electric eye. Air conditioning added to the inside comfort. Outside, the Barrons built a new marquee and exterior sign. They also replaced the old Grand box office on the north side of the lobby with a new one on the south side.[88] As the lobby was in the Lougheed Building, the Lougheed Estate had to consent to all changes. They did.

Some years later Calgary journalist, Tom Moore, explained the complicated relationship between the two adjacent structures. "As things stand, when you buy a ticket at the box office you are standing in the Lougheed Building. When you sit down, you are in the Grand Theatre Building. If you go to a washroom, you find yourself back in the theatre building. The stairways to the balcony are in the Lougheed building which also houses the theatre office."[89]

Definitely one of the finest weeks for the theatre in the Barron years was the first week of February 1946. Paul Robeson, the great African American singer and actor, visited the Grand on February 5th, by chance the theatre's 34th birthday. The management placed extra seats on the stage to allow the greatest number to hear the celebrated bass-baritone perform spirituals and the folk songs of other lands sung in their own languages. For his performance 350 people sat on the stage behind him, raising the numbers in the Grand that night to nearly two thousand. Robeson, a courageous fighter against racism in his own country, received a standing ovation before he even uttered a note.[90]

As segregation existed in Calgary, Robeson's welcome included a strong dash of Calgarian hypocrisy. In 1946, many Calgary hotels still refused rooms to African Canadians.[91] Marian Anderson had broken the colour bar at the Palliser, where Robeson and his accompanist Lawrence Brown also stayed, but it remained up at other hotels. After the performance Bob Barron, one of J. B.'s sons, suggested to Paul Robeson that conditions were better for Blacks in Canada than in the United States. As Bob told *Calgary Herald* heritage columnist David Bly in early 2004, "I'll never forget what he said: 'You are absolutely wrong. The American Negroes have great difficulty in getting to the top in whatever they're doing but we have, nonetheless, lawyers and doctors and professors, although very rarely can a Negro rise to that level. In Canada, the highest a Negro can rise in his profession, if you can call it that, is a railway porter'."[92] The great baritone added, "Prejudice is wide-open in your city." Just that morning Lawrence Brown had walked over from the Palliser to a neighbouring barbershop hoping to get a haircut only to be told, "We don't serve Negroes."[93]

An important event at the Grand for Calgary's Chinese community was the presentation of two Chinese light operas on 13 April 1947. The Chinese Dramatic Club of Vancouver performed in connection with the national convention of Chinese Free Masons being held in Calgary that week. *The Calgary Herald* reported the next day: "A capacity audience, composed of most of Calgary's Chinese population and a number of prominent citizens from public, business and professional life, attended Sunday night's unique presentation."[94]

The hosting of the Dominion Drama Festival at the Grand in May 1950 also proved a cultural highlight for the city. Doug Doherty, house manager for the event, and Alberta Lieutenant-Governor John J. Bowlen, both arrived on opening night in white tie, tails and white cowboy hats.[95] Eight groups from across Canada competed for the Bessborough Trophy, awarded for the best presentation at the festival. Director General Michel Saint-Denis of the Old Vic Theatre Company in London, England, served as adjudicator for the festival. Unfortunately Calgary's Workshop 14, directed by Betty Mitchell, did not win top honours. The Bessborough Cup went to the Belmont Group Theatre of Toronto.[96]

Although the Calgary Symphony of the 1930s had expired by 1939, Jascha Galperin, Garbovitsky's concertmaster, had sown seeds for the orchestra's rebirth. With the Mount Royal Conservatory Galperin first organized a "Baby Symphony" of conservatory music pupils between the ages of four and twelve. They gave their first concert in the Grand Theatre on 15 June 1938.[97] A year later the Baby Symphony graduated into the Mount Royal Junior Symphony composed of young performers under the age of eighteen. Wood winds, brasses and drums were added to the original strings. By the time of their 1942 concert at the Grand, hundreds could not obtain tickets as the concert sold out early. In 1944 the orchestra's name changed again to the Mount Royal College Symphony Orchestra. They also played regularly at the Grand.[98]

After Jascha Galperin left Calgary in 1945 for Vancouver, the Ontario-born conductor Clayton Hare succeeded him.[99] In 1949 the Mount Royal College Symphony became the new Calgary Symphony Orchestra. It played at the Grand from 1949 until 1955, the year it became part of the Calgary Philharmonic Orchestra. In order to help the symphony, Jack Barron rented the Grand to them for $500 to cover his costs, rather than at the commercial rate of $850.[100]

To Calgarian Don Palmer belongs the distinction of having played in all five groups, from the Baby Symphony to the Calgary Philharmonic Orchestra. Both his parents were very musical. His father loved opera and sang Italian arias while he worked. The English-born plumber from Manchester did not know Italian, but to many non-Italian speakers it sounded as if he did. Don began to learn at age eight to play the cello from Harcourt Smith, a member of the Calgary Symphony. His career highlight as a musician came at the Grand on the evening of 2 May 1949. That evening he performed as the soloist and principal cellist of the Mount Royal College Symphony Orchestra. Shortly after his performance he entered into the printing business in Calgary, but played occasionally with the Calgary Symphony under Clayton Hare, and then on a number of occasions with the early Calgary Philharmonic.[101]

In its last years as a legitimate theatre the Grand had one final period of glory between 1949 and 1957. Highlights included: Donald Wolfit (who had appeared at the Grand in 1931 with the Barry Jackson Players) and his London company who performed three Shakespeare plays (12–14 February 1948); the Passion Play of the Black Hills (18–23 October 1948); two visits of George Formby, the legendary British music hall star (27–29 October 1949 and 23–25 October 1950); two big Broadway shows— "Brigadoon" (6–10 September 1949) and "Oklahoma!" (17–22 November 1952). For the last Jack Barron had to hire twenty-seven stage hands to accommodate the huge sets.[102] A big production like "Oklahoma!" did not pay off for a theatre like the Grand. For a large gross, big touring companies need gigantic auditoriums. Large touring attractions such as Sadler's Wells Ballet, Old Vic and London Festival Ballet could not book Calgary because of a lack of adequate facilities before the Jubilee Auditorium opened in 1957.[103]

In this time period the Grand could accommodate Canadian ballet companies. Both the Winnipeg Ballet (21–22 January 1952, 19–20 January 1953; 17–18 May 1954) and National Ballet Company of Canada (17 October 1952 and 29–31 March 1954) visited. Judy Rogers Dundas' memory of the Winnipeg Ballet's first visit to Calgary in 1952 speaks volumes of Calgary's continuing cultural impact on southern Alberta. The ballet student and her mother drove over gravel roads in the middle of winter from their home in Drumheller, 200 kilometres northeast of Calgary, for the performance. Judy still vividly remembers that evening in the gorgeous theatre, "lots of people and excitement and the opening curtain revealed the magic of the ballet—can you imagine never having seen a real ballet dancer before and suddenly seeing the ballet." After the performance came the highlight of the evening. She and her mother went backstage and met Eva von Gencsy, the prima ballerina.[104]

Betty Mitchell's Workshop 14 performed several plays during the mid-1950s in the venerable old playhouse.[105] Both "Pygmalion" (3 February 1952) and "The Apple Cart" (1 May 1955) had packed houses.[106] Dr. Jim Black, Professor Emeritus, Department of English, University of Calgary, was in the audience for "The Apple Cart." He recalls: "I had not long before come to Canada, and eventually to Calgary, from Ireland. That Workshop 14 special performance in the Grand was the first time I'd ever seen a play performed live in a real theatre. It was an epiphany. A superb performance in a perfect resonating setting—and I make that judgement from a subsequent lifetime's experience of theatre going."[107] The last two plays performed by Workshop 14 in the Grand were "Picnic" (29 April 1956) and "The River Line" (6 May 1956).

In 1929 Betty Mitchell helped to found the Green Room Club, an organization that worked to further interest in drama throughout Alberta.[108] Seven years later the young teacher began the first high school credit course in drama in Canada at Calgary's Western Canada High School.[109] She was greatly admired by Mrs. Lydia Winter, who constituted the living force of theatre in the city from the late 1890s to her death in 1939.[110] Betty Mitchell replaced Mrs. Winter as Calgary's leading lady of the stage from the 1940s to 1960s. Her Workshop 14 won many awards provincially, and in the Dominion Drama Festivals. Incidentally, like Mrs. Winter, Betty Mitchell loved the

A good shot of the auditorium of the Grand Theatre in the mid-1940s, perhaps the major innovation that was made in the auditorium in the Barron's first years of ownership was the removal of the boxes probably in 1944. They have been taken out by the time of this photograph. Photo by Joseph L. Rosettis. Courtesy of Robert H. Barron.

Extensive alterations were made to the Grand Theatre in the winter of 1947/48. In this photo appear, from left to right, at the extreme left, Edgar Lougheed; fourth from the left, Dick Barron; fifth from left, Jack Barron. Photo by Joseph L. Rosettis. Glenbow Archives/PA-3463-26.

A photo taken by the Calgary Herald, and used in their issue of 5 February 1948, the theatre's thirty-sixth birthday. The shot taken from outside the Grand Theatre shows some of the alterations made the winter of 1947/48. Glenbow Archives/PA-3463-3.

An autographed copy of the program for Paul Robeson's performance at the Grand, 5 February 1946. That evening marked the theatre's thirty-fourth anniversary. Courtesy of Ed Bredin.

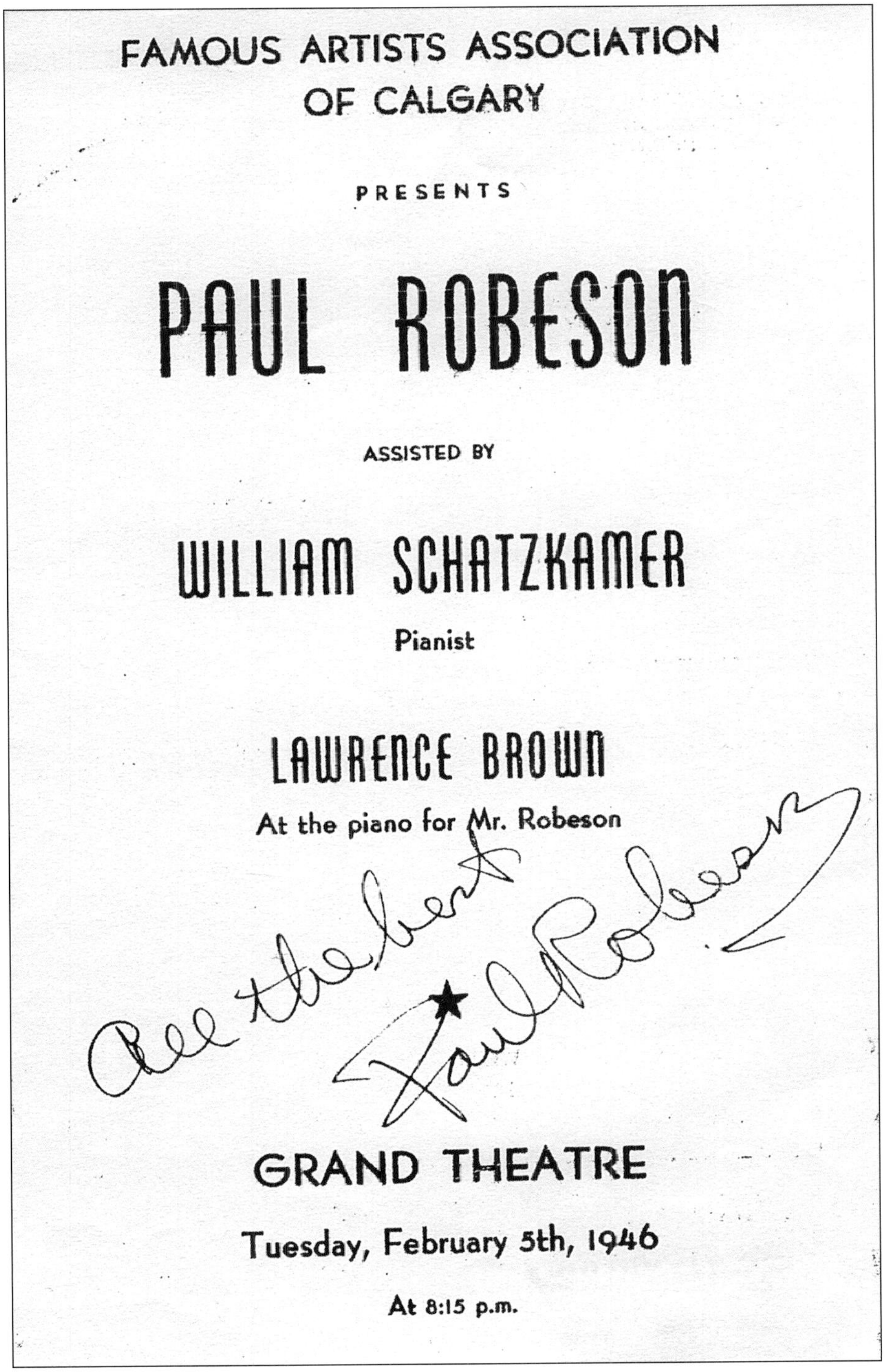

FAMOUS ARTISTS ASSOCIATION
OF CALGARY

PRESENTS

PAUL ROBESON

ASSISTED BY

WILLIAM SCHATZKAMER

Pianist

LAWRENCE BROWN

At the piano for Mr. Robeson

All the best ★ Paul Robeson

GRAND THEATRE

Tuesday, February 5th, 1946

At 8:15 p.m.

The Dominion Drama Festival,
Grand Theatre, 8-13 May 1950.
From left to right: Michel Saint-
Denis, Festival Adjudicator; Pauline
McGibbon, member of the executive
committee of the Dominion Drama
Festival; and J.B. Barron. Photo
courtesy of Robert H. Barron.

Crowd in the lobby of the Grand
Theatre, 24 October 1949. The
first performance of the Calgary
Symphony Orchestra, the first
in ten years, was that evening.
Glenbow Archives/NA-5093-22.

Calgary Symphony Concert, 5 December 1949. Photo by Joseph L Rosettis. Photo courtesy of Colin Catley.

Grand's sound: "The acoustics were superb—flawless!" In retrospect this was a turning point. Betty wanted to buy the Grand but Workshop 14 did not have the necessary $30,000 to purchase. The opportunity passed.[111]

With the completion of the Jubilee Auditorium in 1957 the Grand's days as a live theatre facility ended. The Jubilee's location out of the downtown, on the top of the North Hill, illustrated the suburban drift of the 1950s. The new Calgary Philharmonic formed in 1955 played at the Jubilee, not the Grand. In the early spring of 1957 the Canadian Players from Stratford, Ontario, performed the last two stage plays in the theatre: Shaw's "Man and Superman" (April 1) and "Othello" (April 2). Only three months later special Stampede visitor Leo Carillo, who played "Pancho" in the TV series "The Cisco Kid," paid a nostalgic visit to what was now strictly a movie house. The former vaudeville artist had fond memories of the "old" Grand,[112] where he had performed four times in the 1910s and 1920s.[113]

During the post-1947 oil boom J. B. Barron built a modern office building to respond to the growing demand for office space. Architect Jack Crawston, who completed his renovations of the Grand Theatre Lobby in 1947–1948, designed the eleven-story Art Deco structure. The Barron Building at 610, 8th Avenue S.W., built between 1949 and 1951, proved central to making Calgary the provincial oil capital.[114] The office district that grew in the western end of downtown became known as the oil patch. It incorporated office and retail space, and included a $1 million movie theatre, the Uptown, on the ground floor. Once Mobil, Shell and the Sun Oil Company moved into the Barron building, Calgary definitely confirmed that it was Alberta's oil capital.[115]

The president of J. Arthur Rank organization in Canada flew out for the official opening of the Uptown Theatre in late June 1951. The newly appointed president of Odeon Canada was none other than Leonard Brockington, whom J. B. had known for over thirty years when he was Calgary's City solicitor.[116] In a *Calgary Herald* interview that year Jack Barron announced the new direction for the Grand. It would continue to present stage shows and concerts: "No stage work would be presented at the Uptown since it was designed solely as a motion picture theatre." The ultra-modern Uptown would obtain the more "sophisticated" type of films, while the Grand's billings would concentrate on "action" movies.[117]

During the Grand's "Barronial Era" the Lougheed Building underwent a major transformation, just as the city's economy moved from dependency on agriculture to a reliance on oil and gas production. In the late 1940s the exciting tenant was Home Oil. It had a long history in the building. Originally organized by "Major" Jim Lowery (everyone called him "Major"), an Ontario school teacher who came to Alberta in 1905 and made a fortune. Home Oil first rented space in the building in 1938. It remained there until 1956. During visits from his home in Vancouver in the 1940s, the Major lived in the penthouse, which still had a completely unbroken view of the Rockies to the west.[118] The company had been successful in the Turner Valley field, largely due to Dr. "Pete" Sanderson, a Yale and University of Toronto-trained geologist who opened an office at the Lougheed in the early 1930s. He was a grandson of James F. Sanderson, a Metis trader in Medicine Hat at the same time James Lougheed lived there in 1883.[119]

The Mount Royal Symphony, with Jascha Galperin, on the stage of the Grand Theatre, late 1930s. Glenbow Archives/ND-10-218.

Don Palmer as a member of the Mount Royal Junior Symphony. On his lapel Don is wearing the wolf badge of the Cubs, Central United Troop. Photo by Stillings, lent for copying by Don Palmer.

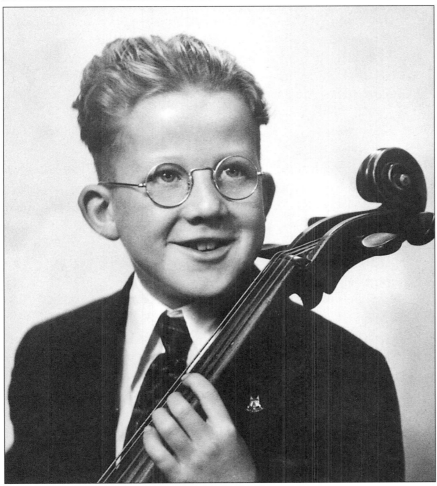

"Pete" advised Home Oil (correctly) to obtain extensive acreage in the northern flank of Turner Valley. Home Oil wisely followed his advice and profited from it.[120]

"Pete" Sanderson was a most relaxed employer. Jim Nicoll helped with drafting. Before service overseas in the World War One, Jim attended the first University of Calgary, where he won the Dr. T. H. Blow prize for English.[121] After the war he had entered engineering at the University of Alberta, and graduated in 1924.[122] But his real love was painting. He and his wife, Calgary art instructor and painter, Marion Nicoll, lived for art. Whenever it was a good sketching day, "Pete" encouraged Jim to make up his hours on another day.[123] A decade earlier another tenant in the Lougheed Building employed another well-known Calgary artist, W. L. Stevenson, who worked as a clerk for the Alberta Wheat Pool in the late 1920s and early 1930s.[124]

The discovery of the Leduc oilfield south of Edmonton in 1947 came at a most opportune time for Calgary, since Turner Valley's output had begun to decline. Moreover, Calgary oil refineries were just on the verge of arranging crude oil imports from the United States. Leduc suddenly transformed Alberta into an oil surplus region once again. The fact that the oil refineries were already located in Calgary, as were the headquarters of most oil companies operating in the Canadian West, gave the city an advantage in maintaining its position as Canada's oil and gas administrative and financial centre.[125] Top-flight office buildings like the Barron Building, the first major postwar building to respond to the new demand for office space, also helped the city.[126] With the availability of such modern accommodation as the Barron Building, oil companies had little incentive to move their headquarters to Edmonton, even though it was adjacent to the new oil field at Leduc.

Oil and gas after 1947 raised Alberta into a "have" province, from one with a per capita income nine percent below the national average in 1945, to one in the 1950s with a per capita income well above it.[127] Calgary tripled in population from a small provincial community of less than a hundred thousand in 1946 to an urban metropolis of 315,000 by 1965. The new wealth transformed the city physically with towering skyscrapers, sprawling suburbs reaching out in all directions and suburban shopping centers diminishing the power of the downtown core. By 1965 about half of Calgary's rapidly expanding population owed their jobs to oil and gas.[128] The influx of so many superimposed a sizeable population of newcomers onto a relatively small nucleus of Calgary-born residents.[129]

Bob Brown, Jr., was one of the few Calgary-born residents in the new post-Leduc Alberta to become a major player in the oil business. By 1955 Home Oil had become one of the largest independent Canadian producers of oil and gas.[130] Throughout the early 1950s Home Oil increasingly took over more space in the Lougheed Building, particularly after 1951 when Brown's Federated Petroleum, also a tenant in the Lougheed, merged with it. Bob's mother knew the Lougheed Building area well. Christina McLaughlin Brown had grown up just two blocks away at 126 6th Avenue S.W.[131] Home Oil remained in the Lougheed until their three-story office building was finished in 1955.[132]

Celia Franca, director, National Ballet of Canada, discusses the choreography of "Casse Noisette," performed at the Grand, 30 March 1954. The photograph by Jack De Lorme appeared in the Albertan, 29 March 1954. Glenbow Archives/ NA-5600-7223a.

Mayor Don Mackay, wearing a white hat, greets Leo Carillo, "Pancho" in the TV children's series, "The Cisco Kid." He appears holding his gift, a white hat, received on his arrival at the Calgary airport, 6 July 1957. That year he was the special stampede guest. Glenbow Archives/PA-2864-564.

With the onset of the oil and gas boom accounting firms like Harvey and Morrison moved into the natural resources field even as they maintained their old ties with established organizations like the Alberta Wheat Pool. Although Frank Harvey died in 1938 the firm continued on in the Lougheed Building as Harvey Morrison and Co. for more than two additional decades.[133] Ken Morrison continued to give his best to his work, serving as both president of the Institute of Chartered Accountants of Alberta before the war and president of the Dominion Association of Chartered Accountants in 1950. He also generously donated time as a volunteer to his community. In a tribute to his friend after his death, Eric Connelly enumerated Morrison's gifts to Calgary: "His church was important to him—he taught Sunday School at Knox United and was clerk of the session for 32 years. He was active with Mount Royal College, Woods Christian Home, Foothills Hospital, in charge of budget for the Community chest, president of the Chamber of Commerce..." So loyal was he to Calgary that in his retirement Ken Morrison bore only one regret—that following the death and illness of his two partners in 1959, he had turned his local Calgary practice over to Clarkson Gordon & Co., a national firm of chartered accountants. He believed that "he had let the City down."[134] The accounting profession in Calgary did not agree. As part of the Calgary Chamber of Commerce's centennial in 1991, five Calgary CA firms raised approximately $20,000 to sponsor a meeting room at the chamber offices, the Kenneth John Morrison, FCA, Room, in commemoration of the Calgarian who did so much for the accounting profession.[135]

Law firms like Porter Allen also adjusted to the new conditions. Marsh Porter, a vice-president and counsel for Home Oil, realized the need for reinforcements due to the sudden and steadily mounting oil and gas business. Two of the first law students recruited by Porter Allen were Dick Matthews and Steve Wood.[136] Marsh Porter continued as Alberta Wheat Pool counsel until called to the Bench in 1954, at which point Steve Wood succeeded him.[137] Matthews moved into oil and gas work.[138] By the mid-1950s Gordon Allen already represented a significant number of oil and gas corporations.[139] (Just like Ken Morrison, lawyer Dick Matthews did not become swallowed up by his work. In 1955 he became president of the Calgary Symphony Orchestra. One of his first duties was overseeing of the amalgamation of the Calgary Symphony with the fledgling Alberta Philharmonic to create the Calgary Philharmonic in 1955.[140])

Right up to the mid-1950s agriculture remained the chief player in Alberta's economy. As late as 1952, in fact, the value of wheat production alone was nearly double the value of petroleum and natural gas.[141] The Alberta Wheat Pool continued into the 1950s as the Lougheed's major tenant. It still had 165 employees in 1959, its last year in the Lougheed.[142] As in other downtown offices at the time a strict dress code applied. Men came to work wearing ties. Women were always well-dressed.[143] Yet, despite the formality at work, the Alberta Wheat Pool had a warm friendly atmosphere. The Pool's social and recreational club, the Wheat Kernels, helped to foster this. In the 1950s the Kernel's executive organized golf tournaments, a softball team in the City Commercial League, participation in the Grain Trade Curling League, a bowling league, challenge hockey games with the UGG, an annual train excursion to Banff, the annual Wheat

Jim Nicoll and his wife, Marion, on a
Calgary street, around 1943–1944.
Shot taken by a street photographer.
Glenbow Archives/PA-2435-4.

Kernel Banquet and many other social events as well.[144] In the mid-1950s a popular group was the Wheat Kernel Choir, formed in 1952 under the baton of Doug Parnham of the Payroll Department on the fifth floor.[145]

The Grand Cigar Store and Tea Rooms continued to give the Lougheed a community feeling. Office workers spent their breaks there or came for a quick lunch. Harry Epstein worked endless hours at the Tea Rooms to send all three of his children to university, which he and his wife managed to do in the midst of the depression.[146] His son Bill won the gold medal in law when he graduated from the University of Alberta in 1935.[147] On scholarship he attended the London School of Economics. After military service in the Canadian Army in World War Two, Bill Epstein joined the United Nations and went on to become director of the UN's Disarmament Affairs Division from 1954 to 1972.[148]

After Harry Epstein sold the Grand Cigar Store and Tea Rooms in the early 1940s Morris and Joe Smith purchased the business. They operated it for about ten years. As a young teenager in the mid-1950s Stan Smith helped his father Morris by working as the cashier.[149] Today he is an eye doctor in Calgary. After the Smiths sold the store, a major change occurred: coffee defeated tea. Fred Wolf and Nate Greenberg, the new owners, changed the shop's name to the Grand Tobacco and Coffee Shop Ltd.[150]

Fred Wolf dealt with Peter Lougheed about the lease and had a good working relationship with him. Every once in a while his mother Edna Lougheed dropped by. After Edgar's death in 1952, Mrs. Lougheed had helped with business matters for the Lougheed Estate.[151] As the Alberta Wheat Pool moved out in late 1959, Fred and Nate were able to obtain space in the basement for a bakery.[152] Ernie Hutchinson, a recently retired Alberta Supreme Court judge, was then a young lawyer with Allen, MacKimmie, Matthews. He recalls going to the Grand Coffee Shop regularly for lunch, where he often saw Bert Baker of the Pool, or perhaps even John Brownlee of the UGG. It was very democratic; "really a family."[153]

Another aspect of community involved the Christian Science Reading Room located on the Lougheed's ground floor, 6th Avenue side, from 1957 to 1974. The staff had an arrangement with the Grand Coffee Shop. If someone came into the reading room looking hungry or out of work, they would send them over to the restaurant. The understanding was that the Coffee Shop would feed them and send the bill to the reading room.[154]

Right until the end of the 1950s the Alberta Wheat Pool was the largest tenant. Its accountants and lawyers also had their offices in the Lougheed, lending another element to the building's community atmosphere. For many years Ken Morrison spent most of one day at the annual Wheat Pool meetings reading and explaining the accounts to delegates. Marsh Porter, and later Steve Wood, represented the Pool before various commissions relating to the grain trade, in presentations to government and in the negotiations over federal income tax. They frequently attended Pool directors' meetings and the annual delegates' meeting.[155] Although the UGG remained for another twenty years, the Wheat Pool's departure in 1959 really marked the end of agriculture's dominance in the Lougheed Building. Wheat Pool lawyers (Allen, MacKimmie,

The law firm of Allen, Mackimmie, Matthews, Wood, Phillips, and Smith, December (Christmas decorations are on the tree) late 1950s. Marsh Porter, member of the Supreme Court of Alberta, Appellate Division, Calgary (appointed in 1954) was paying a visit to the office. From left to right: (standing) Gordon Allen, Ross Mackimmie, Marsh Porter, Rhoda Fenton (office manager), Ernie Hutchinson, Dick Matthews; (kneeling) Jim Millard, Fred Phillips, and Steve Wood. Photo courtesy of Rhoda Fenton, copy also in The Legal Archives Society of Alberta.

Executive meeting of the Kernels, the Alberta Wheat Pool social club, Lougheed Building, 1953. Left to right: Bud Notland, Ed Patching, Alice Duke, Gordon Palmer, Doreen Himmelreich (Secretary), Ruby Beck, Joe Dabinett (President), Harlow Tripp (Vice-President), Jack Warren (Treasurer). Photo courtesy of Harlow Tripp.

Matthews, Wood, Phillips & Smith—formerly Porter Allen) and accountants Harvey and Morrison (later to become Clarkson, Gordon & Co.) followed. Similarly the theatre was on the cusp of major changes.

J. B. Barron kept in step with Calgary's changing society. With the decline in downtown movie-going occasioned by television's impact and the development of suburban theatres, the Barron family again altered the Grand to reverse the trend of declining attendance. In the mid-1960s they invested $500,000 to transform the Grand into a totally modern movie theatre.[156] They removed the stage with its two large dressing rooms, and also took out the smaller dressing rooms in the basement. The old interior décor went as well. They moved the movie screen back twelve metres (forty feet) to the rear wall.[157] The Barrons used the extra space to increase the size of the lobby. They also installed new seats and a new sound system. As Jack Barron explained: "We would like to have kept up the Grand as a site for legitimate theatre, but we just couldn't compete with the Jubilee Auditorium with its seating capacity and modern sound and stage equipment."[158] It became in form what it had been in fact since 1957—a movie house. Four years after Jack Barron's death in 1965 the Barron family sold the Grand to Odeon, ending the Grand's Barronial era.[159]

Alberta Wheat Pool Choir, directed by Doug Parnham, Lougheed Building, December 24, 1952. Photo courtesy of Doug Parnham.

The Grand Theatre and Lougheed Building, 5 July 1959. Don's Hobby Shop had just moved to the Building, and stayed nearly half-a-century. The Alberta Wheat Pool was just about to leave. Glenbow Archives/5093-688.

Alberta Chief Justice Clinton J. Ford
cuts the green and gold ribbon
across the main stairway in the Arts
and Education (now Administration)
building, 28 October 1960. From
left to right: President Walter Johns
of the University of Alberta, Chief
Justice Ford, and Dr. Malcolm Macleod,
chair of the Board of Governors.
Photo by Harold Paskall. University
of Calgary Archives/UARC 92.076.

Chapter Thirteen

MODERN TIMES

THE 1960s TO 2005

ALMOST HALF-A-CENTURY AFTER THE FIRST UNIVERSITY OF CALGARY DIED, the second one was born. On 28 October 1960, Alberta Chief Justice Clinton J. Ford officially opened two rectangular shaped university buildings—Arts and Education (now Administration) and Science and Engineering (now Science A). They stood alone on a vast desolate field in northwest Calgary. Earthmovers had smoothed the large track of land in preparation for further construction. That fall the University of Alberta in Calgary, a satellite campus of the University of Alberta, welcomed eleven hundred full-time students.[1] Since 1946 the Calgary University Committee had fought for permanent university facilities in Calgary. William Reid, a former articling student in the accounting firm of Harvey and Morrison in the Lougheed Building, initially led the campaign until his death in 1952.[2]

Throughout the 1950s Calgary's suburbs expanded ever further over the surrounding grasslands.[3] The windswept tract of land in the northwest corner of the already sprawling city still had some grazing land and a few old farmsteads around it; but development already surrounded the infant campus on three of its four corners. To the west stood Montgomery and the new suburb of Brentwood was situated to the east. The Brentwood Shopping Centre would be built the next year. To the southeast stood the "ancient" suburb of Banff Trail—dating back to the early 1950s.[4] The just completed McMahon Stadium emerged to the south, and further in that direction one reached Calgary's second oldest golf club, the former Calgary St. Andrews, now the suburb of St. Andrews Heights.

Calgary St. Andrews had held its last annual general meeting in 1927 in the Board of Trade rooms in the basement of the Lougheed Building, just before it folded as a private club.[5] It became a single owner operated course until a developer purchased the site shortly after World War Two. In the early 1950s one of city's newest subdivisions welcomed new residents.[6] When Doug Parnham of the Alberta Wheat Pool and his wife Elizabeth moved to St. Andrews Heights in 1953 friends joked that they were moving out to the gates of Banff.[7] With the completion of 16th Avenue N.W. as part of the TransCanada Highway in 1959, St. Andrews actually gained a direct link to the mountain paradise.[8] In late 1959 the provincial government announced that it would build Calgary's new Foothills Hospital in the western portion of St. Andrews, just south of the TransCanada.[9]

In 1955 the City of Calgary offered land for a permanent Calgary Branch campus of the University of Alberta. At the time the Calgary Branch called home the west wing of the Provincial Institute of Technology and Art (renamed the Southern Alberta Institute of Technology, or SAIT, in 1960). The Calgary Branch began when the Calgary Normal School joined the University of Alberta's Faculty of Education in 1945.[10] Courses in arts, science, commerce and engineering were gradually added to the core education program. In July 1957, needing more space for its Calgary operation, the University of Alberta signed a one dollar lease for the three-hundred acre Banff Highway property.[11] On 1 November 1958, Fred Colborne, minister without portfolio in the Alberta government, turned the first sod of the new campus at a spot just west of the site of the arts and administration building.[12] In his speech the provincial cabinet minister and long-time Calgarian told those present: "This is a day that will be long remembered in Calgary. It marks the beginning of a new kind of life for us. Calgary in the next few years will become a university city in every sense of the word. The thousands of young students who will live their university lives here will bring changes to the character of our city. In the future, a much higher percentage of Calgarians and southern Albertans will receive the benefits of a university education."[13]

The Grand Theatre could claim a tiny, tiny portion of the credit for Fred Colborne's excellent address. Two early Grand appearances helped him hone his public speaking skills. As a boy of five he performed in the McDonald's Dancing Academy show, "Revue of 1922." *The Calgary Herald* praised his performance, noting that "he recited his lines with a real power and deep feeling which, to judge by the applause he received immediately afterwards, must have moved every heart in the house."[14] Years later he acted again at the Grand in a play entered in the 1936 Alberta Drama Festival.[15] The provincial cabinet minister had another link with the Grand: his brother Blair had been one of the extras in the 1942 blockbuster, "49th Parallel," which had its Calgary premiere at the Grand.

During the University of Alberta's fiftieth anniversary in 1958 the provincial government officially announced their plans for a permanent Calgary campus for the University of Alberta in Calgary (UAC). The Foothills City found it offensive to be called a "branch" of anything, especially something originating in Edmonton. Hence the new title. Two years later UAC's first two buildings were ready, with the gymnasium and library (temporarily located in the arts and education building) to follow.[16] On display at the official opening of the campus's first two buildings on 28 October 1960 stood the engraved sod-turning spade Fred Colborne used two years earlier, visible proof of his promise of 1 November 1958 to transform Calgary into a university city.[17]

At the 1960 opening ceremony Chief Justice Ford cut the green and gold ribbon across the main stairway at the north end of the new arts and education building.[18] The late October festivities came with a surprise. An early winter blizzard forced the event organizers to move the ceremonies indoors.[19] The inclement weather brought with it one advantage: the ground was frozen hard. Stripped as it was of all natural vegetation in spring, summer and fall, the site became a mud bowl; without rain it was a drifting

dust bowl.[20] On opening day the guests saw no mud and no drifting soil—just white clean snow.

With Dr. Walter Johns, president of the University of Alberta on one side, and Dr. Malcolm Macleod, chair of the University's Board of Governors on the other, Chief Justice Ford performed his official duties. Throughout the ceremony he seemed quite moved. Why? It could not have been the architecture of the buildings constructed by the Alberta Public Works Department. In one observer's eyes the structures looked "more like factories than faculties."[21] The platform party stood just several metres or so away from the entrance to what is today the Executive Suite of the University of Calgary, the location of the offices of the president and vice-presidents.

What thoughts ran through Judge Ford's mind on 28 October 1960? A clue appears in his speech: "This is the fulfillment of long, long wishes, even prayers, of many public-spirited people in Alberta that Calgary, worthy as it is, would some day have its own university." His reference to prayers indicates that the seventy-eight-year-old judge belonged to a far more religious era than did many of the young people before him, who had grown up in an increasingly secular post-war society.

To the younger of the invited guests, and certainly to the undergraduates standing before him, Judge Ford belonged to a very different age. If they had the opportunity to visit his Supreme Court office they would have gained a clearer idea of his guiding principles. The distinguished jurist had a plaque hanging on the wall behind his desk outlining his personal philosophy:

"To steel our souls against
        the lust of ease,
"To find our welfare in the
        general good.
"To hold together, merging
        all degrees in one wide
        brotherhood.
"To teach that he who saves
        himself is lost.
"To bear in silence 'tho our
        hearts may bleed.
"To spend ourselves and
        never count the cost, for
        others' greater need."[22]

No one can know, of course, the exact thoughts of the chief justice that afternoon, but one supposition can safely be made. He thought of two friends: Fred Albright and Charles Ward, faculty members of the first University of Calgary. He had known both men at Victoria, the Methodist College at the University of Toronto. In Calgary Fred Albright taught economics and later helped with the University of Calgary's law program as well.[23] Moved by Albright's subsequent death at Passchendaele forty years earlier,

Clinton wrote a tribute to him in *The Christian Guardian*, the Methodist national newspaper. He summarized his friend's sacrifice in the essay's title: "A True Soldier of Jesus Christ."[24]

Charles Ward had taught French at the first University of Calgary. Like Clinton and Fred he believed in the Social Gospel—the necessity of working to create a better world on earth. In the winter of 1913–1914 the French professor had organized a well-received course of twenty public lectures for Calgarians on the great social needs of the day.[25] In the last months of the University of Calgary's existence he had married a Calgary girl, Muriel Robertson.[26] Annie Glen Broder provided incidental music at the wedding held at Muriel's parents' home.[27] But, without the prospect of a university job, Charles could not stay. He returned to the University of Chicago, where, several years earlier, he had obtained his Ph.D.

Judge Ford served as the City of Calgary solicitor in the 1910s. The City of Calgary Archives contains two letters that Charles Ward sent him in the summer of 1915. In the first, written on August 16th, Dr. Ward suggested that, "the largest city in Alberta, in view of its wealth, population etc.," might itself continue the University of Calgary. To eliminate it on the grounds of fiscal restraint "would be considered (in view of its possibilities as an *asset* with the training it might afford) just about the same kind of economy that would cause a man to try & reduce expenses by cutting off his meals."[28] Charles waited until the last minute before finalizing his plans. On September 17th he wrote Ford about his recent appointment to Rice University in Houston, Texas: "But if Calgary should need me *now* or later, *I would somehow manage to get free and go there even at this eleventh hour*, for I feel that our work in Calgary was not really started."[29] But the city was preoccupied with the war. Wary of any further investment in the university in a time of economic decline, it did nothing. The first university died.

In 1960 one of the most important participants in Calgary's first university experiment still lived in Alberta. Kent Power had organized the university's law courses. During its last months the first university's acting dean of law worked from his law office, room 402 in the Lougheed Building.[30] In 1949 *The Calgary Herald* ran an entertaining article about him in which he recalled his early deanship. Already the experiment had been largely forgotten (historical amnesia is nothing new in Calgary), as the *Herald* writer commented: "It will come as a surprise to many Calgary citizens to learn that there ever was a University of Calgary and Mr. Power, in reminiscent mood, told how in 1912 he was dean of the law school at that university." Learning of his early administrative career at the University of Calgary, the writer called the well-respected Calgary legal author,[31] the "Dean of Local Lawyers."[32] Kent Power died in Edmonton after a lengthy illness in 1961.[33]

Two former law instructors, Lloyd Fenerty and J. E. A. Macleod (today's huge Calgary law firm, Macleod Dixon, bears his name) still lived in the city. Another individual the chief justice knew with a University of Calgary connection was Carson MacWilliams, a son of Rev. Andrew MacWilliams, the last registrar of the University of Calgary.[34] The following year Carson became the City of Calgary's solicitor, the job Clinton held nearly forty years earlier.[35]

Children of three important backers of the first University of Calgary still resided in the city. The energetic Eva Reid tracked them down for her regular column in *The Albertan*, "Evesdrop with Eva."[36] She located Wilda Blow Bernard, daughter of the foremost advocate of the institution, Dr. Thomas Blow; Mae Tregillus, daughter of Will Tregillus, secretary of the Board of Governors; and Elizabeth (Dolly) Skinner Richardson, whose father, Thomas Skinner, donated $35,000 for the university's history chair. Mrs. Richardson summarized for Eva her feelings about the opening of the new campus: "We feel our fathers laid the foundation and we are gratified it has come to pass."[37]

Two former professors at the first University of Calgary, now both retired, lived in distant Vancouver. Whether or not they actually knew of the physical establishment of a permanent university campus in Calgary is unknown. Mack Eastman, the first and only occupant of the Skinner Chair, had gone on to found the University of British Columbia Department of History. He later served as a senior civil servant in the International Labour Office in Geneva, Switzerland.[38] The second individual, Walter Sage, who took over Fred Albright's economics course and who also taught English and history, followed Mack Eastman as chair of UBC's history department.[39] Eastman and Sage did not attend the ceremony, but close to the Chief Justice sat his wife, Phyllis Chapman Ford, who did have close family ties to the first university. Mrs. Ford was a niece of Will Tregillus.

Phyllis Ford, a respected music teacher and musical performer in the community, came to Calgary in 1913 as a young girl with her parents. Her father, Alfred Chapman, later became city engineer for the City of Calgary. Her mother, Bee Tregillus Chapman, taught and played the organ at First Baptist Church. In Calgary Phyllis studied musical theory under Annie Glen Broder, and later attended McMaster University, then in Toronto.[40] She knew that directly southwest of the new campus, across the Bow, had once stood her uncle's large ranch house, Roscarrock.[41] Just beyond it, in what today is known as Strathcona Heights, you could see the land her uncle had given the first University of Calgary. This visionary, who believed totally in the value of education, once told the annual convention of the United Farmers of Alberta in 1912: "Knowledge is power, gives light, independence, and freedom; while lack of knowledge—ignorance—is weakness, darkness, dependence, and bondage."[42]

Phyllis must have thought of her uncle before the ceremonies of Friday afternoon, October 28th. Will Tregillus had done so much to try to make the experiment of a university in Calgary work. Just before the opening ceremony we do know that she visited the building where the secretary of the University of Calgary had his office.

The reason for her stopover is simply explained. Phyllis regularly visited the Lougheed Building, going there several times a month, and always before important events. Why? Ever since the ancient Greeks developed a liking for curls, a well-coiffed head became a mark of elegance.[43] Phyllis Chapman Ford came regularly to the Lougheed Building, as did women from across the city, to have their hair done at the Peter Pan Beauty Salon on the second floor.[44] Other women present at the opening ceremony did so as well,[45] including art professor Helen Stadelbauer, the founding member

Ethel King, advisor to women students and assistant professor of education, arranges a gift corsage for Phyllis Ford, wife of Chief Justice Clinton Ford, before the ceremonies to open the Arts and Education Building, 28 October 1960. University of Calgary Archives/ UARC 82.010, file 1.13. Calgary Herald Photographic Collection.

of the university's art department,[46] and Aileen Fish, who in the early 1960s became one of the early advisors to women students.[47] Eva Reid herself went there.[48]

Doug Doherty, operator of the Lougheed Building's salon for over two decades by 1960, had one of the most successful hairdressing businesses in the city. In addition to providing the latest styles, he offered something more: intelligent and informed conversation. He enjoyed talking with his customers and listening to them. "Women," he said, "are stimulating conversationalists. They are interested in just about everything. They have opinions, they express themselves on any topic and have much broader interests than men have. Men talk sports, politics or business. Women can talk on literature, art, theatre, politics, children psychology … you name it."[49] When his clients wanted to focus on their children he could certainly do that as well. Doug and his wife Hilda had four of their own, which made for rich and enjoyable conversations.

The expert hairdresser had a deep personal interest in music, art, drama, literature and current affairs. His friendship with Richard Needham, a future winner of the 1967 Stephen Leacock award for humour (for *Needham's Inferno*), confirms his conversational range.[50] When the star columnist worked in the 1940s for *The Calgary Herald*, they met at the Grand Tea Rooms twice a week.[51] The irreverent Needham immigrated to Canada at age sixteen from Britain, arriving in Alberta, via Ontario, in his late twenties.[52] Needham's conversations with Doherty enriched his Calgary experience, which he greatly enjoyed: "Coming from the smoky old East, we were enchanted by the clear, tangy air; by the sense of freedom and adventure, by the feeling that we were spiritually, as well as physically, on top of the world."[53]

Through his volunteer work in the late 1940s and 1950s with Calgary's Allied Arts Centre, the city's community arts centre, Doherty knew a wide range of people. Since the late 1930s he had been a leading figure in the city's amateur theatre movement, directing one play each year.[54] Well-respected in city drama circles, he worked as the house manager at the Grand when Calgary hosted the Dominion Drama Festival in 1950.

1960, the year Calgary finally obtained a permanent university campus, proved a milestone year in the Lougheed Building's development. Doug Doherty stayed until he retired in the late 1970s; but suddenly in 1960 nearly one half of the Lougheed community departed. After nearly forty years the Alberta Wheat Pool went to its new skyscraper, followed by its lawyers and accountants. In search for new tenants to fill the vacated space, the Lougheed Estate prepared a prospectus with interior photos.[55] The booklet emphasized the modern aspect of the building. The estate had just installed a modern automatic elevator service, at a cost of over $125,000. Since the Lougheed's opening in 1912 an elevator operator, in uniform, had been available at all times in the evening. During the day two men worked each of the elevators. A rotating shift of four elevator operators running three shifts had made this system possible.[56] But now in the modern world of the 1960s the automatic elevators did all the work, running from the basement to the sixth floor.

After the Wheat Pool's departure the UGG became the building's major tenant. By the 1960s the amount of paper involved in the UGG's business had reached

In October 1945 Doug Doherty directed
Noel Coward's "Blythe Spirit" in the
Western Canada Auditorium. The
Calgary Civic Theatre production starred
(left to right): Florence Thorpe, Tom
Rannie, and Doug's wife, Hilda Doherty.
Glenbow Archives/NA-4217-11.

enormous proportions. The Alberta Wheat Pool had installed computers in the basement where the Board of Trade, and then the Knights of Columbus, had once been.[57] With the IBM's all the office work became so much simpler, but the computers went with the Wheat Pool's departure. So in the 1960s the UGG struggled on, handling tons of paper. The UGG located its computers in the Winnipeg head office, not in Calgary. In 1974 the UGG's Calgary mailing department dealt with half a million pieces of mail each year. Every day they handled reports and correspondence to and from 250 elevator points in Alberta and British Columbia, as well as mail to headquarters in Winnipeg and other area offices.[58]

The UGG cherished its own history. One of the highpoints of the UGG in Calgary came in 1956. To mark the 50th Anniversary of the formation of the Grain Growers Company, one of its two founding organizations along with the Alberta Farmers' Co-operative Elevator Company, the UGG invited Canadian historian Donald Creighton to address their anniversary banquet at the Palliser Hotel. The University of Toronto Department of History Chair spoke on "The Past Half-Century."[59]

Part of the reason for the UGG's sense of history came from the length of service of several long-serving administrators: George Edworthy worked for the UGG for almost half-a-century, from 1917 to 1964, rising from the post of ledger-keeper to Western Division manager in charge of UGG's operations in Alberta and British Columbia.[60] George Herriott put in forty-eight years, beginning as a relief elevator agent in 1917 and later superintendent of the UGG's farm supplies department to his retirement in 1965.[61] Harry Francis began as an office boy in 1920 and retired in 1969 as superintendent of grain sales for UGG's Western Division.[62] And, of course, John Brownlee towered over all others in seniority. As a young man he had helped craft the agreement that united the two companies to form the UGG in 1917. From 1948 to his death in 1961 he served as the UGG's president.

John Brownlee had a strong sense of history. In Calgary he and his wife lived in the Donegal Apartments on Memorial Drive. They loved to walk along the pathway on the north side of the Bow River under the trees planted as saplings in the early 1920s as living memorials to the Calgary soldiers killed overseas in World War One, men like his best friend Fred Albright. Then one day he heard that Calgary traffic planners intended to cut down the trees to widen Memorial Drive. The former premier acted immediately. He called the mayor, registering his strongest objections. Thanks to John Brownlee's intervention Calgary's memorial trees were saved.[63]

Ethel Garnett, another long-serving member of the UGG staff in Calgary, worked for over twenty-five years for UGG Insurance Agencies, a division of the company that offered farmers a range of insurance services. Beginning as a secretary in 1946 she rose to head the claims department, processing on average about fifteen hundred claims a year.[64] Ethel liked the old building. Every morning she went for coffee at the Grand Coffee Shop. Frequently she had her hair done at the Peter Pan Beauty Salon.[65] She enjoyed the UGG's social activities. The UGG Calgary Staff Association in the 1950s and early 1960s organized an annual summer outing to Banff, a fall corn roast, a special Christmas party in the Lougheed Building and an annual banquet in the Crystal

The 25th anniversary of the Peter Pan Beauty Salon, April 1964. Left to right: Kit Dingle, personal friend and actress; Marjory Sword, managing secretary of the Lougheed Building; Ivy Gilday, operator; and Doug and Hilda Doherty. Courtesy of Hilda Doherty.

UGG Christmas Party, December 1950, in the Lougheed Building. The UGG employees are enjoying the antics and music of the "Three Melody Men." Photo courtesy of Ivan Radke.

Ballroom of the Palliser Hotel each winter.[66] With the downsizing of the Calgary office in the early 1970s the UGG transferred her to the city with the company's computers to become UGG claims supervisor, but she returned to Calgary from Winnipeg upon her retirement several years later.

In the 1970s the UGG operation at Lougheed radically changed. Instead of perhaps two to three hundred employees, the number by 1979 had shrunk to maybe thirty when Winnipeg centralized its work force.[67] Long-term Calgary employee Ivan Radke was raised on a farm near Hand Hills Lake southwest of Hanna, Alberta. He came to Calgary after high school and worked for two years as a bank teller until joining the UGG in 1958. As the staff shrunk in the 1970s, he recalled it became impossible to have a UGG baseball team as so many co-workers had been transferred to Winnipeg.[68] Finally, it no longer made any sense to occupy such a large amount of space for such a reduced operation. While UGG Western Manager Gordon Moss, the last in the Lougheed, considered it a "glorious building," he moved the offices to more appropriate quarters in Airways Industrial Park near the Calgary airport in 1979.[69]

Like the UGG, the Workmen's Compensation Board (WCB) had a long history in the Lougheed. Provincial legislation passed in 1918 introduced guaranteed compensation for injured workers. Employers bore the cost of workplace injuries, but in return for this non-fault approach employees waived their right to sue for damages.[70] An independent board, the WCB was set up to handle the compensation process and adjudication. From 1938 to 1965 the Lougheed housed the WCB Calgary branch office. The board in 1938 first took a ground floor office at the corner of 6th Avenue and 1st Street West, later moving to new quarters on the second floor in the mid-1950s.[71] It later relocated upstairs from the second floor in 1960 to the fifth floor where they remained until 1965, when they left the building.

As in many other offices at the time, women in the WCB faced discrimination. During the war female staff took over male staff duties as many joined the armed services. The position of claims officer, up to that point exclusively handled by men, became open to women, but with the end of the war the WCB again classified claims officer as a "man's job." Another inequality arose over pay. During the war years the women who worked as claims officers were not called that. The WCB instead termed them "claims clerks," which meant they received less pay than did the males doing the same work. Another grievance concerned female employees marrying; if a woman married, and continued to work, she forfeited her pension. Finally, another grievance from an age in which the health hazards of smoking remained little known: men could smoke in their offices—nice big ashtrays sat on their desks—but the women had to go to the washroom if they wanted to light up.[72]

Like the UGG and WCB, the Bank of Nova Scotia was a large tenant in the early 1960s. Marsh Porter of Porter Allen, then a director of the bank, had originally recommended a branch be established in the Lougheed.[73] Edna Lougheed, Edgar's widow, handled the lease negotiations.[74] Several factors led the bank to follow Marsh Porter's advice. First, as the bank's main office on 8th Avenue was becoming very congested, another branch nearby would relieve the pressure. Secondly, the location was

good, as the bank's investigative report revealed: "Pedestrian traffic is heavy at this intersection because of the telephone, light, water and gas offices and parking facilities are more readily available than in the congested area of 8th Avenue West especially in the vicinity of our main Calgary Branch."[75]

The bank took the space in 1955 and remained there to 1979. Momentarily they considered following the Alberta Wheat Pool to their new building, then under construction two blocks away. "Undoubtedly," the branch manager wrote the supervisor in Winnipeg on 3 January 1958, "the business area of this city is moving westward which could well mean that within a short period some of the legal firms, doctors, accountants etc. who have been long established in the building we occupy and others close to our site could move to more pretentious office buildings."[76] But for the immediate future the bank decided to remain. Their quarters in the Lougheed meant considerably lower rent than in a new modern building.[77]

When the WCB left the Lougheed in 1965 the Bank of Nova Scotia took over their old space on the fifth floor. The bank wanted only one major alteration in what was to become their provincial headquarters for eight years: air conditioning. This necessitated correspondence with Lougheed Investments, directed by Peter Lougheed. After several years with Mannix Corporation, one of Western Canada's largest private companies, he had just entered into private legal practice with John Ballem and Marvin McDill. On 11 August 1965, J. V. Hunt of Hunt Real Estate Corporation, who was arranging the lease with the Bank of Nova Scotia, wrote Peter Lougheed, at Lougheed, Ballem, and McDill, 1600 Elvedon House: "It is generally considered that the central system with ducts to the various parts of the space would be most suitable but the architect might have some additional ideas for you."[78]

Air conditioning was but a minor problem for Senator Lougheed's grandson, who had just become the Alberta Progressive Conservative leader, a party without a single seat in the legislature. He had his hands full in his effort to transform the moribund provincial Conservatives into a fighting force. After first establishing a party office at Edmonton in April 1966, he opened another in Calgary.[79] What was badly needed was a central location with rent as low possible. The party chose the penthouse of the Lougheed Building.[80]

As Peter Lougheed lived in Calgary, the Lougheed Building office became the party's central command post. Ted Mills, his key constituency organizer throughout Alberta, recalls the planning sessions held in the penthouse leading up to the provincial elections of 1967, in which the party became the official opposition. Similar planning sessions took place in 1971, when the Progressive Conservatives swept Social Credit from office. Helpers included long-time Conservative Pansy Pue, a former member of the Calgary City Council in the early 1930s.[81] Joe Clark, a future prime minister of Canada, was another frequent visitor, running as a candidate in Calgary during the 1967 provincial election, almost winning the seat.[82] Richard MacInnes and Don Sinclair regularly participated in Calgary West constituency executive meetings held here in the late 1960s. Peter's riding was Calgary West. Richard served as his first constituency

Peter Lougheed was admitted to the Alberta bar, 6 October 1955. W.A. McGillivray presented him to the bar. Special guests during the welcoming ceremony were Jean Lougheed, Peter's wife; and Edna Lougheed, his mother. W.A. McGillivray appears on the far right, and Peter Lougheed on the far left. Jean Lougheed stands between her husband, and her mother-in-law. Photo by Jack De Lorme, published in the Albertan, 7 October 1955, City News Page, p. 3. Glenbow Archives/NA-5600-8520a.

president and Don as a party worker.[83] The Conservatives kept their penthouse office until 1971.

In addition to the Lougheed's trio of large tenants, many smaller tenants remained. The lineage of the chartered accounting firm of Roberts, Gibson and Fraser went back to 1920. John H. Williams, C.A., established his office in the building that year, and he stayed there until his death in 1942.[84] Nearly a decade after the war Dave Williams, who had been in partnership with his father, entered into partnership with Lorne Roberts.[85] Williams and Roberts became, after Dave Williams left the firm, Roberts, Gibson and Fraser. After Harvey Morrison & Co. moved out in 1960 they took over their office space and remained there for ten more years. When their record is combined with that of the J. H. Williams firm, Roberts, Gibson and Fraser had a half-a-century of residency in the Lougheed.

The law firm of Milne and Davis also had a long history in the Lougheed. George Milne articled in the building with Bill Hall, the UGG's lawyer whose association with the Lougheed dated back to the early 1920s until 1952. Art Davis later articled with George Milne and became his partner. First located on the second floor, they took over the fifth floor offices of Roberts, Gibson and Fraser when they moved out. Milne and Davis still had a number of Bill Hall's rural clients into the 1970s, but as more lawyers established themselves in the smaller communities around Calgary, Milne and Davis's rural practice diminished.[86] They left the Lougheed in 1976.[87]

James Cleave was the Lougheed's longest single tenant. In 1915 he came to the main floor, 6th Avenue side, and remained to the mid-1960s. A workaholic to say the least, the Cornish-born Cleave still put in ten-hour workdays after he passed the age of seventy-five.[88] In his younger years the insurance broker and real estate agent devoted an enormous amount of time to the Alberta Motor Association (AMA). In the mid-1940s he served as AMA president, and contributed a monthly column to the *Voice of Motordom*, the AMA's news bulletin.[89] He was a highly respected tenant. When Marjorie Sword, the Lougheed Estate's very efficient office manager, retired in 1965, *The Albertan* covered the farewell party in the UGG board room: "All the tenants of the Lougheed Building gathered to honor Miss Marjorie Sword who is retiring as managing secretary of the building after 32 years… Mr. James Cleave, who has been a tenant in the Lougheed Building for 52 years, was among the well-wishers who gathered to bid Miss Sword goodbye."[90]

Several years before James Cleave left the building Don Spicer of Don's Hobby Shop moved in. The hobby shop sold costumes, masks, make-up and theatrical supplies. The shop took retail space in 1959 on the main floor, 1st Street side, when the Lougheed Estate still owned it. As Don recently told David Bly, heritage writer for *The Calgary Herald*: "We needed a new location and the rent was reasonable. With the Lougheeds, it was almost a gift when we moved in here, the rent was low." The rent rose with the new owners in the 1970s and after that as well, but still, he added, "it's still fair compared to other locations."[91] Don retired in 2003. Scott Bennie operated Don's Hobby Shop in the same location until the late spring of 2004, when forthcoming renovations in the Lougheed obliged him to relocate to Centre Street North, south of 16th Avenue N.W.

In the 1960s the Lougheed had a prestigious link to the province's rapidly expanding oil and gas sector. The Alberta Society of Petroleum Geologists (now the Canadian Society of Petroleum Geologists) had their headquarters in the building from the mid-1960s to late 1970s. While in the Lougheed the Alberta Society of Petroleum Geologists published Stan J. Nelson's monumental *The Face of Time: The Geological History of Western Canada* (1970), designed for those interested in geology: students, teachers and members of the general public. The title paper contains in bold letters: "Published by the Alberta Society of Petroleum Geologists, Calgary, Alberta, 612 Lougheed Building, Calgary, Alberta, Canada." As the book was displayed at the Eighth World Petroleum Congress in Moscow in 1972 the address of its publisher, "612 Lougheed Building," obtained international exposure. The fate of the book in the Alberta school system proved challenging, as a group calling itself the "True Education Committee" disliked its introduction of the theory of evolution. Subsequently Alberta's junior and senior high school science curriculum committees delayed adding the book to their recommended reading lists for two years.[92]

An era ended on 30 March 1973 with the sale of the Lougheed Building by Lougheed Investments. It sold for a sum of one million dollars.[93] For five years it was owned by Louis Desrochers, a Quebec-born lawyer raised in Alberta. The French-speaking Albertan had contributed greatly to French-language organizations in the province, to the University of Alberta and to the Canada Council. In 1970 he began a four-year term as chancellor of the University of Alberta.[94] Formerly his University of Alberta appointment would have made him the titular head of the University of Alberta at Calgary, but in 1966, UAC ended its branch plant existence and achieved full independence as the University of Calgary. He sold the building in 1977 to Dynacorp Group of Calgary. A year later Dynacorp sold it to three investors: Clive Beddoe, Harley Hotchkiss and Jim Palmer.

John Moreau and Jim Ogle, both newly minted University of Alberta lawyers, came into the Lougheed toward the end of Louis Desrochers's period of ownership. While John was from Edmonton, Jim came from Calgary, completing his undergraduate degree in economics at the University of Calgary. Interestingly Jim had articled in Calgary under Bill Wuttunee, a Cree lawyer, one of the first First Nations lawyers in Canada. The Moreau Ogle lease with Louis Desrochers included a demolition clause in the event he decided to tear down the building. The two partners liked the building but moved to other quarters after their three-year lease expired.[95]

English-born Clive Beddoe, who had trained as a chartered surveyor in Britain, came to Calgary in late 1970. He arrived with just $999 in his bank account. At first he worked in property management for the CPR's Marathon Realty, which still owns large tracts of downtown Calgary from its original land grant. After several months with Marathon a new career opportunity arose, a chance to become the development manager for the Cascade Group of Companies, which owned real estate and nursing homes in Western Canada. In Calgary it ran a construction company and apartment buildings. The English-trained land surveyor helped Cascade move into the development of office buildings in Calgary. He acquired the land, negotiated the permits, and oversaw the construction of such Cascade projects as the Norcen Tower, the Exchange Tower and the Sun Oil building.[96]

After seven years Beddoe had accumulated enough capital and Alberta experience to strike out on his own. The former surveyor started his own commercial development company with $100,000 and named it Hanover Management after London's Hanover Square, where he had once worked. It had a nice sound to it. Hanover had been the family name of the royal house of Great Britain until the First World War. In 1917 King George V renounced the German name in favour of the present name, Windsor. After his abdication as King Edward VIII in 1936, the man Calgary knew so well as Edward, Prince of Wales, had become the Duke of Windsor.

Beddoe made a specialty of buying older downtown office buildings such as the Lougheed. He purchased the Lougheed/Grand Theatre from Dynacorp Group of Calgary in 1979. They had only owned it just one year. With that purchase he brought in two partners: business leader Harley Hotchkiss, originally from Ontario, and lawyer Jim Palmer, originally from Prince Edward Island, both highly respected members of the Calgary community.[97] Looking ahead to developing the larger site the group of three also purchased the Grand from the Odeon Theatre chain, and then leased it back to them.

In 1979–1980 Calgary approached the summit of its greatest economic boom since 1909–1912. In 1980 more new office space was built in Calgary than in New York City and Chicago combined.[98] Just before the crash of the winter of 1981–1982, historians Max and Heather Foran noted: "The high-rolling mentality is reminiscent of the pre-1914 era. Land speculation is as rife today as it was then."[99]

The post-Leduc boom impacted a number of historically significant buildings in the city. The building frenzy led to their destruction. Included amongst the heritage buildings lost from the 1950s to 1970s were: the Pat Burns mansion in 1956;[100] "Bow Bend Shack," William Pearce's home in 1957;[101] Braemar Lodge, the hotel where Forbes-Robertson stayed when he came to open the Grand, in 1964;[102] "Langmore," William Roper Hull's mansion, in 1970.[103] During the Second World War Pierre Berton had been stationed in Calgary as an infantry instructor at Currie Barracks for a year and a half. He never forgot the nickname of the Palliser Hotel. "We called it the Paralyser, because we came here for parties and drank a little."[104] On a book promotion tour in mid-September 1980 the popular Canadian historian commented on how the city had changed in the thirty-five-year interval: "All this talk about Alberta's heritage—where is it? Buildings are torn down and put up again. Calgary looks like it was built yesterday… There's no texture of the past, no sense of its generations of citizens."[105] The assessment of Calgary's history made in 1960 by *Calgary Herald* columnist Ken Liddell still dominated.[106] In his book, *Alberta Revisited*, he wrote: "Calgary is not a place with any great historical background. Actually, it is so young it has none."[107]

One long-term resident disagreed. Dr. Harry Gibson, a Calgarian who had first come to the city from Kingston, Ontario, in 1904, fiercely believed in the importance of a community knowing itself, of preserving important landmarks.[108] On 8 November 1973, one the oldest living members of the Class of Medicine '03 sent a note to the

View of downtown Calgary from
the roof of the Glenbow Museum,
1984. The Lougheed Building, once so
prominent forty years or so earlier,
is now hidden among new high-rise
buildings. It now stands in the shadow
of the tallest building on the horizon,
the West Tower of the Petro-Canada
Centre. Photograph: John Dean.

director of Queen's alumni affairs. He expressed interest in the well being of the old Queen's Arts Building, and then he talked about Calgary and its lack of care for its older structures: "The new buildings can never match the old ones. I have watched this city grow from the size of a town to that of a huge city, & it is still growing at a tremendous rate...My home is on what was almost the extreme limit of building—now is about 5 miles from the limit of building. The business area has also grown very quickly—too quickly I should think to have solidity & permanence. The tendency seems to have a building only built to last about 20 years, then destroy it & a new & better (?) one built."[109]

Yet slowly several newly-formed heritage organizations won back some lost ground. Beginning in 1956 with the appointment of Hugh Dempsey, the library and archives of the newly formed Glenbow Foundation energetically began collecting important records of Western Canada's past. The Glenbow missed out by one year on the acquisition of the voluminous William Pearce Papers, which went in 1955 to the University of Alberta Archives.[110] However, after 1956, incredible finds like the Hardisty Papers, essential for any understanding of fur trade Alberta, went to the Glenbow Archives.[111] By the early 1960s the Glenbow Library and Archives were open to the public. The original Calgary Public Library (now the Central Memorial Park), home of the first University of Calgary, housed the Glenbow Library and Archives from 1965 to 1976, at which point the Glenbow Museum moved to its present quarters in the Glenbow Centre, 130, 9th Avenue S.E. One of Canada's largest non-government repositories, the Glenbow has become a major research centre for historians, writers and students.[112]

Eric Harvie, a millionaire Calgary oilman who had struck his bonanza in his mid-fifties with the discovery of oil at Leduc, set up the private Glenbow Foundation in 1954. He had been a law student at the first University of Calgary. In the photo taken on the library steps on opening day, 4 October 1912, he stands immediately beside fellow law student Ernie Pinkham, killed in Flanders in 1916. Eric Harvie knew the Lougheed Building well as he was the lawyer for pioneer Turner Valley oilman Archibald Dingman, who had his office in the building for over two decades.[113]

More good news followed Eric Harvie's establishment of the Glenbow. On 1 July 1964, Heritage Park, a portrayal of life in Western Canada before 1914, officially opened to the public. Located by the Glenmore Reservoir in southwest Calgary, the historical village included original buildings moved to the park, as well as other structures replicated on site.[114] Included among the historic structures from across Western Canada is an exact replica of the 1914 Dingman Well No. 1.[115] Eric Harvie wanted this replica included out of respect for his former client.[116]

Immediately after the establishment of Heritage Park came another victory, this time at the junction of the Elbow and the Bow. Alderman John Ayer successfully led the struggle to save the site of the original Fort Calgary. Interestingly, the Fort Calgary Steering Committee included Dave Coutts of the Historical Society of Alberta.[117] Over half-a-century earlier he was the little boy Evelyn Albright had taken to church, the day before she received the telegram announcing her husband's death at Passchendaele.[118] In May 1978 the interpretive centre of Fort Calgary Historic Park officially opened.[119]

The late Harold Hanen, a great urban visionary, revisited the Penthouse of the Lougheed Building, 27 June 2000. Here, on the roof, with the York Hotel in the background, he discusses the possibilities of restoring the building with Dennis Burton, then resident in the Penthouse. Photo by Donald Smith.

Other campaigns followed. In 1980, the Burns Building from which Marcell had shot his wonderful 1912 photos of the Stampede Parade was saved from demolition by one vote in City Council.[120] The Society for the Protection of Architectural Resources in Calgary (SPARC) led the struggle to save the Burns Building. That battle won, SPARC's attention shifted to 8th Avenue, the Stephen Avenue Mall, which contained some of the best examples of structures from the sandstone era of the 1890s, as well as some fine brick and stone buildings from the early twentieth century.[121]

At this time Harold Hanen, one of Western Canada's most distinguished planners and architects, had his office in the penthouse of the Lougheed Building.[122] While an employee of the City of Calgary in the late 1960s he introduced the concept of the Plus 15, the popular elevated walking system between downtown buildings. After starting his own architectural firm in the 1970s he developed downtown plans for several Western Canadian towns. He also worked in the field of historical architecture, carefully preserving the exteriors of both the Clarence Block and the Lancaster Building while redesigning the interiors to meet contemporary needs.[123] In 1979 his restoration of the Clarence Block on Stephen Avenue, where Senator Lougheed and R. B. Bennett once had their offices, won a City of Calgary Urban Design Award. By a strange coincidence architect Lanier R. Wardrop's office had been in the Clarence Block in 1911–1912 when he supervised the building of both the Grand Theatre and the Lougheed Building.[124] The following year Harold's refurbished Lancaster Building, also on Stephen Avenue, won Heritage Canada's National Award of Honour in 1980 for an outstanding contribution to heritage conservation in Canada.[125] The noted architect had his office in the penthouse from 1975 to 1981.[126] One of his biggest project ideas was his concept of an ambitious new civic centre complex for Calgary. He worked with Raymond Moriyama, the well-known Toronto architect, on a bold concept, which narrowly went down to defeat by less than one percent in a 1980 city plebiscite.[127]

On 27 January 1981, Clive Beddoe hired Tom Anderson, his first employee, for the maintenance of the Lougheed Building and Grand Theatre, to start 1 March 1981. Anderson worked for sixteen years in the insurance business as an underwriter, but went back to school in his early forties. He did so to avoid the frequent company transfers that made life so very difficult for his wife and young family. With fellow students half his age he attended SAIT to learn the skills needed for the maintenance of large buildings, a job that would finally keep him in one place.[128] Hanover's first property supervisor for the two old buildings was supposed to very short-term, as the company planned to tear both structures down on 31 March 1981. Tom recalls Clive telling him: "Tom you are going to have a new building to look after."[129] All the plans were in place for a new twenty-two-story office building.

John Bascom, a University of Calgary graduate in history who later entered law at the University of Alberta, moved into the Lougheed with law partner Chris Evans at the time Hanover took over the building. The UGG, the building's longest tenant—over sixty years—was still there. As soon as you stepped off the elevator in the morning onto the fourth floor you could tell what day it was from the smell from the UGG cafeteria—onion soup, it must be Wednesday. When the two lawyers met with Clive

Beddoe he told them the building would be up for another six months only, then the demolition clause would be enforced. Yet, as it turned out Chris Evans stayed for about a decade, and John Bascom spent a quarter-of-a-century there, right to early 2004.[130]

No demolition followed on account of the city's biggest economic crash since 1913. The federal government's National Energy Program (NEP), unilaterally introduced by Ottawa on 28 October 1980 without consultation with Alberta, increased Ottawa's share of energy revenues. The NEP also contributed to the decision of many oil companies to downsize or leave Calgary. The real-estate market crashed, and the idea of a new building went with it. The fall in world oil prices through 1981–1982, from the $40 range to $30 a barrel, also contributed to Calgary's abrupt fall from incredible prosperity. In 1982 more people left Calgary than moved there.[131]

The lowest point in the Lougheed Building's fortunes came in 1981. The year ended in a grotesque, horrible way. On Friday, 4 December 1981, Eugene Schoenberger, owner of Gene's Jewelery, one of shops on the 6th Avenue side of the building, was found dead at his business. The shop owner was slain during a robbery. The murderer escaped with $60,000 in jewellery. Although public aid was sought the murder still remains unsolved.[132]

Under the changed economic circumstances of the early 1980s Hanover worked to keep the Lougheed Building well-serviced, with a very attractive rental structure based on the lack of amenities.[133] Hanover held meetings of their maintenance staff once or twice a week with an eye to keeping all their properties in immaculate condition. Tom liked the tenants and the work, but always believed that one day the buildings would go down and a new one go up. Then finally he would become the property supervisor of a brand new office building.

The economy did improve, but the Lougheed stayed. The big changes occurred instead immediately to the north, in the adjacent block between Centre Street and 1st Street S.W., and 5th and 6th Avenues S.W. where Petro-Canada, the federal government's national oil company, erected the Petro-Canada Centre. The complex had two towers connected by an expansive atrium. The Crown Corporation angered the city's sensibilities by building its fifty-two-story West Tower twenty-four metres higher than Calgary's downtown icon, the Calgary Tower, built during Canada's centennial in 1967.[134]

Before construction of the complex began the Lougheed's old basement tenant, the Calgary Board of Trade (now the Calgary Chamber of Commerce), intervened. The chamber came forward with a plan to purchase and restore a heritage building on the city block. The Oddfellows Temple at the corner of Centre Street and 6th Avenue S.W. had been previously designed as a provincial historic site, which meant that its size and exterior must be preserved. The Chamber of Commerce purchased it, then sold the air rights above their new premises to Petro-Canada, which now could build higher than the City ordinarily permitted under the its formula of building height to base area. The sale raised two and a half million dollars—enough to fund completely the chamber's building renovations.[135]

Shortly after its completion in late 1984 about 5,000 people, more than the entire population of Calgary in 1901, worked in the newly-completed Petro-Canada Centre.[136] The complex soon gained the nickname of "Red Square" on account of Petro-Canada's creation in 1975 by the "leftist" Trudeau government.[137] Many Calgary oil people saw the Crown Corporation as an intruder backed by Ottawa's cash and given preferential treatment denied to privately-owned companies.[138] One *Calgary Herald* writer called the complex "a twin-towered, $200-million monument to socialism."[139] In 1984, Peter Lougheed, then Alberta's premier, blamed Petro-Canada for bringing about the collapse of a real-estate boom in Calgary's downtown by flooding the market with new office space.[140] Ironically, during the last phase of the Petro-Canada's construction in 1983-1984, the complex's project office had been located in the adjacent building to the south named after his grandfather.[141]

Barry Nelson wrote an insightful sketch of the Lougheed in *The Calgary Herald* of 16 November 1987: "Lougheed Building home to low-cost operations." The "A+" office building of 1912 had tumbled to a Class C.[142] The Lougheed's penthouse lacked the luxury of the executive offices on the Petro-Canada's top two floors, which featured three-metre wide corridors, triple insulation for soundproofing, a fully equipped kitchen, an executive dining area and spacious offices with up to 7.5 metres by 10.5 metres in floor space.[143] Yet, the writer found the "C"-rated Lougheed full of life, "funky," a place where people could begin a business with nothing more than a desk, a phone and business cards on account of the incredibly low rent. "It's a vibrant business community, throbbing with activity that makes other downtown spots seem dozy. It's a fun place, packed with grassroots entrepreneurs who are hustling hard to make a buck."

The building, Nelson reported, hosted an incredibly vast array of tenants, from the *Renters Guide* that sold listings to landlords, to Homelocators, which charged to consult with people looking for a place to live. Software Express sold IBM and Apple Macintosh software at well below the standard price. Another tenant ran a training school for bus tour guides. Small oil companies wishing to watch drilling sites owned by other companies could hire Jim Morris's Ireland Field Scouting Service. The Beltone Hearing Aid Centre had an office here. The Aadon Denture Clinic, Don's Hobby Shop, the Shaver Shop and the two hairstylists, Coleen Kauth of The Hair Nook and Bill Yee of Lily's, were all there by 1987, and remained in the building until 2004. Start-up companies began there, such as QC Data Collectors, which provided a well log digitizing service. It stayed for several years until it could acquire needed additional room in the late 1980s for its expanding operation. QC Data had added two hundred employees in its new quarters.

From Clive Beddoe, the spokesperson for the owners, Barry Nelson learned that "the site is a likely candidate for redevelopment within three to five years." But for the interim the business writer concluded: "I personally think it is Calgary's best sounding business address and is available at the right price. Folks from Bay Street to Zurich and Kuwait could be impressed by the right letterhead sent from: The Penthouse, Lougheed Building, 604 1st St. S.W., Calgary, Alberta."

The Lougheed Building and Grand
Theatre, December 1984. Seven
years later the decorative sheet
metal cornice along the roof line
was removed. Photograph by Bow
Valley Photographic Services Ltd.

Actually the penthouse from 1989 to 1995 really was a fun place. Ken Knudsen and two partners rented it as a rehearsal and recording studio. During the day, and particularly the early evening they recorded many bands throughout the city, from "local buttheads" to "wannabees." Some of the groups actually performed in the Penguin Pub in the basement; they could warm up in the penthouse, walk down to the 6th floor and ride the elevator directly to the pub. At the time Ken worked evenings at "The Den" at MacEwan Hall on the University of Calgary campus, booking bands and being the "D.J." He only got off work at midnight, at which time he went down to the penthouse. After the last set many groups playing in bars wanted some "after hours time," an opportunity to unwind. Some of Calgary's best groups played in the penthouse after 2 a.m. Often Ken was up to 6 a.m. before driving back to his home in nearby Bankview. He loved the building, a "lively, creative, inspiring place."[144]

A few years later one tenant on the street floor, 6th Avenue side, went a little too far. In early January 1913 Sarah Bernhardt had entered the Parisian Delicacies on the same side to buy some "gateaux." She compared the pastries she purchased to what she herself could buy back home in Paris.[145] Times change. Seventy-six years later the Fantasia Bikini Bar, an exotic entertainment establishment, rented the same space that the French bakery once occupied eighty-six years earlier. For six weeks in the late spring of 1999 the bar owner put dancing bikini-clad women in Fantasia's windows between 4 p.m. and 6 p.m. to entertain men grid locked in rush hour traffic and to entice customers. One Calgary alderwoman called the bikini-clad window dancers brazen. After a Calgary alderman asked police to look into whether the scantily clad women were breaking the Highway Traffic Act by distracting drivers' attention, the bar owner backed down and pulled the curtains.[146]

Since its construction in 1912 the Lougheed Building has reflected changes within the city. From the 1960s onward a noticeable ethnic development occurred, as Calgary became increasingly global and multicultural. As late as the 1961 census almost sixty percent of Calgary's population identified themselves as being of "British" background.[147] But in the 1960s and 1970s Calgary became more cosmopolitan, with increasing numbers of immigrants from outside of Britain and the United States. One of the first examples of a more international presence in the Lougheed came with the arrival of the Norwegian Vice-Consulate (later Consulate) in a rental unit on the 6th Avenue side of the Lougheed from the late 1950s to late 1960s.[148] Bill Yee, originally from Hong Kong, established Lily's Hairstyling (named after his wife), also on the 6th Avenue Side, in the early 1970s. He remained until 2004. Hak Kim from Korea took over the vacant basement in the Lougheed in 1985, and transformed it into the popular Penguin Pub, which became a popular "watering hole" for many in the building and neighbouring high-rises.[149] In the late 1980s the House of Persian Rugs became a tenant, staying until 2004. They offered the finest selection of Iranian rugs in Canada. The Calgary Consulate for the Philippines moved to the Lougheed in the early 2000s. By 2004 the face of the Lougheed had changed from the first decades of its history, like the city it had became truly cosmopolitan.

Among the multicultural tenants in the Lougheed Building in the 1980s was artist Chin Shek Lam (1918-1990). The Chinese-born artist whose art is a unique combination of East and West had his studio in the Lougheed for several years in the mid-1980s. Calgary's Triangle Gallery of Visual Arts held a special exhibit of his art in late 2001. Photo by Davis Maksins. Courtesy of Myken Woods.

Harold Cardinal shown talking with Her Majesty Queen Elizabeth II. Premier Peter Lougheed appears directly behind her, on the far right, Calgary International Airport, 5 July 1973. Glenbow Archives/NA-2464-23281 #11.

Also very pronounced in recent years is the re-emergence of a Native face both to Calgary and to the Lougheed. The Alberta Indian Health Care Commission had its office in the Lougheed in the late 1980s. The organization advocated for comprehensive health care for First Nations people. Recently the Aboriginal Society for Aboriginal Youth was located there, and the office of YMCA's Aboriginal Recreational Coordinator. But the building's strongest link with Aboriginal Canada dates back to the late 1960s. From 1957 to 1971 the Western Canadian office of Time Canada was located on the second floor of the Lougheed. Ed Ogle, the magazine's Calgary bureau chief, had a deep interest in the North and in Aboriginal Canada.[150] The American journalist had worked for *The New Orleans States* before joining *Time* in News Orleans, and later Denver,[151] before becoming the magazine's bureau chief in Calgary. When Mel Hurtig sought out an editor for the book he requested in 1969 from Harold Cardinal, the young Cree president of the Indian Association of Alberta, he approached Ed. [152]

The Unjust Society, which appeared in late 1969, became an immediate bestseller. Directly it stated the issues, the first line setting the tone for what followed: "The history of Canada's Indians is a shameful chronicle of the white man's disinterest, his deliberate trampling of Indian rights and his repeated betrayal of our trust."[153] In his acknowledgements the young Cree warmly thanked Time Canada's Western Canada bureau chief: "I am particularly grateful for the assistance of Ed Ogle of Calgary, who gave so generously of his time to discuss the manuscript with me."[154]

Other Native connections existed in the building. Several lawyers worked in the field of Aboriginal Law, including Karen Gainer, a lawyer in the Lougheed in the early and mid-1990s. John Bascom and Clayton Rice of the law firm Ouellette Rice, tenants in the building from the late 1990s to 2004, had cases in Native law. Another First Nation reference was the YMCA's popular Camp Chief Hector, named after Hector Crawler, the early twentieth century Nakoda (Stoney) chief.[155] It had its office in the Lougheed from the late 1990s to 2004. At the original Camp Chief Hector on the Nakoda Reserve near Morley half-a-century earlier, the Indian Association of Alberta had held one of their most important meetings. *Calgary Herald* journalist Fred Kennedy attended and summarized Chief Rueben Bull's plea that the First Nations, "no longer be kept as hewers of wood and drawers of water but that they be recognized as human beings to whom God had also given the spirit of life."[156]

Over the years the Lougheed Building changed and so did the theatre. The development of suburbs from the 1950s onward led to the building of massive shopping centers with cinemas. Drive-ins catering to the automobile culture also became popular from the 1950s to 1970s. Odeon, who took over from the Barrons in 1969, tried to adapt in 1972 by dividing the auditorium into two twin theatres: two long boxcar-shaped rooms each with its own tiny balcony. The theatres had approximately 625 seats each, separated by a solid, sound-proof wall fourteen inches thick.[157] Nevertheless, large movie audiences did not return to the downtown. Odeon seemed to have run out of ideas to turn the market around. *Calgary Herald* music critic Eric Dawson visited the Grand in the early 1980s. In an article on classical music in Calgary he recalled the days of the great touring artists, when some of the finest instrumentalists of the twentieth century played at the Grand: "Memories are short, and no one would now think to mount a plaque on the walls of the Grand—these days divided into two cinemas specializing largely in soft-core porn and kung-fu movies—stating that 'Artur Rubinstein played here'."[158]

Odeon became Cineplex Odeon in the summer of 1983. Hanover, which now owned both the Lougheed Building and the theatre, seeing no immediate re-development on the site, worked with Cineplex Odeon the following year to modernize the theatre complex further, this time by separating the balcony from the main floor. The work was estimated to cost $500,000. The renovation converted the 1,139 seat side-by-side twin theatre to an up-and-down twin theatre with a total capacity of 1200—750 downstairs and 450 upstairs. The main floor became one auditorium and the old balcony upstairs a separate viewing space. The theatres, both equipped with 70-mm wide screen projection and Dolby stereo sound, opened with a new moniker the following December, the Showcase Grand.[159] Cineplex Odeon celebrated the re-opening of Calgary's oldest movie theatre with two of the Christmas season's major attractions: "A Chorus Line" and "Out of Africa."[160]

Despite the half million dollar renovation the theatre still struggled in the 1990s. The competition from home videos, multiple movie outlets at suburban shopping centers and the difficulty of parking downtown during the day created enormous problems for downtown cinemas, almost all of which had closed by the mid-1990s. Cineplex Odeon announced that they would not renew their lease in 1999.[161] At the same time the cost of running the two eighty-five-year-old buildings was becoming increasingly problematic These developments, coupled with a momentary need for more downtown Calgary office space, led the owners to bring forward their development plans again, after a lapse of nearly twenty years.

On 3 June 1998, *Calgary Herald* columnist Peter Stockland alerted Calgarians to the fact that the Grand Theatre was once again threatened with demolition. The owners sought a development permit for the Lougheed Building site. The columnist's article began: "One of these days, this city will stand firm against pulverizing it past." The Alberta Historical Preservation and Rebuilding Society formed a support group to help save both the Grand and the Lougheed. University of Calgary student Cara Fast acted as the chair of the organization meetings, and nurse Alison Robertson agreed to become the permanent chair. The Save the Grand Lougheed Committee collected 4,000 signatures on a petition asking the Alberta minister of community development to designate the buildings as a provincially protected historic site.[162]

The City of Calgary's Heritage Advisory Board had listed the buildings on the City of Calgary's Inventory of Potential Heritage Sites as a "Category A" site. It gave this, the highest ranking, only to buildings or sites that are notable, unique or rare. Section 33 of the Historical Resources Act allows the minister of community development, or his designate, to demand an impact assessment of all proposed development, an impartial process based on professional review. In 1991 the provincial government issued an order to assess the Lougheed's and Grand's historic significance. At their own expense the owners commissioned a Historical Resource Impact Assessment. To complete the report they hired Gerald Forseth, architect, and project leader David Mittelstadt, historian, along with Colin Campbell, engineer (structural assessment) in August 1998. The final report bore the full title, "Historical Resource Impact Assessment of the Lougheed Building for Prairie Fund Management" or, in short form, the Forseth Report.

When approached by the Save the Grand Lougheed Committee, Clive Beddoe, spokesperson for the three owners of the building and theatre, agreed to meet with a small group of those concerned with the development proposal. On 18 September 1998 he explained the deficiencies of the buildings. He ruled out the possibility of the owners attempting to save the Lougheed Building/Grand Theatre: "The building has come to the end of its economic life." The full range of the owners' concerns became apparent in the late fall when the Forseth Report entered the public domain. The report included the owners' list of deficiencies as of 18 August 1998:

> "Electrical: The existing electrical service is inadequate for today's office user and the building is seriously underpowered... Fire alarm system does not meet current code requirements... Mechanical: No fire suppression equipment i.e., fire hoses, sprinklers or stand pipe. Boilers date back to the early 60's and have reached the end of their economic life...Elevators: Elevator cabs, controls and hoist mechanisms, are all original and have reached the end of their useful life. Architectural: The roof was repaired some time ago with a single membrane. Patching the repair is now a regular maintenance item. Structural: Concrete deterioration is evident."[163]

In its "mitigation recommendations" the Forseth Report recognized the challenges of maintaining these two nearly century-old structures. The report confirmed the need for substantial work on the interior: the outdated and underpowered electrical systems, the lack of air conditioning, the replacement requirements of plumbing pipes and fixtures, the need to upgrade fire safety systems all needed attention, and the roof needed replacement as it required constant maintenance. Yet, on the positive side, it reported that the building appeared structurally sound from basement to roof. The brick façade appeared in excellent condition. Most important of all, the authors stated that the buildings had considerable historical importance. Overall they concluded: "This report assesses the Lougheed Building as an important historic structure in Alberta, worthy of preservation and protection; and capable of continuing usefulness into the future with controlled renovations and modifications that involve sensitive repairs, replacement, and upgrades."[164]

For over a year the provincial government considered the issues at hand. Finally the minister of community development made known his decision. In November 1999, he refused to designate the Lougheed and the Grand Theatre as a provincial historic site against the current owners' wishes. Upon learning of the minister's refusal, the City of Calgary, on the recommendation of its Heritage Advisory Board, requested provincial designation again. In June 2000 he again declined. In a subsequent letter, then Minister of Alberta Community Development Stan Woloshyn explained his reasoning: "After a through review of all factors associated with the possible preservation of the Lougheed

5 February 1999, the Grand Theatre's 87th birthday. Outside Don's Hobby Shop, left to right, David Smith, soon to become the Save the Grand Lougheed Committee's webmaster; Alison Robertson, committee chair; David Marshall, the Grand's last projectionist; and Mike Kampel, committee member. Photo by Donald Smith.

Building in Calgary, I determined that it was not in the public interest to designate the structure as an Historic Resource under the terms of the *Historical Resources Act* of Alberta."[165]

Calgary's oldest continuous theatre closed in late November 1999. Eager to obtain a short-term tenant for the theatre the owners succeeded in locating Terry Carter, who set up and operated the Players Grand Golf Centre in the old theatre. After considerable renovation the golf facility opened in January 2001. The golf centre, and the surplus of available downtown retail space, took the heat off the threatened demolition for the short term.

Diehard Save the Grand Lougheed Committee members, including chair Alison Robertson and, among other key volunteers, Anne Birch, Roseleen Heddinger, Mike Kampel, Nance Kuenz, Patti LaPorte, Ralph Thurn, Bob van Wegen, myself and my fifteen-year-old son, David Smith, who volunteered as our webmaster, kept up the struggle. With the assistance of many others we fought to convince the City of Calgary to declare the Lougheed Building/Grand Theatre a municipal historical resource. A key meeting came on 5 April 2000 with our appearance before the City's Operations and Environment Committee at the old City Hall.[166] To our great joy the Committee voted to recommend that the Calgary City Council request again that the Province of Alberta reconsider its previous decision and designate the buildings as provincial historic sites. If such a measure failed (it did, the minister again declined the move in June), it was recommended that council set up a committee to investigate the possibility of the City buying the buildings.

In City Council we came very close to obtaining the City's intervention, but the tied vote (7–7) on 24 July 2000, was a lost one. The motion that highly recommended the retention of the Lougheed Building and Grand Theatre, and that the City of Calgary enter into negotiations with the owners with respect to the acquisition of the property, or its municipal heritage designation, went down to defeat.[167] On 1 November 2000 the Calgary Planning Commission gave the green light for a twenty-two-story office tower on the downtown site of the Lougheed Building and Grand Theatre. The City of Calgary now granted the development permit.

In the long term both heritage structures seemed destined for the wrecking ball. But two years later an unexpected turning point occurred. Early in 2003, Neil Richardson, who had previously brought and restored the exteriors of two important city heritage buildings, the Lorraine Apartments and the Northwest Travellers Building, purchased both the Lougheed and the Grand Theatre. He announced, financing permitting, his intention of restoring and rehabilitating the Lougheed Building. City Council's decision of 22 March 2004 to contribute financially to the restoration greatly assisted him. This decision now allowed him to apply for additional help to other levels of government, as well as to the private sector. The fact that the city lost the historic St. Mary's School to demolition in 2002 no doubt helped to awaken council to the necessity of saving the Lougheed. Councillors Druh Farrell (Ward 7) and Madeline King (Ward 8) both played crucial roles in advancing the issue in council.

City Council's decision on March 22nd contained the additional recommendation that "best efforts" be made "to ensure that the Grand Theatre continues to provide performance space." A week later Theatre Junction stepped up to the plate. On March 30th General Manager Carol Armes and Artistic Director Mark Lawes signed a deal for the purchase of the theatre. The sale went through on 2 September 2004 with the transfer of a symbolic key from Neil Richardson to Mark Lawes in what was once the historic theatre. As so little remains of the original 1912 structure, after so many renovations, Theatre Junction plans to make the main theatre area over into a contemporary and flexible performance space, to reopen in late 2005 as a "culture house," supporting "contemporary performance in theatre, dance, music, and film."[168]

"Not in the public interest"? Fiscal responsibility is essential. Quite correctly not every memory, every ancient structure, can be, or should be saved by the private and public sector. But in terms of their historic importance to Alberta the Lougheed Building and Grand Theatre are exceptional. Life is not all dollars and cents. A need exists for a sense of place—knowledge of a shared past—a sense of belonging to a community.

Almost a century ago James and Belle Lougheed got it exactly right: business, the office building, and culture, the theatre, provide the perfect mix. Today the Government of Alberta entirely agrees. In the fall of 2004 they committed $2.7 million to Theatre Junction's $10.5 million fundraising campaign to remake the Grand Theatre into a modern performance space. Then, on 11 May 2005, Gary Mar, Minister of Alberta Community Development, designated the Lougheed Building as a Provincial Historic Resource under the Alberta Historical Resources Act. More good news: the Government of Canada's Commercial Heritage Properties Incentive Fund has recently approved a $1 million restoration grant for the Lougheed. *Calgary's Grand Story* celebrates both the Lougheed Building and the Grand Theatre, invaluable city landmarks, in the year of the province's 100th birthday, 2005!

Letter from Stan Woloshyn, Minister,
Alberta Community Development, to
Donald Smith, dated February 7, 2001

ALBERTA

COMMUNITY DEVELOPMENT

*Stan Woloshyn, Minister
MLA, Stony Plain Constituency*

AR66727

February 7, 2001

Professor Donald Smith
Department of History
University of Calgary
2500 University Drive N.W.
Calgary, Alberta
T2N 1N4

Dear Professor Smith:

Thank you for your letter of January 23, 2001, concerning the designation of the Lougheed Building in Calgary as a Historic Resource under the terms of the *Historical Resources Act* of Alberta.

After a thorough review of all factors associated with the possible preservation of the Lougheed Building in Calgary, I determined that it was not in the public interest to designate the structure as an Historic Resource under the terms of the *Historical Resources Act* of Alberta. Factors that I assessed in making this decision included, among other things, the views of the current owners of the structure, and the fact that little remains of the Grand Theatre or its 1948 Art Deco alterations.

If you have any further questions concerning this matter, please feel free to contact me at your convenience.

Yours truly,

Stan Woloshyn
Minister

204 Legislature Building, Edmonton, Alberta, Canada T5K 2B6 Telephone 780/427-4928, Fax 780/427-0188
Constituency Office: 4995 - 53 Ave., Stony Plain, AB, Canada T7Z 1V4 Telephone 780/963-1444 Fax 780/963-1730

♻ Printed on recycled paper

Appendix 2

"Wilf Carter vs George Bizet" by Christopher Dyke

Alan Hustak writes in the introduction of his manuscript history of early theatre in Calgary, "'Curtain Up. Performing the Arts in Calgary: 1893–1918," now deposited in the Glenbow Library in Calgary: "Theatre history is a sensory, not a literary experience. It is the most ephemeral of the arts. It lasts only in the memory of those who have experienced it. No writer a century after the fact can really restore the breathing presence of the actors, the sense of space or occasion, or the heartbeat of an audience so long ago."

Fortunately in the mind of one individual memory of a remarkable 1938 operatic performance at the Grand has remained alive for nearly two-thirds of a century. In late 1999 Christopher Dyke wrote to Jeff Collins of the CBC Radio's Calgary Eye Opener his remarkable story, "Wilf Carter vs George Bizet." During the great debate about the future of the Grand Theatre the popular CBC radio personality had requested listeners to write memorable stories of the days when the Grand was the centre for outstanding live entertainment in Calgary. In chapter twelve of "Calgary's Grand Story" a short reference appears to the event, but Christopher Dyke himself best tells the story of seeing his first opera:

"Many years ago, during the bad old depression, when there was precious little outside entertainment passing through small town Calgary, we were lucky to receive a visit by the San Carlo Opera Co., here to perform four operas at the Grand Theatre. My wise old Mother, a violinist herself, promptly decided I would have to attend at least one performance of the great masters. This she felt, would offer some much needed balance to my unseemly attraction to the cowboy songs of Wilf Carter... She chose Bizet's Carmen as a rousing production to inspire my young and unaffected musical experience.

"How right she was. I sat spellbound throughout all four acts. In the final scene, on hearing the triumphant march of the victorious Toreador approaching, Carmen flaunts her fickle affections in the face of the jilted Don Jose, who enraged opens a long flashing knife with teeth and stabs her fatally right through her breast! Paralyzed by fright over this dastardly deed, my quick witted Mother grabbed me just in time as I nearly fell over the balcony rail.

"This grand presentation I have never forgotten although it took some time for my parents to convince me that this was just skilled play acting and that the leading lady would surely survive to play her part in the next night's performance. From that day forth I have continued to attend and rejoice in the magic of both grand and light operas. But I also revere the memory of the legendary Wilf Carter and his country music. I later took up playing both guitar and 5 string banjo. Sorry Mum.

"Yours truly and long live the Grand Theatre."

Appendix 3:

THE MAN WHO BEGAN "CALGARY'S GRAND STORY"

Damian Petti, President of Local 212, the Calgary stagehands and projectionists union, phoned me late one Wednesday afternoon in February 2005. Aware that the 100th anniversary of the original Calgary stagehands union approached in 2011, he had begun the search for historical materials. He phoned me as he had heard of my book project on the Lougheed Building and Grand Theatre. Did I have any information on Calgary's early stagehands? I am so glad that he called.

That evening, 9 February 2005, I carefully went through a number of my Grand Theatre files. I found some information about an early stagehand, a key individual in "Calgary's Grand Story." Six years earlier I located my first reference to Percy "Frenchie" Giroux in the wonderful clipping files of the Glenbow Library. I found a short article by Eva Reid from *The Albertan* (24 May 1962), which described the 13-part CBC radio series, "Canadian Theatre – Fact and Fancy." Grace Lydiatt Shaw, a daughter of Jeff Lydiatt, an early manager of the Grand Theatre, prepared the series on the history of Canadian Theatre. In Eva Reid's article I learned that she interviewed Percy Giroux, the stagehand who pulled the curtains back on the Sherman Grand's opening night.

Thanks to Gordon Lydiatt, a cousin of Grace's in Calgary, I reached her in Vancouver in early fall of 1999. She referred me to the National Archives of Canada, which held her interviews, including that with Percy "Frenchie" Giroux. I first heard his deep voice on that tape. Frenchie and fellow stagehand Jimmy Silcox discussed the days of vaudeville in Calgary half-a-century earlier. They talked about the Lyric and Grand Theatres, manager Bill Sherman, and how the stagehands created sound effects to accompany the early silent films. Percy also recalled the evening he knocked down the great Sir Harry Lauder. During an impossibly short scene change he collided in the dark with the great British music hall entertainer.

Another interesting reference to Frenchie came in a *Calgary Herald* story by Tom Primrose, entitled, "Old Grand Theatre Holds Memories. Many World-Famous Performers Trod the Boards in Early Days" (17 September 1960). Again Gordon Lydiatt helped, as he gave a copy of the article to me. The reference to Percy reads: "'Frenchie' Giroux pulled the first curtain opening night at the Grand, he was with the theatre, off and on, for 28 years. He has an intimate backstage knowledge of many of the players at the Grand."

On Thursday, February 10th Damian told me that had a terrific photo of Frenchie receiving his 50th anniversary "gold card" in 1960. He had joined the stage-hands union in 1910 in Quebec. More good news followed. On Friday Lindsay Moir, the head librarian at the Glenbow Library, located the obituary of "Leon Percival (Frenchie) Giroux," which appeared in both *The Albertan* and *The Calgary Herald* in late June 1977. He died on 24 June at the age of 86. The short entry states that Percy, born in Quebec in 1891, came to Calgary in 1912, and was "an honorary life member of International Theatrical Stage employees" (*Calgary Herald*, 27 June 1977, p. 41). A quick email from John King, Senior Editor of the University of Calgary Press, late Friday afternoon gave me the green light to add this, the third and final appendix, to the manuscript.

Tuesday morning, February 15th, Damian arranged for me to meet Mel Merrells, the most senior member of the stagehands, the only one with the 50-year card. Michele Merrells, Mel's daughter, joined us. Instantly Mel recognized Frenchie's deep voice on the tape. Often in the late 1950s Mel had driven Frenchie to work at the Jubilee Auditorium. He remembered his Quebec origins well, and recalled that the former Montrealer at different times had a very slight French accent when he spoke English. He had known Frenchie and his brother Bernie Giroux. A close friend of Bernie's, Mel had served as one of his pallbearers.

What a morning it was, as we listened to the tape, and Mel talked about the challenges of working in the old "hemp houses," the theatres like the Grand that were fully equipped with hemp ropes. Mel spoke of Frenchie, Jimmy Silcox, and a host of other characters who had "checked out," departed long before. He recreated the back-stage world entirely. I was transformed with his talk of Frenchie's work as a "fly man," up in the "fly floor," the nest of ropes, twenty to thirty feet above the "deck" or stage floor. Mel Merrells had known personally the individual who began "Calgary's Grand Story."

A NOTE ON SOURCES

To write the story of two buildings without an existing archives, or collection of papers, posed formidable challenges. The children of three managers of the Grand made it possible to complete the history of the Grand Theatre: the Lydiatts (Margaret, Grace and Jeff, the children of Jeff Lydiatt), Bill Joiner (son of Maynard Joiner) and the Barrons (Bob and Dick, sons of Jack Barron, who was both manager and owner). I cannot thank them enough for the family records and stories they generously shared with me. Without the photographs in the Barron family collection our visual record of the interior of the theatre would be almost minimal. Essential for the description of the Lougheed's first prime tenant was the information supplied by his niece Peggy Tregillus Raymond, and his great-grandson Robert Tregillus.

I located some caches of private papers, particularly in the early period, with valuable references to the Lougheed Building and the Grand Theatre, particularly in the 1910s, the privileged decade of this study. By far the richest are the letters of Fred Albright and Evelyn Kelly Albright, held in the University of Western Ontario Archives. John Lutman of the Archives and the Archives staff helped with several enquiries about the collection. Fortunately Lorna Brooke has transcribed the majority of the letters and made them available on the website: <http://ca.geocities.com/echoinmyheart@rogers. com> While the Calgary dailies for the 1910s provide a good exterior life of the city in this decade, the Albright/Kelly correspondence allows an intimate look at the interior—my warmest thanks to my colleague Sarah Carter in the University of Calgary History Department for informing me of their existence, and to my colleague David Marshall for sharing his printed copies with me. Lorna Brooke has made an invaluable contribution by making these letters available to all.

Fortunately, for the early years three Calgary dailies provided a wealth of material on both the theatre and the office building. Each paper had its own personality: *The Calgary Herald*, arch-Tory in its outlook: *The Albertan*, strongly Liberal; *The Calgary News-Telegram*, in many ways beyond description—often not much more than a daily gossip sheet. The *News-Telegram* proved the richest source of information. I am deeply indebted to Kathleen Renne for her meticulous search through the *News-Telegram* from 1911 to 1918. In addition I looked up a number of reviews of important performances in the Grand Theatre in the 1910s reported in the *Herald* and the *Albertan*. I also examined selected issues from 1906 to 1922 of that incredible source of Calgaryiana, the occasionally published but dependably outrageous *Calgary Eye Opener*. Its editor, the irascible Bob Edwards, Eye Opener Bob, made an invaluable contribution to *Calgary's Grand Story*.

After the First World War, the *News-Telegram* disappeared, leaving just the two Calgary dailies, the *Albertan* and the *Herald*. Of the two the *Herald* included more extended discussions of theatrical events, hence it became the favoured source of information for the 1920s onward. Once again I am most indebted to several individuals who helped me with my review of activities at the Grand in these years. Sara House examined the *Herald* from 1920 to mid-1923; Oliver Jull from mid-1923 to late 1925; and Kathleen Renne (once again, thank you, Kathleen!) from 1926 to the end of 1929. Jason Chan identified articles for selected months in *The Calgary Herald Saturday Magazine*, between 1939 and 1944. For the post-1929 period at the Grand Elaine Gibson helped enormously. On my behalf she read the *Herald*'s entertainment page from 1930 to the end of 1958, an enormous stretch. In the late 1950s the Grand became exclusively a movie house. For spot checks of specific issues of the *Herald* and the *Albertan* in the early twentieth century I greatly appreciated the reproduction of many issues of both Calgary newspapers in the Alberta Heritage Digitization Project, available on the World Wide Web <www.ourfutureourpast.ca>.

The staff of the Glenbow Archives and Library proved invaluable. Doug Cass, in particular, assisted again and again with guidance in their rich archival collections. The collection of reviews of productions at the Grand Theatre from 1919 to 1922 (M2314) was very helpful. Jim Bowman, Antonella Fanella, Susan Kooyman, Pat Molesky-Brar, Harry Sanders and Lynette Walton greatly assisted as well at the Glenbow. I warmly thank as well Lorain Lounsberry and Frances Roback of the Glenbow's Cultural History Collections. Kathleen Renne searched on my behalf through the papers at the Glenbow of geologist Pete Sanderson. Dr. Brad Rennie examined the records of the United Farmers of Alberta, the Calgary Board of Trade (Calgary Chamber of Commerce), and the Alberta Society of Petroleum Geologists. I appreciate the help of Clara King with the Alice Murdoch papers. Lindsay Moir, Jennifer Hamblin and Shona Gourlay of the Glenbow Library helped with countless requests over a six-year period. The clippings collections led me to many additional sources of information that greatly enriched this study. Alan Hustak's manuscript, "'Curtain Up' Performing the Arts in Calgary: 1893–1918," held in the library, contains a good overview of productions at the Grand from 1912 to 1918. Extremely valuable as well are the two manuscript reports by David Mittelstadt, "A Biographical and Social History of Mount Royal, Calgary," and "A Social and Biographical History of Elbow Park," both also in the library. In gratitude for their assistance on this project (and on many other Western Canadian topics over the last three decades) all royalties from *Calgary's Grand Story* will be donated to the Glenbow Library and Archives.

The Lougheed House Collection provided invaluable information on the lives of James and Belle Hardisty Lougheed. Trudy Cowan, Janet Wright, Marg Exton, and Sandra Grainger helped me begin my research in Lougheed House's holdings. More recently Jennifer Cook Bobrovitz has assisted me. Thanks to Jennifer's phenomenal research many new details of James and Belle Lougheed's lives have come to light. David Hall, of the University of Alberta Department of History kindly shared with me his summaries of Senator Lougheed's interventions in the *Senate Debates* from 1890 to

1925. He also generously allowed me complete access to all of the research material he gathered for our joint sketch of Sir James Lougheed to appear in the volume 15 of the *Dictionary of Canadian Biography*.

Calgary resources also included the valuable clippings and Grand Theatre programs held in the Local History Room of the Calgary Public Library, Macleod Trail Branch. Karen Crosby and Norma Marr of *The Calgary Herald* responded to my numerous requests. Ken Beckie, historian of the Knights of Columbus in Calgary allowed me to examine his records. I also thank Kirsten Olson and Tanya Barber of The Legal Archives Society of Alberta in Calgary for their help with questions about Calgary lawyers with connections to the Lougheed Building. The City of Calgary Archives has valuable archival items, all indicated in the footnotes. I also thank Jean Brunet and Diane Theriault at the Land Titles Office in Calgary. Pat McCann, General Manager of the Ranchmen's Club in Calgary helped with a number of enquiries, as did Jonathan Hanna, Corporate Historian, CP Rail in Calgary. Jim Mackie assisted me greatly with my research in the archives of the Southern Alberta Pioneers and their descendants.

The University of Calgary helped considerably with my research. The University Archives has useful material on the history of the first University of Calgary, and the origins of the second. I thank Suzanne Ell, Lisa Atkinson, Karen Buckley, Judy Loosemore and Jennifer Willard for their assistance. Both Apollonia Steele and Marlys Chevrefils of Special Collections, University of Calgary Library, helped greatly with books and manuscript material on Calgary authors. The Canadian Architectural Archives at the University of Calgary Library contains architectural drawings and plans for both the Grand Theatre and the Lougheed Building. Linda Fraser introduced me to this rich collection. Cindy Murrell of the Theatre and Music section of the University of Calgary Library helped with many research questions. Many thanks as well to John Reid and to the staff of the Canadian Music Centre–Prairie region, located in the main university library, for their assistance.

A number of archives and libraries in Toronto also contributed. The University of Toronto Archives contains newspaper clippings on many of its graduates, several of whom appear in these pages. Kathleen McMorrow, University of Toronto Faculty of Music Library, assisted with the Kathleen Parlow Papers held in their archives. The Toronto Public Library helped with the Ontario side of the story, as did the United Church Archives at Victoria College, University of Toronto, for all Methodist connections. My thanks to Gail Donald and Brent Michaluk, CBC Radio Archives in Toronto, for access to a number of CBC radio documentaries, particularly Grace Lydiatt Shaw's 1964 series, "Canadian Theatre—Fact and Fantasy." I thank Donna Murphy, Corporate Archivist for her help with items in the Manulife Financial Archives; also Ian Wolfe, Assistant Archivist, Group Archives, for assistance at the Scotiabank Archives.

Important collections of papers elsewhere in Canada also surfaced. Raymond Frogner of the University of Alberta Archives helped with my examination of the William Pearce Papers, which contain the correspondence of William Pearce with his son Seabury Pearce, a tenant in the Lougheed in the mid-1910s. The University of British Columbia Archives hold the papers of both Mack Eastman and Walter Sage, both former instructors at the first University of Calgary, in existence from 1912 to 1915. Chris Hives and Leslie Field aided with my consultation of these records. I thank Susan Bellingham for access to the Elaine Catley Papers, held in Special Collections, Dana Porter Library, University of Waterloo. Many thanks to Lewis Stubbs and his staff in the Department of Archives and Special Collections, University of Manitoba Libraries, for their help in allowing me to consult the United Grain Growers Papers. Garth Clarke assisted with my research on the Parlby Family Papers in the Red Deer and District Archives.

Photos constitute a vital part of this study. I am most grateful to Dave Brown and Jim Burton of the Image Centre at the University of Calgary for copying dozens of old photos lent to me by present and former residents of Calgary. Ellen Bryant, Ron Marsh, and Owen Melenka at the Glenbow helped with numerous photo orders. Other repositories assisted, the credit lines indicating the provenance of each shot.

A SELECT BIBLIOGRAPHY

All those wishing to pursue further investigation of Calgary's rich history should consult: Jennifer Bobrovitz, Marianne Fedori, Catherine Mayhood and Maria Murray, "Calgary—A Select Bibliography," which appears in Donald B. Smith, ed. *Centennial City: Calgary 1894–1994* (Calgary: University of Calgary, 1994), 82–88. For all those seeking a firm foundation in the history of the Foothills City three books remain essential: Max Foran, *Calgary: An Illustrated History* (Toronto: James Lorimer, 1978); Max Foran and Heather MacEwan Foran, *Calgary: Canada's Frontier Metropolis* (n.p.: Windsor Publications, 1982); Hugh A. Dempsey, *Calgary: Spirit of the West* (Calgary: Fifth House, 1994). Max Foran and Sheilagh S. Jameson, eds., *Citymakers: Calgarians after the Frontier* (Calgary: Historical Society of Alberta, Chinook Country Chapter, 1987) contains valuable biographical portraits of twentieth century Calgarians. For an overview of the province's history see Howard and Tamara Palmer, *Alberta: A New History* (Edmonton: Hurtig, 1990).

The best starting point for any study of the Lougheed Building and Grand Theatre is the excellent manuscript report, a copy of which is now in the Glenbow Library, "Historical Resource Impact Assessment of the Lougheed Building, Calgary for Prairie Fund Management, August 1998," prepared by Gerald Forseth, architect; David Mittelstadt, historian; and Colin Campbell, structural engineer. For background on the golden age of live theatre in the Grand, consult Alan Hustak's "Curtain Up! Performing the Arts in Calgary: 1893–1918," prepared in 2000, a copy of which is also at the Glenbow Library. Also very useful, particularly for its emphasis on the possibilities of restoration of two Calgary landmarks, is the thesis by Jacqueline M. Durrie, "Come to the Cabaret; Adaptive Re-Use of the Lougheed Building," prepared as a masters' degree project for the Faculty of Environmental Design, University of Calgary (Master of Architecture, 2003).

For an understanding of Alberta's and Calgary's nineteenth and early twentieth century history I have relied particularly on five books: J. G. MacGregor, *Senator Hardisty's Prairies 1849–1889* (Saskatoon: Western Producer Prairie Books, 1978); Henry C. Klassen, *Eye on the Future: Business People in Calgary and the Bow Valley, 1870–1900* (Calgary: University of Calgary Press, 2002); A. W. Rasporich and Henry Klassen, eds., *Frontier Calgary: Town, City and Region 1875–1914* (Calgary: McClelland and Stewart West, 1975); David Bright, *The Limits of Labour: Class Formation and the Labour Movement in Calgary, 1883–1929* (Vancouver: UBC Press, 1998). Grant MacEwan's lively biography, *Eye Opener Bob: The Story of Bob Edwards* (1957, reprint; Calgary: Brindle and Glass, 2004), captures the personality of early Calgary. The new edition is superbly annotated by James Martin. For the late twentieth century see

Robert M. Stamp, *Suburban Modern. Postwar Dreams in Calgary* (Calgary: TouchWood Editions Ltd., 2004).

For an understanding of agriculture, and its political as well as economic aspects, I relied especially on Bradford James Rennie's *The Rise of Agrarian Democracy: The United Farmers and Farm Women of Alberta, 1909–1921* (Toronto: University of Toronto Press, 2000). Three older studies also helped: William Kirby Rolph, *Henry Wise Wood of Alberta* (Toronto: University of Toronto Press, 1950); R. D. Colquette, *The First Fifty Years: A History of United Grain Growers Limited* (Winnipeg: The Public Press, 1957); Leonard D. Nesbitt, *Tides in the West* (Saskatoon: Modern Press, 1962).

Many studies of Alberta's politics proved helpful in preparing "Calgary's Grand Story." Four were of the greatest assistance: Franklin Foster, *John E. Brownlee: A Biography* (Lloydminster, Alberta: Foster Learning Inc., 1996); James H. Gray, *R. B. Bennett: The Calgary Years* (Toronto: University of Toronto Press, 1991); John J. Barr, *The Dynasty: The Rise and Fall of Social Credit in Alberta* (Toronto: McClelland and Stewart, 1974); Allan Hustak, *Peter Lougheed: A Biography* (Toronto: McClelland and Stewart, 1979). The recent edited work by Bradford J. Rennie, *Alberta Premiers of the Twentieth Century* (Regina: Canadian Plains Research Center, 2004), is invaluable for an overview of Alberta's premiers in the last century.

As so many popular articles and books on Calgary's past are undocumented I have made a special effort in the text to provide full references. Those wishing to learn the source of information are encouraged to check the footnotes. Please note the original reviews of many of the performances at the Grand are available on the Web, as many issues of *The Calgary Herald* and *The Albertan* for the early twentieth century have been digitalized. The provincial history by Howard and Tamara Palmer, *Alberta: A New History* (cited above), is also now available on the Web in the "Local Histories" section of this web source. The Web address for "Our Future Our Past. The Alberta Digitization Project" is http://www.ourfutureourpast.ca.

Very useful for a follow-up to *Calgary's Grand Story* is Harry M. Sanders, *Historic Walks of Calgary. Ten Walks to Points of Historical Architectural Interest* (Calgary: Red Deer Press, 2005).

NOTES

Notes to Introduction

1 For a full account of the fire see "Scorched Site Wins Council Tax Reprieve," *The Calgary Herald*, 11 March 2004.
2 Mark Lawes quoted in Eva Ferguson, "Theatre Poised for Facelift," *The Calgary Herald*, 6 November 2004.
3 Archibald Oswald MacRae, "Charles Traunweiser," in *History of the Province of Alberta*, vol. 2 (n.p.: The Western Canada History Co., 1912), 832.
4 Constance Martin, "A Calgary Walking Tour," *Western Living* (October 1981): 190.
5 Nellie McClung, *The Complete Autobiography: Clearing the West and The Stream Runs Fast*, eds. Veronica Strong-Boag and Michelle Lynn Rosa (Peterborough, Ontario: Broadview Press, 2003), 312.

Notes to Chapter 1

1 Lawrence Ira Eilenberg, "Johnston Forbes-Robertson: Actor-Manager: A Study of his Theatrical Style" (Ph.D. diss., Yale University, 1975), 71, 141. Jerome K. Jerome, *The Passing of the Third Floor Back. An Idle Fancy In a Prologue, a Play, and an Epilogue* (1905; reprint, London: Samuel French, 1948).
2 Johnston Forbes-Robertson quoted in "Calgary Delights Forbes-Robertson," *Calgary News-Telegram*, 6 February 1912.
3 E. Joyce Morrow, *"Calgary, Many Years Hence": The Mawson Report in Perspective* (Calgary: University of Calgary, n.d.), 18.
4 Johnston Forbes-Robertson quoted in "Calgary Delights Forbes-Robertson."
5 Sir John Martin-Harvey reportedly said this to Malcolm Morley, Dominion Drama Festival adjudicator, prior to his departure from England to Canada in 1934. See "Merry Widow Proves Notable Presentation of Light Opera Group," *The Calgary Herald*, 21 November 1935.
6 For a description of the dressing rooms see the article on the theatre in *The Albertan*, 28 October 1911.
7 *The Albertan*, 28 October 1911; Fire Insurance Map (1914), Glenbow Library.
8 "Mrs. L. M. Roberts, Mrs. Charles Clark, Mr. and Mrs. J. S. Jones, Mr. and Mrs. Ballachy [Balachey], High River, and Mrs. W. M. Campbell, Macleod, are guests at the Alberta," *The Albertan*, 6 February 1912. Mrs. Clark was the grandmother of Joe Clark, a future prime minister of Canada. See *The High River Times*, 8 February 1912, Local and General News section. Edited by Charles Clark, this paper reported, "A number of our townspeople took in the opening of the new Sherman Grand Theatre in Calgary on Monday last …"
9 Climatic details of 5 February 1912 provided by Scott McCormick, Environment Canada (Calgary), telephone conversation with author, 15 August 2002.
10 "M. S. Joiner Gets Big Appointment," *The Calgary Herald*, 6 August 1929. Article states that the future Grand orchestra leader, and later manager, "went into the orchestra pit of the Grand on its opening night."
11 "Beautiful Paintings in Grand Theatre Brought to Light during Reconstruction Work under Direction of Hungarian Artist," *The Calgary Herald*, 3 September 1937.
12 The English pastoral scene appears on the fire curtain in the drawing of the theatre that appeared in both *The Calgary Herald*, 21 September 1912; and *The Western Standard* (Calgary), 12 June 1913.
13 "Forbes Robertson Opens Playhouse," *The Albertan*, 6 February 1912.
14 Ibid.
15 For a short, untitled update on the theatre stating that the seats were "upholstered in leather" see *The Albertan*, 28 October 1911. For an account mentioning that the chairs were to be green in colour see "Forbes Robertson to Open Calgary's Fine New Theatre Feb. 5," *The Calgary Herald*, 22 January 1912.
16 For the best descriptions of the theatre in late January and early February of 1912 see: "Forbes Robertson to Open Calgary's Fine New Theatre Feb. 5." *The Calgary Herald* 22 January 1912; see also "Calgary Delights Forbes-Robertson," *Calgary News-Telegram*, 6 February 1912; "Forbes Robertson Opens Playhouse," *The Albertan*, 6 February 1912; "Opening of the Sherman Grand," *Calgary News-Telegram*, 7 February 1912. Three details appear in *The Calgary Herald* piece of 22 January 1912, that the other later accounts do not reference. It states: "Mr. Robertson has been specially invited to read the opening speech before the curtain goes up, and at the conclusion of the play Mr. Sherman has arranged for a public reception on the stage, so that those who are present at the first night of the Sherman Grand may inspect the theatre and its appointments. Afterwards a banquet will be held to celebrate the occasion." The opening speech, public reception and celebration banquet were not cited in the other contemporary sources listed above. Hence, they are not referenced here, as I suspect the initial plans were altered. Unfortunately there is no surviving copy of *The Calgary Herald* for 6 February 1912. For the invaluable program for the opening night, see *Program, Sherman Grand Theatre, 5 February 1912*, Glenbow Library. The call number is, 792.097123 S553p Pam. I have made approximations of the attendance numbers based on the plan of the theatre in the program. The balcony held 541 seats, and 813 more were located in the orchestra or main floor. If the twelve loges, which sat six people, were full, that would add 72 people to the total number. If the twelve boxes, which also each accommodated six individuals, were also full, another 72 could be seated. The seating capacity was thus 1498 or, as stated, approximately, 1,500. Useful secondary accounts on the theatre include Tom Ward, *Cowtown. An Album of Early Calgary* (Calgary: McClelland and Stewart West, 1975), 459, and Alan Hustak, "The Grand Lady of First Street," *City Scope* 2, no. 3 (September 1985): 53–54, 77.
17 "Forbes Robertson to Open Calgary's Fine New Theatre Feb. 5."
18 Hustak, "The Grand Lady of First Street," 53.
19 *Program, Sherman Grand Theatre, 5 February 1912*.
20 Norman J. Kennedy, "The Growth and Development of Music in Calgary" (M.A. thesis, University of Alberta, 1952), 91. Notes

written by Professor Augade's son, Louis Augade, 2 February 1973, Lucien Albert C. Augade Fonds, M36, file 7, Glenbow Archives.

21 "Mostly About Women," *The Albertan*, 7 February 1912.

22 Eva Reid, "Eavesdrop with Eva," *The Albertan*, 18 May 1961.

23 Jack Peach, "Historic Theatre Stately Old Lady with Grand Past," *The Calgary Herald*, 6 April 1985.

24 "Theatres and Music," *The Albertan*, 11 March 1911.

25 "Real Estate," *The Albertan*, 3 May 1911; "Whole Alexander Corner to be Remodelled," *Calgary News-Telegram*, 3 May 1911.

26 "Pete Egan's Movie Beat," *The Albertan*, 18 June 1959.

27 Eilenberg, "Johnston Forbes-Robertson," 43, 131.

28 Ibid., 42–43. Also useful for this sketch of Forbes-Robertson's background is his autobiography, *A Player Under Three Reigns* (New York: Benjamin Blom, 1971) and Frances Donaldson, "Sir Johnston Forbes-Robertson 1853–1937," in *The Actor-Managers* (London: Weidenfeld and Nicolson, 1970), 123–40.

29 "Russian Dancers Opening Attraction at Sherman Theatre," *Calgary News-Telegram*, 23 December 1911.

30 "Mr. Sherman Defends Advertising Curtain," *Calgary News-Telegram*, 20 March 1912.

31 For information on Bill Sherman, see Archibald Oswald MacRae, "William B. Sherman" in *History of the Province of Alberta*, vol. 2 (n.p.: The Western Canada History Co., 1912), 944–946; Andrew King, *Pen, Paper and Printing Ink* (Saskatoon: Western Producer Books, 1970), 86–88; Hustak, "Grand Lady."

32 "Forbes-Robertson at Maxine Elliott's Theatre," *Leslies' Weekly* (21 October 1909), Robinson Locke Collection of Dramatic Scrapbooks, vol. 213, Forbes Robertson, vol. 2, p. 3, New York Public Library.

33 Two excellent biographical accounts of Annie Glen Broder's life can be found in the Annie Glen Broder Papers, MG 258, file 1, Glenbow Archives. These are Dorothy J. Currie, "Annie Glen Broder—Pioneer Musician of Calgary," and "Memoirs of a Musical Pioneer," presumably written around 1931 by Mrs. Broder herself. The archival guide to the Annie Glen Broder Paper suggests that she was born about 1857. Mrs. Broder's physical description provided by a former student, Phyllis Chapman Ford, telephone interview with the author, 1 January 2003.

34 "Mrs. Annie Broder," in *The Canadian Men and Women of the Time*, ed. Henry James Morgan (Toronto: William Briggs, 1912), 144-145. Nancy Stevenson, "William Glen (1779-1849)," *Biographical Dictionary of Christian Missions*, ed. Gerald H. Anderson (New York: Macmillan Reference USA, 1998), 244.

35 Sir Arthur Sullivan quoted in Morgan, *The Canadian Men and Women*, 145. Annie Glen Broder, "An Appreciation," *The Calgary Herald*, 3 March 1927.

36 S. M. Kooyman, "Glenbow Alberta Institute, Archives Department, Annie Glen Broder Papers, 1880–1949," (1990): 1. "Mrs. Annie Glen Broder. Alberta Women We Should Know," *The Calgary Herald*, 26 November 1932.

37 "The Ride of the R.N.W.M.P. Song with Chorus by A. Glen Broder," Annie Glen Broder Papers, M6268, file 27, Glenbow Archives.

38 "Mrs. Annie Glen Broder, Well Known Musician, Dies," *The Calgary Herald*, 19 August 1937.

39 "Mother of Art and Drama in Calgary's Early Days, Mrs. W. R. Winter is Dead," *The Calgary Herald*, 16 October 1939.

40 Eve Crawford, "... and she always carried a gold-headed cane," *Canadian Golden West* 6 (Winter 1970–71): 26. I am indebted to Eve Crawford for depositing the research notes for her wonderful article with the Glenbow Archives.

41 "Music and Drama: 'The Mikado'," *The Calgary Herald*, 24 February 1911.

42 Crawford, "... and she always carried," 27.

43 Ibid.

44 E. M. Catley, "Calgary 35 years Ago ...," *The North Hill News* (Calgary), 2 September 1955.

45 For the best source regarding Bob Edwards see Grant MacEwan, *Eye Opener Bob* (Edmonton: The Institute of Applied Art Ltd., 1957), 16. Local historian James Martin recently discovered Bob Edward's

birth certificate. Although Edwards gave 1864 as his date of birth, he was actually born on 17 September 1860. "Extract of an entry in a Register of Birth, Robert Chambers Edwards, District of Saint Andrew, Burgh of Edinburgh, Scottish Registry Office, Edinburgh."

46 "The Calgary Eye Opener," *The Calgary Herald*, 27 April 1909.

47 Bob Edwards to Miss Ross, 7 February 1915, Bob Edwards Papers, M 8804, Glenbow Archives.

48 For *Calgary Eye Opener* circulation figures see MacEwan, *Eye Opener Bob*, 125, 134. See also *Calgary Eye Opener*, 9 March 1912; p. 1. For examples of Edwards' writing see Hugh A. Dempsey, ed., *The Best of Bob Edwards* (Edmonton: Hurtig, 1975) and Hugh A. Dempsey, ed., *The Wit and Wisdom of Bob Edwards* (Edmonton: Hurtig, 1976).

49 *Calgary Eye Opener*, 27 January 1912.

50 "Davidson Back From the Orient," *The Calgary Herald*, 26 March 1931. For the best review of Davidson's life, see Robert Lampard, "Making New Friends: James Wheeler Davidson and Rotary International," *Alberta History* 52, no. 3 (Summer 2004): 2-10.

51 Ruth Gorman, "Jim W. Davidson," *My Golden West*, Stampede Issue (1968): 32. Davidson gave his height as nearly 5' 11" in an excerpt from his diary of Peary's second expedition (1893-94) shown to me by his daughter Marjorie Davidson Abramson, Ladner, B.C., 5 September 2000.

52 Sam Coultis, unpublished speaking notes from a speech to the club concerning the history of Calgary's Rotary Club, p. 3. I have added punctuation to the selected quote. My thanks to Sandra Elliott, Executive Secretary, the Rotary Club of Calgary, for bringing these notes to my attention.

53 Harry Hutchcroft, "The Life and Work of Jim Davidson," speech to the Calgary Rotary Club, July 15, 1947. Notes shown to me by Marjory Davidson Abramson, Ladner, B.C., 5 September 2000.

54 Lillian Dow Davidson, *Making New Friends* (Chicago: Rotary International, 1934), 139.

55 Harry M. Sanders, "Beiseker," in *The Story Behind Alberta Names* (Calgary: Red Deer Press, 2003), 46.

56 "Late C. H. Davidson A Friend of Alberta," *Calgary News-Telegram*, 5 February 1915; "C. H. Davidson, Banker, Dies after an Operation," *Minneapolis Morning Tribune*, 30 January 1915.

57 The best contemporary description of Jim Davidson appears in Archibald Oswald MacRae, *History of the Province of Alberta* (n.p.: The Western Canada History Co., 1912), 565–66. A good short overview is "J. W. Davidson, Noted Rotary Worker, Dies," *The Albertan*, 19 July 1933. I am very grateful to Jim Davidson's daughter, Marjorie Abramson, for supplementary information. Bob Lampard has recently written an excellent summary of his life, "Making New Friends: James Wheeler Davidson and Rotary International," *Alberta History* (Summer 2004): 2-10.

58 James W. Davidson, "Canada's Finest Theatre," *The Albertan*, 6 February 1912. A Calgary weekly later claimed that the Sherman Grand's stage was "one foot larger than that of the Royal Alexandra in Toronto." See *The Western Standard*, 12 June 1913.

59 *Calgary* (London: Hodder and Stoughton, n.d.), 1.

60 Hugh A. Dempsey, *Calgary: Spirit of the West* (Calgary: Fifth House, 1994), 98.

61 Fred Kennedy, "When Subdivision Stakes Sprouted Over Vast Areas," *The Calgary Herald*, 21 January 1933.

62 Conflicting reports exist of when Forbes-Robertson gave his speech. "Forbes Robertson Opens Playhouse," *The Albertan*, 6 February 1912, reports it was after the third act. "Forbes-Robertson Warmly Welcomed by Local Audience," *Calgary News-Telegram,* 6 February 1912, states it was after the second. Unfortunately, no issue of *The Calgary Herald* survives for that date. I believe *The Albertan*, a morning paper, erred, for it contains the false information that Belle Lougheed "was in attendance for a short time, before departing for Ottawa by the midnight train." This is incorrect. "Mainly About Women," *The Albertan,* 7 February 1912 corrected the earlier error and noted that Mrs. Lougheed had postponed her visit to Ottawa to host a theatre supper at the Alexandra Hotel after the play. Press reviews of Forbes-Robertson's other North American presentations

of "The Passing of the Third Floor Back" indicate that when he made a short speech to an audience, it came after the second act. See: "Robertson's Art Makes Play Great Lesson," *Vancouver World*, 25 January 1912, p. 50; Sidney Ormont, "Forbes-Robertson Casts Spell Over his Audience," *Atlanta Constitution*, 9 April 1912, p. 55. The play's author argued that the interruption would best come between the second and third acts for dramatic purposes. See Jerome K. Jerome, *The Passing of the Third Floor Back* (London: Samuel French Ltd., 1948). For all these reasons, I believe that he made his speech after the second act.

63 "Grand Opening: Calgary's New $500,000 Theatre," *The Provincial Standard*, 3 February 1912.

64 Details regarding anthem singing confirmed by Dick Barron, interview with author, 21 January 2004. Dick Barron helped his father at the Grand from the moment of purchase in 1937. It remained customary to sing the anthem after the Second World War as well. "Are Calgary Audiences Crude?" *Calgary News-Telegram*, 13 February 1917, confirms that "God Save the King" was sung after each performance in Calgary theatres in the 1910s.

65 Annie Glen Broder, "Forbes-Robertson. An Appreciation," *The Provincial Standard*, 10 February 1912; Mrs. W. Roland Winter, "Thirteen Years at Calgary Theatres," *The Western Standard*, 12 June 1913; *Calgary Eye-Opener*, 10 February 1912.

66 "Forbes-Robertson Warmly Welcomed by Local Audience," *Calgary News-Telegram*, 6 February 1912.

67 "Local and General News," *High River Times*, 8 February 1912.

68 "Sen. Lougheed Congratulated," *Calgary News-Telegram*, 7 February 1912.

69 This program is now housed in the Glenbow Library. For details regarding Henry Orr Beattie see his obituary in the *Salmon Arm Observer*, 29 July 1981.

70 Wesley F. Orr to Mrs. Addie C. Wood, London, Ontario, dated Calgary, Christmas 1893, Wesley F. Orr Papers, Glenbow Archives.

71 For more on Wesley Orr see Max Foran, "The Making of a Booster: Wesley Fletcher Orr and Nineteenth Century Calgary," in *Town and City: Aspects of Western Canadian Urban Development*, ed. A. F. J. Artibise (Regina: Canadian Plains Research Centre, 1981), 289–307.

72 Agnes Ballentine, "A Woman's Impressions of Calgary," *The Colonizer* 17, no. 203 (November 1912): 576.

73 "Wild Descriptions of Early Calgary by Dr. McDougall," *Calgary News-Telegram*, 20 January 1912.

74 "Old Times Lecture Very Interesting," *The Calgary Herald*, 27 January 1912.

75 James H. Gray, *R. B. Bennett The Calgary Years* (Toronto: University of Toronto Press, 1991), 128.

76 "Table VII: Ethnic Origins of Calgary's Population, 1901–1961," in Max Foran, *Calgary. An Illustrated History* (Toronto: James Lorimer & Company, 1978), 178.

77 "Table VIII: Major Religious Affiliations of Calgary's Population, 1901–1961," in Foran, *Calgary*, 178.

78 Alberta West [Ethel Heydon Davidson], "Forbes-Robertson's Farewell Offering of Sermon Play," *The Albertan*, 9 February 1915. This article was actually written three years later, when Forbes-Robertson returned to Calgary, and presented the play once again.

79 "Mrs. W. M. Davidson," *The Alberta Club Women's Blue Book* (Calgary: Calgary Branch of the Canadian Women's Press Club Publishers, 1917), 120; "Was First to Blaze Trail for Women in Newspaper World," *The Toronto Star*, 17 January 1923.

80 "Table II: Number of Males Per 1,000 Females in Calgary, 1891–1971," in Foran, *Calgary*, 174.

81 "Forbes-Robertson Warmly Welcomed by Local Audience," *Calgary News-Telegram*, 6 February 1912.

82 R. J. C. Stead, "Observations," *High River Times*, 15 February 1912.

83 Earl Grey to Robert J. C. Stead, 6 March 1911, Stead Papers, box 1, file 14, National Archives of Canada, quoted in Clarence Karr, *Authors and Audiences. Popular Canadian Fiction in the Early Twentieth Century* (Montreal: McGill-Queen's University Press, 2000), 95, 265.

84 Paul Voisey, *High River and the Times* (Edmonton: University of Alberta Press, 2003), 35.

85 Robert J. C. Stead, *The Empire Builders and other Poems* 4th ed. (Toronto: William Briggs, 1910), 20. While he originally objected to the immigration of non-white races to Canada, by 1918 he changed his mind and ended his opposition to "Hindoos and Chinese" entering the country; see footnote 23 in Karr, *Authors and Audiences*, 266.

86 "Table VII: Ethnic Origins of Calgary's Population, 1901–1961" in Foran, 178; Bryan P. Melnyk, *Calgary Builds. The Emergence of an Urban Landscape, 1905-1914* (Regina: Canadian Plains Research Centre, 1985), 22.

87 James H. Gray, *Red Lights on the Prairies* (1971, reprint; Scarborough, ON: New American Library, 1973): 152.

88 Ethel Heydon Davidson to "E. R." [unidentified correspondent], 17 May 1962, William and Ethel Davidson Papers, M514, Glenbow Archives.

89 Text of R. B. Bennett's speech from *First Annual Report of the Canadian Club of Calgary for the Year 1907* (Calgary: Canadian Club of Calgary, 1907), 45–46.

90 See Donald Smith, "Historic Mount Royal has a Few Secrets," *The Calgary Herald*, 31 July 2002.

91 Title deed in the name of James W. Davidson, 21 October 1909, reprinted in Elise A. Corbet and Lorne G. Simpson, "Calgary's Mount Royal. A Garden Suburb," paper prepared for the Planning and Building Department, the Heritage Advisory Board, City of Calgary, September 1994, p. 81. The Corbet and Simpson report is the best source on the question of the naming of Mount Royal's streets, particularly pages 21 to 23; my thanks to Harry Sanders for bringing it to my attention.

92 Gray, *R. B. Bennett*, 120.

93 Marjorie Davidson Abramson, telephone conversation with author, 6 July 2000; Marjorie Davidson Abramson, interview with the author, Ladner, BC, 13 November 2000. Jim Davidson's full knowledge of the theatre's physical dimensions, as revealed in his newspaper article on the Sherman Grand's opening, helps to confirm this story.

94 Paul Voisey, "In Search of Wealth and Status: An Economic and Social Study of Entrepreneurs in Early Calgary," in *Frontier Calgary, Town, City, and Region 1875–1914*, ed. Anthony W. Rasporich and Henry C. Klassen (Calgary: McClelland and Stewart West, 1975): 233.

95 Ticket prices appear in the *Calgary News-Telegram*, 26 January 1912; "Cowboys' and Cowgirls' Performance Nothing Short of Hair-Raising," *Calgary News-Telegram*, 3 September 1912. This second article noted that "twenty cents an hour is a pretty fair average wage for western Canada."

96 Bank of Canada Inflation Calculator, http://www.bankofcanada.ca/en/inflation_calc.htm. It states that a "basket" of goods and services that cost $100 in 1914 would cost $1,576.71 in 2003. Hence I write that $5 in 1912 would be nearly $100 in 2004 terms.

97 *Montreal Gazette* quoted in Henry James Morgan, *The Canadian Men and Women of the Time* (Toronto: William Briggs, 1912), 606.

Notes to Chapter 2

1 The Mace [pseud.], "Turning a New Leaf," *Saturday Night*, 30 May 1925, p. 4.

2 Max Foran, "W. A. 'Billy' Griesbach and World War One," *Alberta History* 32, no. 3 (Summer 1994): 4.

3 W. A. Griesbach, *I Remember* (Toronto: Ryerson, 1946), 130.

4 Emil Longue Beau, "The Confessional. No. 45—Sir James Lougheed," *Toronto Star Weekly*, 30 July 1921.

5 Beckles Willson, *The Life of Lord Strathcona and Mount Royal* (London: Cassell, 1915), 83; quoted in J. G. MacGregor, *Senator Hardisty's Prairies 1849–1889* (Saskatoon: Western Producer Prairie Books, 1978), 2. McGregor also adds that Richard successfully applied for script at Edmonton in 1885 under Certificate No. 734 on account of his mother's Metis background.

6 Belle Hardisty, Richard's niece, visited her in Lachine before her grandmother's death in 1876; see "Canadian Women in the Public Eye. Lady Lougheed," *Saturday Night*, 16 September 1922, p. 27.

7 MacGregor, *Senator Hardisty's Prairies*, 147, 182.

8 Pierre Berton, *The Last Spike. The Great Railway 1881–1885* (Toronto: McClelland and Stewart, 1971), 111

9 For a good review of the Hardisty family see Donna McDonald, *Lord Strathcona: A Biography of Donald Alexander Smith* (Toronto: Dundurn Press, 1996), 65–67.

10 MacGregor, *Senator Hardisty's Prairies*, 182.

11 For a short summary of Richard Hardisty's career in the Hudson's Bay Company see Shirlee Anne Smith, "Richard Charles Hardisty," *Dictionary of Canadian Biography*, vol. 11, *1881–1890* (Toronto: University of Toronto Press, 1982), 383–84.

12 Richard Hardisty to J. A. Grahame, dated Edmonton, 20 June 1882, Hudson's Bay Company Archives, D 20/23 folio 161 d, Provincial Archives of Manitoba. My thanks to Henry Klassen for this quotation.

13 Henry C. Klassen, *Eye on the Future. Business People in Calgary and the Bow Valley, 1870–1900* (Calgary: University of Calgary Press, 2002), 76.

14 Here I follow her age as given in the registration of her marriage: 16 September 1884, Methodist Church Mission Morleyville, Northwest Territories, Marriage Register, McDougall Family Papers, M732, folder 13, Glenbow Archives. Interestingly her name is given in the document as "Bella," only later in Calgary did she become known as "Belle." A Photostat of entries from the Lougheed Family Bible in the Lougheed House Collection lists her full name as "Isabella Clark Lougheed," and gives her date of birth as 18 April 1861. The same photostat shows that Belle had a younger sister, Mary Louise Hardisty (later Hackland), who was born on 8 May 1877. She also had seven brothers; two died as infants and five survived to adulthood.

15 Senator G. D. Robertson quoted in Senate, *Debates*, 12 January 1926, 7.

16 J. Fraser Perry, ed., *They Gathered at the River* (Calgary: Central United Church, 1975), 123.

17 John Blue, *Alberta, Past and Present*, vol. 3 (Chicago: Pioneer Historical Publishing Co., 1924), 160; Perry, *They Gathered at the River,* 161, 176.

18 "Pay Last Respects Sir James Lougheed; Hundreds View Remains Today; Service at All Saints Church," *The Ottawa Citizen*, 3 November 1925; "Thousands Pay Last Respects to Memory of Senator Lougheed," *The Calgary Herald*, 10 November 1925. His funeral in Ottawa was held at All Saints Church; and the Calgary funeral at the Anglican Pro-Cathedral Church of the Redeemer. Interestingly, however, as late as 1923 he told a reporter that he still considered himself a Methodist. See: "The Spotlight. Sir James Lougheed," *The Toronto Star*, 21 June 1923, p. 6.

19 Elizabeth B. Price, "Alberta's Woman Pioneers Will Form Organization," *The Calgary Herald*, 21 March 1922.

20 The very successful novelist Onota Watanna (or Mrs. Winnifred Eaton Babcock Reeve), wrote an inscription in the presentation copy of her novel, *Cattle*, which she gave to Belle Lougheed in Calgary in December 1923; the copy is now housed in the Margaret P. Hess Collection of the University of Calgary Library. It reads, "To Lady Lougheed—a picturesque and delightful personality, with the regard of the author." Mrs. Reeve lived on a ranch just sixty kilometres west of Calgary at the time. See Elizabeth Bailey Price, "Onota Watanna has Written a New Book," *Canadian Bookman* 4 (April 1922): 123-125. In my opinion, this short assessment by one of Canada's most successful authors is the best summary of Belle Hardisty Lougheed. For a full biography of Winnifred Eaton see Diana Birchall, *Onota Watanna. The Story of Winnifred Eaton* (Urbana: University of Illinois Press, 2001).

21 "Concert," *The Calgary Herald*, 16 April 1884; quoted in Jennifer Cook Bobrovitz and Trudy Cowan, "Reasoned Speculation: The Challenge of Knowing Isabella Clarke Hardisty Lougheed," (unpub-

lished manuscript, 2003), p, 3, the Lougheed House Collection. The church is described in Perry, *They Gathered at the River*, 35.

22 Mrs. William Pearce's invitation to the wedding and the reception has survived in her papers: Mrs. William Pearce Papers, MU 85, Glenbow Archives. The Glenbow also has the registration of the marriage: McDougall Family Papers, Methodist Church Mission, Morleyville, North West Territories, Marriage Register, M 732, folder 13, Glenbow Archives.

23 In Toronto, among his boyhood friends, he was always just "Jim." William Lewis Edmonds, "Lougheed is an Old Toronto Boy," *Toronto Star Weekly*, 29 September 1917, 13.

24 See the Toronto directories for 1867/68, 1870, 1874 and 1875 under "John Lougheed" on Queen St. East; see also the City of Toronto Assessment Rolls for St. David's Ward, Queen St. East, for 1866, 1870 and 1872.

25 For an excellent summary of nineteenth century Cabbagetown see J. M. S. Careless, "The Emergence of Cabbagetown in Victorian Toronto," in *Gathering Place: Peoples and Neighbourhoods of Toronto, 1834–1945*, ed. Robert F. Harney (Toronto: Multicultural History Society of Ontario, 1985), 25, 31.

26 Careless, "Cabbagetown," 35.

27 "Noted Western Statesman and Pioneer Passes," *The Calgary Herald*, 2 November 1925.

28 This book is now in the possession of the Lougheed House Collection. The volume includes eight sketches of Christian leaders; two of those selected are St. Augustine and Charles Wesley. My thanks to David Hall, University of Alberta Department of History, for identifying the source of the quote in the King James Version of the Bible.

29 "Religion Half Century Ago Simple, Stern, Says Judge," *The Toronto Star*, 26 February 1940.

30 "The Spotlight: Sir James Lougheed," *The Toronto Star*, 21 June 1923, p. 6.

31 William Pearce quoted in "Remembers late Sir James as Boy…," *The Albertan*, 3 November 1925.

32 William Pearce to Phina Pearce, 20 May 1909, William Pearce Papers, (hereafter cited as Pearce Papers), 74-169/810, University of Alberta Archives

33 V.B. Wadsworth, "History of Exploratory Surveys Conducted by John Stoughton Dennis, Provincial Land Surveyor, in the Muskoka, Parry Sound and Nipissing Districts 1860–1865 and Incidents of the Surveys and Succeeding History of the Principal Events of my Life," mimeographed, February 1926, pp. 19, 98, Toronto Public Library.

34 William Pearce quoted in, "Remembers late Sir James as Boy…"

35 Edmonds, "Lougheed is an old Toronto Boy," 13.

36 "Seventy-One Tuesday: Sir James Lougheed," *The Calgary Herald*, 1 September 1925.

37 Sam Blake quoted in "Noted Western Statesman," *The Calgary Herald*, 2 November 1925. James Lougheed himself must be the unidentified source of the information. His friend Senator Raoul Dandurand repeated it in his tribute in the Senate on 12 January 1926. Dandurand, who had known James Lougheed from 1898 until his death, told the story this way: "In his early teens he began life seriously, preparing for the carpentry trade, a trade which requires intelligence and which affords scope for artistic values. At the same time, being anxious to learn, he attended regularly the Sunday school classes of the Hon. Samuel Blake. That honourable gentleman, recognizing his ability and his desire to learn, and seeing in him talents which would fit him for professional life, suggested that he should prepare himself for a higher station in society. This advice did not fall upon unproductive soil. Young Lougheed decided to make an effort to advance himself by studying the classics, he devoted all his spare time to self-improvement, and the moment came when he entered upon the study of law." See Senate, *Debates*, 1926, 4. For Sam Blake's background see John D. Blakewell, "Samuel Hume Blake," *Dictionary of Canadian Biography*, vol. 14, *1911–1920* (Toronto: University of Toronto Press, 1998): 85–89.

38 Senate, *Debates*, 1926, 4.

39 My thanks to Orlando Martini for assistance with James Lougheed's attendance at Weston High School. The best source on the school is Dora E. Wattie, *One Hundred Years, A Retrospect 1857–1957: Weston Grammar School to Weston Collegiate and Vocational School* (n.p, 1957). Page 26 of Weston High and Vocational School's first yearbook, *Conning Tower*, Easter 1927, mentions James Lougheed's attendance at the school, as does "Noted Western Statesman and Pioneer Passes," *The Calgary Herald*, 2 November 1925.

40 "Noted Western Statesman and Pioneer Passes."

41 The organization included an Anderson, a Self, a Coatsworth, and the two Lougheeds.

42 "Awscal Literary Society, Toronto, 30 December 1876: Report of Oyster Supper." Note in the possession of Jamie Coatsworth, grandson of Emerson Coatsworth, Jr.

43 The Wanderer [pseud.], "I First Saw," *Winnipeg Evening Tribune*, 16 June 1923.

44 "Hon. Senator Lougheed, Calgary, N.W.T.," *Prominent Men of Canada*, ed. G. Mercer Adam (Toronto: Canadian Biographical Publishing Company, 1892), 118.

45 A conversation with James Lougheed in the early 1920s ("shortly before his death"—Lougheed died in 1925) recalled by Z. M. Hamilton, in Z. M. Hamilton, "Nicholas Flood Davin," SHS 14, Saskatchewan Archives Board, University of Regina. George Bennett, the man executed, was accused of the murder of George Brown, editor of the *Toronto Globe*. He was hanged on 23 July 1880.

46 Ibid.

47 P. B. Waite, "Reflections on an Un-Victorian Society," in Donald A. Swainson, ed., *Oliver Mowat's Ontario* (Toronto: Macmillan, 1972), 26.

48 J. V. McAree, *Cabbagetown Store* (Toronto: The Ryerson Press, 1953), 100.

49 Ibid., 92.

50 Hereward Senior, *Orangeism: The Canadian Phase* (Toronto: McGraw-Hill-Ryerson, 1972), 73.

51 For an excellent summary of the Orange Lodge in mid-nineteenth century British North America see Scott W. See, "The Orange Order: Institutionalized Nativism," chap. 4 of *Riots in New Brunswick: Orange Nativism and Social Violence in the 1840s* (Toronto: University of Toronto Press, 1993), 71–111.

52 McAree, *Cabbagetown Store*, 94.

53 Cecil J. Houston and William J. Smyth, *The Sash Canada Wore: A Historical Geography of the Orange Order in Canada* (1980; reprint, Milton, ON: Global Heritage Press, 1999), 49.

54 William Jenkins, "Between the Lodge and the Meeting-House: Mapping Irish Protestant Identities and Social Worlds in late Victorian Toronto," *Social and Cultural Geography* 4, no. 1 (2003): 79.

55 Jim would have been active in the Young Britons in his late teens, and perhaps during his early twenties. We can say this with precision as the Orange Young Britons were only formed in 1869; see Houston and Smyth, *The Sash Canada Wore*, 90. See the following footnote for reference to testimony from Jane and Elizabeth.

56 Interview with Misses Jane and Elizabeth Lougheed, by B. Phillips, 3 April 1936, Perkins Bull Papers, p. 36765 Archives of Ontario; see also William Perkins Bull, *From the Boyne to Brampton, or John the Orangeman at Home and Abroad* (Toronto: The Perkins Bull Foundation, 1936), 228. Jane was 86 years old in 1936, and her sister Elizabeth was 74. Jane was four years older than Jim, and Elizabeth eight years younger than him.

57 "Noted Western Statesman"; Mercer, *Prominent Men of Canada*, 118. For all genealogical information on the Lougheed family see "James Lougheed of Britannia," third up-date, October 1998, compiled by Jopie Loughead, Viviane McClelland, and Frank Ellis Wickson, Lougheed House Collection. Mary Ann Alexander Lougheed's death appears on page 19.

58 Jennifer Cook Bobrovitz, personal communication, Lougheed House, 18 October 2004.

59 W. Stewart Wallace, "Sir James Albert Manning (1851-1929)," *The Macmillan Dictionary of Canadian Biography* 3rd. ed. (Toronto: Macmillan, 1963), 4.

60 Alan F.J. Artibise, *Winnipeg. A Social History of Urban Growth, 1874–1914* (Montreal: McGill-Queen's University Press, 1975), 44.

61 Valerius Geist, *Buffalo Nation. History and Legend of the North American Bison* (Calgary: Fifth House, 1996), 110.

62 Senate. *Debates*, 12 January 1926, 5. The chief engineer was Herbert Holt, later to become one of Canada's leading financiers; see Wallace, "Herbert Holt," *The Macmillan Dictionary of Canadian Biography*, 326.

63 Peter Turner Bone, *When the Steel Went Through: Reminiscences of a Railway Pioneer* (Toronto: The Macmillan Company of Canada, 1947), 45.

64 James A. Lougheed to Laura L. Lougheed, Port Carling, Ontario, dated Ottawa, 14 February 1911, Lougheed House Collection.

65 James F. Sanderson, "Indian Tales of the Canadian Prairies," *Alberta Historical Review* 13, no. 3 (Summer 1965): 16–17. For a sketch of Sanderson's life see L. J. Roy Wilson, "James Francis Sanderson," *Dictionary of Canadian Biography*, vol. 13: *1901–1910* (Toronto: University of Toronto Press, 1994), 921–22.

66 "Horse Trouble," *The Regina Leader*, 12 July 1883; reprinted in *Alberta History*, 31, no. 3 (Summer 1983): 21.

67 L. J. Roy Wilson, "Thomas Andrew Tweed," *Dictionary of Canadian Biography*, vol. 13: *1901–1910* (Toronto: University of Toronto Press, 1994), 1043.

68 John K. Warkentin, "Western Canada in 1886," *Papers Read before the Historical and Scientific Society of Manitoba* 3, no. 20 (1963–1964): 108.

69 This approximation is based on the size of the Indian reserves in the Treaty Seven area of Southern Alberta in the late nineteenth century. This region encompasses approximately 50,000 square miles. Throughout what is now the province of Alberta, "[reserves] comprise 0.95% of the total area." Norman C. Conrad, *Reading the Entrails. An Alberta Ecohistory* (Calgary: University of Calgary Press, 1999), p. 177, n 17.

70 Turner Bone. *When the Steel Went Through*, 46.

71 Senator J. A. Lougheed, "Why Go To Canada? The City of Calgary," Supplement to *Calgary Daily Herald* [1910], James Lougheed clipping file, Glenbow Library.

72 Burns and Elliott, *Calgary, Alberta: Her Industries & Resources* (1885; reprint, Calgary: Glenbow-Alberta Institute, 1974), 53.

73 "He Remembers Sir James as Boy in Toronto Law Office," *The Albertan*, 3 November 1925. Forty-two years later, Turner Bone remembered precisely where they pitched their tent during the early part of the winter of 1883-34: "Where the Robin Hood flour mill now stands." Gulf Canada Square occupied this spot in 2005.

74 Ibid., 58.

75 John Egan to William Van Horne, quoted in Dave Jones, *Alberta Then & Now: The Second Coming of the Railway to Calgary* (n.p.: CP Rail System, 1996), 1.

76 Max Foran, "Early Calgary 1875–1895: The Controversies Surrounding the Townsite Location and the Direction of Town Expansion," in A. Ross McCormack and Ian MacPherson, eds., *Cities in the West: Papers of the Western Canada Urban History Conference, University of Winnipeg, October 1974* (Ottawa: National Museum of Man, 1975), 31.

77 Canadian Pacific Railway Town Sites, Sales Book, Canada North West Land Company Papers, vol. 24, Calgary, 15 January 1884, pp. 125–126, Glenbow Archives. For James Lougheed's recollections of the land sale see "Lougheed was First Lawyer when Calgary was Mushroom Town," *The Albertan*, 2 June 1925.

78 Janice Dickin McGinnis, "Birth to Boom to Bust: Building in Calgary, 1873-1914", in *Frontier Calgary: Town, City, and Region, 1875-1914*, Anthony W. Rasporich and Henry C. Klassen, eds., (Calgary: McClelland and Stewart West, 1975), 10.

79 Turner Bone, *When the Steel Went Through*, 63.

80 Rev. Joshua Dyke quoted in *The Calgary Herald*, 9 April 1907; cited in Hugh A. Dempsey, *Calgary: Spirit of the West* (Calgary: Fifth House Publishers, 1994), 41.

81 Mr. Justice J. C. Major, Excerpts from Speaking Notes, "The Bennett and Lougheed Feud," Legal Archives Historical Dinners, September 19 and 20, 1995, *The Legal Archives Society of Alberta Newsletter*, Fall 1995, p. 4.

82 Burns and Elliott, *Calgary, Alberta*, 53.

83 Civic Committee Minutes, box 1, file 1, 1884, City of Calgary Papers. My thanks to Jennifer Cook Bobrovitz for this information.

84 The brand appears in the *North West Territories Brand Book* (Calgary: *The Calgary Herald*, 1903), and is cited and reproduced in George Edworthy, "By Their Brands Ye Shall Know Them," in Elsie C. Morrison and P. N. R. Morrison, *Calgary 1875–1950. A Souvenir of Calgary's Seventy-fifth Anniversary* (Calgary: Calgary Publishing Company, 1950), 136.

85 Details on Sam Lougheed came from the following sources: Lougheed [et al], "James Lougheed of Britannia," 40; Alexander Sutherland to John Nelson, 15 April 1895, Alexander Sutherland Letter Book, United Church Archives, Toronto; Walter J. Wasylow, "History of Battleford Industrial School for Indians," (Master's thesis, University of Saskatchewan, 1972), 346, 350, 354, 358. My thanks to Uta Fox for this reference.

86 Klassen, *Eye on the Future*, 65.

87 Henry C. Klassen, "Lawyers, Finance, and Economic Development in Southwestern Alberta, 1884 to 1920," in *Essays in the History of Canadian Law. Beyond the Law: Lawyers and Business in Canada, 1830 to 1930*, ed. Carol Wilton (Toronto: The Osgoode Society, 1990), 304.

88 James A. Lougheed to Mr. Hardisty, dated Calgary, 25 November 1885, M508/1688, Glenbow Archives.

89 Province of Manitoba, Department of Health and Public Welfare, Certificate of Death for Richard Hardisty, 12 May 1885, issued 12 April 1930, enclosed in William Lucas Hardisty Estate, McLaws Redman Lougheed and Cairns Fonds, Fond 37, file 173, folder 2, The Legal Archives Society of Alberta, Calgary.

90 Frank Hardisty quoted in Victor V. Murray, "Personality Parade. 'Have a Good time – Live a Long Time'," *The Winnipeg Tribune*, 15 May 1945.

91 *The Ottawa Citizen*, 2 November 1925. My thanks to David Hall for this reference.

92 "Wedding Bells," *The Calgary Tribune*, 11 September 1889. My thanks to Jennifer Cook Bobrovitz for this reference.

93 For James Lougheed on the death of Lord Strathcona, see Senate, *Debates*, 20 January 1914, 15.

94 Louis Knafla and Richard Klumpenhouwer, *Lords of the Western Bench. A Biographical History of the Supreme and District Courts of Alberta, 1876–1990* (Calgary: The Legal History Archives Society of Alberta, 1997), 17–18.

95 "Sir John's Visit," *The Calgary Herald*, 17 July 1886.

96 Klassen, *Eye on the Future*, 333.

97 Bobrovitz, personal communication.

98 Ibid.

99 An article in *The Calgary Tribune*, 18 December 1889, estimated the value of the property he held at "nearly $70,000 worth." See also McGregor, *Senator Hardisty's Prairies*, 182. He lists Richard Hardisty's net worth in the early 1880s.

100 C. E. D. Wood, "On the Road to Banff, 1890," *Alberta History* 25, no. 3 (Summer 1977): 7.

101 James Lougheed cited by Beau, "Sir James Lougheed," 10.

102 Beverley A. Stacey, "D. W. Davis: Whiskey Trader to Politician," *Alberta History* 38, no. 3 (Summer 1990): 1–11.

103 John McDougall, *On Western Trails in the Early Seventies* (Toronto: William Briggs, 1911): 69, 191; the quote appears in Hugh A. Dempsey, *Firewater. The Impact of the Whisky Trade on the Blackfoot Nation* (Calgary: Fifth House, 2002), 102. Davis died in 1906.

104 *The Calgary Herald*, 18 April 1888; quoted in Allan Connery, comp., *As Reported in the Herald* (Calgary: *The Calgary Herald*, 1982), 35.

105 Peter McCarthy to John A. Macdonald, 21 October 1889, John A. Macdonald Papers, 238100–238102, National Archives of Canada. My thanks to David Hall for this reference and also for information on James Lougheed's Senate career from 1889 to 1925.

106 Rev. Leo Gaetz to G. Foster, 25 October 1889, John A. Macdonald Papers, 7980, National Archives of Canada.

107 The dates in office of Senators Wark and Dessaulles appear in J. K. Johnson, ed., *The Canadian Directory of Parliament, 1867–1967* (Ottawa: Public Archives of Canada, 1968), 592, 164.

108 See the two photos in the short report by Audrey Dubé, Office of the Curator, House of Commons, "The Room of the Francophonie" (1997), 2. Named in 1993, the room used to be the old Senate Smoking Room.

109 Raoul Dandurand recorded in Senate, *Debates*, 12 January 1926, 5.

110 Edmonds, "Lougheed is an Old Toronto Boy," 13.

111 Robert A. Mackay, *The Unreformed Senate of Canada,* Revised ed. (Toronto: McClelland and Stewart, 1963), 9.

112 Robert MacGregor Dawson, *The Government of Canada,* 3rd ed. (Toronto: University of Toronto Press, 1957), 339.

113 Beau, "Sir James Lougheed," 10.

114 Bobrovitz, personal communication.

115 The Senator mentioned both the Russell Hotel and the Rideau Club in his defence against the accusations of Peter McCarthy; see: Examination of J.A. Lougheed, 20–21 March 1894, Edwin R. Rogers, Clerk of the Court, McCarthy vs. Lougheed, p. 12, Civil Cases, accession number 79.266, file number, 3369, box 36, Provincial Archives of Alberta, For a reference to the Rideau Club consult John H. Taylor, *Ottawa: An Illustrated History* (Toronto: James Lorimer, 1986), 55, 72.

116 Statement of Claim, Supreme Court of the Northwest Territories, Calgary, Civil Cases, accession number 79.266, file number 3369, box 36, "Peter McCarthy v. James A. Lougheed," 19 June 1893, Provincial Archives of Alberta.

117 Senator James Lougheed quoted in C. B., "Sir James Lougheed—Gentleman" *The Ottawa Citizen*, 2 November 1925.

118 Statement of Claim, "Peter McCarthy v. James A. Lougheed," 19 June 1893.

119 Examination of James A. Lougheed, 20–21 March 1894, 10, 13, 15, 19. See also: "Death of Peter M'Carthy, K. C.," *The Calgary Herald*, 8 October 1901.

120 Bobrovitz, personal communication.

121 On Calgary in the 1890s, see Donald Smith and Henry Klassen, "Onward! Calgary in the 1890s," in Donald Smith, ed., *Centennial City* (Calgary: The University of Calgary, 1994), 1–14.

122 "Still Lives in 'Bow Bend' Home," *The Calgary Herald*, 18 November 1933.

123 Jennifer Bobrovitz, "Mansion home to 'Czar of the West'," *The Calgary Herald*, 9 November 1997.

124 "The Buildings of 1891," *The Calgary Weekly Herald*, 6 January 1892. See also Jennifer Bobrovitz, "Stately Mansion Scene of Many Historic Events," *The Calgary Herald*, 15 June 1997. I have taken details on Beaulieu's roof from the pamphlet, "Beaulieu Gardens, Historic Mansion, Carriage House, Step Two," (n.d, n.p.), 6.

125 Canada, Census of Canada, 1901, Province of Alberta, District of Central Alberta, p. 13, microfilm reel T-6550. My thanks to the Lougheed House Collection for this reference.

126 Western Canadian Census, 1906, Calgary Section 26 D, district 19, p. 40, microfilm reel T-18362. My thanks to David Elliott for this reference. Interestingly, in the era of the high head tax against Chinese immigrants, the senator wanted to allow the entry into Canada of the wives of Chinese immigrants, "in the interests of morality." See Senate, *Debates*, 14 March 1911, 328–29. My thanks to David Hall for this reference.

127 "A Great Housewarming. The Elite of Calgary at Senator Lougheed's Friday Night," *The Calgary Tribune*, 17 February 1892.

128 David Mittelstadt, "A Biographical and Social History of Mount Royal, Calgary," July 2002, p. 11, manuscript report, Glenbow Library.

129 Bryan P. Melnyk, *Calgary Builds. The Emergence of an Urban Landscape 1905–1914* (Regina: Alberta Culture/Canadian Plains Research Centre, 1985), 50–51.

130 Charles Bruce, *News and the Southams* (Toronto: Macmillan, 1968), 116–123.

131 Harold M. Daly, "Sir James Lougheed," "Memoirs, autobiographical notes," M.G. 27, series 111F9, volume 2, p. 1, National Archives of Canada. For a reference to Harold Daly see John English, *The Decline of Politics: The Conservatives and the Party System, 1901–20* (Toronto: University of Toronto Press, 1977), 99.

132 James Gray, *R. B. Bennett: The Calgary Years* (Toronto: University of Toronto Press, 1991), 13.

133 Ibid., 31.

134 Ibid., 240.

135 Ibid., 138, 72.

136 Daly, "Sir James Lougheed."

137 See the advertisement for "Lougheed, Bennett, Allison and McLaws," in Lougheed, "Why Go to Canada."

138 Klassen, "Lawyers, Finance, and Economic Development," 305.

139 Bruce, *News and the Southams*, 123.

140 Joan Mattie, "Walker Theatre, Winnipeg," Historic Sites and Monuments Board of Canada Agenda Paper, reference number 1991-19A, p. 23, footnote 22.

Notes to Chapter 3

1 Tom Ward, *Cowtown: An Album of Early Calgary* (Calgary: McClelland and Stewart West, 1975), 456, 458.

2 James W. Davidson, "Canada's Finest Theatre," *The Albertan*, 6 February 1912.

3 Her presence is noted at the performance of Richard Crooks, the renowned New York Metropolitan Opera tenor, at the Grand, 9 October 1935; and at the recital of the Moscow Cathedral Choir at the Grand on 16 November 1935. See: "Huge Crowd Gathers to hear Crooks," *The Calgary Herald*, 10 October 1935; "Grand Crowded for Recital By Moscow Choir," *The Calgary Herald*, 18 November 1935. She died on 13 March 1936.

4 Belle's name appears in a number of college catalogues under the name of "Bella Hardisty" during some years and as 'Isabella Hardisty" during others. The entries are for the academic years, 1868/69 to 1875/76. Muriel MacLeod to M[arg] H. Exton, 6 March 1996, Lougheed House Collection.

5 On the college see Bert Den Boggende, "'The Vassar of the Dominions': The Wesleyan Female College and the Project of a Women's University," *Ontario History* 85, no. 2 (June 1993): 95–117, and Johanna M. Selles, *Methodists and Women's Education in Ontario, 1836–1925* (Montreal: McGill-Queen's University Press, 1996), 82–87; 104–11.

6 Jennifer Cook Bobrovitz and Trudy Cowan, "Reasoned Speculation: The Challenge of Knowing Isabella Clarke Hardisty Lougheed," (unpublished manuscript, 2003), p. 5, Lougheed House Collection

7 Elizabeth B. Price, "Alberta's Women Pioneers Will Form Organization," *The Calgary Herald*, 20 March 1922.

8 Wesleyan Ladies College, *Catalogue 1891/92*, quoted in Selles, *Methodists*, 105–6.

9 Belle's father, W. L. Hardisty mentions "Beaulieu and his sons" in a letter William McMurray of the Hudson's Bay Company, dated Fort Chipewyan, 12 January 1871; reprinted in Clifford Wilson, "Private Letters from the Fur Trade," *Papers Read before the Historical and Scientific Society of Manitoba* III, no. 5 (1950): 45. On the Beaulieu family see Chris Hanks, "Francis Beaulieu II: The origins of the Metis in the Far Northwest," *Selected Papers of Rupert's Land Colloquium 2000, May 24–28, 2000* (Winnipeg: The Centre for Rupert's Land Studies, 2000): 111–26.

10 Jennifer Bobrovitz, compiler, "James Alexander and Isabella Lougheed. A Chronological History," Lougheed House Conservation Society (19 August 2003): 1–5.

11 W. L. Hardisty to Miss Davis, dated Fort Simpson, 20 November 1869, Davis Family Correspondence, General no. 22, Hardisty Family file 1, P1110-1122 (1869–70), Provincial Archives of Manitoba.

12 Charles Camsell, *Son of the North* (Toronto: Ryerson Press, 1954), 9. See also the reminiscences of his sister, Louise Camsell Mills, "Seventy Years Ago in the North West Territories," circa 1950, 74.1/88, box 3, Provincial Archives of Alberta.

13 Belle Lougheed quoted in Elizabeth Bailey Price, "Alberta's Women Pioneers Will Form Organization," *The Calgary Herald*, 20 March 1922.

14 James Lockhart to Robert Kennicott, dated Fort Resolution, 21 November 1864; and James Lockhart to Robert Kennicott, dated Fort Resolution, 26 June 1865; quoted in Debra Lindsay, ed., *The Modern Beginnings of Subarctic Ornithology: Correspondence to the Smithsonian Institution, 1856–1868* (Winnipeg: The Manitoba Record Society, 1991), 170, 191. As the references are to Mrs. Hardisty of Fort Simpson, I assume they refer to Mary Hardisty, Belle's mother.

15 A fragment of one of Elizabeth Bailey Price's articles about Belle survives, but it is incomplete. The title of the article is: "Lady Lougheed's First Home Still Standing." The undated, unidentified newspaper article, the first page of which is in the Lougheed House Collection, states that the family had First Nation and Metis servants as staff at the "Big House" inside the fort. Elizabeth Bailey Price wrote it, as several of the lines are identical to those in her other two articles about Belle: see "Alberta's Women Pioneers Will Form Organization," *The Calgary Herald*, 20 March 1922, and "Canadian Women in the Public Eye. Lady Lougheed," *Saturday Night*, 16 September 1922.

16 Mills, "Seventy Years Ago," 1–2; W. J. Healey, *Women of Red River* (Winnipeg: Russell, Lang & Co., 1923), 169–71; Camsell, *Son of the North*, 3.

17 Belle Lougheed quoted in Price, "Alberta's Women Pioneers Will Form Organization."

18 Louise Camsell Mills quoted in Healey, *Women of Red River*, 170–171.

19 Eva Reid, "Eavesdrop with Eva," *The Albertan*, 22 August 1962; this article contains the detail that Norman and Mary were already engaged at the time of the Banff auto trip.

20 C. B. Fisher, "Banff or Bust!" *Golden West* (September 1977): 46–48. C. B. Fisher obtained the story from Mary Stringer Lougheed. For an earlier more abridged version see Eva Reid, "Eavesdrop with Eva," *The Albertan*, 22 August 1962.

21 Belle Lougheed to Eliza McDougall Hardisty, 24 November 1903, Hardisty Fonds, series 23-7, M5908/1779, Glenbow Archives.

22 "Political At Home," *The Calgary Herald*, 26 November 1898.

23 "Did Milner Buy Lands," *The Calgary Herald*, 3 October 1908. During his visit, Mrs. Annie Glen Broder had tea with him in his special railway car; they were life-long friends. See also "The late Viscount Milner: His Calgary Visit Recalled," *The Calgary Herald*, 14 May 1925.

24 "Earl Grey Guest of Calgary Today," *The Calgary News*, 30 September 1909. See also *The Albertan*, 2 October 1909, p. 7. My thanks to Jennifer Cook Bobrovitz for these references.

25 David Bly, "A Daughter of the West Who Made a Difference," *The Calgary Herald*, 30 December 2001.

26 Ibid.

27 "A 'Dansant'," *The Albertan*, 5 January 1914.

28 For an account estimating that about sixty friends of Dorothy and Edgar were present at the "dansant" see "Jolly Dansant is Given by Mrs. Lougheed," *Calgary News-Telegram*, 6 January 1914. See also "Calgary Society" *The Calgary Herald*, 5 January 1914.

29 Jean Leslie, "Southern Alberta's 'Bob Hope'," in Jean Leslie, *Glimpses of Calgary Past* (Calgary: Detselig, 1994), 98.

30 Marjorie Norris, *A Leaven of Ladies: A History of the Calgary Local Council of Women* (Calgary: Delselig, 1995), 27–29.

31 Helen English, Victorian Order of Nurses Program Coordinator, to Janet Wright, Lougheed House Conservation Society, n.d., Lougheed House Collection.

32 Shauna Wilton, "Manitoba Women Nurturing the Nation: The Manitoba IODE and Maternal Nationalism, 1913–1920," *Journal of Canadian Studies* 35, no. 2 (Summer 2000): 152.

33 Katie Pickles, *Female Imperialism and National Identity. Imperial Order Daughters of the Empire* (Manchester: Manchester University Press, 2002), 16

34 Norris, *A Leaven of Ladies*, 69.

35 Marriage Certificate for James A. Lougheed and Bella C. Hardisty, 16 September 1884, Methodist Church Mission, Morleyville, North West Territories, Marriage Register, McDougall Family Papers, M732, folder 13, Glenbow Archives. The other witness was H. B. Andrews.

36 *The Calgary Tribune*, 11 September 1889. My thanks to Jennifer Cook Bobrovitz for this reference.

37 "A Great Housewarming: The Elite of Calgary at Senator Lougheed's Friday Night," *The Calgary Tribune*, 17 February 1892. On the evening of Saturday, 9 April 2005 the first post-restoration event at Lougheed House was a gala housewarming ball, commemorating the one given by the Lougheeds 113 years earlier. Lougheed House opened to the public on Sunday, 1 May 2005, as a Public Heritage Centre, see: "Experience Lougheed House," *The Calgary Herald*, 1 May 2005.

38 Note written by Rev. J. C. Herdman, Knox Church, 2 February 1896; also George Hamilton to Captain Harrison, dated Calgary, 2 February 1896; Parlow Papers, Faculty of Music Library, University of Toronto (henceforth cited as Parlow Papers).

39 "Kathleen Parlow Related How She Became Violinist," *The Calgary Herald*, 12 April 1921.

40 These biographical details are taken from Maida Parlow French, *Kathleen Parlow. A Portrait* (Toronto: The Ryerson Press, 1967), 1–6.

41 Tully Potter, program notes for "The Recorded Violin: The History of the Violin on Record, Vol. 1," (n.d.), p. 6, Pavilion Records, Pearl BVA 1, Music Library, University of Calgary

42 Kathleen Parlow, "Student Days in Russia," *The Canadian Music Journal* 6, no. 1 (1961): 19.

43 Ibid., 150.

44 Belle served as one the honorary patrons of the Calgary Symphony Orchestra in the 1930s until her death in 1936. Her name is listed at the outset of each of the published programs.

45 French, *Kathleen Parlow*, 21.

46 Photos indicate Belle was quite short; in contrast, Jean Pinkham was quite tall; see Doris Anderson, "Encounter: Jean Drever Pinkham," *The Beaver* (August-September 2004): 53. Belle briefly appears in a film made around 1930 by Dr. Burwell J. Charles. A video copy is held by the Glenbow Archives, F168, VHS#31. The video is entitled "Old Timers of Southern Alberta."

47 Mrs. W.C. Pinkham, "Selections from the Unpublished Recollections of Mrs. W.C. Pinkham, an Early Manitoban," part 2, *Manitoba Pageant* 19, no. 3 (Spring 1974): 20.

48 Mrs. W.C. Pinkham, "Selections from the Unpublished Recollections of Mrs. W.C. Pinkham, an Early Manitoban," part 3, conclusion, *Manitoba Pageant* 20, no. 1 (Autumn 1974): 11.

49 Mary Dover (great-niece of Margaret Drever Mackay), interview with the author, 18 March 1993.

50 Cyprian Pinkham, "Autobiography," p. 30, Pinkham Papers, M 978, folder 1, Glenbow Archives.

51 "Cree Bible Completed," *Prince Albert Times*, 21 October 1908, p. 4.

52 George F.G. Stanley, "The Naming of Calgary," *Alberta History* 23, no. 3 (1975): 7–10.

53 Nancy Walton, telephone interview with author, 12 April 2001; Jean's granddaughter described her as "very dominating."

54 Pinkham, "Selections," *Manitoba Pageant* 20, no. 1 (Autumn 1974): 13.

55 Ibid.

56 Molly, "The Women's Hospital Aid", *Calgary News-Telegram*, 20 July 1914.

57 Jean A. Pinkham to Kathleen Parlow, dated Calgary, 20 February 1911, Parlow Papers. Also printed in Cordelia, "'Thro' Milady's Lorgnette," *Calgary News-Telegram*, 22 February 1911.

58 Program, *Philharmonic Society of New York, 19 March 1911,* Parlow Papers.

59 Geoffrey Ridout, "Kathleen Parlow," *Encyclopedia of Music in Canada*, 2nd ed., eds. Helmut Kallmann and Gilles Potvin (Toronto: University of Toronto Press, 1992), 1019.

60 *New York Herald* quoted in French, *Kathleen Parlow*, 40–41.

61 The Parlows stayed at the Lougheed's between 18 and 20 February 1911; see Kathleen Parlow, Diary for 1911, Parlow Papers. The Senator spoke in the Senate on 15 and 23 February 1911, which confirms his absence in Ottawa at the time; see Senate, *Debates,* 210–11, 278–82. My thanks to David Hall for these references.

62 Kathleen Parlow, Diary for 1911, entry for Sunday, 19 February 1911, Parlow Papers.

63 Cordelia, "Thro' Milady's Lorgnette."

64 French, *Kathleen Parlow*, 2–3.

65 Geographical Board of Canada, *Place-Names of Alberta* (Ottawa: King's Printer, 1928), 23.

66 Dempsey, *Calgary: Spirit of the West* (Calgary: Fifth House, 1994), 4.

67 Hugh Dempsey, "The Place of Indians in Western Canadian History" (n.p.: 1968, mimeographed), 12.

68 Maureen K. Lux, *Medicine That Walks: Disease, Medicine, and Canadian Plains Native People, 1880–1940* (Toronto: University of Toronto Press, 2001), 7.

69 Constance Backhouse, *Colour-Coded: A Legal History of Racism in Canada, 1900–1950* (Toronto: University of Toronto Press, 1999), 6.

70 Howard Palmer, *Patterns of Prejudice. A History of Nativism in Alberta* (Toronto: McClelland and Stewart, 1982). This book remains the classic study of ethnic prejudice in Alberta.

71 Pickles, *Female Imperialism*, 38.

72 Speech by R. B. Bennett given in Toronto, 24 May 1914; quoted in Carl Berger, *The Sense of Power: Studies in the Ideas of Canadian Imperialism, 1867–1914* (Toronto: University of Toronto Press, 1970), 230–231.

73 "Negroes Not Wanted In Province of Alberta: Calgary Board of Trade Endorses the Edmonton Resolution to Exclude Negro," *The Albertan*, 20 May 1911.

74 "Keep the Negroes Out," *The Albertan*, 6 April 1911, cited in David Bright, *The Limits of Labour: Class Formation and the Labour Movement in Calgary, 1883–1929* (Vancouver: University of Calgary Press, 1998), 44.

75 "The King George Hotel," *Calgary, Sunny Alberta: The Industrial Prodigy of the Great West* (Calgary: Jennings Publishing Company, 1911), 182.

76 "Louie Kheong Returns to His Ancestors. Calgary Chinese Mourn Old Friend with Ancient Rites," *The Calgary Herald*, 27 April 1939.

77 Luey Kheong, letter to the editor, *The Calgary Herald*, 6 October 1910; cited in Brian Dawson, *Moon Cakes in Gold Mountain: From China to the Canadian Plains* (Calgary: Detselig Enterprises, 1991), 51.

78 B. O. K. Reeves, "'Kootisisaw': Calgary Before the Canadians," in *Frontier Calgary: Town, City, and Region 1875–1914*, eds. A. W. Rasporich and Henry Klassen (Calgary: McClelland and Stewart West, 1975), 20.

79 For a brief introduction to the First Nations in southern Alberta see Hugh Dempsey, *Indian Tribes of Alberta* (Calgary: Glenbow Museum, 1997).

80 Dudley McClean, "Ancient and Tribal Customs Are Still Clung to by Fast Declining Race in Sun Dance," *The Calgary Herald*, 25 August 1923.

81 "J. Keir Hardie, "A Scamper Round the World—In Canada," *The Voice* (Winnipeg), 29 November 1907, p. 1, col. 1–2.

82 "Steeles' Scouts: Presentation of Medals by Madame Rouleau," *The Calgary Herald*, 4 September 1886.

83 Dempsey, *Calgary: Spirit of the West*, 58. See also p. 157, n. 7. Hugh Dempsey has successfully identified her last name.

84 "Horrible Murder," *The Calgary Tribune*, 6 March 1889.

85 *Calgary Eye Opener*, 23 October 1920. My thanks to Hugh Dempsey for this reference. "Cappy" Smart, a long-time Calgary resident, recalled the brutal murder in his column, "I Remember Calgary When—," *The Calgary Herald*, 6 and 13 May 1933. Actually Fisk's sentence was for only seven years, not fourteen; see Donald Smith, "Bloody Murder Almost Became Miscarriage of Justice," *The Calgary Herald Sunday Magazine*, 23 July 1989, 12–15.

86 *The Calgary Tribune*, 17 April 1889.

87 See the following scrip files in R.G. 15, Department of the Interior, series D-11-8-c, National Archives of Canada for: Mary Louise Hardisty Hackland, vol. 1350, reel C-14972; Frank Allen Hardisty, vol. 1350, reel C-14975; William Lucas Hardisty, vol. 1350, reel C-14975; Mary Allen Hardisty Thomas, vol. 1369, reel C-15006; Mary Allen Hardisty Thomas, vol. 1369, reel C-15006. My thanks to Pat Cleary for these references.

88 Edmund Taylor to William Pearce, 6 November 1923, William Pearce Papers, 74–169/442, University of Alberta Archives.

89 Edmund Taylor, "Western Canada in the Making," written for the Calgary Historical Society by Edmund Taylor, January 1924, George B. Coutts Papers, M279, file 41, Glenbow Archives.

90 "Edmund Taylor Dies Suddenly Following Brief Indisposition," *The Calgary Herald*, 3 October 1929. The phrase "Hudson Bay families" appears in the article. Henry Klassen provides background on Taylor's business career in his *Eye on the Future. Business People in Calgary and the Bow Valley, 1870–1900* (Calgary: University of Calgary Press, 2002), 285–87.

91 James H. Gray, *R. B. Bennett: The Calgary Years* (Toronto: University of Toronto Press, 1991), 138.

92 Elizabeth B. Mitchell, *In Western Canada before the War* (1915; reprinted, Saskatoon: Western Producer Prairie Books, 1981), 34.

93 Mrs. Louise E. Ramsay Purchase, "A Sketch of Janet (Nettie) T. Coatsworth Ramsay. Mistress of English Literature, 1875–1879. Hamilton Ladies' College," archives file, "Wesleyan Ladies College," Hamilton Public Library. My thanks to Jennifer Cook Bobrovitz for a copy of this memoir by Nettie Coatsworth's oldest daughter, written at Albright Gardens, Beamsville, Ontario, May 1962. By a strange coincidence Nettie Coatsworth was a sister of James Lougheed's closest boyhood friend, Emerson Coatsworth.

94 Chief Buffalo Child Long Lance, "Indians of the Northwest and West Canada," *The Mentor* 12, no. 3 (March 1924): 6.

95 Quoted in Backhouse, *Colour-Coded*, 3–4; 283–84.

96 Census of Canada, 1901, Alberta, District of Central Alberta, microfilm reel: T-6550, p. 13.

97 Backhouse, *Colour-Coded*, 283–84.

98 Henry Youle Hind, *Narrative of the Canadian Red River Exploring Expedition of 1857 and of the Assiniboine and Saskatchewan Exploring Expedition of 1858* (Edmonton: Hurtig, 1971), 178–79.

99 As previously mentioned it was so commonplace that writer Chief Buffalo Child Long Lance, who had lived in Calgary from 1919 to 1922, included this line in his article, "Indians of the Northwest and West Canada": "Some of western Canada's best citizens are of Scotch and Indian descent. Lady Lougheed, wife of Sir James Lougheed, minister of the interior, is a half-breed."

100 In an interview with Calgary journalist Elizabeth Bailey Price, Belle apparently made this remark to distinguish herself from the Metis: "In Calgary's early days it was almost impossible to get help. The squaws and half breed women were all that were available. They could wash but could not iron, and they were never dependable." See *Saturday Night*, 16 September 1922. This quotation appears in the longer version of the article, which is printed unsigned, but is clearly written by Elizabeth Bailey Price; the typed copy of the story appears in her papers, Manuscripts and Clippings, 1920s-1950s, biographies, L–Z, Alberta, M1000, Glenbow Archives. The shorter version,

which contains many of the identical sentences used in the *Saturday Night* article, appeared in Elizabeth B. Price, "Alberta's Women Pioneers Will Form Organizations," *The Calgary Herald*, 20 March 1922. A fragment of an article, "Lady Lougheed's First Home Still Standing," undated and unidentified, also survives in the Lougheed House Collection.

101 Elizabeth Bailey Price, "Preserving the Red River Jig for posterity," *Toronto Star Weekly*, 7 April 1928.

102 Norman became involved with the Western Canada College Old Boys' Association; see *The Albertan*, 21 December 1911. Edgar went to McGill University after Western Canada College in 1911.

103 Archibald Oswald MacRae, *History of the Province of Alberta* (n.p.: The Western Canada History Company, 1912), 430.

104 "Alberta Women We Should Know: Lady Lougheed," *The Calgary Herald*, 17 December 1932.

105 Biographical treatments of her life include: Linda Popp Di Biase, "The Alberta Years of Winnifred Eaton," *Alberta History* 39, no. 2 (Spring 1991): 1–8, and a full biography by her grand-daughter Diana Birchall, *Onoto Watanna. The Story of Winnifred Eaton* (Urbana: University of Illinois Press, 2001).

106 Marmie Hess, long-time Calgarian, telephone conversation with the author, 10 November 2004. My thanks to her for this wonderful description.

107 Many of Winnifred Eaton's works are available on the World Wide Web; see the Winnifred Eaton Digital Archives, edited and compiled by Jean Lee Cole, hosted and maintained by the University of Virginia Library, <http:etext.lib.virginia.edu/users/cole/>

108 The inscribed copy is in the Margaret P. Hess Collection, Special Collections, University of Calgary Library. Winnifred Eaton in her inscription used the short form, "Decr," for December." My thanks to George Melnyk for telling me about this inscription copy.

109 "Royal Visitors Will Occupy Lougheed Home While Here," *Calgary News-Telegram*, 31 August 1912; "Ducal Party Cancelled Early Arrangements and Spent Quiet Evening at Lougheed Home," *Calgary News-Telegram*, 5 September 1912.

110 W. A. Griesbach, *I Remember* (Toronto: Ryerson Press, 1946), 130.

111 H. F. Gatesby, "The Borden Cabinet—X: The Government Leader in the Senate," *The Canadian Liberal Monthly* (July 1914): 123.

112 *The Eye Opener*, 16 June 1906, p. 1, col. 1.

113 Griesbach, *I Remember*, 129–30.

114 Pamela Clark, Registrar, the Royal Archives, letter to the author, 28 October 2003. My thanks to Miss Clark for the quotation from the Duchess of Connaught's diary, entry for 5 to 7 September 1912.

115 Apparently they had moved in by mid-September; see A. M. Terrill's ad by the article, "The Lougheed Building; Calgary's Finest and Most Up-to-Date," *The Calgary Herald*, 14 September 1912. It reads: "In our new and up-to-date store, with all modern conveniences, we are in a position to offer all seasonable cut flowers and house plants…"

116 "Royal Visitors Will Occupy Lougheed Home While Here," *Calgary News-Telegram*, 31 August 1912.

117 George Aston, *His Royal Highness the Duke of Connaught and Strathearn* (London: George G. Harrap, 1929), 91.

118 "Calgarians Present at first Ottawa State Ball of Season," *The Albertan*, 5 December 1912. See also, "A Daughter of the West", *The Western Standard*, 12 June 1913. The Duchess of Connaught presented the gift to Belle at Calgary.

119 "Society," *The Albertan*, 1 September 1911; "Calgary Society," *The Calgary Herald*, 9 January 1913; "In the Social World," *Calgary News-Telegram*, 8 September 1914; "In the Social World," *Calgary News-Telegram*, 14 December 1914.

120 John Cowan, *Canada's Governors-General, 1867–1952* (Toronto: York Publishing Co., 1952), 91; Robert M. Stamp, *Royal Rebels. Princess Louise and the Marquis of Lorne* (Toronto: Dundurn Press, 1988), 206. Interestingly, the Duke of Connaught, who was the godson of the famous Duke of Wellington, became in turn the godfather of Queen Elizabeth II.

Notes to Chapter 4

1 Liesbeth Leatherbarrow summarizes the challenges in her article, "Calgary Horticultural Society" *Alberta History* 46, no. 3 (Summer 1998): 21.

2 Information on the Terrills appears in: Archibald Oswald MacRae, *History of the Province of Alberta* (n.p.: The Western Canada History Co., 1912), 624–25; "John E. Terrill," in John Blue, *Alberta Past and Present. Historical and Biographical*, vol. 3 (Chicago: Pioneer Historical Publishing Co., 1924), 436–37.

3 Leishman McNeill, *Tales of the Old Town* (Calgary: The Calgary Herald, 1960), 16.

4 Allan Connery, comp., *As Reported in the Herald* (Calgary: The Calgary Herald, 1982), 80. Excerpt cited from *The Calgary Herald*, 10 July 1923.

5 Editorial, "Keep Up Stray Stock," *The Calgary Herald*, 15 August 1904.

6 Hugh A. Dempsey, *Calgary: Spirit of the West* (Calgary: Fifth House, 1994), 70.

7 "Veteran Calgary Barrister, J. P. J. Jephson, is Dead," *The Calgary Herald*, 15 June 1923.

8 David Mittelstadt, "A Social History of Cliff Bungalow-Mission" (manuscript report, 1997), Glenbow Library. See entry under "The Jephsons."

9 In the newspaper references various spellings of her first name are given: Christina, Christine and Christian. Christin is the spelling given in Sherrill MacLaren, *Braehead: Three Founding Families in Nineteenth Century Canada* (Toronto: McClelland and Stewart, 1986). 91, 131-132, 204, 208-209, 219. Here I follow the spelling, "Christian", suggested by her great-granddaugher, Jane Vincent, email, sent 18 December 2004.

10 Linda Curtis, "The Real Story of Calgary's Early Colourful History Lies Buried Beneath the Eaves of its Oldest Houses," *The Calgary Herald* [l953], exact date unknown; clipping in the Jean Drever Pinkham file, Glenbow Library.

11 The Ranchmen's Club, *A Short History of the Ranchmen's Club: A Light-hearted Account* (Calgary: The Ranchmen's Club, 1975), 2.

12 "Veteran Calgary Barrister, J. P.J. Jephson, is Dead," *The Calgary Herald*, 15 June 1923.

13 Ibid.

14 Editorial, "The Late Mr. Jephson," *The Calgary Herald*, 16 June 1923.

15 MacRae, "Alfred Marmaduke Terrill," *History of the Province of Alberta,* 625.

16 The quotation appears in James H. Gray, *Red Lights on the Prairies* (Scarborough: New American Library, 1973), 150.

17 The following description of Calgary at the turn of the century is based on the one found in Donald Smith and Henry Klassen, "Onward! Calgary in the 1890s," in Donald Smith, ed. *Centennial City. Calgary, 1894–1994* (Calgary: The University of Calgary, 1994), 1–14.

18 MacRae, "Alfred Marmaduke Terrill," *History of the Province of Alberta*, 624.

19 For a review of sandstone buildings in Calgary see Richard Cunniffe, *Calgary—In Sandstone* (Calgary: Historical Society of Alberta, 1969).

20 For an analysis of the challenges of tree-planting and general horti-culture in Calgary see Sue Anne Donaldson, "William Pearce: His Vision of Trees," *Journal of Garden History* 3, no. 2 (1983): 238.

21 For details on Samuel Barber consult Henry C. Klassen, *Eye on the Future: Business People in Calgary and the Bow Valley, 1870–1900* (Calgary: University of Calgary Press, 2002), 135–36.

22 "P. W. King, Once Sheriff of Calgary, is Dead: Came to Calgary in 1886 and was first Sheriff of this District," *The Albertan*, 28 August 1920; "Ex-Sheriff King Leaves $257,382 to Alberta Poor," *Alberta Farmer*, 17 March 1921, Peter Willoughy King clipping file, Glenbow Library.

23 "Sheriff King Home given $300,000 boost," *The Calgary Herald*, 15 May 2004.

24 South Alberta Land Registration District Office, Calgary.

25 McNeill, *Tales of the Old Town*, 23.

26 See the column, "Up-to-date Florist," *The Calgary Herald*, 5 October 1912.

27 "Royal Visitors will Occupy Lougheed Home While Here," *Calgary News-Telegram*, 31 August 1912.

28 "Florist Business Grew with Calgary," undated typed manuscript, Terrill Florists Fonds, M1500, Glenbow Archives.

29 Ibid.

30 Heber C. Jamieson, *Early Medicine in Alberta. The First Seventy-Five Years* (Edmonton: Canadian Medical Association Alberta Division, 1947), 50.

31 See photo with "Birthplace of Kathleen Parlow in Calgary," *The Albertan*, 9 April 1921.

32 McNeill, *Tales of the Old Town*, 32.

33 Advertisement for "A Grand Amateur Dramatic and Musical Entertainment will be given in the Opera House, Calgary, on Thursday, March 17," *Calgary Weekly Herald*, 9 March 1892.

34 "Then and Now: Hull's Opera House," *The Calgary Herald*, 5 February 2003.

35 [Ruth Gorman], "People of the West. Mrs. R. A. Brown, Sr.," *My Golden West* 2 (Spring 1967): 22, 33. I have supplemented this de-scription of the 6th Avenue and Centre Street neighbourhood with information from the City of Calgary directories; see those for 1906 and 1908–1912.

36 Shelagh Nolan, "A Young Girl in the Old West," *The Beaver* 66, no. 4 (August-September 1986): 56

37 P. M. Plunckett [Evelyn Sparrow], "A History of the Sparrow Family," p. 9, Sparrow Papers, 72.288, Provincial Archives of Alberta.

38 Grant MacEwan, *Fifty Mighty Men* (1958; reprint, Saskatoon: Modern Press, 1967), 67.

39 My thanks to James Martin for this information; he located Bob Edwards's birth registration from the General Register Office, Edinburgh, Scotland. He was born in the St. Andrew District, Edinburgh, on 17 September 1860; and not in 1864 as stated in his obituary, "Has Crossed the Great Divide," *Calgary Eye Opener,* 25 November 1922.

40 Louis A. Knafla, "Patrick James Nolan," *Dictionary of Canadian Biography* , vol. 14, *1911-1920* (Toronto: University of Toronto Press, 1998), 782; Grant MacEwan, *He Left Them Laughing When He Said Good-bye: The Life and Times of Frontier Lawyer Paddy Nolan* (Saskatoon: Western Producer, 1987), 166; Donald B. Smith, "Alberta's Foremost Storyteller," *Alberta History* 49, no. 1 (Autumn 2001): 20.

41 Grant MacEwan, "The Town-Country Background at Calgary," in *Frontier Calgary. Town, City, and Region 1875–1914* (Calgary: McClelland and Stewart West, 1975), 5.

42 Grant MacEwan, *Calgary Cavalcade: From Fort to Fortune* (Saskatoon: Western Producer Book Service, 1975), 93. The street address was 612 6th Av. S.W. The home was demolished in 1962. Information from the "Home Sweet Heritage Home. Bigraphies of Famous Calgarians and Their Homes", website, Calgary Public Library, 2000. Web address: <http://collections.ic.gc.ca/calgary/res31.htm>

43 The first quotation is one from James Lougheed; the second is the reporter's summary of his remarks; see "Fulham vs. Jacques," *The Calgary Tribune*, 2 December 1891.

44 *The Calgary Herald*, 12 October 1901; quoted in Grant MacEwan, "Caroline 'Mother' Fulham: The Lady Kept Pigs," in *... And Mighty Women Too* (Saskatoon: Western Producer Prairie Books, 1975), 125.

45 MacEwan, *He Left Them Laughing*, 50.

46 Robert E. Gard, *Johnny Chinook* (Toronto: Longmans, Green & Company, 1945), 153.

47 The election would have been in either 1899 or 1902; see David Hall, "Arthur L. Sifton, 1910-1917," in *Alberta Premiers of the Twentieth Century*, ed. Bradford J. Rennie (Regina: Canadian Plains Research Center, 2004): 22-23.

48 Senator James Lougheed quoted in Emil Longue Beau, "Sir James Lougheed," *Toronto Star Weekly*, 30 July 1921, p. 10.

49 Knafla, "Patrick James Nolan," 783; see also MacEwan, *He Left Them Laughing*, 66.

50 See, for example, Nolan, "A Young Girl in the Old West," 55.

51 *Calgary Eye Opener*, 8 March 1913, cited in Grant MacEwan, *Eye Opener Bob* (Edmonton: The Institute of Applied Art, 1957), 138. Bob Edwards wrote in his friend's obituary, "Brilliant though Paddy undoubtedly was in the court room, his brilliance shone with its most dazzling effect when he was completely ensconced in an armchair at home or at the club, surrounded by a group of congenial spirits."

52 MacEwan, *Eye Opener Bob*, 165–66.

53 Jacqueline Mary Durrie, "Come to the Cabaret; Adaptive Re-use of the Lougheed Building" (master's degree project, University of Calgary, 2003), 35–38.

54 Max Foran, "Land Speculation and Urban Development: Calgary, 1884-1912," in *Frontier Calgary. Town, City, and Region. 1875-1914*, eds. Anthony W. Rasporich and Henry C. Klassen (Calgary: McClelland and Stewart West, 1975), 215.

55 McNeill, *Tales of the Old Town*, 23.

56 "Passing of Last Central Garden: A. M. Terrill Sells First Street and Sixth Avenue Lots For $100,000," *The Calgary Herald*, 11 March 1911.

57 South Alberta Land Registration District Office, Calgary.

58 "Hudson's Bay Company Paid $250,000 for Site for Store," *The Albertan*, 16 March 1911.

59 Henry C. Klassen, "Lawyers, Finance, and Economic Development in Southwestern Alberta, 1884 to 1920," in *Essays in the History of Canadian Law: Beyond the Law: Lawyers and Business in Canada, 1830 to 1930*, ed. Carol Wilton (Toronto: The Osgoode Society, 1990): 305.

60 "Plans Completed for Sen. Lougheed's Hotel and Theatre," *Calgary News-Telegram*, 23 May 1911. "Contract Let Today by Senator Lougheed for Office Building," *The Calgary Herald*, 3 August 1911.

61 Max Foran, "The Civic Corporation and Urban Growth: Calgary, 1884–1930" (Ph.D. diss., University of Calgary, 1981), p. 145, n. 1; Earl A. Levin, "City History and City Planning. The Local Historical Roots of the City Planning Function in Three Cities of the Canadian Prairies" (Ph.D. diss., University of Manitoba, 1993), 611.

62 City of Calgary Papers, vol. 8. City of Calgary Archives.

63 Assessment Cards, vol. 11, City of Calgary Archives.

64 Ibid.

65 My thanks to David Hall, University of Alberta Department of History, for this insight.

66 The lengthy article, "Sherman Theatre," *The Albertan*, 28 October 1911, does not have a caption. It is a fabulous source of information on the Grand in its final construction phase. The article contains the vital information that "the Lyric Theatre will be devoted to vaudeville operation on the Sullivan and Considine circuit who control the chain of theatres known as the Empress theatres." Bill Sherman was the manager of the Lyric at this time. He must have linked the senator to the Sullivan and Considine people, who told him about their new theatre, then under construction, in Salt Lake City.

67 Anthony Slide, "John W. Considine," *The Encyclopedia of Vaudeville* (Westport, Connecticut: Greenwood Press, 1994), 112.

68 "Society on Hand at Empress," *Salt Lake Telegram*, 4 November 1911. My thanks to Matt McLain for this reference.

69 Lanier R. Wardrop was very hard to trace. In the article, "Canada's Finest Theatre," *The Albertan*, 6 February 1912, James W. Davidson mentioned, "In order that the building should follow the latest and best lines of theatre construction, Mr. L. R. Wardrop, a well known theatrical architect, was engaged and personally superintended the entire construction." The Register for the Alberta Society of Architects, Canadian Architectural Archives, University of Calgary Library, contains his name, dated 1 April 1912, on page 265. The *Calgary Henderson's Directory*, 1912, lists "Robert Lanier Wardrop,

architect at 15, 122 8th Avenue W., with his residence at 1504 22nd Avenue W (p. 760). The senator gave him an office in the Clarence Block (122 8th Avenue where Lougheed Bennett had their office, right beside the Lyric at 126 8th Avenue W.). For information on the Lyric see Jeffrey Goffin. "Lyric Theatre", in Eugene Benson and L.W. Connolly, eds., *The Oxford Companion to Canadian Theatre* (Toronto: Oxford University Press, 1989), 316. The floor plans for the office building and theatre. which are reproduced in "New Buildings, Calgary, Alta.," *Construction* 6 (October 1913): 376, list the architect as "R. Wardrop." But from where did he originate? Jacky Durrie put me on the trail to solving the puzzle as to the identity of "Lanier R. Wardrop." In late 2002 she found in a web search using <http://www.ancestry.com> the name of a "Lanier Rumel Wardrop", born 10 September 1883, at Salt Lake City, Utah, and died 14 April 1954. In particular I thank Matt McLain, Periodicals Department, the Salt Lake City Public Library System, for sending me two obituaries of him: *The Deseret News*, 15 April 1954, p. C-6, and "Retired Lumber Manager Dies on Vacation Trip," *Salt Lake City Tribune*, 16 April 1954. The obituary in the *Tribune* states that he designed with his partner D. C. Dart, "such landmarks as the Judge Building, Covey Apartments, Uptown Theatre and the Keyser warehouse." I did not follow this any further until one of the two academic reviewers of the first draft of my manuscript discovered the same reference and urged me to pursue it. I did on 11 November 2004, beginning my search with queries about the Uptown Theatre in Salt Lake City. Quickly I learned that the *Henderson's Calgary Directory* had incorrectly transcribed Lanier Rumel Wardrop's middle name as "Robert" and not "Rumel." Grant Smith, website, "Cinema Treasures—The Uptown Theatre," <http://www.cinema-treasures.org/theatre/1471>, relates that the Uptown was originally called the Empress when it opened in 1911 at 53 South Main Street in Salt Lake City. It was torn down in 1971 to make way for the ZCMI Centre. My debt to Matt McLain is considerable, as he also sent me the article from the *Salt Lake Telegram* on the opening of the Empress, "Society on Hand at Empress: Salt Lake's Newest Playhouse Presents Bright Scene at Opening," 4 November 1911. This article contains the information that with the opening of the Empress, Sullivan and Considine Vaudeville had arrived in Salt Lake City. For pictures of the theatres see the Utah State Historical Society website, <http://history.utah.gov/Photos/C275/indexform.html>. Type "Empress" in the "search for a term in any field" box. Twenty-five photos will appear. The interior shots show a very close similarity with the Grand. This physical similarity as well as the Sullivan and Considine Vaudeville connection between the Empress and Calgary's Lyric, confirm that Lanier Rumel Wardrop was the architect for both the Grand Theatre and the Lougheed Building. One final surprise entered into the "search for Wardrop." Academic review is a strictly confidential process. Except with the reviewer's permission, his or her identity is never revealed. In this case, I was so curious to learn the identity of the second reviewer who urged me to pursue the identity of Lanier Rumel Wardrop of Salt Lake City, I asked the University of Calgary Press to contact the individual. The reviewer gave the Press permission to reveal his identity to me. My joy was a thousand fold to learn that the reviewer was Calgary historian Harry Sanders, a former student of mine nearly fifteen years ago. Full circle—the student has become the teacher.

70 "Contract Let Today by Senator Lougheed for Office Building," *The Calgary Herald*, 3 August 1911.

71 This detail is contained in the Memorandum of Agreement, 1 August 1941, between the Royal Trust Company and National Theatres Limited, Land Titles, Grand Theatre 8761 FA, Alberta Registries.

72 Durrie. "Come to the Cabaret," 38, 45.

73 My thanks to Robert Seiler of the University of Calgary's Faculty of Communications and Culture for his help with this description of the exterior of the office building. The floor plans included in the article, "New Buildings, Calgary, Alta.," *Construction* 6 (October 1913): 376, are invaluable.

74 "Forbes Robertson to Open Calgary's Fine new Theatre Feb. 5," *The Calgary Herald*, 22 January 1912.

75 For details on all aspects of the Lougheed Building see Gerald Forseth, David Mittelstadt and Colin Campbell, "Historical Resource Impact Assessment of the Lougheed Building, Calgary for Prairie Fund Management August 1998," Glenbow Library.

76 Durrie, "Come to the Cabaret," 48.

77 "The Lougheed Building; Calgary's Finest and Most Up-to-date," *The Calgary Herald*, 14 September 1912, p. 12. On the same page an advertisement appears announcing that Lougheed and Taylor are handling the rental arrangements.

78 If you examine the photo of the Lougheed Building appearing with the article, "New Buildings, Calgary, Alta.," *Construction*, 6 (October 1913): 377, you will see "P.J. Nolan Law Offices" on two windows on the third floor on the First Street West side of the building. The city directories for 1912 and 1913 do not list him in the Lougheed Building; he died too soon to be included. Alfred Terrill's shop, the directories indicate, remained next to the Grand Theatre until 1922. He retired that year, as mentioned in "Terrill's ... The Florist Business that Grew with Calgary," *Calgary 1875–1950*, ed. Elsie C. Morrison and P. N. R. Morrison (Calgary: Calgary Publishing Company, 1950), 88.

79 "Professional Directory: Solicitors," *The Calgary Herald*, 6 September 1912 and 12 October 1912.

80 "Calgarians Pay Last Respects to late P. J. Nolan," *Calgary News-Telegram*, 13 February 1913.

Notes to Chapter 5

1 Honoré J. Jaxon to his wife (Aimée), his mother and brother, Eastwood, dated Calgary, 20 March 1909, Jaxon Papers in posses-sion of Lorne Grant, great-nephew of Honoré Jaxon. In the letter he mentions: "Letter (registered) or telegram should be addressed to Honoré J. Jaxon, care of Mrs J. H. Kerr, 130 Sixth Ave West, Calgary, Alberta." Mrs. J. H. Kerr is identified as "Mrs. J. H. Kerr, widow" in *Henderson's Calgary Directory,* 1908, 225.

2 *Henderson's Calgary Directory,* 1908, 225–26.

3 "Socialist Meeting: Party held a Business Meeting on Sunday Night," *The Calgary Herald*, 29 March 1909. My thanks to David Bright for this reference.

4 "Coxey's Indian Ally," *The Woman's Tribune* (Washington, D.C.), 12 May 1894.

5 "Who's Who—And Why: Serious and Frivolous Facts about the Great and the Near Great," *The Saturday Evening Post*, 1 June 1907.

6 William H. Jackson to "My Dear Family," 19 September 1885, MG 3 C20, Archives of Manitoba.

7 "Socialist Meeting," *The Calgary Herald;* "Socialists Discuss Religion in Schools," *The Albertan*, 21 June 1909, p. 1.

8 *Fair Play and Free Play*, 29 October 1908, Jaxon Papers. This was actually a newspaper, only one issue of which survives.

9 William Pearce, "Memorandum: Department of the Interior," in "Documents of Western History. Louis Riel's Petition of Rights, 1884," *Saskatchewan History* 23, no. 1 (Winter 1970): 24.

10 Belle told her grandson Don Lougheed about his great-uncle, who was killed at Batoche. As he added: "She would be terribly upset with all this talk of Riel today." Don Lougheed quoted in David Bly, "A daughter of the West who made a difference," *The Calgary Herald*, 30 December 2001, A11.

11 Ethel (Mrs. W. M.) Davidson, "About the Author," in William McCartney Davidson, *Louis Riel 1844–1885* (Calgary: The Albertan Publishing Company Ltd., 1955).

12 "J. M. Davison, Editor and Manager of the Albertan, Calgary," *The Voice* (Winnipeg), 14 July 1905.

13 Honoré used the letterhead for his letters to his family near Prince Albert, dated 11, 23 and 29 June 1909, Jaxon Papers.

14 "Honore Jaxon out for Persians," *The Albertan*, 16 February 1912.

15 Cyril Alwin Tregillus, "Reminiscences," p. 35, typed copy of the original manuscript in the possession of Richard Tregillus, Pincher Creek, Alberta. A copy has been deposited in the Glenbow Library.

16 David Bright, *The Limits of Labour: Class Formation and the Labour Movement in Calgary, 1883–1929* (Vancouver: University of British Columbia Press, 1998), 38.

17 Joe Cherwinski, *Early Working-Class Life on the Prairies,* Canada's Visual History Series, vol. 69 (Ottawa: National Museum of Man, n.d.), 5.

18 Max Foran, *Calgary. An Illustrated History* (Toronto: James Lorimer, 1978), 116.

19 *The Albertan*, 4 March 1902, quoted in Bright, *Limits of Labour*, 72.

20 S. J. Ferns and H. S. Ferns, *Eighty-five Years in Canada* (Winnipeg: Queenston House, 1978), 70.

21 Arthur Stringer, "Mr. Optimist of Calgary," *Canada West* 6, no. 1 (May 1909): 6.

22 Colin K. Hatcher, *Stampede City Streetcars: The Story of the Calgary Municipal Railway* (Montreal; Railfare Enterprises, 1975), 11, 17.

23 Archibald Oswald MacRae, "John W. Mitchell," *History of the Province of Alberta* (n.p.: The Western Canada Co., 1912), 328.

24 The constitution then in force was that of the Grand Lodge in Manitoba, from which the quote is taken; see: Patricia Jasen, "The Oddfellows in Early Calgary," *Alberta History* 35, no. 3 (Summer 1987): 9.

25 Jasen, "The Oddfellows," 10.

26 MacRae, "Alfred Marmaduke Terrill," *History of the Province of Alberta*, 625.

27 MacRae, "Thomas John Searle Skinner," *History of the Province of Alberta*, 515.

28 "D. E. Black," *Calgary, Sunny Alberta: Merchants and Manufacturers Record* (Calgary: Jennings Publishing Company, 1911), 160.

29 Bright, *Limits of Labour*, 58.

30 Jennifer Bobrovitz, "A History of Service to the Community," *The Calgary Herald*, 23 January 2000.

31 MacRae, "Richard Addison Brocklebank," *History of the Province of Alberta*, 866.

32 Bright, *Limits of Labour*, 71–72.

33 Foran, *Calgary*, 105.

34 Bright, *Limits of Labour*, 41.

35 Calgary Trades and Labour Council cited in Bright, *Limits of Labour*, 45.

36 Ibid., 44–45.

37 "Fifty Carpenters on New Theatre Strike," *The Calgary Herald*, 17 November 1911. My thanks to Norma Marr for this reference.

38 "Real Estate," *Calgary News-Telegram*, 3 May 1911. This mentions that work on the theatre has been underway "for the past two weeks."

39 Senate, *Debates*, 3 May 1897, 250–51. My thanks to David Hall, University of Alberta Department of History, for this reference.

40 Senate, *Debates*, 29 April; 17 and 22 July 1903, 143–44, 644–45. My thanks again to David Hall.

41 Bob Edwards in the *Calgary Eye Opener*, 6 October 1906.

42 "Senator Lougheed Made No Reply," *The Albertan*, 23 November 1911.

43 The B.C. Federationist of "last week," quoted in *The Albertan*, 9 December 1911.

44 For a full list of the buildings under construction in late 1911 see Bryan P. Melnyk, *Calgary Builds. The Emergence of an Urban Landscape, 1905–1914* (Regina: Canadian Plains Research Centre, 1985), 127-148.

45 "Calgary Gets C.P.R. Car Shops," *The Calgary Herald*, 4 October 1911.

46 James A. Lougheed to William Pearce, dated Calgary, 3 November 1911, William Pearce Papers, acc. no. 74-169, file 67.8, University of Alberta Archives.

47 "Work Resumed on Sherman's Theatre," *Calgary News-Telegram*, 24 November 1911.

48 Stephen Avenue Heritage Area Society, *Stephen Avenue and Area Historical Walking Tour* (Edmonton: Alberta Community Development, n.d.), 6.

49 Donna Livingstone, *The Cowboy Spirit: Guy Weadick and the Calgary Stampede* (Vancouver: Douglas and McIntyre, 1996), 38.

50 Robert M. Seiler and Tamara P. Seiler, "The Social Construction of the Canadian Cowboy: Calgary Exhibition and Stampede Posters, 1952–1972," *Journal of Canadian Studies* 33, no. 3 (Autumn 1998): 60.

51 Simon M. Evans, "The End of the Open Range Era in Western Canada," *Prairie Forum* 8, no.1 (Spring 1983): 71–88.

52 Robert M. Seiler, "M. B. ('Doc') Marcell: Official Photographer of the First Calgary Stampede," *The American Review of Canadian Studies* 33 (Summer 2003): 219–20; letter of Maria Marcell, El Paso, Texas, in "You Asked Us…," *Glenbow* (September-October 1984): 15.

53 I follow here the description provided in "'Frontier Days' Celebration Attracted Tens of Thousands and was Thoroughly Enjoyed," *Calgary News-Telegram*, 3 September 1912.

54 Livingstone, *The Cowboy Spirit*, 42.

55 "First White Boy Born in Calgary Here on Visit," *The Albertan*, 3 September 1912.

56 "Majestically Superb in all Wonder of Primitive Plains Life, Great Historical Celebration has Become Living Reality," *The Calgary Herald*, 3 September 1912.

57 Jacqueline Mary Durrie, "Come to the Cabaret: Adaptive Re-Use of the Lougheed Building" (master's thesis, University of Calgary, 2003), 52. As she points out, in contrast, retailers in shopping malls today want wide storefronts and shallow interiors to maximize exposure to window shoppers.

58 "The Lougheed Building," *The Calgary Herald*, 14 September 1912.

59 "The Lougheed Building," *The Calgary Herald*, 28 September 1912.

60 "The Lougheed Building," *The Calgary Herald*, 21 September 1912.

61 *The Albertan*, "Phil W. McCrystle," in *The 100,000 Manufacturing, Building and Wholesale Edition of the Morning Albertan* (Calgary: The Albertan, 1914), 13.

62 "The Lougheed Building," *The Calgary Herald*, 28 September 1912. See also Kate Reeves, *Rosedale Stories: A Community Remembers* (Calgary: Two Printers, 2000), 3, 194.

63 "M. J. Sheedy Has Removed to His New Store 129 Sixth Avenue West Lougheed Block" (advertisement), *Calgary News-Telegram*, 3 September 1912; "Long Illness Fatal to M. J. Sheedy, 64," *The Calgary Herald*, 26 December 1939.

64 "Calgary Just Like Paris, says Divine Sarah Bernhardt," *Calgary News-Telegram*, 15 January 1913.

65 Durrie, "Come to the Cabaret," 57–58.

66 "The Lougheed Building," *The Calgary Herald*, 28 September 1912. For a good review of the Flesner Marble and Tile Company see the entry in *The Albertan, The 100,000 Manufacturing, Building and Wholesale Edition*, 135.

67 "The Lougheed Building," *The Calgary Herald*, 28 September 1912.

68 *Henderson's Calgary Directory*, 1912, 599; *Henderson's Calgary Directory,* 1913, 65.

69 "The Lougheed Building," *The Calgary Herald*, 28 September 1912; *Henderson's Calgary Directory*, 1913.

70 *Henderson's Calgary Directory*, 1913.

71 MacRae, *History of the Province of Alberta*, 929; *The Albertan*, "Dowler & Stevenson Architects," *The 100,000 Manufacturing, Building and Wholesale Edition*, 97; Lyn Hancock, with Marion Dowler, *Tell Me, Grandmother* (Toronto: McClelland and Stewart, 1985), 13–14; *Henderson's Calgary Directory*, 1912.

72 MacRae, "Robert H. L. O'Callaghan, M.D., F.A.C.S.," vol. 3 *History of the Province of Alberta*, 364–65.

73 *The Albertan*, "Hook Construction Company," *The 100,000 Manufacturing, Building and Wholesale Edition*, 151.

74 "Calgarians in Caricature: Harry James Finch," *Calgary News-Telegram*, 13 June 1913; see *The Calgary Herald*, 28 September 1912, for H. J. Finch, Broker, advertisement.

75 "Pinkham & Macleod," *Calgary, Sunny Alberta*, 110; *Henderson's Calgary Directory*, 1913; "The Realty Mart," *Calgary News-Telegram*, 16 January 1913; "Obituaries: James Pinkham," *The Calgary Herald*, 23 June 1941.

76 *Henderson's Calgary Directory*, 1914; *Tregillus-Thompson Calgary Directory*, 1913; Dave Green, "Profile, Walter Kingsley Jull," *The Calgary Herald*, 7 February 1959. Oliver Jull, a great-grandson of Walter Jull, helped me with my research on the Grand Theatre in the mid-1920s.

77 Louis I. Dublin, *A Family of Thirty Million, The Story of the Metropolitan Life Insurance Company* (New York: Metropolitan Life, 1943) 285; "[I]n 1912 the Metropolitan had already achieved more business in force in Canada than any other company—a leadership it has continued to maintain." My thanks to Daniel B. May, MetLife Company Archivist, One Madison Avenue, New York, for this reference. The information on the tenants in the building comes from the *Henderson's Calgary* directories, 1912 and 1913.

78 *Henderson's Calgary* directories, 1912–1922; "Openings Available for Capable Men," *Calgary News-Telegram*, 8 July 1915.

79 *Henderson's Calgary* directories, 1912–1914; Jennifer Bobrovitz, "Gargoyles Top Heraldic Building," *The Calgary Herald*, 12 October 1997.

80 *Henderson's Calgary* directories, 1912–1914; Canadian New Town Co. Limited, Lougheed Building poster, undated, circa 1912 or 1913 (before the economic boom ended!), "Land and Immigration Posters," file 2, Glenbow Archives.

81 Advertisement for "The Lougheed Building," *Calgary News-Telegram*, 3 April 1915.

82 My thanks to Lois Daly for showing me these two transoms, and to Jim Cameron for putting me in touch with her.

83 "Death Comes to Geo. Edward Rutley," *The Albertan*, 22 November 1913. *Henderson's Calgary* directories, 1912–1913.

84 For the price tag of the Calgary Hudson's Bay Company store see J. Brown, "Calgary—The City of the Foothills," *The Beaver* (April 1922): 3.

85 Jennifer Bobrovitz, "Hudson's Bay Opening Celebrated with Parade," *The Calgary Herald*, 28 September 1997; *Henderson's Calgary Directory*, 1913; "New H.B. Store Will Be Opened on August 18. Commissioner Burbidge will Remain Here until Big Structure is Occupied," *Calgary News-Telegram*, 16 July 1913.

86 *Henderson's Calgary* directories, 1912–1915. Listed under "Matthew Dougherty," his name also appears in the *Tregillus-Thompson Calgary Directory*, 1913, 289. There he is shown as living on the "seventh floor" as "manager of building."

87 *Henderson's Calgary* directories, 1914–1919. Listed under "Grenville K. Jack."

88 "The Lougheed Building: Calgary's Finest and Most Up-to-Date," *The Calgary Herald*, 14 September 1912.

Notes to Chapter 6

1 The office locations appear in the directory that he published in 1913, *Tregillus-Thompson Greater Calgary Directory*, 1913, 287–88.

2 "W. J. Tregillus, Head United Farmers, Dead," *The Albertan*, 13 November 1914.

3 W. T. Tregillus [W. J. Tregillus], "Agriculture as a Profession. The Dignity, Importance and Possibilities," *The Grain Growers' Guide* (12 December 1910): 12.

4 "Will Municipal Elections Next Year be Run on a New Reform Ticket?" *Calgary News-Telegram*, 22 July 1912.

5 "Ald. Tregillus to be Made Acting Mayor," *Calgary News-Telegram*, 17 July 1913; "Property owners object to C.N.R. Crossing Street," *Calgary News-Telegram*, 2 January 1914.

6 The best summaries of Will Tregillus's life include: "William John Tregillus 1858–1914," Biographical Information, Calgary, 1982, M6286, Glenbow Archives; Max Foran, "William John Tregillus," *Dictionary of Canadian Biography*, vol. 14: *1911–1920* (Toronto: University of Toronto Press, 1998), 1006–1008; Norman F.

Priestley and Edward B. Swindlehurst, *Furrows, Faith and Fellowship* (Edmonton: Co-op Press Limited, 1967), 36–38; Archibald Oswald MacRae, *History of the Province of Alberta* (n.p.: The Western Canada Co., 1912), 1000–1001; "W.J. Tregillus, Head United Farmers, Dead," *The Albertan*, 13 November 1914. Probably the best source of all is Cyril Tregillus, "Reminiscences": My thanks to Robert Tregillus for showing this mimeographed family history to me. A copy has been deposited in the Glenbow Library.

7 Tregillus, "Reminiscences," 34.

8 "Calgary has at Least Sixteen Millionaires, of Whom Fifteen Made Their Fortunes in This City," *Calgary News-Telegram*, 15 July 1912.

9 Charles Parish Church, Plymouth, RBMB, 167/14, Devon Record Office, West Devon Area, Plymouth, England, cited by Foran, *Dictionary of Canadian Biography*, 1008. Some sources list 1859 as the date of his birth, but Foran establishes that it was 2 May 1858.

10 "Brothers Recall Calgary Mostly Tents in 1880s," *The Edmonton Journal*, 14 July 1950.

11 Greg Oleksiuk, "The Tregillus Era in Barkerville," Curatorial Intern Report, 2000/2001, 30 March 2001, p.3, Barkerville Historic Town. My thanks to Bill Quackenbush of Barkerville, B.C., for sending me a copy of this report.

12 Oleksiuk, "The Tregillus Era," 5; John F. Moore, "Fred Tregillus," *Western Producer Magazine* (Saskatoon), 9 May 1963.

13 "A Pretty Spot in South Devon. Loughtor Mills, Plymouth," *Milling* (6 July 1907): 48. My thanks to Bill Quackenbush of Barkerville, B.C., for this article. John Tregillus retired in 1902.

14 "Issue of John Tregillus (circ 1830–1909) of Devonshire, England," prepared 1 July 1977. My thanks to Robert Tregillus of Pincher Creek, Alberta, for lending me a copy of the family tree.

15 "A Pretty Spot in South Devon," 48–49.

16 Ibid., 48.

17 W. J. Tregillus quoted in "Farmers Foregather Here to Consider Matters of Vital Importance to Them," *Calgary News-Telegram*, 22 January 1913.

18 Priestley and Swindlehurst, *Furrows*, 37; "A Pretty Spot in South Devon," 48.

19 Tregillus, "Reminiscences"

20 Ibid., 10.

21 Ibid., 5–7.

22 Ibid., 7–8.

23 Ibid., 15.

24 *Kelly's Directory of Southampton*, 1894 (London: Kelly and Co., 1894), 10, 18. The history of Freemantle and neighbouring Shirley appears in: Philippa Newnham, "The Southampton District of Shirley," in *Shirley from Domesday to D Day*, ed. John Guilmant (Southampton: Community History Unit, 1997), 19–28.

25 C. A. Dawson and Eva R. Younge, *Pioneering in the Prairie Provinces: The Social Side of the Settlement Process* (Toronto: Macmillan, 1940), 31–32; quoted in Dick Harrison, *Unnamed Country: The Struggle for a Canadian Prairie Fiction* (Edmonton: The University of Alberta Press, 1977), 38.

26 "Farmers at Ottawa," *The Grain Growers' Guide*, 21 December 1910; R.D. Colquette, *The First Fifty Years. A History of the United Grand Growers Limited* (Winnipeg: The Public Press, 1957), 140–41.

27 Nathan S. Elliott, "'We have Asked for Bread, and You Gave Us a Stone': Western Farmers and the Siege of Ottawa" (master's thesis, University of Saskatchewan, 2004), 114.

28 George Edworthy, "Wildwood" (typed manuscript), p. 7, Glenbow Archives.

29 "The Death of Mr. Tregillus," *The Grain Growers' Guide*, 18 November 1914.

30 Tregillus, "Reminiscences," 4, 7.

31 Ibid., 21.

32 Ibid., 22–23. On Joseph Butlin and family see Southern Alberta Pioneers and their Descendants, *Pioneer Families of Southern Alberta* (Calgary: Southern Alberta Pioneers, 1993), 45.

33 Ibid, 28. Cyril is slightly incorrect on the purchase of the three quarter-sections of CPR land; the 480 acres were transferred by the CPR on 10 October 1902, only a few weeks after the Tregillus's arrival in Calgary. See CPR Database, vol. 91, contract number 21325, Glenbow Archives. My thanks to John Hawitt for this information.

34 Accounts by Calgary Authors, *Communities of Calgary. From Scattered Towns to a Major City* (Calgary: Century Calgary Publications, 1975), 13.

35 Tregillus, "Reminiscences," 36.

36 For information on the name "Roscarrock" see A. L. Rowse, "Nicolas Roscarrock and his Lives of the Saints," *The Little Land of Cornwall* (Gloucester, England: Alan Sutton Publishing, 1986), 145–77. "Roscarrock" is the spelling W. J. Tregillus used, see his letter to Sydney, 24 March 1913, William J. Tregillus Papers, M8316, Glenbow Archives. In error the City of Calgary has added a second "s," and refers to the district named after the Tregillus home as "Rosscarrock."

37 Georgina Thomson, "Colorful Rosscarrock," *The Calgary Herald*, 31 May 1958.

38 "A Jolly Dance," *Calgary News-Telegram*, 7 January 1914.

39 Photo and undated newspaper article on the occasion of A. S. Chapman's retirement in the mid-1930s in the possession of Mrs. Margaret Tregillus Raymond. See also Tregillus, "Reminiscences," 47-5.

40 Tregillus, "Reminiscences," 3, 7, 18–19. Miss Susie M. Holland is listed as a "companion" at the W. L. Tregillus residence at 43 Shirley Road, Southampton, in the 1901 Census, Public Record Office, RG 13/1074, 98 South Stoneham 3D Millbrook, fiche no. 3. Her age is given as 31.

41 "Tregillus," M6286, Glenbow Archives.

42 "Tregillus"; MacRae, *History of the Province of Alberta*, 1001.

43 For details of Will's 1911 European tour see *The Albertan*, 3, 13, 15, 21 and 28 June, 6 July 1911.

44 "Through the Low Countries of the Continent of Europe," *The Albertan*, 6 July 1911.

45 "To Represent Calgary at the Coronation," *The Albertan*, 25 April 1911.

46 Henry James Morgan, *The Canadian Men and Women of the Time* (Toronto: William Briggs, 1912), 666; "Canada at Cross Roads Now, States Senator Lougheed," *The Calgary Herald*, 25 July 1911.

47 James Cameron, "The Late Alderman Tregillus. Glasgow, December 11, 1914," *Calgary News-Telegram*, 28 December 1914.

48 In May the cost was estimated at $500,000; see "Another New Industry," *Calgary News-Telegram*, 1 May 1912. Six months later, it had doubled; see "Tregillus Clay Products Company About Ready to Commence Operations," *Calgary News-Telegram*, 21 October 1912.

49 "Tregillus Clay Products Limited," 1 July 1913, p. 4, document in the possession of Robert Tregillus.

50 "The Tregil Clay Products Give Satisfaction," *Calgary News-Telegram*, 1 March 1913.

51 Tregillus, "Reminiscences," 47-5.

52 W. J. Tregillus quoted in "Farmers Foregather here to Consider Matters of Vital Importance to Them," *Calgary News-Telegram*, 22 January 1913.

53 W. J. Tregillus quoted in UFA, film BR, "Minutes and Reports of Annual Convention," 1912, p. 9, Glenbow Archives.

54 *Preliminary Announcement of the University of Calgary, July 1912*, p. 7, University Archives, University of Calgary.

55 "Funeral of Ald. Tregillus is Impressive," *The Albertan*, 17 November 1914.

56 O. S. Chapin, E. A. Dagg and D. Hope, "Why W. J. Tregillus Deserves Well at the Hands of the Electors of Calgary," *Calgary News-Telegram*, 7 December 1912.

57 "Calgary University is Now in Working Order," *Calgary News-Telegram*, 23 September 1912; *Preliminary Announcement of the University of Calgary*, 13.

58 *Preliminary Announcement of the University of Calgary*, 6.

59 William J. Tregillus to "Mr. Crearer" [Thomas Crerar], 1 November 1912, Thomas Crerar Papers, Queen's University Archives.

60 "The University Project," *The Albertan*, 20 May 1911.

61 "Mr. Tregillus Replies," *The Grain Growers' Guide*, 13 July 1910, p. 13. My thanks to Brad Rennie for this reference.

62 Donald Blow, interview with Dr. Henry Klassen, 26 April 1975. I am indebted to my late colleague, Henry Klassen, professor emeritus, University of Calgary Department of History, for the notes of his interview with Dr. Blow's son. A sketch of Dr. Blow's early life appears in MacRae, *History of the Province of Alberta*, 636–38.

63 "Blow House," *Driving Tour: Inglewood and Mount Royal, Calgary* (Edmonton: Alberta Culture n.d.), 22.

64 *Preliminary Announcement of the University of Calgary*, 12.

65 "Will Apply For University Charter," *The Calgary Herald*, 2 June 1910; *Preliminary Announcement of the University of Calgary*, 4.

66 "Healthy Wallop is Taken at Trusts by Ald. Tregillus," *Calgary News-Telegram*, 7 March 1914.

67 "Calgarians Leaving Because of Promotion Honoured by Friends," *Calgary News-Telegram*, 10 July 1913.

68 "Tregillus, Special Advertising Department," *Henderson's Calgary Directory*, 1912, 94–95.

69 Will Tregillus to Sydney Tregillus, dated Roscarrock, Calgary, 24 March 1913, William J. Tregillus Papers, M8316, Glenbow Archives.

70 Peggy Tregillus Raymond, interview with the author, Calgary, 7 February 2002.

71 Tregillus, "Reminiscences," 39; "Tregillus Clay Products Company About Ready to Commence Operations," *Calgary News-Telegram*, 21 October 1912; *Tregillus-Thompson Calgary Directory*, 1913, 288.

72 "No Reason for Gloom in West over Outlook," *Calgary News-Telegram*, 15 March 1913.

73 Will Tregillus to Sydney Tregillus, dated Roscarrock, Calgary, 24 March 1913, William J. Tregillus Papers, M8316, Glenbow Archives.

74 Ibid.

75 Norman Leslie McLeod, "Calgary College 1912–1915: A Study of an Attempt to Establish a Privately Financed University in Alberta" (Ph. D. diss., Department of Educational Foundations, University of Calgary, 1970), 112. This thesis is the best source of information on Calgary's first university.

76 Henry Marshall Tory, "Autobiography 1907–1915," M.G. 30, series D115, vol. 27, pp. 29–32, National Archives of Canada.

77 McLeod, "Calgary College," 107.

78 My thanks to Jens Blecher of the Universitätsarchiv, Leipzig, for forwarding references to Dr. MacDougall's attendance at the University of Leipzig. My thanks to Gaby Divay, for her help in contacting him.

79 "Another Addition to Staff of University," *The Calgary Herald*, 6 September 1912.

80 "Dr. Mack Eastman to fill Skinner Chair in Local University," *Calgary News-Telegram*, 27 April 1912.

81 "W. Kent Power, 76, Dies in Edmonton," *The Albertan*, 16 October 1961.

82 *The University of Calgary, Calgary, Alberta: First Annual Calendar, Session 1913–1914*, 19–21, University Archives, University of Calgary.

83 Walter Sage, "Calgary College 1912-1915," Walter N. Sage Papers, box 31, folder 8, University of British Columbia Archives.

84 Edward Braithwaite quoted in H. Jeffs, *Homes and Careers in Canada* (London: James Clarke and Co., 1914), 137. My thanks to Doug Francis for pointing out this reference.

85 The University of Calgary, *Second Annual Calendar, Session* 1914–15, p. 6, University Archives, University of Calgary.

86 "University Wants to Secure Portion of Sarcee Reserve," *Calgary News-Telegram*, 5 March 1913.

87 McLeod, "Calgary College," 132.

88 "The Province Must Be Unified in System of Education, Says Expert," *Calgary News-Telegram*, 6 May 1913.

89 "President Falconer Makes Plea for Unity," *The Albertan*, 6 May 1913.

90 "French Club Formed," *Calgary News-Telegram*, 16 January 1914.

91 Walter Sage to Harry Gerrans, dated Calgary, 16 December 1913, Walter N. Sage Papers, box 31, folder 29, University of British Columbia Archives.

92 George F. Chipman, Editor, *Grain Growers' Guide*, to W. J. Tregillus, dated Winnipeg, 23 March 1914, S. Mack Eastman Papers, box 1, folder 2, University of British Columbia Archives.

93 Mack Eastman, "Farmers and Militarism," *Grain Growers' Guide*, 20 May 1914.

94 McLeod, "Calgary College," 144.

95 Tregillus, "Reminiscences," 47-6.

96 "Suit Entered Against Ald. W.J. Tregillus," *Calgary News-Telegram*, 13 February 1914.

97 "$165 311.00 Writ Against the W.J. Tregillus Estate," *Calgary News-Telegram*, 23 September 1915.

98 "Varsity Official Resigns," *Calgary News-Telegram*, 30 July 1914.

99 W. J. Tregillus to "Mr. T. A. Crerar," 11 August 1914, Thomas Crerar Papers, Queen's University Archives.

100 McLeod, "Calgary College," 177–78.

101 *Calgary Eye Opener*, 13 January 1912.

102 "Death of W. J. Tregillus," *Grain Growers' Guide*, 18 November 1914.

103 "W. J. Tregillus, Head United Farmers, Dead," *The Albertan*, 13 November 1914.

104 "Flag at Half Mast," *Calgary News-Telegram*, 13 November 1914.

105 "Funeral of Ald. Tregillus is Impressive," *Calgary News-Telegram*, 17 November 1914.

106 The Lorraine is named in the caption of the photos entitled "The Tregillus Clay Products Co.," in the booklet, *The Story of Calgary—Alberta—Canada: Issued in Commemoration of the International Irrigation Congress, October 5–9, 1914*, 45. The Glenbow Library has a copy.

107 His photo is quite visible in the picture accompanying the article, "District Managers Meet," *UGG News* (April 1975): 8. The photo is the same shown in *The Story of Calgary—Alberta—Canada*, 44.

Notes to Chapter 7

1 Fred Albright Members File, Law Society of Alberta, The Legal Archives Society of Alberta.

2 Lorna Brooke (ed.), "An Echo in My Heart: The Letters of Elnora Evelyn (Kelly) Albright and Frederick Stanley Albright," http://ca.geocities.com/echoinmyheart@rogers.com. More than 550 of Fred and Evelyn Kelly Albright's letters are available on the internet; this and all subsequent references to them in this chapter are taken from this electronic source. They are transcribed from the originals held by the University of Western Ontario Archives.

3 "University Lectures on Political Economy. Fred S. Albright, a Graduate of Toronto University, Will be in Charge," *The Albertan*, 24 October 1912.

4 Fred Albright to Evelyn Kelly, dated Calgary, 1 June 1913, on "University Club of Calgary" letterhead, "An Echo in My Heart."

5 "University Club" is an entry in the *Henderson's Calgary Directory* for 1912 (room 615). "University Club Rooms," appears in the *Henderson's Calgary Directory* for 1913 (room 615), and 1914 (room 613). The reference in the *Tregillus-Thompson Directory* for 1913 is to "University Club" (rooms 613, 615 and 617); hence they had a suite of three rooms. The "University Club of Calgary" hosted the informal dinner at the Palliser Hotel in honour of the three visiting university presidents, members of the commission appointed to consider the granting of degree-conferring powers to Calgary College, hence my inference that it was a support organization for the young university. See "Varsity Club Honours Noted Educationists," *Calgary News-Telegram*, 21 November 1914.

6 For a full review of Brownlee's and Albright's friendship at the University of Toronto and in Calgary see Franklin L. Foster, *John E. Brownlee. A Biography* (Lloydminster, Alberta: Foster Learning Inc., 1996), 13–30.

7 Foster, *John E. Brownlee*, 19.

8 For Brownlee's height see Foster, *John E. Brownlee*, 9; Fred Albright's height appears in his Attestation Paper, Canadian Over-Seas Expeditionary Force No. 895173, 21 June 1916, National Archives

of Canada. The attestation papers of all servicemen attached to the Canadian Expeditionary Force can be viewed online at <http://www.collectionscanada.ca/02/020106_e.html>.

9 Clinton J. Ford, "A True Soldier of Jesus Christ—A Tribute," *Christian Guardian* (24 March 1920): 9.

10 Foster, *John E. Brownlee*, 16.

11 Hon. J. E. Brownlee, recorded interview with Una Maclean, 28 March 1961, tape accession no. RCT-14-1, transcript, p.4, M4079, Glenbow Archives.

12 *Henderson's Calgary* directories, 1910, 1911, 1912 and 1913; Fred and Clinton roomed together until Clinton married in 1913.

13 For a wonderful sketch of Maitland McCarthy see David Mittelstadt, "A Social and Biographical History of Elbow Park" (unpublished manuscript, October 2000), 121–22. My thanks to David Mittelstadt for allowing me to see it.

14 "University Lectures on Political Economy," *The Albertan*, 24 October 1912.

15 Ford, "A True Soldier," 9

16 Foster, *John E. Brownlee*, 21; *Henderson's Calgary* directories, 1910, 1911 and 1912.

17 "Dr. James Muir, Dean of Alberta Bar Society, Dead," *The Calgary Herald*, 23 February 1926.

18 "Final Basis of Agreement is Reached in Establishment of the United Grain Growers," *Calgary News-Telegram*, 29 March 1917.

19 "Giant Amalgamation May Purchase Lougheed Block," *Calgary News-Telegram*, 26 October 1917.

20 Foster, *John E. Brownlee*, 29.

21 My thanks to Sarah Carter for bringing these letters to my attention and to David Marshall for allowing me to use his printed copies of the transcribed letters.

22 Lorna Brooke, introduction, "An Echo in My Heart."

23 Evelyn to Fred, 14 October 1913, "An Echo in My Heart."

24 Evelyn to Fred, 7 July 1917, "An Echo in My Heart."

25 "New H. B. Store Will Be opened on August 18," *Calgary News-Telegram*, 16 July 1913.

26 Fred to Evelyn, 2 March 1914, "An Echo in My Heart."

27 Sir John Martin-Harvey, *The Autobiography of Sir John Martin-Harvey* (London: Sampson, Low, Marston & Co., n.d.), 500. His company played the 2,000th performance of the play on 22 December 1921.

28 Edythe Rosen Pearlman, interview with the author, 24 September 1999. As a young woman in her late teens, Edythe Rosen Pearlman worked at the Grand in the mid-1920s; she remembered seeing the inscription. A photograph of the Grand's stage in the Glenbow Photo Library (NA-4560-4) shows the inscription clearly on the proscenium arch over the stage. My thanks to Jim Black, professor emeritus, University of Calgary Department of English, for the identification of the quote.

29 David Gardner, "A Life in the Theatre," *The Beaver* (February/March 1990): 52–53.

30 Stanley Morgan-Powell, "Margaret Anglin: Star of Canada," from *Memories That Live* (Toronto: Macmillan, 1929); reprinted in Don Rubin (ed.), *Canadian Theatre History. Selected Readings* (Toronto: Copp Clark, 1996), 34.

31 Fred to Evelyn, 5 November 1913, "An Echo in My Heart.".

32 David R. Elliott and Iris Miller, *Bible Bill. A Biography of William Aberhart* (Edmonton: Reidmore Books, 1987), 27. David Elliott, e-mail message to author, 15 January 2003.

33 Charles W. Ross, *Calgary Knox 1883–1983* (Altona, Manitoba: D.W. Friesen & Sons, 1983), 30. Also see "Knox Church is Under the Ban of the City Building Inspector," *The Albertan*, 28 November 1912.

34 "At Sherman's Theatre," *The Albertan*, 29 April 1912.

35 J. Fraser Perry, ed., *They Gathered at the River* (Calgary: Central Book Committee of the Central United Church, 1975), 98–100, 143.

36 *Edmonton Bulletin*, 14 January 1913; quoted in James Sheremeta, "A Survey of Professional Entertainment and Theatre in Edmonton, Alberta before 1914" (master's thesis, University of Alberta, 1970), 226.

37 "Divine Sarah Bernhardt is in Love with Work," *The Calgary Herald*, 15 January 1913.

38 "This is the Day When the Jersey Lily Comes," *The Albertan*, 19 December 1912; "Lady de Bathe Prefers Calgary to Edmonton," *Calgary News-Telegram*, 27 December 1912. Lily herself became caught up in the city's land boom and bought property here; she lost money after the boom ended. See "City Acquires Lady de Bathe's Property Here. Comprise 25 Feet on Eighth Ave. Adjacent to the Princess Theatre," *The Calgary Herald*, 4 March 1922, p. 4; see also *Calgary Eye Opener*, 28 August 1920, p.1, col.1.

39 "Nethersole's Brother Comes to Calgary," *The Albertan*, 15 April 1912.

40 Alberta West [pseud.], "Miss Olga Nethersole talks of 'Sapho,' one of the First of the 'Sex' Dramas," *The Albertan*, 20 February 1914.

41 "Dramatic Gossip…" *The Albertan*, 14 February 1914.

42 W. C. A. Moffatt, "Pte Albright was Man of Promise," *Toronto Star Weekly*, 15 December 1917, p. 13.

43 Fred to Evelyn, 7 February 1913, 19 October 1913, and 22 February 1914, "An Echo in My Heart."

44 The phrase, "feast of good things" appears in two articles: "Fifth Evening Concert of Symphony Orchestra Success in Every Way," *The Calgary Herald*, 17 February 1914, and "Sixth Symphony Concert One of the Most Interesting of Season's Programme," *The Calgary Herald*, 24 March 1914.

45 "Orpheum's New Bill will be a Good One," *The Calgary Herald*, 5 October 1912.

46 "Wild Dance of the Argentine to be Investigated," *The Albertan*, 5 February 1914.

47 "University 'Prom' will not Permit of the Tango," *The Albertan*, 26 January 1914.

48 "A 'Dansant,'" *The Albertan*, 3 January 1914, p. 4. My thanks to Jennifer Cook Bobrovitz for bringing this reference to my attention.

49 "Wild Dance of the Argentine to be Investigated," *The Albertan*, 5 February 1914; "Bishop M'Nally Has Not Decided to Ban The Tango. At the Same Time Catholic Prelate Thinks It Isn't Respectable," *The Calgary Herald*, 19 March 1914.

50 Jim Nicoll quoted in "Wild Dance of the Argentine to be Investigated," *The Albertan*, 5 February 1914.

51 Fred to Evelyn, 26 October 1915, "An Echo in My Heart."

52 Fred to Evelyn, 26 October 1913; 11 and 13 January 1914, "An Echo in My Heart."

53 Foster, *John E. Brownlee*, 44–46.

54 Ibid., 50.

55 Fred to Evelyn, 2 October 1915, "An Echo in My Heart."

56 "Calgary St. Andrews Golf Club is Formed," *The Calgary Herald*, 29 April 1912; Donald Smith, "History Close at Hand: The Story of St. Andrew's on the Bow," *Legacy* (August–October 1998): 26–28. For the history of Calgary's oldest golf club see Tyler John Trafford, *Calgary Golf and Country Club: 1897–1997: more than 18 holes* (Calgary: The Club 1997).

57 "Purchase of St. Andrew's Golf Course. Progressive Calgary Club now in Tip Top Shape—Many Improvements to be made," *Canadian Golfer* (January 1921): 618.

58 Minutes, 23 May 1912, Calgary St. Andrew's Golf Club, M 1675, Glenbow Archives. The club was so popular that it reached its maximum membership of 200 men and 50 women by 13 May 1912. On 10 June 1912 the minutes record that the club extended the number of possible members. The minutes record 326 members on 13 March 1914. Some avid Calgary golfers belonged to both the Calgary St. Andrew's Golf Club and the city's older Calgary Golf and Country Club. See, for instance, the biography of Fred Shouldice, a law partner of Fred Albright's, in John Blue, *Alberta Past and Present. Historical and Biographical*, vol 2 (Chicago: Pioneer Historical Publishing Co., 1924), 152.

59 For account of Rev. MacWilliams winning the club's Martin Trophy in 1915 consult *Canadian Golfer* (December 1915): 507; see also his obituary, *The Calgary Herald*, 20 November 1944.

60 Art Tregillus is listed as a member in the minutes, 9 May 1913.

61 Bertha Hart Segall, "'Bob' Edwards," *Canadian Cattlemen* (June 1950): 42.

62 He had two shares; the certificate is in M 65 f.7, Glenbow Archives.

63 "Social Notice," *Calgary News-Telegram*, 8 September 1914: "To watch part of the golf tournament at St. Andrew's on Friday. Mrs. J. A. Lougheed, Mrs. E. M. Adams, Mrs. Nourse, and Mrs. Atkinson motored to the links." Clarence's and Edgar's names appear in the minutes for 1914 of the Calgary St. Andrew's Golf Club.

64 Tony Cashman, *A Picture History of Alberta* (Edmonton: Hurtig Publishers, 1979), 49.

65 *First programme, Calgary Symphony Orchestra, 1913/1914*, p. 12, Glenbow Library. The call number is 784.2097123 C151f.

66 See the entries in *Henderson's Calgary* directories from 1912 to 1955. By 1912 their company history states: "As a matter of fact, in 1912 the Metropolitan had already achieved more business in force in Canada than any other company--- a leadership it has continued to maintain." Louis I. Dublin, *A Family of Thirty Million. The Story of the Metropolitan Life Insurance Company* (New York: Metropolitan Life, 1943), 285. My thanks to Daniel B. May, Company Archivist, Metropolitan Life Assurance Company, New York, for this reference.

67 The full title appears in their ad in the *Henderson's Calgary Directory*, 1912, 146.

68 *Henderson's Calgary* directories indicate that Phil McCrystle had his shop in the Lougheed from 1913 (on the Sixth Avenue side, at 127); and, in 1914, on the 1st Street side (at 602a), where Doherty had been. Doherty seems to have downsized as they gave up their 602 space on 1st Street in 1914, but kept their store at 137 on 6th Avenue. By 1915 both Doherty and McCrystle had left the Lougheed Building. For details on Phil McCrystle and his shop in the Lougheed, see *The Albertan*, "Phil W., McCrystle," in *The 100,000 Manufacturing, Building and Wholesale Edition of the Morning Albertan* (Calgary: The Albertan, 1914), 13.

69 Note on Mrs. Maud St. Clair Pinkham, Pinkham Family Papers, Miscellaneous, 1979, M978, Glenbow Archives; *Henderson's Calgary* directories, 1911–1915; "Social Column," *Calgary News-Telegram*, 18 July 1914; "Obituaries, James Pinkham," *The Calgary Herald*, 23 June 1941. My thanks as well to Stephen Francom, Archivist, Corporate Archive, Royal Bank of Canada, and to Nancy Walton, daughter of Jim Pinkham.

70 *Henderson's Calgary* directories, 1915 to 1965; Dave Green, "Profile: James Cleave," *Calgary Herald Magazine* (19 April 1958).

71 David Finch and Gordon Jaremko, *Fields of Fire. An Illustrated History of Canadian Petroleum* (Calgary: Detselig, 1994), 27.

72 Douglas E. Cass, "Investment in the Alberta Petroleum Industry, 1912–1930" (master's thesis, University of Calgary, 1985), 57.

73 See Ed Bredin, "Leonard W. Brockington C.M.G., LL.D, D.C.L., K.C.," in *Citymakers: Calgarians after the Frontier*, ed. Max Foran and Sheilagh S. Jameson (Calgary: The Historical Society of Alberta, Chinook Country Chapter, 1987), 83–94. I am indebted to Ed Bredin, Brockington's biographer, for showing me his notes he prepared for a talk to the Chinook Country Historical Society, November 2001. For a contemporary view of "Brock" see Eric Hutton, "… and now, a few words from Leonard Brockington," *Maclean's* (15 April 1953): 24–25, 64–68. A. M. Laverty contributes a warm, intimate portrait of him in, "Leonard W. Brockington 1888–1966," *The Queen's Review (Kingston, Ontario)*, (September-October 1966): 120–22. See also "Ladies and Gentlemen, Mr. Brockington," a one-hour tribute to the memory of Leonard Brockington played on CBC radio network, 2 November 1966, prepared by Harry Boyle, CBC Radio Archives, Toronto. My thanks to Brent Michaulak for access to this item.

74 Fred to Evelyn, dated Bramshott, England, 27 July 1917, "An Echo in My Heart."

75 For a collection of George B. Coutts's correspondence with Leonard Brockington see M279, Glenbow Archives.

76 Foster, *John E. Brownlee*, 36.

77 Perry, *They Gathered at the River*, 37, 165.

78 Attestation Paper of Fred Albright, Canadian Over-Seas Expeditionary Force, No. 895173, 21 June 1916, National Archives of Canada.

79 Fred Albright to George Coutts, dated Bramshott, England, 20 August 1917, George B. Coutts Correspondence, M279, file 3, Glenbow Archives.

80 The dining room service began on 1 August 1917. "Board of Trade Elects Officers for Coming Year," *The Calgary Herald*, 27 December 1917.

81 Evelyn Albright, "Letters to Fred Albright Written in a Notebook after his Death," transcribed by Lorna Brooke. See the letter of 2 December 1917. My thanks to Lorna Brooke for showing me these recently located additions to the Albright letters.

82 We know that word of Fred's death reached Calgary on Monday morning thanks to the following newspaper account: "According to word which was received in Calgary this morning, F.S. Albright, well-known barrister and church worker, has been killed at the front." "F.S. Albright Killed on Western Front," *The Calgary Herald*, 12 November 1917.

83 Victor W. Wheeler, *The 50th Battalion in No Man's Land* (Calgary: Alberta Historical Resources Foundation, 1980), 224.

84 "Frederick Stanley Albright," biographical information supplied by Evelyn Kelly Albright, A73-0026/003 (87), University of Toronto Archives.

85 "Fred Albright," *The Calgary Herald*, 14 November 1917.

86 Brownlee, interview with Una Maclean, 4.

87 The biographical details are taken from "Looking Back at 50 Years in Law," *The Albertan*, 24 February 1961; "Clinton J. Ford," *Alberta: Past and Present*, vol. 3 (Chicago: Pioneer Historical Publishing Co., 1924), 525–26. My thanks to Lorna Brook for identifying the letters in the Albright Papers that refer to Clinton Ford; see particularly, Fred's letters for 25 January 1911; 2 February 1913; 15 June 1913, "An Echo in My Heart."

88 Fred to Evelyn, 17 October 1910, "An Echo in My Heart."

89 Evelyn to Fred, 18 June 1917, "An Echo in My Heart."

90 Ford, "A True Soldier."

91 Lorna Brooke, postscript, "An Echo in My Heart."

Notes to Chapter 8

1 "W. R. Sherman Sells Theatrical Interests to a New Company," *The Calgary Herald*, 6 June 1914.

2 His height was 5' 11"; recalled by Grace Lydiatt Shaw, interview with author, Vancouver, 12 November 2000.

3 Dorothy Lydiatt Vokes, interview with Grace Lydiatt Shaw, 1962, Grace Lydiatt Shaw Collection of interviews on the history of Canadian theatre, National Archives of Canada. Born in Winnipeg in 1903, Dorothy was the Lydiatts' oldest child. She knew Bill Sherman as a young girl in Calgary and made this comparison.

4 Andrew King, *Pen, Paper and Printing Ink* (Saskatoon: Western Producer Prairie Books, 1970), 87–88. For a short overview of the both fire curtain and the Daniels law suit in early 1914 see Alan Hustak, "The Grand Lady of First Street," *City Scope* 2, no. 3 (September 1985): 53–54, 77.

5 "Sherman Corrects Misstatements Re Advertising Curtain," *Calgary News-Telegram*, 21 March 1912.

6 "Mr. Sherman Defends Advertising Curtain," *Calgary News-Telegram*, 20 March 1912.

7 "Sherman Gets Handsome Christmas Present," *The Albertan*, 17 December 1912.

8 "Sherman Corrects Misstatements."

9 "The New Theatrical Merger," *Calgary News-Telegram*, 1 May 1912.

10 "Orpheum Circuit Opens at the Sherman Grand with Splendid Program," *The Calgary Herald*, 6 September 1912. "William B.

Sherman," *The Albertan*, 2 November 1912. Later this scheduling was reversed with road attractions from Thursday to Saturday, and vaudeville acts from Monday to Wednesday; see the advertisement for the Grand on p.153, from S. Arnold Wark, comp., *Calgary. The City of Calgary Year Book* (Calgary: n.p., 1919).

11 David Gardner, "Vaudeville," in *The Oxford Companion to Canadian Theatre*, ed. Eugene Benson and L. W. Conolly (Toronto: Oxford University Press, 1989), 579.

12 "This is the Day When the Jersey Lily Comes," *The Albertan*, 19 December 1912.

13 "Sarah Bernhardt Warmly Greeted By Calgarians," *The Calgary Herald*, 15 January 1913.

14 "Week's Orpheum Bill Leads All the Rest," *The Albertan*, 11 October 1912.

15 "Changes in the Local Theatre World Rumoured," *Calgary News-Telegram*, 13 August 1913. My thanks to Harry Sanders for this important article.

16 C. H. Daniels appears as "CPR inspector" in the *Henderson's Calgary* directories for 1912–1913; he was listed as "chief inspector" in 1914–1915 and then as a "porter" in 1916. The inspector's role was that of a foreman; for instance, they checked to see if the sleeping cars were cleaned properly. They obtained higher pay. Ralph Budd, interview with author, Toronto, 8 September 2001. Mr. Budd worked as a CPR porter in the late 1930s.

17 "A Colored Man Sues a Theatre," *Calgary News-Telegram*, 7 February 1914.

18 Ibid.; "Barney Collison Dies at 78," *The Calgary Herald*, 20 October 1958. Barney Collison, Calgary criminal lawyer, was mentioned by Eva Reid in, "Bob Edwards' Widow Dies," *The Albertan*, 27 May 1968.

19 James Thomas Leatherby, Birth Certificate, Registration District, Uxbridge, Sub-district of Hillingdon, County of Middlesex, issued 18 May 1883, born 8 April 1883. His father's occupation is listed as "Brickfield Labourer." My thanks to Gwen Kingsley for obtaining James Leatherby's birth certificate for me.

20 Attestation Paper, James Thomas Leatherby, Canadian Expeditionary Force, R.G. 150, acc. 1992-93/166, box 5492, sequence 13, regimental number 1188, National Archives of Canada.

21 "Dies in France: Jimmie Leatherby," *Calgary News-Telegram*, 12 March 1915.

22 "Will discriminate against Negroes," *The Albertan*, 10 February 1914.

23 Peter Turner Bone, *When the Steel Went Through* (Toronto: Macmillan 1947), 66; "February, Journal of Remarkable Occurrences—1884," *The Dominion Annual Register and Review, 1884*, ed., Henry J. Morgan (Toronto: Hunter, Rose & Company, 1885), 319.

24 Letterhead for "The Hottest Coon in Dixie: Tour Opens May, 1905," Riveredge Foundation Fonds, M 4843, file 14, Glenbow Archives.

25 "Hotels Refuse Admission To Colored Jubilee Singers—Advance Agent Makes His Complaint, A letter to the Herald from Wm. Irle," *The Herald Calgary*, 5 May 1906; Abridged version of the letter appears in "Herald at 100," *The Calgary Herald*, 31 August 1983, Special Section, G20.

26 Owen Stone is listed as the janitor, or caretaker, of the Grand Theatre in the *Henderson's Calgary* directories for 1912 to 1919. His wife, Alice Stone, is listed as the "matron" in the directories for 1914 and 1915. When she was a young girl in the mid- and late 1910s, Mrs. Stone used to take her neighbour's daughter, May Smitten, from the age of five to eight, to the Grand for the Saturday afternoon matinees. While Mrs. Stone did her cleaning duties May watched the performances. As a result of this early exposure to live entertainment, May has had a life-long interest in the theatre. I interviewed May Smitten in Edmonton, 23 January 2003.

27 Howard and Tamara Palmer, "Urban Blacks in Alberta," *Alberta History* 29, no. 3 (Summer 1981): 9. In 1911, seventy-two lived in the city. The Calgary community was composed primarily of porters and their families.

28 Stanley G. Grizzle, with John Cooper, *My Name's Not George: The Story of the Brotherhood of Sleeping Car Porters in Canada* (Toronto: Umbrella Press, 1998), 41.

29 Sarah-Jane Mathieu, "North of the Colour Line: Sleeping Car Porters and the Battle Against Jim Crow on Canadian Rails, 1880–1920," *Labour/ Le Travail* 47 (Spring 2001): 10.

30 Grizzle, *My Name's Not George,* 37.

31 "Negro Gets Damages from Local Theatre," *The Albertan*, 26 March 1914. Sherman threatened to appeal this decision, see "Defence Filed by Theatre in Daniels Suit," *Calgary News-Telegram*, 7 April 1914. As no further newspaper articles appeared on this topic, apparently he did not proceed with his appeal.

32 "W.B. Sherman Sells Theatrical Interests to a New Company," *The Calgary Herald*, 6 June 1914.

33 "Renovated Grand Theatre Reopens Monday August 10. C.P. Walker, Manager of Winnipeg Theatre of That Name, Will in Future Control Booking for This House, Now probably the Handsomest and Best Equipped in Canada," *Calgary News-Telegram*, 8 August 1914.

34 "R. J. Lydiatt Goes East," *Calgary News-Telegram*, 23 June 1914.

35 The temporary manager, George Dumond, left in late December; see "Popular Young Manager of the Grand is Going," *Calgary News-Telegram*, 26 December 1914. For the first reference in the *Calgary News-Telegram* to Jeff Lydiatt as the Grand Theatre manager see "Col. Mason's Battalion Invited Out," *Calgary News-Telegram*, 15 January 1915.

36 Grace Lydiatt Shaw, interview, 12 November 2000.

37 Margaret Lydiatt, interview with author, Kelowna, B.C., 28 September 2000. She is their daughter.

38 Margaret Lydiatt, letter to author, dated Kelowna, 13 August 2001.

39 Photos in an unidentified church publication in the possession of Grace Lydiatt Shaw show captions indicating their positions.

40 Margaret Lydiatt, interview with author, Kelowna, 12 November 2000.

41 My thanks to David Odgen, their grandson, for showing me the photo.

42 *Might's Toronto* directories for the years 1895, 1896, 1897 and 1898, list Jeff Lydiatt as a clerk at H. H. Fudger.

43 My thanks to their son, Jeff Lydiatt, Jr., for showing me their marriage certificate. *Might's Toronto* directories for 1901 and 1902 indicate that he was a CPR clerk in Toronto.

44 Grace Lydiatt Shaw, interview with author, Vancouver, 6 September 2000.

45 Grace Lydiatt Shaw, interview, 12 November 2000.

46 "R. J. Lydiatt to Leave Railway Work," *The Albertan*, 4 October 1912; "Reginald Jeffrey Lydiatt," *Who's Who and Why, 1921*, ed. B. M. Greene (Toronto: International Press Ltd., 1921), 523; "Alfred Price," *The Canadian Men and Women of the Time*, ed. Henry James Morgan, 2nd ed. (Toronto: William Briggs, 1912), 917.

47 Victoria Freeman, *Distant Relations: How My Ancestors Colonized North America* (Toronto: McClelland and Stewart, 2000), 359–60.

48 "Alfred Price," *Canadian Railway and Marine World* (August 1922): 412.

49 *The Albertan*, 28 February 1913; cited in Henry C. Klassen, *A Business History of Alberta* (Calgary: University of Calgary Press, 1999), 127.

50 Max Foran, *An Illustrated History of Calgary* (Toronto: James Lorimer, 1978), 70; David Jones, *Alberta Then and Now: The Second Coming of the Railway to Calgary* (n.p.: CP Rail System, 1996). This item is a very readable fourteen page booklet.

51 "Plans of the New Home of A. Price, Superintendent of the C.P.R. Now Being Erected in Mount Royal," *The Calgary Herald*, 17 June 1912.

52 "Over Two Hundred Calgarians Attend Farewell Dinner," *The Calgary Herald*, 10 July 1913; "Alfred Price," *Canadian Railway and Marine World,* 412.

53 See for example the references in the *Calgary News-Telegram*, 4 and 5 May 1911; 3 May 1912; 25 June 1912; *The Albertan*, 9 June 1912.

54 "Calgary Has the Biggest Y.M.C.A. Membership, in Proportion to Population, of any City in America," *Calgary News-Telegram*, 31 January 1912.

55 William Pearce to Phina Pearce, 12 July 1912, William Pearce Papers, 74-169/810, University of Alberta Archives (henceforth identified as Pearce Papers).

56 E. Alyn Mitchener, "William Pearce and Federal Government Activity in Western Canada 1882–1904," 2 vols. (Ph.D. diss., University of Alberta, 1971), 90–98.

57 William Pearce to Miss Phina Pearce, 25 July 1912, Pearce Papers, 74-169/810.

58 William Pearce to W.H. Aldridge, 5 April 1909, Pearce Papers, 74-169/791.

59 William Pearce to Mrs. Macdonnell, 23 August 1909, Pearce Papers, 74-169/801.

60 William Pearce to Phina Pearce, 20 May 1909, Pearce Papers, 74-169/810.

61 William Pearce to Frances Pearce, 9 March 1912, Pearce Papers, 74-169/784.

62 William Pearce to Seabury Pearce, 21 September 1908, Pearce Papers, 74-169/791.

63 William Pearce to Harry Pearce, 1 June 1915, Pearce Papers, 74-169/796.

64 William Pearce to Seabury Pearce, 22 March 1909, Pearce Papers, 74-169/791.

65 For the dates of birth of the Pearce children see the genealogy of the Pearce family in the William Pearce Papers, M4845, file 34, Glenbow Archives.

66 William Pearce to Harry Pearce, 4 May 1912, Pearce Papers, 74-169/796.

67 Grace Lydiatt Shaw, interview, 6 September 2000; Margaret Lydiatt, telephone conversation with author, 21 October 2000.

68 Archibald Oswald MacRae, "Thomas Henry Blow, M.D." *History of the Province of Alberta*, Vol. 2 (n.p.: The Western Canada History Co., 1912), 636–38. Donald Blow, interview with Henry Klassen, Calgary, 26 April 1975. My thanks to Henry Klassen for providing me with a copy of his interview with Dr. Blow's son.

69 "Jeff Lydiatt at Series," *Calgary News-Telegram*, 17 November 1912.

70 "Lydiatt Banquet is Successful Affair," *The Calgary Herald*, 31 October 1912.

71 "Friends of R. J. Lydiatt Meet at Banquet Board," *The Albertan*, 31 October 1912.

72 Both the *Tregillus-Thompson* and the *Henderson's Calgary* directories for 1913 list "R. Jeffery Lydiatt real est." for 212 7th Avenue S.W.; in the *Henderson's Calgary Directory*, 1913, he is also listed as "sec Dr T H Blow."

73 "Mainly About Women," *The Albertan*, 27 December 1912.

74 Anne Crawford, "Concern Voiced as Early Homes Bite the Dust," *The Calgary Herald*, 12 August 1990. My thanks to Gordon Lydiatt who saved this clipping, and to Jeff Lydiatt, Jr., who showed it to me.

75 "No Changes in Local Political Situation on Nomination Day," *Calgary News-Telegram*, 11 April 1913.

76 Grace Lydiatt Shaw, telephone interview with author, 28 October 1999. Grace Lydiatt Shaw, interview with author, Vancouver, 11 February 2001. For confirmation that it was through the efforts of Jim Davidson that Jeff "went into the theatrical business," see George Treadwell, "'He Had a Genius for Friendship'," *The Rotarian* (December 1927): 28.

77 "Symphony Orchestra for Calgary is a Certainty. Scheme of Organization is Outlined at Meeting of the Directors," *The Albertan*, 5 May 1914.

78 Judge Winter quoted in "Symphony Orchestra Suggestion," *Calgary News-Telegram*, 11 April 1914.

79 Norman J. Kennedy, "The Growth and Development of Music in Calgary (1875–1920)," (master's thesis, University of Alberta, 1952), 95–96, The Glenbow Library contains a copy of the first evening program of the Calgary Symphony Orchestra, 10 November 1913. The call number is 784.2097123 C151f

80 B. M Greene, ed., *Who's Who and Why, 1921* (Vancouver: International Press Limited, 1921), 523, states that he was "associated with Sir James Lougheed at Calgary, October 1912, to November 1919"; this cannot be, as he worked for Dr. Blow in late 1912 and early 1913.

81 "The Pipes of Pan will Charm every Calgary Child," *The Albertan*, 5 June 1913; "Maude Adams Delightfully Charming in J. M. Barrie's Fairy Play 'Peter Pan'," *The Calgary Herald*, 10 June 1913.

82 Grace Lydiatt Shaw, interview with her sister, Dorothy Lydiatt Vokes, 1962, CBC Radio Archives, Toronto.

83 James W. Davidson, Club Historian, "History of the Calgary Rotary Club," unpublished manuscript, 1923, p. 1, Rotary Club of Calgary Fonds, M1700 file 98, Glenbow Archives.

84 Davidson, "History of the Calgary Rotary Club," 3; "Rotary Club Meets," *The Calgary Herald*, 17 February 1914.

85 "R. J. Lydiatt New President of the Calgary Rotary Club," *Calgary News-Telegram*, 29 May 1917. Gordon Anderson and John Stevenson, comps., eds., *An Historical Summary of the Rotary Club of Calgary, Alberta, Canada* (Calgary: McAra Printing Limited, 1985), 6–7.

86 "Supreme Event of the Season In Forbes-Robertson," *The Calgary Herald*, 8 February 1915.

87 "The Church and the Stage," *Calgary News-Telegram*, 16 February 1915.

88 "War Announcement Gives Rise to Great Outburst of Patriotic Feeling," *The Calgary Herald*, 5 August 1914.

89 Sir Johnston Forbes-Robertson, *A Player Under Three Reigns* (1925, reprint; New York: Benjamin Blom, 1971), 272. See also: "Actor Visits Troops," *The Calgary Herald*, 12 February 1915.

90 Sir Johnston Forbes-Robertson quoted in "Forbes-Robertson on Attitude of the United States," *The Albertan*, 9 February 1915.

91 He appears there in the *Henderson's Calgary Directory*, 1914, but not in 1915, when his office as manager would be in the Grand Theatre.

92 "Recruits Needed by Princess Pats," *Calgary News-Telegram*, 22 November 1915; "Another University Company Recruiting. Particulars may be Obtained. Dr. R. B. O'Callaghan, Lougheed Building," *The Calgary Herald*, 7 December 1915.

93 "Dr. O Callaghan Returning after Active Service," *Calgary News-Telegram*, 6 September 1917.

94 "Urgent Appeal Is Being Made for Recruits," *Calgary News-Telegram*, 5 August 1914; "Second Naval Contingent on Way to Coast," *Calgary News-Telegram*, 10 August 1914.

95 "Soldiers' Club's Headquarters in Lougheed Block," *Calgary News-Telegram*, 1 November 1915; "I.O.D.E. Khaki Club to Be Opened Monday," *Calgary News-Telegram*, 25 November 1915.

96 "Patriotic Fund is Forced to Remove," *The Calgary Herald*, 27 December 1916.

97 "Physical Standard is Lowered for the Army Medical Corps," *Calgary News-Telegram*, 20 April 1917.

98 "Many Scouts are now in the Army," *Calgary Canadian (Calgary News-Telegram)*, 12 April 1918; *Henderson's Calgary* directories for 1916-1919.

99 Accounts by various Calgary authors, *Scouting in Calgary: Boy Scout Groups and Activities, 1910-1974* (Calgary: Century Calgary Publications, 1975), 7, 10.

100 Robert H. MacDonald, *Sons of the Empire: The Frontier and the Boy Scout Movement, 1890-1918* (Toronto: University of Toronto Press, 1993), 186.

101 Ibid., 188, 201.

102 Accounts by various Calgary authors, *Scouting in Calgary*, 17.

103 Mack Eastman quoted in "M. Eastman Volunteered Although Anti-Militarist," *Calgary News-Telegram*, 23 October 1914.

104 "Prof. Eastman Debarred," *Calgary News-Telegram*, 31 August 1914.

105 The University of Calgary, *Second Annual Calendar, Session 1914/15*, 4. See also unidentified clipping, March–April 1962, Former Student Files, Queen's University Archives, Kingston, Ontario.

106 J. H. Woods, Hon. Secretary of the Belgian Relief Committee, dated Calgary, 4 May 1915, S. Mack Eastman Papers, box 1, file 3, University of British Columbia Archives. In the same collection are some press clippings (undated) of his Calgary talks (box 1, file 33), as well as lecture notes on Belgium's history (box 2, file 7). The article, "Belgium Subject of Lecture Series," *Calgary News-Telegram*, 13 January 1915, lists the Alberta towns visited. See also for Eastman's role, "A Worthy Movement in Behalf of Belgium," *Calgary News-Telegram*, 14 January 1915. For references to his talks outside of Calgary, consult the *Calgary News-Telegram*, 17 February, 17 April and 3 May 1915.

107 Eastman to Edward Braithwaite, dated Calgary, 28 December 1914, Braithwaite Papers, University of Western Ontario Archives, University of Western Ontario. Eastman gave his home address as 2420, 5th Street West. The *Henderson's Calgary Directory*, 1915, lists 2420 5th Street West as the address of "George B. Coutts." See also Evelyn Albright to Fred Albright, 30 September 1915, in Lorna Brooke (ed.), "An Echo in My Heart: The Letters of Elnora Evelyn (Kelly) Albright and Frederick Stanley Albright," http://ca.geocities.com/echoinmyheart@rogers.com. Of David Coutts she writes, "[he] is a smart kiddie, isn't he, and a lovely child."

108 Walter Sage to Leila Gerrens (his aunt), 24 November 1914, Walter N. Sage Papers, box 31, file 29, University of British Columbia Archives. Apparently Walter Sage taught six courses in English literature, three courses in history and two in economics. *Sunday Vancouver Province* 325 (February 1932), clipping in the Walter Sage vertical file, University of British Columbia Archives.

109 Typed sheet in the Mack Eastman Papers, box 1, file 3, University of British Columbia Archives. Professor G. M. Wrong of the University of Toronto termed it "sound and erudite." William Bennett Munro, review, *Review of Historical Publications Relating to Canada* 20 (1915), 24; this Harvard scholar stated it was based "throughout on a painstaking study of the sources."

110 "Calgarian Writes Book That Receives Flattering Reviews," *Calgary News-Telegram*, 26 April 1915. The study is available on microfiche, CIHM no. 9-91867. The CIHM series produced by the Canadian Institute for Historical Microreproduction in Ottawa, is available in many Canadian research libraries. Mack Eastman, *Church and State in Early Canada* (Edinburgh: Printed at the University Press by T. and A. Constable, 1915).

111 Mack Eastman, Attestation Paper, Canadian Over-Seas Expeditionary Force, No. 1090055, National Archives of Canada. He enlisted on 15 December 1916.

112 "Dr. Braithwaite Names Western University Head," *Calgary News-Telegram*, 6 June 1914. Dr. Frank MacDougall, the chemistry professor, succeeded him. He stayed to the summer of 1915. No further information is available.

113 Walter Sage to Leila Gerrans (his aunt), 20 November 1913, Walter N. Sage Papers, box 31, folder 29, University of British Columbia Archives.

114 "Weddings. Sage-Mackinnon," *Calgary News-Telegram*, 7 September 1915. For a full sketch of Sage's life see Margaret Ormsby, "Walter Noble Sage," *Canadian Historical Review* 45 (1964): 180–82.

115 Max and Heather Foran, *Calgary: Canada's Frontier Metropolis* (Calgary: Windsor Publications, 1982), 156.

116 "Col. Mason's Battalion Invited Out," *Calgary News-Telegram*, 15 January 1915.

117 "Grand to Entertain 31st," *Calgary News-Telegram*, 22 February 1915.

118 Jeffrey Goffin, "Lyric Theatre," in Eugene Benson and L.W. Connelly, eds., *The Oxford Companion to Canadian Theatre* (Toronto: Oxford University Press, 1989), 316. The Lyric had become part of the Pantages vaudeville circuit, re-opening on 23 February 1914 as the Pantages Theatre.

119 "Soldiers Were Pleased," *Calgary News-Telegram*, 30 April 1915. While many Calgary soldiers carried with them pleasant memories of the Grand Theatre away to Europe, one did not. Fred Albright's law partner, Fred Shouldice, had his car (a black McLaughlin roadster)

stolen between 10 and 11 o'clock Friday evening, 1 October 1915, near the theatre's entrance, in front of the Lougheed Building, 1st Street West. See *Calgary News-Telegram*, 5 October 1915. Already a lieutenant in the militia, Shouldice left for active service in 1916, and fought at Vimy Ridge in 1917 and at the end of the war in the Cambrai offensive, during which he won the Military Cross at the capture of Tilloy. See his biography, "Captain Fredrick L. Shouldice," in John Blue, *Alberta Past and Present. Historical and Biographical*, vol 2 (Chicago: Pioneer Historical Publishing Co., 1924), 151–52. His militia service is mentioned in Fredrick Lowry Shouldice, Officers' Declaration Paper, Canadian Over-Seas Expeditionary Force, 4 November 1915, National Archives of Canada.

120 Ada Patton Kelter (granddaughter of Millicent McElroy), interview with the author, Calgary, 13 February 2003.

121 "'Lady with the Cornet'," *The Calgary Herald*, 31 August 1945. Anne White, "Songster and Preachers: Female Salvationists in Calgary, 1897-1930," in the Canadian Society of Church History, *Historical Papers, 2001,* 119-120.

122 Ada Patton Kelter, interview, 13 February 2003.

123 The *Henderson's Calgary* directories list his businesses as occupying rooms 423–27 in 1915, and 423 in 1916.

124 William Pearce to Senator James Lougheed, 17 July 1915, 74-169, file 67.8, Pearce Papers.

125 Seabury Pearce to William Pearce, 14 February 1901, 74-169/790, Pearce Papers.

126 Although he appears in the *Henderson's Calgary Directory* for 1915, the first letter to indicate his offices were in the Lougheed Building is dated later—see Seabury Pearce to William Pearce, 9 March 1916, 74-169/792, Pearce Papers.

127 William Pearce to the Archbishop of Rupert's Land, Winnipeg, 20 October 1915, 74-169/802, Pearce Papers.

128 William Pearce to Seabury Pearce, 30 August 1916, 74-169/792, Pearce Papers.

129 William Pearce to J. G. Sullivan, 5 January 1917, 74-169/797, Pearce Papers.

130 Minutes of the Executive, Calgary City Planning Commission. Minutes, 1911–1914, box 1, City of Calgary Archives. See the minutes for the meetings from 22 November 1912 to 7 June 1913. See the minutes for 21 May 1913, the date of Thomas Mawson's visit.

131 Adolphina Tassie, with C. S. Howard, "Prairie Surveys and a Prairie Surveyor," *The Canadian Banker* 60, no. 2 (Spring 1953): 69.

132 For more on the Mawson Report see the short well-illustrated summary by E. Joyce Morrow, *"Calgary, Many Years Hence"* (Calgary: City of Calgary/University of Calgary, 1979) and Max Foran, "The Mawson Report in Historical Perspective," *Alberta History* 28, no. 3 (1980): 31–39.

133 William Pearce to Seabury Pearce, 28 February 1913, 74-169/764, Pearce Papers. Sue Anne Donaldson, "William Pearce: His Vision of Trees," *Journal of Garden History* 3, no. 3 (July–September 1983): 240.

134 Photo NA-3766-38, Glenbow Photo Archives.

135 Donaldson, "William Pearce," 240.

136 *Souvenir. Sixth Annual Assembly of the Royal Architectural Institute of Canada, Calgary, Alberta, Sept. 15 and 16, 1913*, p. 5, Glenbow Library.

137 "A New Policy Needed," *The Calgary Herald*, 28 August 1914.

138 Senate, *Debates*, 19 August 1914, 7.

139 "Dies in France," *Calgary News-Telegram*, 12 March 1915.

140 "Lougheed Quits as Minister of Militia Branch," *Calgary News-Telegram*, 2 September 1915.

141 Clarence Hardisty Lougheed, Attestation Paper, Canadian Over-Seas Expeditionary Force, 27 September 1915, National Archives of Canada.

142 Officers' Declaration Paper, Canadian Over-Seas Expeditionary Force, 24 February 1916. See also his entire military service file housed in the National Archives of Canada. Short news item on Edgar Lougheed, *Calgary News-Telegram*, 3 November 1915, reads

"Mr. Harold Anderson and Mr. Edgar Lougheed, lieutenants in the Army Service Corps, leave shortly for the east, to attend one of the training schools."

143 Senate, *Debates*, 18 January 1916, 14.

144 William Pearce to Frances Pearce, 14 February 1916, 74-169/784, Pearce Papers.

145 For a complete summary of the riots see P. Whitney Lackenbauer, "The Military and 'Mob Rule.' The CEF Riots in Calgary, February 1916," *Canadian Military History* 10, no.1 (Winter 2001): 31–42.

146 William Pearce to Frances Pearce, 14 February 1916.

147 "Soldiers are Armed with Ball Cartridge, and are Placed on Guard at Threatened Places," *Calgary News-Telegram*, 12 February 1916. *The Albertan* states in its issue of 12 February 1916: "Cronn's Rathskeller, in the Lougheed building, First street west, and Kolb's restaurant, 227 Eighth avenue west, were the objective of the mob but were saved by the action of the military authorities in placing strong piquets around them."

148 Leishman McNeill, *Tales of the Old Town* (Calgary: The Calgary Herald, 1966), 63.

149 "Engineers Agree with Laws that Protect Public," *Calgary News-Telegram*, 18 March 1916.

150 See advertisement in the *Calgary News-Telegram*, 1 April 1916.

151 "Cabaret Gardens will be Established Under Grand Theatre. Colored Entertainers Will be Brought from Eastern City to Supply Music," *Calgary News-Telegram*, 23 August 1916.

152 Mark Miller, *Such Melodious Racket: The Lost History of Jazz in Canada, 1914–1949* (Toronto: The Mercury Press, 1997), 47. My thanks to Blane Hogue for this reference.

153 "The Plaza Formerly Cabaret Garden," *Calgary Eye Opener*, 3 March 1917.

154 Miller, *Such Melodious Racket*, 47–49. "Colored Musicians no longer at the Plaza," *The Albertan*, 22 December 1920.

155 "Orpheum Will Be Closed Until The War Is Over," *Calgary News-Telegram*, 13 October 1914; "Orpheum Re-Opens in Calgary," *The Albertan*, 14 December 1915.

156 Hugh A. Dempsey, *Calgary: Spirit of the West* (Calgary: Fifth House, 1994), 106–7.

157 "Letters from Front Tell How 'Dick' Brocklebank Met Death," *Calgary News-Telegram*, 27 July 1916.

158 "Capt. Ernest Pinkham Gives his Life for his Country," *Calgary News-Telegram*, 20 September 1916.

159 "Grand Theatre Will Show Musical Motion Pictures; Sets New Standard Here," *Calgary News-Telegram*, 12 February 1916.

160 Bertha Hart Segall, "'Bob' Edwards," *Canadian Cattlemen* (June 1950): 18, 35, 42. On page 18 she writes, "He avoided social functions but was a lover of the theatre and took in all the plays at the Grand Theatre, including the Orpheum Circuit."

161 Annette Friedman, interview with Bertha Hart Segal, May 1974, transcript, Jewish Historical Society of Southern Alberta Archives.

162 "Publicity Men are named for Victory Loan," *Calgary News-Telegram*, 1 November 1917.

163 "Plans Laid for Big Red Triangle Fund Drive Starting Next Week," *Calgary Canadian (Calgary News-Telegram)*, 4 May 1918.

164 "Red Shield Campaign for the Salvation Army War Work and Children's Home Gets Good Start," *Calgary Canadian (Calgary News-Telegram)*, 11 September 1918.

165 "Wesley Choir Changes," *Calgary News-Telegram*, 25 February 1915.

166 "Grand Theatre Assessment is Cut by $3,000," *Calgary News-Telegram*, 24 January 1916. For background on Patrick Harcourt-O'Reilly see John Blue, *Alberta Past and Present*, vol. 2 (Chicago: Pioneer Historical Publishing Co., 1924), 354–55.

167 Margaret Lydiatt, interviews, 28 September 2000; and 12 November 2000.

168 B. M. Greene (ed.), "Reginald Jeffrey Lydiatt," *Who's Who and Why, 1921* (Toronto: International Press Limited, n.d.), 523.

169 "Determined to Carry on to a Victorious End," *Calgary News-Telegram*, 4 August 1916; "R. B. Bennett to Address Meeting of Red Cross Workers," *Calgary News-Telegram*, 12 August 1916;

"Calgary Greets Premier, Mr. Bennett and Dr. Clark with Greatest Enthusiasm," *The Albertan*, 20 December 1916.

170 "Liberal Government's Leader Tells the Soldiers Why Aliens will be Allowed to Vote in Alberta Election," *Calgary News-Telegram*, 17 May 1917.

171 "Sir Robert Borden Speaks in Grand Theatre Dec. 18," *The Calgary Herald*, 6 December 1916; "Two Great Calgary Audiences Listen to the Prime Minister," *The Calgary Herald*, 19 December 1916.

172 "I Am Out to Win the War, I Have Been from the First and Will Be to the Last," *Calgary News-Telegram*, 13 December 1917.

173 "Principaled by Aberhart, inspired by Famous Five," *The Calgary Herald Neighbours, Zone 1*, 17 August 1995, p. 4.

174 Frances Coulson, "Going to the Movies," in Susie Sparks, ed., *Calgary. A Living Heritage* (Calgary: Junior League of Calgary, 1984), 83–84.

175 This line must have been taken from the press release, as the *Calgary News-Telegram* repeated it verbatim, the same day, "Movies at the Grand," *Calgary News-Telegram*, 12 February 1915.

176 "Forbes-Robertson's Performances Do No Good, Says Pastor," *The Albertan*, 15 February 1915.

177 "Threatens Arrest of Clergyman Unless He Makes an Apology," *The Calgary Herald*, 17 July 1915; "Roman Catholic Church Does Not Approve Action," *The Calgary Herald*, 24 July 1915; "Grace Church Men Support Pastor in fighting Charge," *The Calgary Herald*, 26 July 1915.

178 "'Birth of a Nation': Thrilling Production, Touching and Full of Human Interest, Reproduced on Elaborate Scale," *The Calgary Herald*, 14 December 1915.

179 "'Birth of a Nation' Seat Sale will be Open at Grand Today," *The Calgary Herald*, 21 October 1916; "Birth of a Nation," *The Calgary Herald*, 6 December 1916.

180 Advertisement for "The Birth of a Nation," "D. W. Griffith's 8th Wonder of the World," *The Calgary Herald*, 8 June 1918.

181 "Eminent Actor in Photoplay at the Grand," *The Calgary Herald*, 22 June 1918; "Forbes-Robertson at the Grand," *The Calgary Herald*, 26 June 1918.

182 See J. P. Dickin McGinnis, "A City Faces an Epidemic," *Alberta History* 24, no. 4 (Autumn 1976): 1–11. Her comments on the epidemic, a quarter of a century after the publication of her article, appear in "Pale Horse/Pale History? Revisiting Calgary's Experience of the Spanish Influenza, 1918–19," in *Harm's Way: Disasters in Western Canada*, eds. Anthony Rasporich and Max Foran (Calgary: University of Calgary Press, 2004), 41–45.

183 Clinton Ford quoted in "Retiring Chief Justice pledges Public Service," *Edmonton Journal*, 1 March 1961.

184 "Calgarians in Celebration of Huns' Surrender," *The Calgary Herald*, 11 November 1918; "Hanging the Kaiser by Day and Burning Him by Night at Calgary Celebration," *The Calgary Herald*, 12 November 1918.

185 The story of the San Carlo Opera Company is told in Fortune T. Gallo, *Lucky Rooster: The Autobiography of an Impresario* (New York: Exposition Press, 1967).

186 P. L. Newcombe, "Presentation of 'Madame Butterfly' is Acclaimed Finest of San Carlo Company," *The Albertan*, 25 January 1919.

187 McGinnis, "A City Faces an Epidemic," 1. Forty three individuals died of the "Spanish flu" in 1919.

188 "Influenza Epidemic Ended in City Twenty Years Ago After Striking Many Down," *The Calgary Herald*, 25 November 1938.

189 This information appears in *Program, Grand Opera Festival*, 23, 24 and 25 January 1919, p.17, Non-Circulating Pamphlet, Local History Room, W. R. Castell Central Library, Calgary.

190 Margaret Lydiatt, interview, 11 February 2001; Grace Lydiatt Shaw, interview, 11 February 2001. Grace Lydiatt Shaw, introduction to *Stratford Under Cover: Memories on Tape* (Toronto: N.C. Press, 1977).

191 For a good summary of the opera see Mary Ellis Peltz and Robert Lawrence, *The Metropolitan Opera Guide* (New York: The Modern Library, 1939), 404–10. Far more useful to me was actually seeing

the opera when it played at the Jubilee Auditorium in early spring 2001. Particularly helpful were the program notes in Calgary Opera, *Season Program, 2000–2001,* 22–25. A flyer for the Royal Albert Hall production of "Madame Butterfly" (London, England, 20 February to 2 March 2003) contained several short incisive comments about the opera.

192 Grace Lydiatt Shaw, e-mail to author, 7 October 2004. I am greatly indebted to her for her comments on my first draft of this chapter. She wrote them eighty-five years after her performance as "Trouble" on the stage of the Grand.

193 The opera began that evening at 8:15. Peltz and Lawrence, *The Metropolitan Opera Guide,* 405–9, state that Act One takes forty seven minutes, Act Two forty six minutes and Act Three thirty one minutes. With perhaps two fifteen or twenty minute intermissions added in, 11 o'clock seems a reasonable estimate.

194 Grace Lydiatt Shaw, interviews, 28 September 2000, and 11 February 2001; Margaret Lydiatt, interview, 11 February 2001.

195 P. L. Newcombe, "Presentation of 'Madame Butterfly' is acclaimed Finest of San Carlo Company," *The Albertan,* 25 January 1919.

196 "Former Head of Orpheum Theatre Dies," *Vancouver Sun,* 8 November 1927. "Honored for his Services. Sir James Lougheed," *Calgary News-Telegram,* 3 June 1916.

197 James A. Lougheed to R. J. Lydiatt, dated Calgary, 18 July 1923. The original copy of the letter is in the possession of Jeff Lydiatt, son of R. Jeff Lydiatt.

Notes to Chapter 9

1 Leonard D. Nesbitt, *Tides in the West* (Saskatoon: Modern Press, 1962), 393.

2 "Farmer Members-Elect Unanimous in Support of Man from Westlock," *The Calgary Herald,* 27 July 1921.

3 For a superb account of their rise to political power see Brad Rennie, *The Rise of Agrarian Democracy: The United Farmers and Farm Women of Alberta, 1909–1921* (Toronto: University of Toronto Press, 2000).

4 Ibid., 53.

5 Ibid., 224.

6 Wilfrid Eggleston, *While I Still Remember: A Personal Record* (Toronto: Ryerson, 1968), 172.

7 Nesbitt, *Tides in the West,* 388–89.

8 Ibid., 387.

9 Leonard Nesbitt, "Henry Wise Wood: Philosopher, Logician, Leader and Friend," p. 1, Henry Wise Wood Fonds, Glenbow Archives.

10 Interview with Leonard D. Nesbitt quoted in W. L. Morton, "The Social Philosophy of Henry Wise Wood, The Canadian Agrarian Leader," *Agricultural History* 22 (1948): 116.

11 Rennie, *The Rise of Agrarian Democracy,* 11.

12 Morton, "The Social Philosophy of Henry Wise Wood," 123.

13 William Kirby Rolph, *Henry Wise Wood of Alberta* (Toronto: University of Toronto Press, 1950), 14. This is the best source of biographical information on Henry Wise Wood.

14 Henry Wise Wood quoted in Nicholas North, "That Man from Carstairs," *MacLean's* (1 February 1922): 43.

15 Rennie, *The Rise of Agrarian Democracy,* 37.

16 Gerald Friesen, *Citizens and Nation: An Essay on History, Communication, and Canada* (Toronto: University of Toronto Press, 2000), 151.

17 *Grain Growers' Guide* (14 January 1914). My thanks to Brad Rennie for this information.

18 *Henderson's Calgary* directories, 1917–1921.

19 Rolph, *Henry Wise Wood of Alberta,* 17.

20 Bert Huffman, "Henry Wise Wood, Leader of Farmers' Silent Revolution," *Western Farmer of Weekly Albertan,* 24 March 1927, clipping in the Norman Smith Fonds, file 184, Glenbow Archives. My thanks to Brad Rennie for this reference.

21 Grant MacEwan, "Man from Missouri: Henry Wise Wood" in *Fifty Mighty Men* (Saskatoon: Modern Press, 1958), 61. Henry Wise Wood's friend Lew Hutchinson told this story to Grant MacEwan.

22 Humphrey M. Parlby, "Dr. Irene Parlby," in *Gleanings After Pioneers and Progress,* ed. Beatrice G. Parlby (Alix, Alberta: Alix-Clive Historical Club, 1974), 197.

23 Humphrey M. Parlby, "Walter C. H. Parlby," in *Gleanings After Pioneers and Progress,* 199.

24 Beatrice Parlby, "Memories of Manadon," in *Gleanings After Pioneers and Progress,* 85.

25 Barbara Villy Cormack, "Mary Irene Parlby," *Edmonton Journal,* 2 September 1930.

26 Lois Hollingsworth and Jean Kendrick (granddaughters of Henry Wise Wood), interview with author, Calgary, 18 June 2002.

27 Lois Hollingsworth, interview with Brad Rennie, 25 June 2001. See also the advertisement for the Buffalo Café in the program for the play, "This Thing Called Love," Grand Theatre, Week Commencing Monday, 22 January 1934. My thanks to Brad Rennie for allowing me to see his notes on Henry Wise Wood.

28 Rolph, *Henry Wise Wood of Alberta,* 5.

29 Ibid., 5, 9.

30 Nesbitt, *Tides in the West,* 397.

31 Barbara Villy Cormack, *Perennials and Politics: The Life Story of Hon. Irene Parlby, LL.D.* (Sherwood Park, Alberta: Professional Printing Ltd., 1968), 66.

32 "Both Sections of U.F.A. Convention Honor Mrs. Parlby," *The Calgary Herald,* 24 January 1920.

33 H. W. Wood to Mrs. Irene Parlby, dated Calgary, 28 April 1930, Irene Parlby Papers, Red Deer Archives, Red Deer, Alberta.

34 Franklin L. Foster, *John E. Brownlee: A Biography* (Lloydminister, Alberta: Foster Learning Inc., 1996), 314.

35 "Wheat Pool Anniversary on Tuesday," *The Calgary Herald,* 30 October 1929; Nesbitt, *Tides in the West,* 60.

36 "Honoured for his Services," *Calgary News-Telegram,* 3 June 1916.

37 Rennie, *The Rise of Agrarian Democracy,* 194.

38 *Grain Growers' Guide* quoted in J. Castell Hopkins, *The Canadian Annual Review for 1919* (Toronto: The Canadian Annual Review, 1920), 160.

39 Foster, *John E. Brownlee,* 71.

40 Rev. Bill Sayers, interview with author, 7 May 2003. Rev. Sayers of Knox United Church in Calgary conducted the funeral service for John Brownlee. After her husband's internment in Edmonton, Florence Brownlee gave these three books to Rev. Sayers. The quote is taken from Francis Greenwood Peabody, *Sunday Evenings in the College Chapel* (Boston and New York: Houghton Mifflin Company, 1911), 48. The other two volumes are: *Mornings in the College Chapel. First Series* (Boston and New York: Houghton Mifflin Company, 1896) and *Mornings in the College Chapel. Second Series* (Boston and New York, Houghton Mifflin Company, 1907). Rev. Sayers has donated all three volumes to the Glenbow Library.

41 Foster, *John E. Brownlee,* 74.

42 Ibid., 65, 108.

43 Ibid., 65, 122.

44 Ibid., 202.

45 Chester A. Bloom, "Western Canadian Premiers: Premier Brownlee of Alberta," *Winnipeg Tribune,* 24 September 1927.

46 Foster, *John E. Brownlee,* 222.

47 For a good overview of the case see Patrick Brode, "*MacMillan* v. *Brownlee,*" in *Courted and Abandoned: Seduction in Canadian Law* (Toronto: University of Toronto Press, 2002), 149–73.

48 Ibid., 225.

49 Ibid., 260.

50 Irene Parlby quoted in "Nearly 70 Years of Alberta," *The Western Producer* (Calgary), 20 May 1965, C5.

51 Hollingsworth and Kendrick, interview, 18 June 2002.

52 C. I. Richie, "Brownlee Coming Here for U.G.G.," *The Calgary Herald,* 27 February 1942. John E. Brownlee, interviewed by Una

Maclean, recorded 28 March to 12 May 1961, tape accession no. RCT-14-1, Glenbow Archives.

53 Franklin Lloyd Foster, "John Edward Brownlee: A Biography" (Ph. D. diss., Queen's University, 1981), 634.

54 Foster, *John E. Brownlee*, 309.

55 Franklin Lloyd Foster, "John E. Brownlee," in *Alberta Premiers of the Twentieth Century*, ed. Bradford J. Rennie (Regina: Canadian Plains Research Centre, 2004), 97.

56 "New Features at Bible Conferences in Grand Theatre," *The Calgary Herald*, 4 March 1922, p. 25.

57 David R. Elliott, *Aberhart: Outpourings and Replies* (Calgary: Alberta Records Publication Board, 1991), 23.

58 David R. Elliott and Iris Miller, *Bible Bill: A Biography of William Aberhart* (Edmonton: Reidmore Books, 1987), 64.

59 Ibid., 73.

60 Amelia Turner was the advertising manager for the *UFA*, the publication of the United Farmers of Alberta; see the listing under her name in the *Henderson's Calgary Directory*, 1932.

61 Patricia Roome, "Alberta Socialist: Amelia Turner," in *Citymakers Calgarians After the Frontier* (Calgary: Chinook Country Chapter, Historical Society of Alberta, 1987), 239.

62 Ibid., 237.

63 For details on the group see Meir Serfaty, "The Unity Movement in Alberta," *Alberta Historical Review* 21, no. 2 (Spring 1973): 1–7.

64 Paul I. Farnalls, Correspondence, 1938–1941, M6281, file 33, Glenbow Archives. From their surviving correspondence it appears that they had an office in the building in 1939/1940. The *Henderson's Calgary Directory*, 1939.

Notes to Chapter 10

1 Tom King, "Senate Leaders are very English. Sir James Lougheed Has Appearance and Accent—Senator Bostick Real Thing." *Toronto Star Weekly*, 27 May 1921, p. 10. Actually, as the senator was born on 1 September 1854, he was sixty six and not sixty seven at the time of this article.

2 Desmond Morton and Glenn Wright, *Winning the Second Battle: Canadian Veterans and the Return to Civilian Life, 1915–1930* (Toronto: University of Toronto Press, 1987), 84, 135.

3 Norman Anick, "Agenda Paper on Sir James Alexander Lougheed, 1991," Historic Sites and Monuments Board of Canada, ref. no. 1991–41, 121

4 Morton and Wright, *Winning the Second Battle*, ix, 202.

5 Anick, "Agenda Paper," 126. The *Ottawa Journal* termed his work as minister of the Department of Soldiers' Civil Re-establishment "outstanding"; see "Senate Loses Notable Figure Sir J. Lougheed," *Ottawa Journal*, 2 November 1925.

6 This inscription is below the portrait that now hangs in the Senate Reading Room. For years the painting hung over the fireplace in the Senate Smoking Room. The room was refurbished in 1992-93, and has been renamed by the Senate the "Room of the Francophonie" in honour of the Francophone Union. The portrait now hangs in the Senate Reading Room. Audrey Dubé, "The Room of the Francophonie," a report prepared by the Office of the Curator, House of Commons. The dates in office of Senators Wark and Dessaulles appear in J. K. Johnson, ed., *The Canadian Directory of Parliament 1867–1967* (Ottawa: Public Archives of Canada, 1968), 592, 164.

7 "Sir James Lougheed Will Act as the Prime Minister during Meighen's Absence," *The Calgary Herald*, 2 November 1920; Roger Graham, *And Fortune Fled*, vol. 2 of *Arthur Meighen* (Toronto: Clarke, Irwin & Company, 1963), 105.

8 Grant MacEwan, *Eye Opener Bob: The Story of Bob Edwards* (Edmonton: The Institute of Applied Art, Ltd., 1957), 203.

9 Ibid., 187.

10 C. B., "Sir James Lougheed—Gentleman," *Ottawa Citizen*, 2 November 1925.

11 My thanks to David Hall, University of Alberta Department of History, for his notes on the senator's participation in senate debates from his entry to the senate in 1889 to his death in 1925. The Bulgarian Peace Treaty was debated in April of 1920; the British Columbia Indian Lands Bill between May and June of 1920; Canada's proposed membership in the Court of International Justice was debated in May of 1921.

12 Richard J. Diubaldo, *Stefansson and the Canadian Arctic* (Montreal: McGill-Queen's University Press, 1978), 168–69. William R. Hunt, *Stef: A Biography of Vilhjalmur Stefansson, Canadian Arctic Explorer* (Vancouver: University of British Columbia Press, 1986), 166–69, 135. Copy of letter from Alan Rayburn, Executive Secretary, Geographical Names Board of Canada to P. Gail Armstrong, 4 September 1975. I thank Nancy Pierce of the Secretariat, Geographical Names Board of Canada, for her letter and enclosures of 27 January 2004.

13 Senate, *Debates*, 12 January 1926, p. 6. This documents the tribute by William Benjamin Ross in memory of Sir James Lougheed.

14 Emil Longue Beau [no doubt a pseudonym], "The Confessional: Imaginary Talks with Big Men about Themselves. No. 45—Sir James Lougheed," *Toronto Star Weekly*, 30 July 1921, p. 10.

15 "Tribute of a Loving Cup to Friend of the Blind," *Toronto Telegram*, 8 January 1919, p. 18. "Loving Cup to Pearson: Great Public Testimonial," *The Globe*, 8 January 1919, p. 8. Marjorie Wilkins Campbell, "Keep the Home Fires Burning," in *No Compromise: The Story of Colonel Baker and the CNIB* (Toronto: McClelland and Stewart Limited, 1965), 48-49. 48–49. I thank Jennifer Cook Bobrovitz for pointing out the reference to Sir James in *No Compromise*.

16 "The Spotlight: Sir James Lougheed," *Toronto Star*, 21 June 1923, p. 6.

17 Gunter Gad and Deryck Holdsworth, "Corporate Capitalism and the Emergence of the High-Rise Office Building" in *People Places Patterns Processes, Geographical Perspectives on the Canadian Past*, ed. Graeme Wynn (Toronto: Copp Clark Pitman, 1990), 251–52.

18 Several of Sir James's letters to Emerson Coatsworth have survived. I am grateful to Jamie Coatsworth for showing them to me.

19 The Spotlight [pseud.], "Judge Coatsworth," *Toronto Star*, 15 September 1923.

20 "Emerson Coatsworth," *The Canadian Who's Who*, vol. 2, *1936-37*, ed. Sir Charles G.D. Roberts and Arthur Leonard Tunnell (Toronto: Trans-Canada Press, 1937), 211.

21 The Spotlight [pseud.], "Sir James Lougheed," *Toronto Star*, 21 June 1923.

22 A. B. Watt, "New Empire Theatre Setting for Decade of Productions," *Edmonton Journal*, 30 September 1949.

23 See the company's letterhead in the correspondence in the Edward W. M. Flock Papers, file 1.B5088, University of Western Ontario Archives.

24 Patrick B. O'Neill, "The British Canadian Theatrical Organization Society and the Trans-Canada Theatre Society," *Journal of Canadian Studies* 15, no. 1 (Spring 1980): 62–63.

25 "Canadian Company to Present Tyrone Power in Important Revival," *The Calgary Herald*, 2 February 1920.

26 Advertisement for Chu Chin Chow, *The Albertan*, 30 October 1920; "Gorgeous Exhibition of Crafts of Modern Theater on Huge Scale," *The Albertan*, 2 November 1920.

27 Advertisement for "The Wanderer," *The Albertan*, 9 December 1920.

28 *Henderson's Calgary* directories, 1921 and 1922.

29 "The Late Sir James Lougheed, K.C.M.G.," *Saturday Night*, 14 November 1925.

30 James H. Gray, *Talk to My Lawyer! Great Stories of Southern Alberta's Bar and Bench* (Edmonton: Hurtig, 1987), 31

31 Ibid., 33.

32 James Gray, *R. B. Bennett: The Calgary Years* (Toronto: University of Toronto Press, 1991), 137–38.

33 *Henderson's Calgary* directories, 1920 to 1924. His name does not appear as a tenant in the Lougheed Building, but under "Edmund

Taylor" it states that he lived in the Lougheed's penthouse from 1920 to 1922.

34 "Calgary Oil Co. Has Serious Fire Loss," *Saturday Night*, 6 November 1920.

35 Meeting, Directors of Calgary Petroleum Products Ltd., 20 November 1920, reprinted in *William Stewart Herron: Father of the Petroleum Industry in Alberta*, ed. David H. Breen (Calgary: Alberta Records Publication Board, Historical Society of Alberta, 1984), 61–62.

36 Gray, *R. B. Bennett*, 225–26.

37 Breen, *William Stewart Herron*, xxxiii. A. W. Rasporich, "Oil and Gas in Western Canada, 1900–1980," vol. 70, *Canada's Visual History* (Ottawa: National Museum of Man, 1984), 4.

38 Gray, *R. B. Bennett*, 252.

39 *Henderson's Calgary* directories, 1914 to 1936.

40 Obituary, "James Hunter," *The Calgary Herald*, 22 June 1959, p. 21. My warmest thanks to Lindsay Moir of the Glenbow Library for locating this obituary; it started my search for Jim Hunter's descendants. George Werdon, telephone interview with author, 9 June 2002. Letter, Grant Luck to Ron Campbell, dated Fort St. James, B.C., 1 July 2002. Margaret Moore, telephone interview with author, 13 June 2002. Muriel Hunter Bell, telephone interviews, 25 July 2002 and 1 August 2002. Muriel Hunter Bell, email to author, "Memories of James Hunter. Notes," 29 July 2002. Many thanks to Muriel's grandson, Andrew Simpson (then thirteen years old) who helped with preparing and forwarding this email. See also entries for James Hunter, carpenter; and Alfred Shackleford, engineer, in *Henderson's Calgary* directories, 1926, 1929, 1937 and 1945.

41 Frederick Griffin, *Variety Show: Twenty Years of Watching the News Parade* (Toronto: Macmillan, 1936), 57.

42 For two full accounts of the reception see "Prince Entertained at Delightful Tea Hour Reception at Home of Sir James and Lady Lougheed," *The Albertan*, 15 September 1919, and "Garden Party for Prince Attended by Old Timers. Group of Some of Calgary's Prettiest Girls Also Included Among the Guests—Crowds Greet Prince at Entrance of Lougheed Home," *The Calgary Herald*, 15 September 1919.

43 For details on the dinner see "Prince Guest of Two Local Clubs," *The Albertan*, 15 September 1919; and "Ranchmen's Club Luncheon Proves Brilliant Event," *The Calgary Herald*, 15 September 1919.

44 *Henderson's Calgary* directories, 1913–1921.

45 Ronald Allison and Sarah Riddell, eds. *The Royal Encyclopedia* (London: Macmillan, 1991), 551, 576. My thanks to Miss Pamela Clark, Registrar, the Royal Collection Trust, Windsor Castle, for these references.

46 For a good summary of his political career see "Mr. Dudley Ward Dies in Canada: Liberal M.P. for Southampton for Sixteen Years," *Southern Daily Echo*, 13 November 1946. *The Albertan* mentions he was the Liberal whip; see "Rt. Hon. Dudley Ward Beloved in West, Dead," *The Albertan*, 13 November 1946. For some other references see the Frederick Guest Papers, "William Dudley Ward's work in the Liberal Whip Office," BL 37/3/16, LG F/7/2/32, F/30/3/7, the House of Lords Record Office, London, England.

47 "Mr. William Dudley Ward," *The London Times*, 19 January 1906.

48 "Rt. Hon. Dudley Ward Beloved in West, Dead," *The Albertan*, 13 November 1946.

49 William Dudley Ward to Winston Churchill, dated Knockespock, Clatt, Kennethmont, S.O., Aberdeenshire, Scotland, 10 September 1908, Winston Churchill Papers, CHAR 1/75, Churchill College, Cambridge.

50 "Mr. Dudley Ward, M.P., and Miss Birkin," *The London Times*, 10 July 1913.

51 "Ward Block Remodelled. Renovated Ward Block Makes Fine Addition to City," *The Calgary Herald*, 11 May 1919.

52 "Officers, Members, Constitution and Rules at The Ranchmen's Club of the City of Calgary, 1917, amended to the 12th June, 1917," p. 22. My thanks to Pat McCann, General Manager of the Ranchmen's Club, for showing me this document.

53 Colonel Henderson to the Duke of Devonshire, dated Empress Hotel, Victoria, 24 September 1919, RG 7, G 23, volume 7, file 4, no. 29, National Archives of Canada. My thanks to Simon Evans for this reference. Heather Maki helped me to locate Colonel Henderson's obituary, "Lieut.-Colonel Henderson," *London Times*, 2 November 1922.

54 George Coutts, "Presidents of the Ranchmen's Club, 1891–1953," in *The Ranchmen's Club: A Slight Historical Sketch, 1891–1952* (n.p., n.d.), 27.

55 "George Peet Dies Thursday," *The Albertan*, 4 December 1953. Tyler Trafford, *Toole Peet, 1897–1997: An Enduring Partnership* (Calgary: Toole Peet Company, 1997), 2–4, 32–33.

56 C. W. Mowers, "Two Distinguished Pioneers: Mr. Toole and Mr. Peet of Calgary," *Western Business and Industry* 21, 8: 48.

57 Claude Smith, interview with Grace Lydiatt Shaw, 25 April 1964, Lethbridge, Alberta; tape number 62844, Grace Lydiatt Shaw Collection, National Archives of Canada.

58 Trafford, *Toole Peet*, 4.

59 Edward to Alick Newton, dated New York City, 15 April 1954, reproduced in Tyler Trafford, *Toole Peet 1897–1997. An Enduring Partnership*, 36. The original letter is now at the Ranchmen's Club. My thanks to Pat McCann for showing it to me, 7 June 2001.

60 "Ranchmen's Club Founder. Death of Bob Newbolt Closes a Western Era," *The Calgary Herald*, 29 June 1956. Ken Liddell, "Furrows & Foothills," The Calgary Herald, 9 April 1955.

61 My thanks to Lorraine Lounsberry of the Glenbow Museum for showing me the shirt and its acquisition file, 7 June 2001.

62 "Joseph H. "7 U" Brown, One of Last Alberta Pioneer Ranchers, Dies," *The Calgary Herald*, 23 November 1936.

63 "George Abram Walker," vol. 7, *The Canadian Who's Who, 1955–1957* (Toronto: International Press Ltd., 1952), 1101.

64 The Glenbow Archives has a small collection of his papers.

65 Alfred Shaughnessy, ed., *Sarah: The Letters and Diaries of a Courtier's Wife, 1906–1936* (London: Peter Owen, 1989), 15; Simon Evans, *Prince Charming Goes West: The Story of the E.P. Ranch* (Calgary: University of Calgary Press, 1993), 15.

66 For the location of his suite see "Fair Weather is Forecast for Prince's Visit to Calgary; Arrangements are Complete," *The Albertan*, 13 September 1919, p. 1.

67 Edward, Prince of Wales, to Freda, dated C.P.R. Hotel, Banff, 18 September 1919, *Letters from a Prince: Edward, Prince of Wales to Mrs. Freda Dudley Ward, March 1918-January 1921*, ed. Rupert Godfrey (London: Little, Brown and Company, 1998), 190.

68 Edward, Prince of Wales, to Freda, dated C.P.R. Hotel, Calgary, 15 September 1919, in Godfrey, ed. *Letters from a Prince*, 188; the quote reproduces exactly his spelling, "vewy," and his reference to the "Ranchman's Club" instead of "Ranchmen's Club".

69 The original copy of the prince's "Reply to the Address of the City of Calgary" is in the City of Calgary Archives. This is the text I follow in the above quotation. *The Albertan* prints essentially the same remarks but there are one or two minor differences; see, "Splendid Alien Population Must be Assimilated, Urges Prince of Wales in Address," *The Albertan*, 16 September 1919, p. 1.

70 Brig. General H. F. McDonald, Commanding Military District No. 13, to the Theatre Managers of Calgary, dated Calgary, 28 August 1919. I thank Bill Joiner, White Rock, B.C., son of Maynard Joiner, for showing me this letter in his possession.

71 Program, "The Armouries, Calgary, Alberta, Military Ball Given in Honour of H.R.H. The Prince of Wales by Brig. Gen. H. F. McDonald, C.M.G., D.S.O., and Officers of M.D. No.13, September Sixteenth Nineteen Hundred and Nineteen." I thank Bill Joiner, White Rock, B.C. for showing me this.

72 "Scene of Bewildering Beauty and Brilliancy Greets Prince at Military Ball in His Honour," *The Albertan*, 17 September 1919. The program lists the selections for each dance.

73 Ibid.

74 Ibid.

75 "Stefansson Will Lecture Tonight," *The Albertan*, 18 September 1919. "Canada Best Climate Because it is Conducive to Work, Not to Loafing, Says Stefansson," *The Albertan*, 19 September 1919.

76 Senate, *Debates*, 24 June 1922. 574.

77 Bradford James Rennie, *The Rise of Agrarian Democracy: The United Farmers and Farm Women of Alberta, 1909–1921* (Toronto: University of Toronto Press, 2000), 205.

78 James Lougheed quoted in Emil Longue Beau, "Sir James Lougheed," *Toronto Star Weekly*, 30 July 1921, p. 10.

79 Rennie, *The Rise of Agrarian Democracy*, 199.

80 "Election Results to be Announced at Grand Theatre," *The Calgary Herald*, 3 December 1921.

81 J. M. Beck, *Pendulum of Power, Canada's Federal Elections* (Scarborough, Ontario: Prentice-Hall, 1968), 158.

82 John F. Leslie, "Assimilation, Integration or Termination? The Development of Canadian Indian Policy, 1943–1963" (Ph.D. diss., Carleton University, 1999), 63–64.

83 Letter, Duncan Campbell Scott, Deputy Superintendent General of Indian Affairs, to Sir James Lougheed, Superintendent General of Indian Affairs, dated Ottawa, 1 December 1920, in *Annual Report of the Department of Indian Affairs for the year ended March 31, 1920*, p. 8.

84 Hugh A. Dempsey notes that he fought in 1912 for the First Nations to participate in the Calgary Stampede of 1912 in full costume, to take part in the parades, perform their dances, and set up their tipis at the Stampede grounds. Hugh A. Dempsey, "The Stampede of Native Culture," *Glenbow* (Summer 1992): 6.

85 For background on Long Lance see Donald B. Smith, *Chief Buffalo Child Long Lance: The Glorious Impostor* 2nd ed. (Red Deer, Alberta: Red Deer Press, 1999).

86 Fran Fraser, interview with Hugh Dann, 11 May 1962, tape RCT-12-1, Glenbow Archives. Hugh Dann, interviews with author, Calgary, 21 February 1975 and 18 December 1979.

87 Bill Epstein, interview with author, New York City, 3 June 1999. Bill Epstein's father ran the Grand Cigar Store and Tea Rooms in the Lougheed Building in the 1930s. I am assuming that the photo was placed in the lobby earlier, in the 1920s.

88 George Stanley, letter to author, dated Sackville, New Brunswick, 18 February 1976.

89 "Gen. H. F. McDonald Plans to Retire," *The Calgary Herald*, 9 October 1917, p. 7. His mother was Ellen Inkster, member of an old Hudson's Bay Company family; see Georgina Binnie-Clarke, *Wheat and Women* (1914; reprint, Toronto: University of Toronto Press, 1979), 68.

90 A Lawyer [pseud.], "'Larry Clarke'," *The Calgary Herald*, 13 October 1930. "Saw Entire Legal History of West, Laurence J. Clarke Dies in City," *The Calgary Herald* 1 January 1941. His Native ancestry would be on his mother's side, Jane Bell. She was also member of a long-established Hudson's Bay Company family.

91 "Trans-Canada Theatres in Liquidation," *Saturday Night Magazine*, 11 August 1923.

92 James B. Hartman, "On Stage: Theatre and Theatres in Early Winnipeg," *Manitoba History* 43: 23. O'Neill, "The British Canadian Theatrical Organization Society," 63–64.

93 *Calgary Eye Opener*, 25 November 1922

94 "Fishing Excursion Promised Chaplin on Visit to this City," *The Calgary Herald*, 11 May 1923. Charlie Chaplin apparently did accept; "unless something exceedingly exceptional prevented his coming" he would attend— if a fishing trip was added on. Something "exceptional" apparently did arise as he did not attend the 1923 Stampede.

95 James A. Lougheed to R. J. Lydiatt, 18 July 1923. The letter is now in the possession of Jeff Lydiatt, Jr.

96 Edmund Taylor to R. H. Lydiatt, 18 July 1923. The letter is now in the possession of Jeff Lydiatt, Jr.

97 "Former Head of Orpheum Theatre Dies," *Vancouver Sun*, 8 November 1927. Doug McCallum, *Vancouver's Orpheum: The Life of a Theatre* (Vancouver: Social Planning Department, City of Vancouver, 1984).

98 Grace Lydiatt Shaw, "Orpheum Memories," a letter written to the *Vancouver Sun*, 20 October 2002; email copy sent to author, 29 October 2002.

99 The Ranchmen's Club, "Officers, Members, Constitution and Rules at The Ranchmen's Club (Calgary: The Club, 1922), 17, quoted in Jennifer Cook Bobrovitz, compiler, "James Alexander and Isabella Lougheed: A Chronological History," 19 August 2003, Lougheed House Collection.

100 James A. Lougheed to "Mr. Cross," dated Ottawa, 31 March 1921, A. E. Cross Papers, M154, file 908, Glenbow Archives.

101 Max Foran, *Trails & Trials: Markets and Land Use in the Alberta Beef Cattle Industry, 1881–1948* (Calgary: University of Calgary Press, 2003), 128–30.

102 Gray, *R. B. Bennett*, 219.

103 R. B. Bennett quoted in Gray, *R. B. Bennett*, 219.

104 Copy, Statement of Claim between James Lougheed and R. B. Bennett et al., Supreme Court of Alberta, p. 30, Accession Number: 90-029, The Legal Archives Society of Alberta.

105 Gray, *R. B. Bennett*, 220. Gray states the Southam Building was at the corner of 7th Avenue and 2nd Street S.W., but the correct address is the corner of 7th Avenue and 1st Street S.W.

106 Ibid., 220.

107 Ibid., 221, 225.

108 Ibid., 221–22.

109 Belle Lougheed quoted in "Lady Lougheed Says Paris is Place of Cheer and Charm," *The Albertan*, 3 May 1923, p. 6. I thank Jennifer Cook Bobrovitz for this wonderful reference.

110 *Henderson's Calgary Directory*, 1924.

111 "Senator Lougheed of Canada is Dead," *New York Times*, 3 November 1925.

112 "$1,500,000 Estate Left By Sir James Lougheed," *Alberta Farmer*, 15 May 1926.

113 Senate. *Debates*, 1 February 1923. 15. My thanks to David Hall for this reference and for allowing me to see all his notes on Sir James's senate interventions, 1889 to 1925.

114 "The Income Tax," *Globe and Mail*, 25 July 1995.

115 The Wanderer [pseud.], "I First Saw," *Winnipeg Evening Tribune*, 16 June 1923; reprinted in abridged form in *The Albertan*, 19 June 1923.

116 J. S. Brownlee to Janet Wright, dated Calgary, 8 November 1994, Lougheed House Collection.

117 "Sir James Lougheed Plans South Trip to Recuperate," *The Calgary Herald*, 26 January 1925; Senate, *Debates*, 5 May 1925. On this date he was welcomed back to the senate; I thank David Hall for this reference.

118 The Mace [pseud.], "Turning A New Leaf," *Saturday Night*, 30 May 1925, p. 4.

119 Robert A. Mackay, *The Unreformed Senate of Canada* (Ottawa: McClelland and Stewart, 1963), 74–77.

120 Letter, Arthur Meighen to James A. Lougheed, 13 July 1925, Meighen Papers, 37744-45, National Archives of Canada. My thanks to David Hall for this reference.

121 My thanks to David Hall for this observation, taken from an early draft, November 1999, of our forthcoming joint article on Sir James, for volume fifteen of the *Dictionary of Canadian Biography*.

122 "Senate Loses Notable Figure Sir J. Lougheed," *Ottawa Journal*, 2 November 1925.

123 For a photograph taken at the grave-side at Union Cemetery with Sam indicated see *The Calgary Herald*, 10 November 1925, front page. The information about his residence in Winnipeg appears in Jopie Loughead, Viviane McClelland and Frank Ellis Wickson, compilers, "James Loughead of Britannia," 3rd up-date, October 1998, p. 40. They have found him listed as a CPR carpenter in the Winnipeg directories, 1901–1908. He is almost certainly the "Samuel Lougheed" who died in Vancouver in 1943; see "Samuel Lougheed," *Vancouver Sun*, 22 January 1943. The British Columbia

Archives Death Registry Index indicates that his age was "86," James Lougheed's brother Sam Lougheed was born 13 December 1856, so this fits exactly. The obituary in the *Vancouver Sun* indicates the information is to be reprinted in the Vancouver, Toronto, Winnipeg and Calgary papers—centres in which Sam Lougheed, James's brother, once lived.

124 "Thousands Pay Last Respects to Memory of Senator Lougheed," *The Calgary Herald*, 10 November 1925.

125 Letter, Nellie McClung to Mackenzie King, 4 November 1925, W. L. King Papers, 100683, National Archives of Canada. I thank David Hall for this reference.

126 "Sir James Lougheed's Memory Honored at the Grand Monday," *The Calgary Herald*, 3 November 1925.

127 Rosemary Wood, "Shaw Play Production Captivates," *The Calgary Herald*, 2 April 1957. Rosemary Wood, "Othello Players Impress," *The Calgary Herald*, 3 April 1957.

128 "Announcing 'Twist' Dance Contest for Non-Professional Couples at the Grand Theatre, Jan. 15 to 20. Each Evening at 9 P.M. Sponsored by CHCT-TV; Cash and Other Valuable Prizes; Daily Eliminations Mon. to Fri. Eve; Finals Saturday," *The Calgary Herald*, 12 January 1962, p. 31.

129 Tom Primrose, "Old Grand Theatre Holds Memories. Many World-Famous Performers Trod the Boards in Early Days," *Calgary Herald Magazine*, 17 September 1960. I thank Gordon Lydiatt for this reference.

Notes to Chapter 11

1 "Personal," *The Calgary Herald*, 7 December 1929.

2 L. W. B. [Leonard Brockington], "The Philanderer," *The Calgary Herald*, 9 December 1929.

3 The address today is 803, 15th Avenue S.W., but was originally numbered 1501 7th Street West, the designation "S.W." later replaced "West". My thanks to Al McDowell of Al McDowell and Associates for allowing me to tour the house, 21 and 23 July 2004.

4 The original owner, Harry Blaylock, took out the building permit in August 1907. See City of Calgary Building Permit Register, City of Calgary Archives. Two photos of the living room appear in Harry Hume, compiler, *Prosperous Calgary* (Calgary: *Calgary Daily Herald*, 1908).

5 Dr. Michael McMordie, President of the Calgary Civic Trust.

6 "Weather," *The Calgary Herald*, 6 December 1929; "The Weather," *The Albertan*, 6 December 1929. The day was described as moderately cold, with the high at 52 degrees Fahrenheit, and minimum at 8 degrees Fahrenheit. The sun set at 4:26 p.m. that day, the tea party commenced at 4:30 p.m.

7 A. Ermatinger Fraser, "A Cup of Tea with Nellie McClung," *Canadian Bookman* 10 (August 1928): 236.

8 Ibid., 236–37.

9 Ibid., 237.

10 "Personal," *The Calgary Herald*, 7 December 1929.

11 "Calgary Girl Wins Fame in Old London," *The Albertan*, 11 September 1926. "Young Canadian Actress Visiting Home after London State Successes," *The Albertan*, 9 August 1927. See also the handwritten notes by Irene Gardiner in her "Scrapbook of first date to wedding day for Dr. Harold Price and Irene Elizabeth Gardiner," Price Family Papers, M9000, Glenbow Archives.

12 "Popular London Actress in City on Wedding Trip," *The Calgary Herald*, 6 December 1929.

13 *Glasgow Citizen* quoted in "Calgary Born Actress Scores Success Abroad," *Edmonton Journal*, 7 January 1929.

14 Advertisement in the *Calgary Eye Opener*, 5 February 1921. It played from 7 to 9 February 1921. "Slim Thinks the 'Highwood Trail' was a Crackerjack," *The Calgary Herald*, 8 February 1921. Florence's family was one of the earliest to arrive in Calgary. Her father, Felix McHugh, built the first building on the new townsite, a log building on the northwestern corner of Stephen (8th) Avenue and Osler (1st) Street East, in February 1884. Archibald Oswald MacRae, "Felix

Alexander McHugh," *History of the Province of Alberta* (n.p. The Western Canada History Co., 1912), 548.

15 Maurice Colbourne, *The Real Bernard Shaw* (Toronto: J. M. Dent, 1930), 11.

16 Lord Gardiner, "Mr. Maurice Colbourne," *London Times*, 27 September 1965, p. 12.

17 His biography, *The Real Bernard Shaw,* was published early in 1930 in Toronto.

18 Maurice Colbourne quoted in "Press Club Hears Maurice Colbourne," *The Calgary Herald*, 17 October 1928.

19 Colbourne, *Shaw*, 18.

20 "Press Club Hears Maurice Colbourne," *The Calgary Herald*, 17 October 1928.

21 Wilf Bennett, "Bill accepted a book from Charlie. And the rest is History," *Vancouver Sun*, 9 March 1981.

22 David R. Elliott and Iris Miller, *Bible Bill* (Edmonton: Reidmore Books, 1987), 106–7.

23 Donna Lohnes and Barbara Nicholson, *Alexander Calhoun* (Calgary: Calgary Public Library, 1987), 22.

24 Elaine M. Catley, "Poetry and Prose from Alberta," *The Canadian Doctor* (September 1943): 23. Elaine M. Catley Papers, file 14, Special Collections, Dana Porter Library, University of Waterloo.

25 Candace Savage, *Our Nell: A Scrapbook Biography of Nellie L. McClung* (1979; reprint, Halifax: Biographies, 1985), 166.

26 "Ordination Stand 'Small' Declares Nellie M'Clung," *Toronto Star Weekly*, 24 November 1928.

27 Randi R. Warne, *Literature as Pulpit. The Christian Social Activism of Nellie L. McClung* (Waterloo: Wilfrid Laurier University Press, 1993), 12.

28 "Two addresses for Prohibition Sunday. Rev. F.W. Patterson and Mrs. Nellie McClung Addressed Audiences in the Grand," *The Calgary Herald*, 12 July 1915; "Politics Are an Uncut Book for Women, Nellie McClung Declares," *Calgary News-Telegram*, 17 May 1917; "Premier in Favour of Letting Men of Alien Enemy Birth have Vote," *The Calgary Herald*, 17 May 1917; "Mrs. McClung made Strong Address at People's Forum," *The Albertan*, 4 June 1917.

29 *Calgary Eye Opener*, 14 August 1920.

30 Maxine Pearson, telephone interview with the author, 14 May 2001. Wes's height was recalled for me by his granddaughter, Maxine Pearson. Mark McClung, the youngest son, mentioned his mother's height in a 1975 interview: Mark McClung, "At Guelph: Portrait of My Mother," taped interview, typed transcript, p. 2, Nellie McClung Conference, University of Guelph, 1975.

31 The Manufacturers Life Insurance Company, *The Agents' News-Letter* (April 1923): 89; (February 1928): 44; (August 1929): 360. "M'Clung Hangs up Sixth Win in 'Spiel Play,'" *The Calgary Herald*, 21 January 1928. Ken Penley has written a short sketch of Wes McClung, "Mr. McClung also a leading Calgarian," *Kerby News for Seniors* (January 1990).

32 McClung, "At Guelph," 4.

33 Mary Hallett and Marilyn Davis, *Firing the Heather. The Life and Times of Nellie McClung* (Saskatoon: Fifth House, 1993): 87.

34 Nellie McClung to Mr. F. C. Beech, dated Glenboro, Manitoba, 25 September 1946, McClung Papers, British Columbia Archives, quoted in Savage, *Our Nell*, 37.

35 McClung, "At Guelph," 5.

36 Nellie McClung, quoted in R. E. Knowles, "Radio a Factor in Saving Empire—Nellie McClung: Canadian Women Writer Says Radio Fosters Inter-Canadian Harmony; Husband is Critic," *Toronto Star*, 12 March 1937, p. 1, 3.

37 McClung, "At Guelph," 7.

38 "Petition to Privy Council Outlined by Mrs. McClung," *The Albertan*, 6 December 1929.

39 The Manufacturers, *The Agents' News Letter* (August 1929): 360.

40 The Manufacturers, "The Bunch," *The Agents' News Letter* (November 1914): 95.

41 Letter reprinted in The Manufacturers, *The Agents' News Letter* (March 1927): 96–97.

42 The Manufacturers, *The Agents' News Letter* (January 1924), (August 1929), (September 1929). The addresses of each branch and the name of the manager appear in each issue.

43 See footnote 227, Clarence Karr, *Authors and Audiences: Popular Canadian Fiction in the Early Twentieth Century* (Montreal & Kingston: McGill-Queen's University Press, 2000), 227.

44 Nellie McClung, *The Complete Autobiography: Clearing in the West and the Stream Runs Fast* (Peterborough, Ontario: Broadview Press, 2003), 291. For quote see Savage, *Our Nell*, 32.

45 "Miss Macphail tells of Western Trip," *The Dundalk Herald*, December 1931. A copy of this newspaper from Dundalk, near Flesherton, Ontario, is in Nellie McClung Papers, MSS 10, box 39, British Columbia Provincial Archives.

46 Mark McClung, interviewed by Florence Bird, "The Incredible Nellie McClung," broadcast on CBC radio's *Between Ourselves*, 6 June 1975, quoted in Savage, *Our Nell*, 44.

47 Henry Klassen, "The Role of Life Insurance Companies in the Economic Growth of Early Alberta," unpublished paper presented at Project 2005: an Alberta History Workshop, 12–14 May 1988, Red Deer College, Red Deer, 2–5.

48 The Manufacturers Life Insurance Co., *The First Sixty Years 1887–1947. A History of the Manufacturers Life Insurance Company* (Toronto: The Manufacturers Life Insurance Co., 1947), 136.

49 John Counsell, *Counsell's Opinion* (London: Barrie and Rockliff, 1963), 30.

50 I am extremely grateful to Dr Allan Andrews, Professor of Theatre (retired), Dalhousie University, for sharing with me the draft of a talk he gave to the Association of Canadian Theatre Research in the early 1990s on Maurice Colbourne's tours of Canada in 1928-29, and 1929-30.

51 Fraser, "A Cup of Tea with Nellie McClung." 237.

52 Irene Gardiner, "Calgary's Light Opera Company Gives Its Best; Presents 'A Country Girl'," *The Calgary Herald*, 27 December 1929. This clipping appears in her scrapbook of her own articles, Irene Gardiner Price Papers, M9000, Glenbow Archives.

53 There was no regular vaudeville at the Grand after January 1930.

54 Maurice Colbourne, "The Wounds of the Theatre," *Saturday Night*, 2 August 1930, p. 2.

55 10-12 April 1930; 28–30 December 1931; 1–3 December 1932; 3–4 February 1933. As both *The Calgary Herald* and *The Albertan* are (for the most part) available on the World Wide Web, anyone interested in reading actual reviews can check the website of the "Our Future, Our Past. The Alberta Heritage Digitization Project" at: <http://www.ourfutureourpast.ca/newspapr/>.

56 L. W. B., "Barry Jackson Players Present Fine Performance," *The Calgary Herald*, 29 December 1931.

57 Bill Joiner (Maynard's son), interview with author, White Rock, B.C., 24 November 2000.

58 Eileen Johnson, "Today Maynard Joiner Retires, After 40-Plus Years in Show Business," Vancouver Sun, May 2, 1969. Harry Hutchcroft (words) and Maynard Joiner (music), "C-A-L-G-A-R-Y and that Spells 'Calgary'," (Calgary: The Rotary Club of Calgary, 1926), Glenbow Library. Tom Kayser, "Songwriters' struggles left tuneless town," *The Calgary Herald*, 6 June 1985.

59 "Notes prepared for the sixtieth wedding anniversary of Maynard and Lottie Joiner, December 20th 1977,' shown me by Bill Joiner.

60 "Maynard Joiner Popular as Theatrical Manager," *The Calgary Herald*, 30 December 1919.

61 "Thefts from Grand Theatre Dressing Rooms Reported," *Calgary News-Telegram*, 19 February 1912.

62 "Automobile is Stolen," *Calgary News-Telegram*, 5 October 1915.

63 "Boys Suspected of Robbery at Theatre,' *The Calgary Herald*, 7 September 1927.

64 "Attempt to Rob Theatre," *The Calgary Herald*, 25 July 1928.

65 For a good summary of the tasks involved see "Managing Theatre is Hard Task," *The Calgary Herald*, 21 September 1929.

66 Claude Smith, interview with Grace Lydiatt Shaw, Lethbridge, 25 April 1964. Grace Lydiatt Shaw Interviews, tape number 62844, National Archives of Canada.

67 Zilpha Maxwell, "Harry Lee (Singing Projectionist)," in T. J. Butler, comp., *Alberta Projectionists, Local 302, IATSE*, printed report, no date, p. 87. I thank both Myrna Riches and David Marshall for bringing this valuable history to my attention.

68 "Grand Players Are Celebrating Six Months Here," *The Calgary Herald*, 10 February 1923. Walter, "--And So, Good-Bye," *The Calgary Herald*, 28 April 1923. Edith Elliott and Royal Kemp, interviews with Grace Lydiatt Shaw, Hollywood, 18 and 19 April 1962, Sound Archives, National Archives of Canada.

69 Sir John Martin-Harvey, *Autobiography* (London: Sampson Low, Marston & Co., 1933), 497.

70 14–16 February and 7–9 March 1921; 10–19 April 1924; 4–6 and 24–27 March 1926; 13–15 February and 12–14 March 1928; 14–15 and 21–23 November 1929.

71 Zilpha Maxwell, "Bob Maxwell," in Butler, comp. "Projectionists," 103.

72 Martin-Harvey, *Autobiography*, 437.

73 Ibid., 437–38.

74 E. M. Catley. "Calgary 35 Years Ago…," *North Hill News*, 2 September 1955. "'No Cowtown' Claims Author," *The Calgary Herald*, 5 January 1967.

75 Details of the play and Arliss's role as "Old Heythorp" appear in George Arliss," *George Arliss by Himself* (London: John Murray, 1940), 62–71.

76 Elaine Catley, Diary for 1926, Elaine Catley Papers, Glenbow Archives.

77 Denis Salter, "Julia Arthur (1869–1950)," in *The Oxford Companion to Canadian Theatre*, ed. Eugene Benson and L. W. Conolly (Toronto: Oxford University Press, 1989), 31.

78 "Big Motion Picture Corporation to Take Over Grand Theatre," *The Calgary Herald*, 2 September 1926.

79 "'Talkies' Will Open on Monday," *The Calgary Herald*, 2 November 1928.

80 "Talking Pictures and R-K-O Vaudeville Revolutionize Theatre World During 1929," *The Calgary Herald*, 18 January 1930.

81 "Story of Christian Martyrs Told in Picture 'Quo Vadis.' Spectacular Scenes of Roman History and Realistic Orgies of Nobles Told in Film at Grand Theatre," *The Albertan*, 18 June 1920.

82 See, for instance, the advertisement for "The Sea Beast," *The Calgary Herald*, 24 February 1926, p. 6.

83 "Amusements: Grand," *The Calgary Herald*, 30 November 1927. "First 'Talkie' was Calgary Sensation," *The Calgary Herald*, 13 July 1943.

84 "M. S. Joiner Gets Big Appointment," *The Calgary Herald*, 6 August 1929. Doug McCallum, *Vancouver's Orpheum: The Life of a Theatre* (Vancouver: Social Planning Department, City of Vancouver, 1984), 24. Famous Players would itself buy the Orpheum two years later.

85 "Little Theatres of Four Cities Plan Dramatic Festival," *The Calgary Herald*, 25 January 1930. When the amateur dramatic clubs in Calgary meet in early December 1932 to form the Calgary Theatre Guild, *The Calgary Herald* reported, "in recognition of her many years of service in fostering dramatic endeavour in Calgary, Mrs. W. Roland Winter was made a life member of the guild." See "Theatre Guild Formed Friday," *The Calgary Herald*, 7 December 1932.

86 20–21 February 1931; 22–24 February 1934; 7–9 February 1935; 6–8 February 1936; 17–19 March 1937.

87 "National Dramatic Festival Suggested by His Excellency," *The Calgary Herald*, 17 September 1932. Stuart Townshend, my wife Nancy Townshend's father, acted as stage-manager for both plays.

88 Lord Bessborough's article appeared in the *London Morning Post* in 1936 and is quoted in Betty Lee, *Love and Whisky: The Story of the Dominion Drama Festival* (Toronto: McClelland and Stewart, 1973), 84.

89 "National Dramatic Festival Suggested by His Excellency."

90 Herbert Whittaker, "Dominion Drama Festival," in *The Oxford Companion to Canadian Theatre*, ed. By Eugene Benson and L. W. Conolly (Toronto: Oxford University Press, 1989), 144–45.

91 Lou Laverie, "Musical Instruments Scarce in Early Days," *The Calgary Herald*, 3 September 1955.

92 No complete collection of Calgary Symphony Orchestra programs exists. The respective dates of the programs I have photocopies of are: 20 February, 30 April, 26 November 1930; 28 January, 18 March, 18 May, 26 November (I do not have the program for this concert) 1931; 9 February, 4 April, 28 November 1932; 6 March, 24 April, 6 December 1933; 19 February, 2 April 1934; 18 February, 8 April, 25 November 1935; 4 February, 30 March 1936; 11 January, 22 February, 5 April 1937; 21 February, 25 March, 14 November 1938; 23 January, 27 February 1939.

93 "Our guest artist, Jean de Rimanoczy," Program, *Calgary Symphony Orchestra, Clayton Hare, Conductor, Monday, December 3, 1951, Grand Theatre, Calgary, Alberta*, p. 14. Harcourt Smith, interviews with the author, Edmonton, 10 November 2000, 26 February 2001. Mr. Smith was a cellist with the orchestra in the 1930s. I am also most grateful for his letter of 25 March 2001. "Music is a Pleasure. More Financial Aid Urged for Symphony," *The Calgary Herald*, 4 December 1951.

94 Corolyn Cox, "Russian Violinist in Calgary Heads a Junior Symphony," *Saturday Night*, 15 August 1944.

95 Eva Reid, "Eavesdrop with Eva," *The Albertan*, 16 August 1974.

96 Will Robson, interview with the author, Ottawa, 5 October 2000. Mr. Robson was a violinist with the orchestra in the 1930s.

97 John Murray Gibbon, *Canadian Mosaic. The Making of a Northern Nation* (Toronto: McClelland & Stewart, 1938). See also Stuart Henderson's "'While there is still time…': J. Murray Gibbon and the Spectacle of Difference in Three CPR Folk Festivals, 1928–1931," *Journal of Canadian Studies*, 31, no.1 (Winter 2005), 139–74.

98 "Folkdance, Folksong, and Handicraft Festival," *The Calgary Herald*, 15 March 1930, p. 15.

99 Norma Marr, comp., "The Files: May 16, 1930," *The Calgary Herald*, 16 May 1998.

100 "'Red Square' is Soon to Vanish as Land is Sold," *The Calgary Herald*, 3 June 1932. David Bright, "The State, the Unemployed, and the Communist Party in Calgary, 1930-5," *Canadian Historical Review* 78, no. 4 (December 1997): 549-551.

101 Larry Winter quoted in Elise A. Corbet and Lorne G. Simpson, "Calgary's Mount Royal. A Garden Suburb," a paper prepared for The Planning and Building Department and The Heritage Advisory Board of The City of Calgary, September 1994, p. 24.

102 Hugh A. Dempsey, "The Terrible Floods," in *Calgary: Spirit of the West* (Calgary: Fifth House, 1994), 71-74. Terrible floods included those of 1897, 1902, 1915, 1929 and 1932. The completion of the Glenmore Dam in 1933 has helped to control the Elbow. While the possibility of the Bow flooding its banks still remains, the Bearspaw Dam, completed west of the city in 1954, has lessened the danger of spring and summer flooding.

103 John Sealey, email to the author, 28 February 2003.

104 This was his third visit since the end of the war, and his fourth to Calgary, as he first performed at the Grand from 28 February to 1 March 1918.

105 At the risk of missing several omissions, here is a tentative list: 26–28 February 1920; 17–19 January 1921, 21–23 February 1921; 6–7 and 14–15 February and 13–15 March 1922; 15–16 February 1923; 1–14 February 1925; 10–13 February, 10–13 March and 20–23 December 1926; 10–12 January, 9–12 February and 9–12 March 1927; 30 January–1 February, 6–8 February and 5–7 March 1928; 21–23 January, 25–27 February 1929.

106 Earlier productions included: "Dorothy" (9–11 April 1928); "Florodora" (8–10 April 1929); "A Country Girl" (26–28 December 1929).

107 Annie Glen Broder, "Fine Presentation of 'Hiawatha' is Largely Attended," *The Calgary Herald*, 9 April 1931. "A Saturday Symposium," *The Calgary Herald*, 21 March 1931.

108 "Throngs of Calgarians Hear Salvation Army Head," *The Calgary Herald*, 29 September 1929.

109 Pat Baldwin, letter to the author, September 1999. "Alice Murdoch's School of Dance in Clever Revue," The Calgary Herald, 28 May 1934, p. 15. "Patricia Talerico Baldwin," in *Harvest of Memories: Grand Trunk—West Hillhurst—Calgary* (Calgary: Friesen Printers, 1987), 124–25.

110 Alice Murdoch annual music and dance reviews were frequently held at the Grand; for example: 5 May 1930; 30 May 1931; 21 May 1932; 29 April 1933; 26 May 1934; 27 March 1935; 16 May 1936. For a short sketch of Alice Murdoch Adams see Brian Brennan, *Building a Province: 60 Alberta Lives* (Calgary: Fifth House, 2000), 109–11.

111 "'Stepping Up' Hits High Average for Local Production," *The Calgary Herald*, 8 March 1935.

112 Mabelle Kheong Lee, interview with the author, Calgary, 16 May 2003.

113 "Louis Kheong Returns to His Ancestors," *The Calgary Herald*, 27 April 1939.

114 "Passion Play Tremendously Impressive," *The Calgary Herald*, 3 March 1933.

115 Letter, Bella Hardisty to "Aunt Eliza" [Eliza McDougall Hardisty], dated Fort Providence, 10 December 1877, Richard Hardisty Papers, Series XXIII-3, M 5908/1572, Glenbow Archives.

116 The location is indicated in Alberta Supreme Court, Shepard, J. "Grand Theatre Limited v. Royal Trust Company et al/ Royal Trust Company et al v. Leach et al," *Western Weekly Reports* 2 (1937): 617.

117 "Alberta Women We Should Know. Lady Lougheed," *The Calgary Herald*, 17 December 1932.

118 She is listed in all the symphony programs until her death, 13 March 1936.

119 The file on the William Lucas Hardisty Estate, McLaws Fonds, fond 37, file 173, folder 1, Legal Archives Society of Alberta, is most revealing on this question. The letter from Lougheed, McLaws, Sinclair, & Redman to Lougheed & Taylor Limited, 20 February 1929, provides a good description. For an assessment of the value of the assets four years later see McLaws, Redman, Lougheed & Cairns to The Royal Trust Company, 23 February 1933, McLaws Fonds, fond 37, file 54, The Legal Archives Society of Alberta.

120 David G. Wood, *The Lougheed Legacy* (Toronto: Key Porter Books, 1985), 28. Peter Lougheed, interview with the author, Calgary, 24 July 2000.

121 David Finch and Gordon Jaremko, *Fields of Fire: An Illustrated History of Canadian Petroleum* (Calgary: Detselig, 1994), 56.

122 R. B. Bennett to J. A. Hutchison, dated Ottawa, 2 May 1936, R. B. Bennett Papers, M.G. 26, K, volume 956, p. 605401, National Archives of Canada.

123 "Huge Crowd Gathers to Hear Crooks," *The Calgary Herald*, 10 October 1935.

124 "Grand Crowded for Recital by Moscow Choir," *The Calgary Herald*, 18 November 1935.

125 "Many to pay Last Respects to Lady Lougheed on Monday," *The Albertan*, 14 March 1936.

126 "Associated with Theatres Fifteen Years in Canada," *The Calgary Herald*, 19 July 1923. Grace Shaw, "How Many Please?" in *Calgary: A Living Tradition*, ed. Susie Sparks (Calgary: Junior League of Calgary, 1984), 129.

127 Christine Mayhew Logan, interview with the author, Calgary, 19 March 2004. Mrs Logan worked part-time for Annie Wilson in the 1930s and early 1940s. She called Mrs. Wilson Calgary's "ticket-master" of her day. She is listed as the "Business Executive" of the Calgary Symphony Orchestra in the symphony's programs from late 1930 to early 1935. Her husband John acted as the Symphony's secretary-treasurer, and was on the board from 1934 to 1937.

128 "Stampede Ticket Sale on July 4," *The Calgary Herald*, 22 June 1927.

129 Harcourt Smith, letter to the author, dated Edmonton, 25 March 2001. She also appeared in Grand Theatre programs of the early 1930s, where she is listed in the Second Violin section. Annie Wilson served on the board of the Symphony from late 1930 to early 1935,

and her husband from late 1934 to late 1937. The symphony programs contain this information.

130 "John Wilson called by Death," *The Calgary Herald*, 12 August 1938. His title appears in the *Henderson's Calgary* directories, 1919–1930. Harcourt (Toby) Smith, interview with the author, Edmonton, 10 November 2000. My thanks to Mr. Smith for informing me that Mrs. Wilson's husband ran the Board of Trade.

131 "Calgary Board of Trade," in *Calgary: The City of Calgary Year Book*, compiled by S. Arnold Wark (Calgary: n. p., 1919); see page one of the section on the Board of Trade.

132 *Southern Alberta Pioneers Minute Books*, 1 and 2, Southern Alberta Pioneers Archives, Pioneer Memorial Building, Calgary.

133 "Delightful Affair Marks Anniversary of Literary Club," *The Calgary Herald*, 10 February 1926.

134 "St. Andrew's Club Elects Officers," *The Calgary Herald*, 5 February 1927.

135 *Henderson's Calgary* directories for 1926 and 1927; see also "Corn Show Will Open Thursday for Inspection," *The Calgary Herald*, 12 November 1927.

136 "Board of Trade: It's Place in the Community, 1891–1929," *The Calgary Herald*, 7 December 1929, magazine section.

137 "Bright Luncheon Board of Trade," *The Calgary Herald*, 18 November 1926, p. 11.

138 "Personal," *The Calgary Herald*, 9 April 1927.

139 Jack Peach, *The First Hundred Years: The History of the Calgary Chamber of Commerce* (Calgary: Calgary Chamber of Commerce, 1990), 53.

140 McClung, "At Guelph," 16. Mark McClung recalls his mother regarded him as a "brilliant, first class man."

141 "City Officials Highly Praised by Mrs. M'Clung. Farewell Message Given by Authoress at Board of Trade Gathering," *The Albertan*, 7 July 1932.

142 M. B. Venini Byrne, "Mrs. Frederick Wilson," in *From Buffalo to Cross: A History of the Roman Catholic Diocese in Calgary* (Calgary: Calgary Archives and Publishers, 1973), 523.

143 "The Road to Success," *The Albertan*, 25 April 1961.

144 Rose Wilkinson quoted in Shirley McNeill, "Personality of the Week: Mrs. Rose Wilkinson," *The Calgary Herald*, 29 May 1954.

145 The information on individual apartments and business locations in the Lougheed Building all comes from the *Henderson's Calgary* directories.

146 "George A. Walker," *Who's Who in Canada, 1951–52* (Toronto: International Press Ltd., 1952), 417.

147 James H. Gray, *R. B. Bennett. The Calgary Years* (Toronto: University of Toronto Press, 1991), 236. "James G. Edgar Dies at Clinic." *The Calgary Herald*, 27 April 1937. He lived in the Lougheed Building from 1917 to 1928.

148 He was a tenant in the building from 1917 to 1927; for a brief biographical sketch see "Fred Johnston, Pioneer Calgary Sportsman, Dies," *The Calgary Herald*, 16 April 1937.

149 Leonard D. Nesbitt, "Wheat Pool Began 32 years Ago," *The Calgary Herald*, 3 September 1955.

150 William Kirby Rolph, *Henry Wise Wood* (Toronto: University of Toronto Press, 1950), 207.

151 *Henderson's Calgary* directories. The office was located at 202 in 1936 and 1937; it moved to office 508 in 1938. The Canadian Wheat Board left the Lougheed the following year.

152 Phillip J. Lewis, "The Alberta Wheat Pool, 1923–1935" (master's thesis, University of Calgary, 1980), 172.

153 Ibid., 271.

154 Sheilagh S. Jameson, in collaboration with Nola B. Erickson, *Chautauqua in Canada* (Calgary: Glenbow Museum, 1987), 1–2.

155 Muriel Preston Manning, telephone interview with the author, 1 October 2004.

156 Lougheed Building, list of tenants with dates of leases, prepared in 1931, McLaws, Redman, Lougheed, and Cairns Fonds, fond 37, file 209, folder 2, The Legal Archives Society of Alberta.

157 Lois Hollingsworth (granddaughter of Henry Wise Wood), interview with the author, Calgary, 18 June 2002.

158 Michael Bliss, *Northern Enterprise: Five Centuries of Canadian Business* (Toronto: McClelland and Stewart, 1987), 419. On the company's history see: "Cement for a Growing Industry," *Alberta Business Journal* 1, no. 2 (July-August 1967): 88–89.

159 Advertisement for the Birnie Lumber and Coal Co., Ltd, in *Calgary The City of Calgary Year Book*, compiled by S. Arnold Wark, 114.

160 Bailiff's Sale, 2 May 1932, McLaws, Redman, Lougheed and Cairns Fonds, fond 37, file 209, folder 4, The Legal Archives Society of Alberta.

161 C. L. Dingman, "A. W. Dingman, the Soapman turned Wildcatter," *Western Oil Producer*, 9 July 1955.

162 "S. O. Tregillus Leaves the U.F.A. for New Position," *Calgary News-Telegram*, 5 April 1918.

163 The *Henderson's Calgary* directories indicate that he farmed in 1926 and 1928.

164 Margaret (Peggy) Tregillus Raymond (daughter of Sydney Tregillus), telephone interview with the author, 29 November 2001; Margaret (Peggy) Tregillus Raymond, interview with author, Calgary, 10 January 2003.

165 "Joan Tregillis: Playing in 'The Highwood Trail,'" *The Calgary Herald*, 1 February 1921. "Principals in Musical Comedy Are Announced," *The Calgary Herald*, 16 March 1929. "Joan Tregillus. 'San Toy' to Open Thursday," *The Calgary Herald*, 21 April 1930.

166 "Funeral Next Saturday for Outstanding Figure in Music and City Life," *The Calgary Herald*, 4 August 1938.

167 Mr. Justice Marshall M. Porter, interview with Lynn Huhtala, 11 December 1978, RCT-245, Glenbow Archives. The formal transfer of responsibilities as chief legal counsel for the Alberta Wheat Pool seems to have been in 1928; see Fred Kennedy, "Mr. Justice M.M. Porter Honored by Wheat Pool. Board Counsel for 26 Years Presented with '25 Years Service' Watch by Pool Chairman," *The Calgary Herald*, 30 November 1954. He probably began work with the Wheat Pool earlier; see his obituary, *The Western Producer*, 29 August 1985; it states he began working there in 1925.

168 For biographical information on Bill Hall see "Former City Barrister Dies at West Coast," *The Calgary Herald*, 26 April 1956.

169 "Chronological History of the Law Firm of MacKimmie Matthews, Covering the Period from Inception to November 15th, 1984," 1–7, accession no. 99-016, The Legal Archives Society of Alberta.

170 Louis J. Dublin, *A Family of Thirty Million: The Story of the Metropolitan Life Insurance Company* (New York: Metropolitan Life Insurance Co., 1943), 285. *The Metropolitan Life: A Study in Business Growth* (New York: The Viking Press, 1947), 202.

171 Allan Hustak, *Peter Lougheed* (Toronto: McClelland and Stewart, 1979), 26.

172 R. D. Colquette, *The First Fifty Years: A History of United Grain Growers Limited* (Winnipeg: The Public Press, 1957), 160.

173 Ibid., 172.

174 Graham S. Lowe, "Class, Job and Gender in the Canadian Office," in *Canadian Working Class History. Selected Readings*, Laurel Sefton MacDowell and Ian Radforth, eds. (Toronto: Canadian Scholars' Press Inc., 2000), 382–90.

175 I have made this compilation from the employee list included in the booklet, *A Fortieth Anniversary Presentation. U.G.G. Personalities and their Related Responsibilities of United Grain Grower Limited and Subsidiaries, 1906–1946*, M 8094, file 33, Herriot Papers, Glenbow Archives. In 1946 approximately 70 of the 150 employees were female.

176 James H. Gray, *The Roar of the Twenties* (Toronto: Macmillan, 1975), 187.

177 Ethel Garnett, telephone interview with the author, 21 November 2004.

178 Dave Green, "Profile: James Cleave," *The Calgary Herald Magazine*, 19 April 1958.

179 Tony Cashman, *A History of Motoring in Alberta*, 3rd ed. (Edmonton: Alberta Motor Association, 1990), 15.

180 Tony Cashman, *A Picture History of Alberta* (Edmonton: Hurtig, 1979), 49.

181 "Will Lie Down Town Boulevards," *The Calgary Herald*, 6 August 1929.

182 "Calgary Has Imposing Business Section," *The Calgary Herald*, 18 November 1933.

Notes to Chapter 12

1 For examples see advertisements for the film in *The Calgary Herald*, 29 January 1942, and *The Albertan*, 30 January 1942.

2 An eleven-day period, but only nine days of showings as theatres were closed on Sundays, 1 and 8 February 1942.

3 For this impression of the developments of the war from 1939 to early 1942 see Clifton Daniel, ed., *Chronicles of the 20th Century* (Mt. Kisco, New York: Chronicle Publications, 1987).

4 Ian Christie, *Arrows of Desire: The Films of Michael Powell and Emeric Pressburger* (London: Waterstone, 1985), 53. The best secondary account of the film is chapter two in Anthony Aldgate and Jeffery Richards, *Britain Can Take It: The British Cinema in the Second World War* (Oxford: Basil Blackwell, 1986), 21–43. My thanks to Ben Fullalove for his help with my research on *49th Parallel*.

5 Edward M. Bredin, "Calgary's Silver Tongued City Solicitor: Leonard W. Brockington C.M.G. LL.D. D.C.L. K.C.," in *City Makers. Calgarians After The Frontier*, ed. Max Foran and Sheilagh S. Jameson (Calgary: The Historical Society of Alberta, Chinook Country Chapter, 1987), 91–93. "Funeral Monday for Leonard W. Brockington, 78," *Globe and Mail*, 17 September 1966. Eric Hutton, "… and now, a few words from Leonard Brockington," *Maclean's,* 15 April 1953, 65.

6 "Funeral Monday for Leonard W. Brockington, 78."

7 Michael Powell, *A Life in Movies. An Autobiography* (New York: Alfred A. Knopf, 1987), 349.

8 Grant MacEwan has written his biography but makes no mention of the film in *Tatanga Mani* (Edmonton: Hurtig, 1969).

9 James Montagnes, "Camera Over Canada," *New York Times*, 15 September 1940.

10 Vincent Massey, *What's Past Is Prologue* (Toronto: Macmillan, 1963), 343–44. Powell, *A Life in Movies*, 386.

11 The film is available on video through Vintage Classic (code: 1000650) and Studio Masters (code: RNK 435043). For a full summary see Scott Salwolke, *The Films of Michael Powell and the Archers* (Lanham, MD.: The Scarecrow Press, 1997), 75–83.

12 Salwolke, *The Films of Michael Powell*, 74. "Filming 'The Invaders'," *New York Times*, 15 March 1942. The film was released as *The Invaders* in the United States.

13 Christie, *Arrows of Desire*, 55.

14 "Pick Calgary 'Movie Actors'," *The Albertan*, 13 July 1940. Peggy McGannon Annan, telephone interview with the author, 2 November 2002. Maureen Tighe Colborne, interview with the author, Calgary, 3 April 2003. Mrs. Annan and Mrs. Colborne were both "Calgary extras." I am extremely grateful to another "Calgary extra," Doran Moore (and to his brother Ken Moore for putting me in touch with his brother), for his memories of the filming, as well as for the wonderful still of the "Calgary extras" at the Banff Railway Station, mid-July 1940. Bonar Bain's assistance was also invaluable. In Edmonton, on 28 May 2004, we watched the Banff section of the film together, one of the most enjoyable moments in all of my research for *Calgary's Grand Story*.

15 Peter, the Hutterite leader in *49th Parallel*, quoted in Aldgate and Richards, *Britain Can Take It*, 36.

16 Bonar Bain quoted in David Bly, "War propaganda film a blast for Alberta extras," *The Calgary Herald*, 9 January 2004.

17 Art Evans, "Local Movie 'Star'," *Edmonton Journal*, 5 December 1964, newspaper clipping, Betty Mitchell Papers, M 851, file 164, Glenbow Archives; Bonar Bain, interview with the author, Edmonton, 28 May 2004. The clipping helped me find Mr. Bain.

18 "'49th Parallel' to Continue at Grand Three More Days," *The Albertan*, 6 February 1942.

19 "Jacob Bell Barron," in The Jewish Historical Society of Southern Alberta, *Land of Promise: The Jewish Experience in Southern Alberta* (Calgary: Jewish Historical Society of Alberta, 1996), 246.

20 *Dawson City* directories, 1901 and 1902. "Pioneer to Leave Dawson for Outside," *Dawson Daily News*, 13 August 1915.

21 In the Grace Lydiatt Shaw Collection, National Archives of Canada, there is a tape with J. B. Barron, which consists largely of his memories of the Yukon, recorded in Calgary, 3 July 1963. Only in early September 2004 did I discover that they only had the first half of the tape. Josh Barron, Jack Barron's grandson, located the full interview, which has been copied and is now available at the Glenbow Archives, tape RCT-950 (henceforth cited as Jack Barron Interview). For a short obituary of Jack Barron see "J.B. Barron Dies Here At Age 77," *The Calgary Herald*, 29 September 1965. In the Jack Barron Interview , J. B. Barron states that he and his brother were in the Yukon from 1903–1905, and not from 1903–1907 as stated in the obituary.

22 Bob Barron, interviews with the author, Calgary, 27 October 1998, 1 November 2001 and 15 January 2004. My best source of information on the Barron family and their involvement with the Grand are J. B. Barron's two sons, Robert H. "Bob" Barron and Richard "Dick" Barron. I spoke many times with Bob from 1998 to 2004. My discussions with Dick, who recently moved back to Calgary, have also been invaluable.

23 Bob Barron, interview with the author, Calgary, 9 June 2000.

24 "Amelia Barron," in *Land of Promise*, 246.

25 Floyd S. Chalmers, "The Story of the Allens: How a Business Miracle Came About in Canada," *Maclean's*, 15 February 1920.

26 Annie Glen Broder, "Jascha Heifetz Satisfies Soul-Hunger for Music," *The Calgary Herald*, 2 December 1924.

27 W. H. H., "Heifetz Captured Calgary at his First Appearance," *The Albertan*, 2 December 1924.

28 Jack Barron Interview.

29 Ibid.

30 Tom Keyser, "Golden Years of Theatre are Gone Forever," *The Calgary Herald*, 13 February 1990. Bob Barron, interviews with the author, Calgary, 27 October 1998 and 30 November 2001.

31 "Calgary Boasts of Brilliant Musicians At Home and Abroad," *The Albertan*, 16 April 1932.

32 "Mrs. Annie Glen Broder Praises London String Quartet, Coming to Palace," *The Calgary Herald*, 22 April 1926.

33 David R. Elliott and Iris Miller, *Bible Bill: A Biography of William Aberhart* (Edmonton: Reidmore Books, 1987), 73.

34 "$400,000 Suit Opens Battle for Palace Theatre Properties," *The Calgary Herald*, 5 January 1928. "Barrons Score First Round of Theatre Action," *The Albertan*, 10 January 1928. Jack Barron Interview.

35 "Garbovitsky to End Engagement," *The Calgary Herald*, 26 November 1927.

36 Jack Switzer, "Calgary's Jews Star as Symphonic Conductors, Musicians, Patrons, Teachers," *Discovery. The Journal of the Jewish Historical Society of Southern Alberta* 5, no. 2 (Winter 1995): 1.

37 Frances Maud Ferguson, "Revolution in Russia, Deflation in Germany, Have Given Calgary Music Lovers Their Famous Orchestra Leader," *The Calgary Herald*, 19 February 1938.

38 Lawrence Mason, "Orchestras in the West," *Toronto Globe*, 24 May 1930.

39 Annie Glen Broder, "Real Musical Round-Up At Symphony Concert," *The Calgary Herald,* 19 May 1931. See also her articles, "Symphony concert Thrills Audience," *The Calgary Herald*, 29 January 1931; "Symphony Performance is Artistic Success," *The Calgary Herald*, 27 November 1931.

40 "No symphonies This Winter," *The Calgary Herald*, 2 October 1937.

41 "Musical Instruments Scarce in Early Days," *The Calgary Herald*, 3 September 1955.

Parnham founded the Calgary Boys' Choir, now known around the world. Kerry Williamson, "30th Anniversary Event: Boys Choir Veterans Sing its Praises," *The Calgary Herald*, 5 January 2003.

146 Bill Epstein studied law, his brother medicine and his sister accounting. Bill Epstein, telephone interview with the author, 4 December 1998.

147 "Gold Medallist in Law," *The Calgary Herald*, 14 May 1935.

148 "Bill Epstein's 43-year Mission to the U.N.," *Toronto Star*, 21 May 1989, Section D. "William Epstein," *Canadian Who's Who 1998* (Toronto: University of Toronto Press, 1998), 337.

149 Dr. Stanley Smith, interview with the author, Calgary, 18 November 2002.

150 *Henderson's Calgary* directories, 1956–1957.

151 "Lougheed Funeral Scheduled for Tuesday," *The Calgary Herald*, 2 April 1951.

152 Fred Wolf, interview with the author, Calgary, 15 June 2001.

153 Ernie Hutchinson, telephone interview, 9 July 2004.

154 Blanche Upton, telephone interview with the author, 9 December 2001. She was a former volunteer and later assistant to the librarian, Christian Science Reading Room, Lougheed Building

155 Len Nesbitt, *Tides in the West* (Saskatoon: Modern Press, 1962), 141–42.

156 Parker Kent, "The Grand," *The Calgary Herald*, 10 May 1965. "Twin Theatres Phasing Out of the Grand Old Movie Palaces," *The Calgary Herald*, 27 July 1972.

157 Tom Moore, "Man About Town," *The Albertan*, 18 May 1965. For information regarding the two star dressing rooms on the north side of the stage see Dick Barron, interview with the author, Calgary, 18 May 2004.

158 J. B. Barron quoted in "Grand Theatre Severs a Link with the Past," *The Calgary Herald*, 12 May 1965.

159 "Odeon Group Buys Four City Theatres," *The Calgary Herald*, 30 June 1969.

Notes to Chapter 13

1 "University of Alberta, Calgary," 20 October 1960, file 85.45/2.1, University of Calgary Archives.

2 "W. F. Reid, Former School Trustee, Dies; Was Board Chairman For Four Years, Also Active In Getting University Branch For Calgary," *The Calgary Herald*, 31 March 1952.

3 Air photos of Calgary in the 1950s can be viewed in the Maps, Academic Data, Geographical Information Centre, University of Calgary Library.

4 Banff Trail Community Seniors, *From Prairie Grass to City Sidewalks* (Calgary: Banff Trail Seniors, 1999).

5 Gordon MacWilliams, "Calgary is 'Golfiest' City in Canada," *The Calgary Herald*, 31 May 1930. "St. Andrew's Club Elects Officers," *The Calgary Herald*, 5 February 1927.

6 Audrey Miklos, *History of St. Andrews Heights, 1953–1978* (Calgary: n.p., 1978), 1–6.

7 Doug Parnham, interview with the author, Calgary, 16 September 2002.

8 Merv Anderson, "$10 Million City Hospital Likely Close to University," *The Calgary Herald*, 3 November 1958.

9 "Will Cost $15 Million; New Calgary Hospital One of the Best on Continent," *The Albertan*, 10 September 1960.

10 See Robert M. Stamp, *Becoming a Teacher in 20th Century Calgary: A History of the Calgary Normal School and the Faculty of Education, University of Calgary* (Calgary: Detselig, 2004), 43–59.

11 Joan Van Wagner, "Calgary's 'Battle' is Won," *The Calgary Herald*, 1 November 1958. University of Calgary Physical Plant Pamphlet, "History of the Campus" (March 1992): 5.

12 Dr. Cyril Challice, interview with the author, Calgary, 27 October 1997. Dr. Challice (Professor Emeritus, University of Calgary Department of Physics) was present at the sod-turning.

13 Fred Colborne quoted in "Dream Becomes Reality," *The Albertan*, 3 November 1958.

14 "'Revue of 1922' Scores Big Hit at Initial Showing," *The Calgary Herald*, 22 February 1922.

15 "Calgary Theatre Guild Wins Commendation for Festival Presentation," *The Calgary Herald*, 7 February 1936.

16 Malcolm Taylor, "The Use of the Buildings," 28 October 1960, file 85.45/2.1, University of Calgary Archives.

17 "Ribbon-Cutting Ceremony Launches New University," *The Calgary Herald*, 29 October 1960. The shovel is now in the University of Calgary Archives along with a bag of ceremonial dirt acquired on 1 November 1958! Some name changes followed. In 1961 the University of Alberta in Calgary (UAC) became the University of Alberta, Calgary, then the University of Alberta of Calgary in 1964. Finally independence was gained in 1966, when the University of Alberta of Calgary became the University of Calgary. Robert Stamp, *Becoming a Teacher in 20th Century Calgary: A History of the Calgary Normal School and the Faculty of Education, University of Calgary* (Calgary: Detselig, 2004), 73.

18 Chief Justice Ford quoted in "Ribbon-Cutting Ceremony Launches New University," *The Calgary Herald*, 29 October 1960.

19 "Storm Fails to Dampen Opening of University," *The Albertan*, 29 October 1960.

20 Donna Balzer, "Dustbowl Days Are Over," *AlbertaViews* (January-February 2002): 44–49.

21 Joyce Doolittle, "Calgary, Cowboys, Culture and an Edifice Complex," *Canadian Theatre Review* 42 (Spring 1985): 14.

22 The text is reprinted in "Retiring Chief Justice Pledges Public Service," *Edmonton Journal*, 1 March 1961, clipping, Clinton Ford biographical file, reference A73-0026/105 (54), University of Toronto Archives.

23 See University of Calgary, *First Annual Calendar, Session 1913–14*; and the *Second Annual Calendar, Session 1914–15*, University Archives, University of Calgary.

24 *Christian Guardian* (Toronto), 24 March 1920.

25 W. A. Craick, "The University of Calgary and Social Service," *Christian Guardian*, 18 March 1914, p. 9–10.

26 Muriel M. Robertson, Professional Second Class Certificate, Alberta Department of Education, 20 December 1910; Muriel Macdonald Robertson and Dr. Charles Frederick Ward, Wedding Announcement, 19 December 1914. Both documents are in the possession of Muriel's nephew Don Sinclair.

27 "Weddings Ward-Robertson," *The Calgary Herald*, 21 December 1914.

28 Charles Frederick Ward to Clinton Ford, dated Chicago, 16 August 1915, Calgary College, accession 1999–106, 2-5-4, City of Calgary Archives.

29 Charles Frederick Ward to Clinton Ford, dated Chicago, 17 September 1915, Calgary College, accession 1999–106, 2-5-4, City of Calgary Archives.

30 "Kent Power Moves Office," *Calgary News-Telegram*, 9 December 1914. "Law Lectures to Be Given Here," *Calgary News-Telegram*, 9 October 1915. *Henderson's Calgary Directory*, 1915.

31 "W. Kent Power, 76, Dies in Edmonton," *The Albertan*, 16 October 1961. David Mittelstadt, "W. Kent Power: A Short and Biographical History of Elbow Park," manuscript report, Glenbow Library, October 2000, p. 157–158.

32 "Headed Law School in 1912: Dean of Local Lawyers Observes Anniversary," *The Calgary Herald*, 15 September 1949, p. 19. For a very complete review of Kent Power's career see Jim Senter, "Personality of the Week," *The Calgary Herald*, 16 April 1955, p. 5.

33 "W. Kent Power, 76, Dies in Edmonton," *The Albertan*, 16 October 1961.

34 "Early Calgary Minister Dies," *The Calgary Herald*, 20 November 1944.

35 He was appointed in 1961; see obituary, "A. Carson MacWilliams," *The Albertan*, 15 July 1963.

36 On Eva Reid see Jennifer Hamblin, "Eva Reid: Girl Reporter," *Alberta History* 52, no. 4 (Autumn 2004): 8-21.

37 Eva Reid, "Evesdrop with Eva," *The Albertan*, 2 November 1960.

38 Description of the S. Mack Eastman Fonds, compiled by Christopher Hives (1986), University of British Columbia Archives.

39 Margaret Ormsby, "Walter Noble Sage," *Canadian Historical Review* 45 (1964): 180.

40 J. Fraser Perry, ed., *They Gathered at the River* (Calgary: Central United Church, 1975), 450. She actually attended McMaster, not the University of Toronto as *They Gathered at the River* indicates; see "Chief Justice Ford Weds Phyllis Chapman Clarke," *The Albertan*, 23 February 1959.

41 Georgina Thomson, "Colorful Rosscarrock," *The Calgary Herald*, 31 May 1958. The brick residence was demolished in late 1957.

42 W. J. Tregillus quoted in UFA, film BR, Minutes and Reports of "Annual Convention, 1912," p. 9, Glenbow Archives.

43 "Hairdressing Still Important," *The Calgary Herald*, 28 July 1992.

44 Phyllis Chapman Clarke Ford, telephone interview with author (from her nursing home in Hawaii) 11 January 2003. She passed away at the age of 101 in December of that year. "Phyllis K. Ford, March 23, 1902-December 4, 2003," *The Calgary Herald*, 19 December 2003.

45 A list of several of the Peter Pan's customers appears in the caption to the photo, "Who Says Women Are Fickle?" *The Albertan*, 17 April 1964, p. 6. The list includes Phyllis Ford, Aileen Fish and Helen Stadelbauer; they had all been customers for twenty-five years or more.

46 Biographical sketch in the archival description of the Helen Stadelbauer Fonds, December 1997, accession No. 97.023, University of Calgary Archives.

47 "Leading Civic Affairs Worker Mrs. Frank Fish, Dies at 79," *The Calgary Herald*, 7 March 1977. "Evesdrop with Eva," *The Albertan*, 28 August 1961. Maurice Yacowar, "Letters: Could this be the Ghost of Earth Sciences?" *University of Calgary Gazette*, 11 January 1999.

48 Hilda and Marianne Doherty, interview with the author, Calgary, 11 January 2004.

49 Doug Doherty quoted in Linda Curtis, "Girl Talk," *The Albertan*, 17 April 1964.

50 Richard J. Needham, *Needham's Inferno* (Toronto: Macmillan, 1966).

51 Hilda Dougherty, interview with the author, Calgary, 6 August 2002. For examples of Needham's columns see his *Calgary Herald* articles on atomic energy (4 January 1946); traffic deaths (3 January 1947); the Canadian Senate (9 January 1947); the British economy (5 March 1948), the rearmament of Japan and West Germany (30 December 1948); racial discrimination in Washington, D.C. (4 January 1949).

52 Donn Downey, "Obituary: Richard Needham; Long-time Globe Columnist Struck Chord in Young Readers," *Globe and Mail*, 19 July 1996.

53 Richard J. Needham quoted in Brian Brennan, "Newsman Adored Calgary's Spirit," *The Calgary Herald*, 31 July 1996.

54 Marjorie Fairley, "Talented Calgary Director," *The Calgary Herald*, undated clipping, circa the early 1960s, Doug Doherty Clipping File, Glenbow Library.

55 "Lougheed Building: Calgary, Alberta, Canada," McMillan Fonds, 16A 64:34, Canadian Architectural Archives, University of Calgary Library. From the population cited for the City of Calgary at the time (264,000) and the names of the firms cited as having their offices in the Lougheed Building, this prospectus was most likely prepared in 1961 or so.

56 Millie Stanford Wills, interview with the author, Calgary, 13 August 2001. Elsie Stanford Harrold, telephone interview with the author, 14 August 2001. Their father, Walter Stanford, was one of the elevator men at the Lougheed from the World War One years until his death in 1945.

57 "Office Tour—IBM Section," *Driveway Breeze* (1 August 1957): 2. The computing department was in the basement.

58 "They Move Mountains of Mail," *UGG News* 23, no. 2 (April 1974): 7.

59 They also published his address as *The Past Half-Century: On the Occasion of Dinner Celebrating the Fiftieth Anniversary of United Grain Growers Limited, Calgary, November 1956,* Herriot Papers, M8094, file 34, Glenbow Archives

60 "Former President of Stampede Dies," *The Calgary Herald*, 26 September 1977.

61 "Three Veteran Employees Honored on Retirement," *UGG News* (January–February 1966).

62 Jim Stott, "Personality of the Week: Harry Francis is a Citizen-philosopher," *The Calgary Herald*, 9 August 1971.

63 Franklin Lloyd Foster, "John Edward Brownlee: A Biography" (Ph. D. thesis, Queen's University, 1981), 658.

64 Ethel Garnet, interview with the author, Calgary, 19 August 2002. "Miss Ethel Garnet," *UGG News* (July-August 1965).

65 Ethel Garnet, telephone interview with the author, 15 August 2002.

66 I have examined all the *UGG News* from the 1950s to late 1970s.

67 Gordon Moss, interview with the author, Red Deer, 21 November 2002.

68 Ivan Radke, interview with the author, Calgary, 31 October 2002.

69 Gordon Moss, interview with the author, 21 November 2002.

70 "Highlights, milestones, and turning point," *The WCB Communicator* 24, no. 9 (September 1993): 1.

71 All the details in this chapter on locations of tenants, and at what dates, come from the *Henderson's Calgary* directories.

72 "Highlights, milestones, and turning point," 4–5.

73 H. A. Bell, Manager, to H. M. Dagg, Supervisor, Business Development Department, Calgary 1st St. S.W. and 6th Av. Branch folder, R.G. 024/00/0004/0000/0069 A-86-31, The Bank of Nova Scotia, Toronto, Scotiabank Group Archives, Toronto (henceforth cited as Branch Folder).

74 Manager, Calgary, to the Western Supervisor, 15 December 1953, Branch Folder.

75 "Opening of Branch 1st Street West & 6th Avenue, Calgary, Alberta," authorized by the Board, 29 December 1953, Branch Folder.

76 Manager, First St. W. & Sixth Ave., to the Supervisor, Winnipeg, 3 January 1958, Branch Folder.

77 Manager, 607, 8th Ave. West, to the Supervisor, Winnipeg, 11 December 1957, Branch Folder.

78 J. V. Hunt, President, Hunt Real Estate Corporation Ltd. Realtors to Peter Lougheed, dated Calgary, 11 August 1965, MM1 16A/77.64, Canadian Architectural Archives, University of Calgary Library.

79 Allan Hustak, *Peter Lougheed* (Toronto: McClelland and Stewart, 1979), 87.

80 Peter Lougheed, interview with the author, Calgary, 24 July 2000.

81 Eva Reid, "Loyal to Tories for 69 years," *The Albertan*, 25 January 1980.

82 Ted Mills, interview with the author, Victoria, B.C., 7 September 2000.

83 Richard MacInnes, interview with the author, Calgary, 9 November 2002. Don Sinclair, interview with the author, Calgary, 17 June 2002.

84 "John Williams, Veteran City Accountant, Dies: Started Independent Practice Here In 1908," *The Calgary Herald*, 13 February 1942.

85 Lorne Roberts, interview with the author, Calgary, 12 August 2002. Harold Gibson, telephone interview with the author, 1 July 2002.

86 Art Davis, interview with the author, Calgary, 10 August 2001.

87 This is the last entry for Milne Davis in the *Henderson's Calgary* directories.

88 Dave Green, "Profile: James Cleave," *The Calgary Herald*, 12 April 1958.

89 James Cleve contributed columns to the issues from January 1945 to December 1946.

90 "Building Manager Retires," *The Albertan*, 1 October 1965.

91 Don Spicer quoted in David Bly, "Building's Importance Rests with its People," *The Calgary Herald*, 4 October 2002.

92 David Finch, "Chapter Four" in *Field Notes: The Story of the Canadian Society of Petroleum Geologists* (Calgary: Society of Petroleum Geologists, 2002). Several references to *The Face of Time* are in the papers of the Alberta Society of Petroleum Geologists, M 6442, files, 581, 590, 711, Glenbow Archives. My thanks to Brad Rennie for identifying them for me.

93 David G. Wood, *The Lougheed Legacy* (Toronto: Key Porter Books, 1985), 29.

94 Jim Adams, "Louis Desrochers, Man of 'Meritorious Service'," *Western Catholic Reporter*, 1 December 1974.

95 John Moreau and Jim Ogle, interview with the author, Calgary, 27 August 2003.

96 This biographical information is summarized from Paul Grescoe, *Flight Path: How Westjet Is Flying High In Canada's Most Turbulent Industry* (n.p.: John Wiley & Sons Canada Ltd., 2004), 19–20.

97 Harley Hotchkiss was named to the Alberta Order of Excellence, Alberta's highest honour, in 1998; see: "Flames Owner Joins Alberta Order of Excellence," *The Calgary Herald*, 23 October 1998. The geologist had earlier that year been made an officer of the Order of Canada. For over a decade this member of the Calgary Flames ownership group has served as chair of the National Hockey League board of governors. He co-chaired the Partners in Health Campaign that raised $50 million for health-related initiatives in the Calgary area. Jim Palmer was named in 1999 to the Order of Canada; see "Order of Canada," *The Calgary Herald*, 4 February 1999; and to the Alberta Order of Excellence in 2003. The prominent Calgary lawyer, before his election as Chancellor of the University of Calgary in 1985, had previously served as a director of the Bank of Canada, president and director of the Calgary Philharmonic Society and director of the Alberta Institute of Law Research and Reform; see "U. of C. names new chancellor," *The Calgary Herald*, 3 July 1986. As Chancellor, he chaired the highly successful, "Building on a Vision Campaign," which raised over $46 million for the University of Calgary between 1990 and 1993.

98 Don Martin, *King Ralph: The Political Life and Success of Ralph Klein* (Toronto: Key Porter Books, 2002), 64.

99 Max and Heather Foran, *Calgary: Canada's Frontier Metropolis* (n.p.: Windsor Publications, 1982), 256. For an excellent review of Calgary after World War Two see Robert M. Stamp, *Suburban Modern: Postwar Dreams in Calgary* (Calgary: Touchwood Editions Ltd., 2004).

100 Jennifer Bobrovitz, "Burns Manor Lost out to Colonel Belcher," *The Calgary Herald*, 1 February 1998.

101 Jennifer Bobrovitz, "Mansion Home to 'Czar of the West'," *The Calgary Herald*, 9 November 1997.

102 Jim Stott, "Historic City Landmark Giving Way to Progress," *The Calgary Herald*, 5 November 1964.

103 Jennifer Bobrovitz, "Hull Home Hosted Many Parties," *The Calgary Herald*, 18 January 1998.

104 Pierre Berton, quoted in David Bly, "Calgary a 'Villain' in Tearing Down Historic Buildings," *The Calgary Herald*, 26 October 2001.

105 Pierre Berton quoted in Rosemary McCracken, "Pierre Berton Laments Calgary's Lack of Sense of History," *The Calgary Herald*, 19 September 1980.

106 Brian Brennan, "Columnist Found Interesting Tales in Everyone's Life," *The Calgary Herald*, 23 March 1996.

107 Ken Liddell, *Alberta Revisited* (Toronto: Ryerson, 1960), 127.

108 "Retired Doctor Celebrates his 100th Birthday Today," *The Calgary Herald*, 29 July 1978. Patricia Gibson Blackburn, *Her Memoirs and Her Ancestry in the Families Chalmers, Edwards, Godwin, Gibson*, comp. Robert H. Blackburn (Toronto: University of Toronto Press, 1992). Patricia Blackburn was Harry Gibson's daughter.

109 H. A. Gibson to Herbert J. Hamilton, editor, *Queen' Review*, dated Calgary, 8 November 1973, item 244-1112, Queens University Archives.

110 "A Guide to the William Pearce Papers 1869-1930," Manuscript Group 9/2 (Winter 1987): iii, The University of Alberta Archives.

111 Hugh A. Dempsey, *Treasures of the Glenbow Museum* (Calgary: Glenbow-Alberta Institute, 1991), 68–69.

112 Hugh A. Dempsey, "History of the Glenbow Museum," in *Treasures of the Glenbow Museum* (Calgary: Glenbow-Alberta Institute, 1991), 168, 190-195. For an interesting review of the Glenbow Foundation and Museum see Frances W. Kaye, *Hiding the Audience* (Edmonton: University of Alberta Press, 2002), 99–137.

113 Fred M. Diehl, *A Gentleman from a Fading Age: Eric Lafferty Harvie* (Calgary: The Devonian Foundation, 1989), 21.

114 Fiona Foran, "Heritage Park," in Foran and Foran, *Calgary*, 264–66.

115 Vera Burns, W. J. Campbell and D. H. L. Turner, *The Heritage Park Story* (Calgary: Heritage Park, 1976), 54–56.

116 Diehl, *A Gentleman from a Fading Age*, 21.

117 Hugh A. Dempsey, *Calgary: Spirit of the West* (Calgary: Fifth House, 1994), 138.

118 Evelyn Albright to her late husband, dated 2 December 1917. The passage reads: "Three weeks ago this morning I took David [Coutts] to church, little knowing that at that same time there was a telegram waiting for me, to tell me what has taken the joy, and I might almost say, the purpose out of life." The letter is included amongst "Evelyn Albright's 'Letters' to Fred Albright written in a notebook after his death," University of Western Ontario Archives. Of personal interest to the author, Dave Coutts was also a fellow member of the executive of the Chinook Country chapter of the Historical Society of Alberta, when I, a newly-minted Canadian history professor of two years standing at the University of Calgary, joined the executive in 1976.

119 Ibid, 137-138.

120 Jennifer Bobrovitz, "Burns Building Saved by One Vote," *The Calgary Herald*, 22 August 1999.

121 Walter Jamieson and Alexandra L. Aumonier, "The Mauling of Oil Town: Will Calgary's Stephen Avenue Mall be a Boom or Bust?" *Canadian Heritage* (December 1984-January 1985): 34–39.

122 Donn Downey, "Harold Hanen: Architect Brought Lloyd Wright's Vision to Calgary," *Globe and Mail*, 9 October 2000.

123 Peter Morton, "In the News: Harold Hanen 'In From the Cold' Feels Warmth of Public Spotlight," *The Calgary Herald*, 25 November 1978, F15. The phrase, "redesigning the interior to meet contemporary needs," is Constance Martin's in her excellent sketch, "A Calgary Walking Tour," *Western Living*, October 1981, 182-190, see 184.

124 Lanier R. Wardrop's office is listed as number 15, at 122 8th Street W. which is the Clarence Block. See *Henderson's Calgary Directory*, 1912. The booksellers McNally Robinson occupy the Clarence Block at the present time.

125 Pierre S. Guimond and Brian R. Sinclair, *Calgary Architecture: The Boom Years, 1972–1982* (Calgary: Deselig, 1984), 242–245.

126 *Henderson's Calgary* directories, 1974–1982.

127 Mike Byfield, "Paradise Lost: Civic Centre Pale Shadow of 1980 Plan," *Calgary Sun*, 3 February 1985.

128 Tom Anderson, interview with the author, Lougheed Building, Calgary, 22 April 2004.

129 Tom Anderson, interview with the author, Lougheed Building, 15 August 2003.

130 John Bascom, telephone interviews with the author, 18 October and 25 October 2002.

131 Anne George, "It was Grow, Grow, Grow in '70s Calgary…We Thought They'd Never End," *The Calgary Herald Magazine*, 27 January 1991, p. 11.

132 Belinda Silverman, "Shop Owner Slain as Jewellery Robbed," *The Calgary Herald*, 5 December 1981. David Rooney, "Public Aid Sought in Murder," *The Calgary Herald*, 7 December 1981. "Slaying Rings Wariness: Jewellers Beef up Security," *The Calgary Herald*, 8 December 1981.

133 Tom Anderson, interview with the author, Lougheed Building, 14 April 2004.

134 Scott Haggett, "Outcast Outlives Reviled Status," *The Calgary Herald*, 24 March 2004, D1.

135 Jack Peach, *The First Hundred Years: The History of the Calgary Chamber of Commerce* (Calgary: The Calgary Chamber of Commerce, 1990), 62–63.

136 The figure appears in "Petro-Canada Centre," undated pamphlet, Glenbow Library.

137 Diane Francis, "PetroCan Outgrows its Red Roots," *Financial Post*, 5 October 2002.

138 Haggett, "Outcast Outlives Reviled Status," D1.

139 Ibid.; an unnamed Calgary Herald writer is quoted here.

140 Ibid.

141 *Henderson's Calgary Directory*, 1983/84. The office was in room 526 of the Lougheed.

142 Grescoe, *Flight Path*, 29.

143 Michael Lau, "Trust Leases Top Floors of Petro-Canada Centre; Prime West's Room With a View," *The Calgary Herald*, 17 November 2004.

144 Ken Knudsen, telephone interview with the author, Calgary, 10 August 2004.

145 "Calgary Just Like Paris, says Divine Sarah Bernhardt," *Calgary News-Telegram*, 15 January 1913. "New Tea Rooms in Lougheed Block," *Calgary News-Telegram*, 19 December 1912. Ad for the Parisian Patisserie-Confiseries, Ltd., *Calgary News-Telegram*, 20 March 1913. The office and tea rooms were at 135 6th Avenue, and the bakery at 125.

146 Suzanne Wilton, "Downtown Traffic: Bikini bar says Dancers Lighten Rush Hour," *The Calgary Herald*, 25 June 1999. "Bar Pulls Curtain on Dancers," *The Calgary Herald*, 26 June 1999.

147 Max Foran, "Table VEE: Ethnic Origins of Calgary's Population, 1901–1961," in *Calgary: An Illustrated History* (Toronto: James Lorimer, 1978), 178.

148 Amund Jonassen, Consul Emeritus of Norway, to the author, 3 May 2001.

149 The wooden sign for the Penguin Pub stated that it began in "Anno 1985." *Henderson's Calgary Directory* for 1991 lists "Hak Kim" as the president of the Penguin Pub. Conversation with Cindy Davidson, a former employee of the Penguin Pub, Calgary, at the "Farewell to the Lougheed Building, Penguin Pub and Tom Anderson," Grand Golf Centre, Friday afternoon, 30 April 2004.

150 "Obituary: Ed Ogle; Newsman Loved North," *Globe and Mail*, 14 March 1991.

151 Jim Stott, "Why did I Come up Here? It Looked Like a Great Opportunity to Live the Way I Wanted," *The Calgary Herald Magazine*, 24 April 1979. Stephen Hume, "Lifetime of Words from 'Man Who Never Gets Angry'," *Vancouver Sun*, 13 March 1991. My thanks to John Howse for this article.

152 Mel Hurtig, *At Twilight in the Country: Memoirs of a Canadian Nationalist* (Toronto: Stoddart, 1996), 155–156.

153 Harold Cardinal, *The Unjust Society* (Edmonton: Hurtig, 1969), 1.

154 Ibid., x.

155 Cecil Brown, General Secretary of the Board of the Calgary YMCA in the 1920s, cited in "Origins of Camp Chief Hector," prepared for the Camp Chief Hector Reunion, 1980, mimeograph. My thanks to Jill Jamieson, Camp Director of Camp Chief Hector, for showing me this mimeographed historical summary in December 1998.

156 Chief Rueben Bull of Goodfish Lake quoted by Fred Kennedy, "Alberta Indian Tribes Will Demand New Deal. Revision of Educational System; No Alienation of Treaty Rights and Improvements at Morley Requested by Conference," *The Calgary Herald*, 3 July 1945, p. 13. The camp has now re-located off the reserve to a location farther west, close to the front range of the Rocky Mountains.

157 Jamie Portman, "Twin Theatres Passing out the Grand Old Movie Palaces," *The Calgary Herald*, 29 July 1972. Patrick Tivy, "Theatre Returns Magic to Night at the Movies," *The Calgary Herald*, 20 December 1985. Another development, in the summer of 1969, was the amendment of the Lord's Day Act allowing for the showing of movies on Sunday. "Sunday Movies Are Here," *The Albertan*, 29 July 1969.

158 Eric Dawson, "The Arts: Classical Music," in *The Insiders' Calgary*, ed. Penny Williams (Toronto: Key Porter Books, 1982), 105.

159 Tivy, "Theatre Returns Magic."; Fred Haeseker, "Renovation to bring Grand Theatre into the '80s," *The Calgary Herald*, 23 November 1984, p. F5

160 "Oldest Theatre Re-Opens Doors," *The Calgary Herald*, 22 November 1985, F5.

161 Gerald Forseth, David Mittelstadt, and Colin Campbell, "Historical Resource Impact Assessment of the Lougheed Building, Calgary, for Prairie Fund Management, August 1998 (henceforth cited as the Forseth Report), "Mitigation Recommendations", 3. A copy of the Forseth Report is in the Glenbow Library.

162 Dave Pommer, "Lougheed: City Urged to Save Building," *The Calgary Herald*, 28 April 1999.

163 Statement by the owners included in the Forseth Report, "Mitigation Recommendations," 2–3. Subsequent conversations with Tom Anderson, the Lougheed-Grand property manager, and Don Spicer of Don's Hobby Shop, a tenant of roughly forty years, confirmed the short-comings of the building in its current state.

164 Forseth Report, "Mitigation Recommendations," 6.

165 Stan Woloshyn, Minister, Alberta Community Development, letter to the author, 7 February 2001, file number AR66727. A copy of the letter is included as Appendix 1, at the end of the manuscript. I wrote him on 23 January 2001 to ask if he would please send me, "for possible inclusion as an appendix [in my book]," a full explanation for his refusal to designate the Lougheed Building as a provincial historic site. For the assessment of the process by Rob Graham, then City of Calgary Heritage Planner, see his essay, "The Calgary Context,", in Michael McMordie et al., eds. *Heritage Covenants & Preservation: The Calgary Civil Trust* (Calgary: University of Calgary Press, 2004), 95-117 (see in particular, 110-113).

166 Committee members Alison Robertson and myself spoke, as did other friends of the two buildings: Dennis Burton, Lougheed penthouse tenant; Trudy Cowan, Vice-Chair of the Heritage Canada Foundation; architect Gerald Forseth, who headed the team that prepared the Forseth Report; Larry Gilchrist, former City of Calgary alderman and chair of the Calgary Municipal Heritage Properties Authority; town planner and architect Harold Hanen, former tenant in the penthouse of the Lougheed; Sheila Johnston, past president of the Historical Society of Alberta; Jack Long, a former City of Calgary alderman and well-known architect; Kate Reeves, President of the Chinook Country Historical Society; and Nick Totino, a student at the University of Calgary.

167 City Council Item Number OE2000-31.

168 Mark Lawes and Carol Armes, email to the author, 21 May 2004.

INDEX

Note: Italics indicate photographs.

feature films, 225, 235
financial problem for Lougheed Estate, 233–34
"49th Parallel," 225, 228
golf centre, 289
Joiner as manager, 195, 196
Lydiatt as manager, 140, 142, 145, 150, 154–55, 158, 160, 192
"Neptune's Daughter," 156
Opera Festival, 158
performances in 1920s, 181–82
performances in 1930s, 205–6, 208, 212, 214, 216
performances in 1940s, 235–36, 238–40
purchased by Richardson, 290
renovations under Barron, 234, 238
Robeson's performance, 238
Save the Grand Lougheed Committee, 287–89
Semple McPherson's talk, 216
silent movies, 210
smoking policy, 234–35
sold to Famous Players, 209–10
sold to J.B. Barron, 224, 228, 234
soldiers welcomed to performances, 150
Stefansson's lecture, 188
struggled from 1950s on, 286–87
Theatre Junction purchases, 290
threatened with demolition, 287
transformed into movie theatre, 254. *See also* Sherman Grand Theatre
Grand Tobacco and Coffee Shop Ltd., 252
Gray, James, 18, 19, 42
Great Depression
economic conditions during, 171, 212
financial crisis for Lougheed Estate, 233–34
Grand sold to Famous Players, 209–10
performances at Grand, 205–6, 208, 214, 216
Great West Canadian Folksong–Folkdance and Handicrafts Festival, 212
Green Room Club, 240
Greenberg, Nate, 252
Greenfield, Herbert, 161, 168, 170
Grey, Earl, 48, 50
Griesbach, Gen. William, 21, 62
Griffin, Fred, 183

Hak Kim, 284
Hall, David, 196
Hall, William (Bill), 171, 222, 272
Hanen, Harold, *279*, 280, 289
Hanover Management, 275, 280, 281, 287
Harcourt-O'Reilly, Patrick, 155
Hardie, Keir, 58
Hardisty, Belle (daughter of William and Mary). *See* Lougheed
Hardisty, Frank (brother of Belle), 36
Hardisty, Mary Allen (mother of Belle), 46, *47,* 59
Hardisty, Richard (uncle of Belle), 22, *23,* 24, 35, 37, 40, *44, 278*
Hardisty, Richard (brother of Belle), 36, 82
Hardisty, William (father of Belle), 22, 23, 24, 46, 59, 217
Harling, Fred, 90, 145
Hart, Bertha, 155
Haru Onuki, 158, *159,* 160
Harvey, Frank, 221, 250
Harvey and Morrison, 221, 223, 250

Harvie, Eric, 278
Hearst, Sir William, 181
Heifetz, Jascha, 230, 232
Helal, Elvira, 234
Henderson, Col. H. G., 184, 186
Henderson's Calgary Directory, 94, 113, 224
Heritage Park, 278
Herriott, George, 266
Herron, Stewart, 130
Heydon, Ethel, 17, 18
Higgins, Gen. Edward J., 216
High River Times, 14, 17
Historical Resources Act of Alberta, 287, 289
History of the Province of Alberta, 60–61
Hofmann, Josef, 214
Holland, Susannah, 100, 104
Home Oil, 224, 246, 248
Hook Construction Company, 92
Hotchkiss, Harley, 274, 275
House of Persian Rugs, 284
Hudson's Bay Company store, 120
Hull, William Roper, 40, 275
Hull's Opera House, 69
Hunter, James, 154, 183
Hustak, Alan, 2
Hutchinson, Ernie, 252

immigration policy, 56
Imperial Oil, 182
In Western Canada before the War, 59
Independent Order of Odd Fellows, 86
influenza epidemic, 158
Ives, William C., 171–72

Jack, Grenville, K. 94
Jackson, Sir Barry, 206
Jackson, Will. *See* Jaxon
Jaremko, Gordon, 130
Jaxon, Honoré (Will Jackson), 81–82, *83,* 84–85, 87
Jephson, Jermy, 66, 69, 118
"Jericho," 228
Jerome, Jerome K., 6
Johns, Dr. Walter, 260
Johnston, Fred and Bertha, 220
Joiner, Maynard, 188, 195, 196, 206, *207,* 210
Jones, Barry, 199, 206
Jubilee Auditorium, 240, 246
Jull, Walter, 94

Kadish, Abraham, 90
Kelly, Evelyn. *See* Albright
Kelly, H. and Company, 92
Kennedy, Fred, 286
Kheong, Dorothy, Mabelle and Vivian, 216
Kheong, Louie, 58, 216
King, Andrew, 137
King George Hotel, 56, 230
King, Mackenzie, 190, 226
King, Madeline, 290
King, Peter Willoughby, 68
King, Tom, 177

provided offices for military during World War I, 148, 154
public advocate of western interests, 37–38
racial attitudes, 138, 140
ranchers upset about leasing proposals, 192, 194
rants against high taxes, 195
real estate transactions, 36, 42, 74, 182
received knighthood, 177
senator and cabinet minister, 21, 38–40, 42, 62, 76, 170, 195
sold Grand, 232
visit of Edward, Prince of Wales, 183–84, 190
Lougheed, Jane and Elizabeth (cousins of James), 31
Lougheed, John (father of James), 24, 26, 28, 29, 31
Lougheed, Marjorie (daughter of James and Belle), 48, 49
Lougheed, Mary Ann Alexander (mother of James), 26, 28, 31
Lougheed, Mary Stringer (wife of Norman), 4, 46, 50
Lougheed, Norman (son of James and Belle), 4, 36, 46, 48, 60, 184
Lougheed, Peter (son of Edgar), 176, 233, 252, 270, 282
Lougheed, Sam (brother of James), 24, 26, 28, 31, 35, 196
Lowery, Jim ("Major"), 246
Luxton, Norman, 227
Lydiatt, Dorothy, 145
Lydiatt, Grace, 160
Lydiatt, Jeff, 136, 184
    joined Orpheum Circuit, 192
    manager of Grand, 137, 140, 145, 150, 154–55, 158, 160, 192
    private secretary to Dr. Blow, 144
    Trans-Canada Theatres, 181, 182
    worked for CPR, 141–42
Lyric Theatre, 6, 45, 233

McAree, John, 30, 31
McCarthy, Peter, 37, 38, 39,–40
McCarthy, Maitland, 116
McClung, Mark, 202, 205
McClung, Nellie, 196, 199, 200, 202, 203, 204–5, 218
McClung, Wes, 199, 202, 204–5
McCrystle, Phil, 91, 130, 145
McDonald, Gen. H.F., 188, 191
MacDonald, Robert H., 148
Macdonald, Dr. George, 69
Macdonald, Sir John A., 30 37, 38
MacDougall, Frank, 110, 112
McDougall, Rev. John, 16, 24, 38, 54, 69, 89
McElroy, Millicent, 150
MacEwan, Grant, 70
McGillis, Cuthbert, 70
MacInnes, Richard, 270
Mackay, Don, 236
McLaughlin, Christina, 69–70
Maclean, A. J., 88
Maclean, George (Tatanga Mani), 227
Maclean, Robert, 148
Macleod, J. E. A., 261
McMahon Stadium, 257
MacMillan, Vivian, 171–72
McNeil and Trainer, 92
McNeill, Leishman, 154
McPhail, Agnes, 204
McPherson, Aimee Semple, 216
MacRae, Rev. Archibald, 60–61

MacWilliams, Rev. Andrew, 129, 261
MacWilliams, Carson, 261
"Madame Butterfly," 158, 160
Mahler, Gustav, 53
Manning, Muriel, 221
Manufacturers Life, 204, 205, 221
Marcell, Milward, 88–89
Martin-Harvey, Sir John, 1, 121, 206, 209, 211, 234
Massey, Vincent, 227
Matthews, Dick, 250
Mawson, Thomas, 112, 152
Meighen, Arthur, 21, 178, 190, 195
Melchoir, Lauritz, 236
Menuhin, Yehudi, 236
Metis, 32, 34, 36, 54, 59
Metropolitan Life Insurance, 91, 130, 222
Military Hospitals Commission, 177, 178
Mills, Louise Camsell, 46
Mills, Ted, 270
Milne and Davis, 272
Milne, George, 272
Mitchell, Betty, 239, 240, 246
Mitchell, Elizabeth D., 59
Mitchell, John W., 86
Mittelstadt, David, 40, 288
Monarch Life, 94
Montreal Star, 50, 121
Moore, Tom, 238
Moose Mountain Oil Company, 132
Moreau, John, 274
Morgan-Powell, Samuel, 121
Mornings in the College Chapel, 171
Morrison, Ken, 250, 252
Morton, W.L., 164
Moss, Gordon, 268
Mount Lougheed, 232–33
Mount Royal College Symphony, 239
Munn, Alexandra, 236
Murdoch, Alice, 216
Murdoch, George, 86
Murphy, Emily, 218

National Ballet of Canada, 240
National Energy Program, 281
"Navy Show," 236
Needham, Richard, 264
Nelson, Barry, 282
Nelson, Stan J., 274
"Neptune's Daughter," 156
Nethersole, Olga, 122
New Empire Theatre, Edmonton, 181
New Grass, Rosalie, 58
Newbolt, Bob, 186
Newcombe, Percy Lynn (P.L.), 158, 160
Newton, Alick, 186
Nicholson, Barbara, 202
Nicoll, Jim and Marion, 126, 248, 251
Nolan, Mary Lee (Minnie), 70
Nolan, Paddy, 69–70, 71, 72, 74, 80, 94
Northwest Travellers Building, 290
Norwegian Consulate, 284